Syd Chaplin

Syd Chaplin
A Biography

Lisa K. Stein

McFarland & Company, Inc., Publishers
Jefferson, North Carolina, and London

LIBRARY OF CONGRESS CATALOGUING-IN-PUBLICATION DATA

Stein, Lisa K.
Syd Chaplin : a biography / Lisa K. Stein.
    p.   cm.
Includes bibliographical references and index.
Includes filmography.

ISBN 978-0-7864-6035-9
softcover : 50# alkaline paper ∞

1. Chaplin, Syd, 1885–1965.   2. Actors — United States — Biography.   I. Title.
PN2287.C516S74   2011   791.430'28092 — dc22   [B]   2010040453

British Library cataloguing data are available

©2011 Lisa K. Stein. All rights reserved

*No part of this book may be reproduced or transmitted in any form
or by any means, electronic or mechanical, including photocopying
or recording, or by any information storage and retrieval system,
without permission in writing from the publisher.*

On the cover: Sydney Chaplin, 1918
Front cover by TG Design

Manufactured in the United States of America

*McFarland & Company, Inc., Publishers
Box 611, Jefferson, North Carolina 28640
www.mcfarlandpub.com*

To Kate,
with affection, admiration and gratitude
for your belief in this project

Table of Contents

Abbreviations viii
Preface 1
Introduction 3

1. Kennington Kid 9
2. Downstage to Marquee 27
3. A Keystone Cop Aesthetic 44
4. Surviving Hollywood, 1916–1921 68
5. Rebuilding a Film Career, 1922–1925 103
6. Stardom and a Tenuous Homecoming 126
7. "An Incident at Elstree" 166
8. Travels with Charlie 178
9. Double Exposure: 1932–1938 188
10. Charlie, Gypsy and a Caravan 206

Appendix A: Filmography 227
Appendix B: A Selection of Sydney Chaplin Letters 235
Chapter Notes 243
Bibliography 261
Index 265

Abbreviations

AMPAS	Margaret Herrick Library, Academy of Motion Picture Arts and Sciences
BFI	British Film Institute
CHACHAA	Charlie Chaplin Archive, Cineteca di Bologna, Bologna, Italy
LCLPA	Lincoln Center Library for the Performing Arts
LKSC	Lisa K. Stein Collection
MPN	*Motion Picture News*
MPW	*Moving Picture World*
SOC	Shunichi Ohkubo Collection
USCCAL	University of Southern California Cinematic Arts Library
WGC	Walter Gasparini Collection

Preface

THIS IS THE FIRST-EVER LIFE AND ART STUDY of Sydney Chaplin, Charlie Chaplin's brother, a person notable not only for his importance in establishing his brother's career, but in several other early Hollywood enterprises, including the founding of United Artists and the Syd Chaplin Aircraft Corporation, America's first domestic airline. Sydney also had a very successful film career, beginning in 1914 with Keystone and culminating in a string of films for Warner Bros. in the 1920s that numbered among that company's most popular films for those years. Yet Sydney has received very little recognition in print over the years, beyond the fact that he secured Charlie a million-dollar film contract with Mutual in 1916 due to his negotiating skills.

Film critics have expressed their interest in and curiosity about Sydney for many years. While his brother Charlie's life was punctuated by ups and downs, scandals and miscommunications, Sydney's makes even Charlie's life pale in comparison. Sydney's film career ended abruptly in 1929, for instance, because of an assault charge by a young actress. This incident proved to be only the last in a string of scandals, each causing him to move bag and baggage to another place, another studio, or another business venture. Still, he somehow enjoyed the fidelity of wife Minnie until her death in 1936, then of second wife, Henriette, until his death in 1965. Sydney, despite his disgraceful departure from the film world in 1929, had a facility for business and money that far surpassed his brother. And, it is surely thanks to Sydney that Charlie, too, claimed success and affluence for himself and his progeny.

This is only a small portion of the fascinating story I was to uncover over the next four years.

* * *

Having written my dissertation on Charlie Chaplin's travel narratives, I was a frequent visitor to the Chaplin archive — then in both Paris and Bologna — and often heard tales about Sydney and his mythological exploits. I also heard exclamations of longing on the part of my compatriots there — longing for a book on Sydney. It seemed only fair.

After all, back in 1953, he had been the one to save the very documents we were using when they were in great danger of being taken out to the trash, because moving them all to Europe seemed like an impossible and needlessly expensive task. Even I didn't really know then what all he had accomplished or failed to accomplish in life, but I was interested in finding out. What I found, though, after doing a superficial search, was that Sydney had largely been forgotten. He hadn't garnered a treatment in any book or journal more than a few pages in length.

I knew then that this project would require a staunch commitment of both time and money — that most of my information would have to come from original source materials: letters and film company documents. I knew that I would have to dig deeply into the most respected film industry periodicals, like *Motion Picture News* and *Moving Picture World* and that I would have to spend time trolling through old newspapers. This was my only hope of uncovering enough information to form an interesting narrative. As an established Charlie Chaplin scholar, I was lucky; I had access to a rich diversity of never-before-accessed documents from the Charlie Chaplin archive located at the Cineteca di Bologna in Bologna, Italy, and the Walter Gasparini Collection (a private collection) in Milan, Italy. I collected research for this project at the British Film Institute in London — a place where I also watched films — the Cinema Museum in London, the Margaret Herrick Library at the Academy of Motion Picture Arts and Sciences in Beverly Hills, California, the Santa Catalina Island Historical Society, the Seaver Center at the Los Angeles Natural History Museum, the Warner Brothers archive, part of the USC Cinema Arts Library, the Lincoln Center Library of the Performing Arts in New York, the Library of Congress in Washington, D.C., the Archives des Alpes Maritîmes in Nice, France, and the Archives de Montreux in Montreux, Switzerland, among others. I managed to find a fairly complete set of *The Era*, an important English music hall rag, at Miami University library here in Ohio, which kept me from making too many trips to London to do that very time-consuming work.

Although this book is first and foremost the story of one man's life, it is also the story of Hollywood and the adolescent film industry developing there after 1912. Sydney was instrumental in the formation of United Artists, without which, this industry would have developed in an entirely different way. In fact, he had an uncanny ability to place himself at the threshold of many innovations, well before others came on board. He was an early proponent of talking films and welcomed the opportunity to enter them (his last film, never made, was to have been a talking one). He foresaw the importance of the radio broadcast and the stars that would be made in that medium well before it occurred. In fact, he embraced new technology wherever he found it — in automobiles, in airplanes, in film cameras — and seemed to be skilled at predicting new trends in business. Overall, he was both well-read *and* street savvy, a very potent combination that, combined with his training in the Karno school of physical comedy, should have made him as popular and successful as his brother. Perhaps this last was my greatest motivation for completing the work: Why had Charlie succeeded where Sydney had failed? I welcome the opportunity, with this book, to answer that question at last.

Introduction

THE LIFE OF SYDNEY JOHN CHAPLIN is not the first celebrated one to confound the biographer. In a recent article investigating the prowess of Katherine Anne Porter at fabricating her own background, William Gass aptly quotes Porter's own words on Tolstoy's silence concerning the women in his life: "He did not know the truth about women, not even about that one who was the curse of his life. He did not know the truth about himself. This is not surprising, for no one does know the truth, either about himself or about anyone else, and all recorded human acts and words are open testimony to our endless efforts to know each other, and our failure to do so."[1] Although examples like this one abound, the Chaplin boys (Sydney and Charlie) seemed especially adept at keeping their private lives and especially their childhood as ill-defined as possible. Sydney once wrote in a letter to his friend R. J. Minney, noted British journalist and playwright,

> If I had the energy & desire, I could make a lot of money by writing the true history of the Chaplin family. It would be so startling that the "Confessions of Rousseau" and Harris's "My Private Life & Loves" would read like children's primers along side of it. Nearly everything I have read concerning my brother & I in newspapers, etc., has been mainly bunk. Someday I may sit down & write my memoirs for publication, years after we are dead, that is, if the Chaplin family is of any interest to the public at that time.[2]

This passage is especially interesting, because both Sydney and Charlie were personally involved with the various versions of their own life stories circulating in the press. Perhaps both were thinking about the future day in time in which each would write and publish his own definitive and revealing autobiography — every successful and affluent man's hobby in old age. In fact, Sydney seems to have engineered his own biography in some sense, despite the fact that he himself never wrote it, in that he scribbled meticulous handwritten notes on Charlie's documents to some future biographer, noting his significance at certain points in Charlie's career. He also selectively saved certain documents (and, most likely, culled others) that told the story the way he wanted it told. While we can never know how good this autobiography might have been, what does exist of Sydney's writing is significant, because it is dry, witty, emotional, contradictory, bawdy, and surprisingly grammatically correct, despite his constant indication to professional writers such as Minney to be wary of his "Kennington Road grammar." Because of Sydney's attempts, largely successful, to keep aspects of his life, avocations, and associations secret, this biography will present what facts exist, but also the myths, the stories, and the speculations that must accompany such an enigmatic character.

With an unspoken permission from his mother and society at the time of his childhood to fabricate, fabricate, fabricate, it is no surprise that Sydney adapted his behavior towards people and the world in general to match this behavior. The first stories Sydney heard were wild accounts concerning his conception in a faraway land (South Africa), in circumstances tinged with intrigue, deception and betrayal, accounts that continue to live on in Chaplin family mythology. Perhaps it's not my right as his biographer to suggest a cause-and-effect relationship between Sydney's early exposure to storytelling and his later business and personal dealings. But, as his biographer, I've had to personally come to terms with the Jekyll-Hydeness of his overall character and try to understand it, even justify it — at least to my own mind. It is clear that Sydney suffered from severe mental anxiety and depression. Both of his wives worried constantly about his mental state and the effect certain interactions or situations might have on it. He was obsessive about his hygiene, cleanliness in general, and money. He was a hypochondriac who spent freely on doctors and other medical services and took off long periods of time for recovery, often when others were counting on him to complete a project or fulfill a responsibility long overdue.

At a time in history when Roman Polanski's antics are still in the news — behavior that has failed to halt the release of his latest film — I think about Sydney and the behavior he got away with. It is clear that Sydney was not faithful to his first wife, Minnie, almost flagrantly displaying his young victims in full view of Hollywood society, his family and friends. Being Charlie's less-famous brother, Sydney was often able to fly under the radar, at least until he became more of a box-office commodity himself in the later 1920s. Still, he seemed to be an expert at tempering certain of his less palatable sexual exploits and crimes and then exaggerating others for his own benefit (he once bragged to a correspondent that he had been "raped" by eight different American women on separate occasions[3]).

In money dealings, he was equally unscrupulous, often dealing under the table or outside the law in order to reap the greatest monetary benefit for both himself and his brother, a behavior that was to get both he and Charlie in trouble with the IRS on several occasions. A financial infraction coupled with a sexual encounter gone wrong ended his film career forever in 1929, yet it is rumored that his estate upon his death in 1965 exceeded a million dollars (although this may indeed be a low figure, because his widow was able to accommodate herself at the Beau Rivage Hotel in Switzerland until her death in 1991, with money to spare). Despite his business ethic or lack thereof, he is largely responsible for the founding of United Artists, for Charlie's successful career, for the first domestic American airline, and he was an early promoter and defender of talking films. In many ways, Sydney embraced technological advancement wherever it arose, often well before that advancement was accepted and utilized by others. A scrapbook he created and kept starting in 1909, which would have been during his career as a Karno headliner, is filled with news clippings of such advancements — in aviation especially, but also regarding the automobile and other forms of transportation.

Introduction

The most important aspect of Sydney's "Hyde" persona, however, involved Charlie's children and especially his children with Oona. To each of them I interviewed, Uncle Sydney was a dearly beloved individual, funny and perhaps a bit bawdy at times, but unceasingly caring and generous. None of them knew of his darker side, for clearly much of that misbehavior had disappeared after he married second wife, Henriette (Gypsy). Perhaps it is this relationship between Oona and Charlie's children and Sydney that provided me the most energy in this project and allowed me to bring it to a dignified end.

* * *

This book would not exist without the unflagging support of Kate Guyonvarch, director of Roy Export S.A.S. and the Association Chaplin office. Thanks to Kate, I had the great fortune to be allowed access to all the documents in the Charlie Chaplin archive. With her permission, I visited the Cineteca di Bologna in Bologna, Italy, Archives de Montreux in Switzerland and the Association Chaplin office in Paris over the course of four years in order to glean every pertinent detail. Charlie's archive would not exist but for Sydney's efforts over the years to preserve it and it was Sydney who, in 1953, worked tirelessly in Hollywood, packing up and organizing the Chaplin studio contents to be shipped to Switzerland. It's only right, then, that he eventually profit from these efforts himself through the publication of this life story. In addition, due to the wonders of the Internet, I was contacted by a businessman from Milan, Italy — Walter Gasparini — who informed me that he had purchased a large collection of Sydney's letters at auction some years earlier. Mr. Gasparini's collection of letters *made* this book, in that they provided evidence of the most damning of his lies, Sydney's often near-hysterical paranoia, as well as his unbelievable wit (and intelligence). These letters opened up the idea of Sydney Chaplin and made him human. Yes, they were also largely fabricated (Sydney was always aware of his audience), but they provided glimmers of Sydney that were both compelling and revealing, like no other documents in the Chaplin archive. I consider myself unbelievably lucky to have been given access to them.

I consider David Robinson's definitive and unsurpassed biography of Charlie Chaplin, *Chaplin: His Life and Art* to be the model for this book, in breadth, scope and detail. Whether or not I approached that ideal is up for debate. However, I can't thank David enough for this work and for his support of my project as well. With very little having been written about Sydney in the past, I often looked to David's biography for direction and clarification on the brothers' personal chronologies. It was often the only source—outside of archival documents—on this subject.

Sydney, and first Minnie and then Gypsy, spent much of their lives in Nice, France, with Sydney eventually dying there at the Hotel Ruhl in 1965 on Charlie's birthday. Nice today provides compelling evidence of how expert Sydney was in making himself undetectable to the authorities, for my visit there last summer provided little documentation that he was ever there, yet he lived there nearly six months of every year, starting in 1931. His and Minnie's first apartment in the Palais Rosa Bonheur still exists, and thanks to friend Jean-Paul Woodall, I was invited to visit the couple, M. and Mme. Claude Arcache, who now inhabit it. It was clear from this visit that at the time of its construction, it would have been top-of-the-line in terms of residences for the area, it being a luxury penthouse apartment with a view of the Promenade des Anglais and the ocean beyond. Yet, one of the few documents that remain in the records there — Minnie's death certificate — claims that neither Sydney nor Minnie were residents, thereby allowing them to evade the tax man and other costly authorities. Being in Nice, however, allowed me to see the sort of life Sydney lived in his "exile" and to feel that, despite his palpable regret at losing his film career, there was little about which to feel sorry for him. He clearly lived the life of a very wealthy man of leisure.

Every other archive and research library I visited, from the Margaret Herrick Library in Beverly Hills and the Warner Brothers archive at the University of Southern California to the Library of Congress, the British Library, the British Film Institute and the Cinema Museum in London, answered old nagging questions and uncovered new ones. Obsessed as I am with what "facts" I can bring to light in the telling of this story, I have had to satisfy myself with some subset of the truth, but one I am proud to be able to tell.

One of the most surprising things I uncovered during my research was the knowledge that most of Sydney's films still exist. The only ones I could not find were *The Rendezvous, Her Temporary Husband,* and *The Fortune Hunter,* and this last may, in fact, be tucked away in a vault at Turner. While few of them are available to the average film viewer, I viewed many at the Library of Congress and the British Film Institute. Serge Bomberg of Lobster Films, however, went above and beyond the call of duty when he took two hours of his time in his Paris office to show us one of two existing prints of Sydney's Warner's film *Oh! What a Nurse!* Given the delicate condition of this nitrate print, M. Bomberg was forced to hand-crank the film through the Steenbeck machine so that we could watch it — a selfless act indeed. Other film folk, like Steve Massa, Rob Arkus, Ulrich Ruedel, Richard Roberts, Phil Posner and Rob Farr helped me to find and make sense of Sydney's films and photographs from them that were out there and available, and I thank them gratefully for it. A special thanks is due Brent Walker, for his ready willingness to provide detailed dates and information on the Keystone films.

Other people I wish to thank are, first and foremost, Cecilia Cenciarelli, archivist and head of Progetto Chaplin at the Cineteca di Bologna, who untiringly offered support, friendship and real enthusiasm for the project. Thanks to Evelyne Lüthi-Graf of the Archives de Montreux for suggesting the project to me in the first place. Thanks to Frank Scheide for his information on *King, Queen, Joker* and his energetic support for the project. My student researchers, Kendra Lisum, Crystal Gearhart and Tyler Eyerman helped to make the collection of information easier.

At Association Chaplin in Paris, besides Kate Guyonvarch, I wish to thank Charly Sistovaris and Claire Byrski. Charlie's children who graciously provided their reminiscences of Uncle Sydney included Geraldine Chaplin (and her husband, Pato Castilla), Josephine Chaplin, Michael Chaplin, and Christopher Chaplin. Thanks to other Chaplin relatives who provided their memories and artifacts: Pauline Mason, youngest daughter of Aubrey Chaplin and her daughter Rosemary, and Minnie Chaplin's grandnephews Irvine Gilbert, Jack and Ricky Green. Archivists I encountered who provided much needed assistance include Michela Zegna, Barbara Hall, Faye Thompson, Kristine Krueger, Jeanine Pedersen, Ronald Grant, Martin Humphries, Simon Audley, Mary Hubbard, John Cahoon, Zoran Sinobad, Jonothan Auxier, Kathleen Dickson, Nathalie Morris and Bryony Dixon.

At Ohio University Zanesville, I wish to thank Dean Jim Fonseca, Parinbam Thamburaj, Sheida Shirvani, Billie Mautz, Rosanna St. Clair, Tracey Humphrey, Mike Nern and Chris Shaw for their support. Thanks especially to Betty Pytlik for reading the manuscripts faithfully and offering heartfelt support on the project.

Last but not least are my friends, without whom I would never have mentally or emotionally been able to complete this project, including Michael Cartellone, Nancy Meyer, Hank Tingler, Emery K. Rogers, Jr., and, last but not least, Kris Teters.

CHAPTER 1

Kennington Kid

> To gauge the morals of our family by commonplace standards would be as erroneous as putting a thermometer in boiling water.—Charles Chaplin, *My Autobiography* (1964)

> English people have a great horror of the poorhouse; but I don't remember it as a very dreadful place. To tell you the truth, I don't remember much about it. I have just a vague idea of what it was like.—"Charles Chaplin Was Once in Poorhouse," *Waterloo Evening Courier and Reporter*, June 5, 1915: 11.

HANNAH HARRIETT PEDLINGHAM HILL, daughter of Charles, an Irish cobbler, and Mary Ann (Smith) Hill, grew up to be a young woman full of life and ambition—beautiful and perhaps a little headstrong. Charlie Chaplin, her more famous son, wrote feelingly of his early memories of this young woman "with fair complexion, violet-blue eyes and long light-brown hair that she could sit upon,"[1] a mother both he and half-brother Sydney adored. Imbued with both physical beauty and the ability to sing, dance and mimic much of what she saw, she must have been entrancing—a young lovely who could turn the heads of both the boy down the street and the lord from uptown who was not above a trip across the Thames to experience low entertainment, known as English music hall, and the delights of the young female performers he saw on stage there. Just as Oscar Wilde's protagonist, Dorian Gray, engaged in such frowned-on amusements, it is certain that young affluent men beyond the pages of Victorian novels did the same. Hannah even kept an homage of sorts in her home at one time to Nell Gwyn,[2] the well-known low-class entertainer and paramour of King Charles II. Hannah told her young sons the story of her own such encounter with a wealthy gentleman whose head she had turned, even though she was at the time already acquainted with the man who would be her only husband, Charles Chaplin. She related to them that she made the mistake of going away with this "gentleman" (supposedly Sidney Hawke or Hawkes) on a whim—to Cape Town, South Africa—soon returning in disgrace to south London with a valise choked with broken promises and a belly bulging with what was to be her first baby. Nevertheless, her beauty and vivaciousness soon won over her neglected beau, Chaplin, who agreed to make her a respectable woman, at least for a time. Evidence cannot completely support stories such as this one. Admittedly, Hannah told her boys, Sydney and Charlie, stories to keep them entertained in places and lodgings overwhelmed by misery, their own and others. The life she chose, the loves she experienced, and the emphasis she placed on such "stories," all proved to affect the lives of her first two sons more than anything or anyone else. For her oldest son, Sydney, the promise of such stories and the utility of storytelling in general provided a means of both escape and survival that he was to put to the test more than once in his life.

The young woman, Hannah Hill, gave birth to this first son, named and baptized Sidney John Hill, at 57 Brandon Street in Lambeth, south of London, on March 16, 1885,[3] a home she shared with her half-brother's cousin, Joseph Hodges, and his family, and would just three months later share with her new husband, Charles Chaplin, whom she married on June 22 in St. John's church on Larcom Street. Sydney was not his son. Folklore surrounding the event of Sydney's conception and heritage began to overflow the bounds of even the story Hannah circulated about it. For instance, Charlie believed, at least as a boy, that Sydney was the son of a lord — one who would inherit two thousand pounds someday.[4] This was either a running joke between them or possibly something more. Two pieces of information, though, do complicate the issue: the existence of a signet ring that belonged to Sydney and the mystery of its origin, and an offhand comment Sydney made later in life in a letter to friend R. J. Minney, British journalist and playwright, which suggests that Charlie had recently seen a photograph of Sydney's alleged father, whoever he was:

> Charlie is very busy writing his memoirs, he read some of it to me & it reads very well. He treats the days of poverty with great humour, which will get more laughs than pity. However, I don't know why he should mention that mother made a vaudeville tour in South Africa & came back with a baby as a souvenir. After all, what is the difference? Just a matter of $2 for a marriage license. Charlie said he saw a photo of my father & I look just like him. I consider that a compliment.[5]

Geraldine Chaplin, Sydney's niece and an accomplished actress in her own right, relates that the ring was supposedly forced into Sydney's hand while he was in London one day (as a young man) — the anonymous gentleman saying to him, "This ring is from your father." The ring, still in existence, bears several iconic images suggesting royalty or nobility, such as the double-headed eagle, the lions rampant, the crown, the ball and scepter, and even the motto, which is most familiarly engraved in the walls of Edinburgh Castle and means simply, "Be Trustworthy." Do they add up to one particular family name and, if so, is that name royal or noble? Is Sydney's biological father, then, of this family?[6]

The first photograph in which Sydney is shown wearing the ring is a snapshot taken about 1919 or 1920, suggesting he had acquired it or possibly had it made during his trip back to England in 1919 to film *King, Queen, Joker*. The stone of the ring is carnelian; the ring itself gold. Its size also demands attention, for it is about two inches long and an inch and a half wide, a ring that would have been difficult to wear often and, in fact, he didn't.[7] Impressions from another signet ring in wax used to seal his 1930 correspondence, however, seem to support the ring as a fake — just a tangible item used to bolster a story or stories Sydney had created about himself.

Before and shortly after Sydney's birth, Hannah worked as a soubrette on the music hall stage, usually "in small provincial music halls, and at the bottom of the bill."[8] Her engagements under the name "Lily Harley" largely ended by the end of 1886.[9] Less than three years later, Sydney was presented with his younger half-brother, Charles Spencer Chaplin, on April 16, 1889, changing Sydney's life forever, for now life for each of them would be both enhanced and complicated by the other. Perhaps one of the first written mentions of this phenomenon came from Aunt Kate Mowbray, sister to Hannah, shortly before her death in 1916. "They have been inseparable all their lives," she said, "except when fate intervened at intervals. Syd, of quiet manner, clever brain and steady nerve, has been father and mother to Charlie. Charlie always looked up to Syd, and Sydney would suffer anything to spare Charlie."[10] Aunt Kate, however, never knew Charlie after he had become famous — a situation that was to change the brothers' relationship substantially.

It is likely that these were times of relative financial prosperity for the young family, since Chaplin, Sr. was becoming a sought-after music hall star, even being engaged to tour in the United States in 1890, where he played at the Union Square Theatre in New York City. In his autobiography, Charlie remembers that "our circumstances were moderately comfortable; we lived in three tastefully furnished rooms. One of my early recollections was that each night before Mother went to the theatre Sydney and I were lovingly tucked up in a comfortable bed and left in the care of the housemaid."[11] It is also likely, however, that the union was tumultuous and that Chaplin's accepting the tour of America marked the end of his marriage, in all but legal terms. He was to remain legally married to Hannah until his death in 1901. However, at some point in the late 1880s, Hannah transferred her allegiance to another man, the irascible Leo Dryden (born George Dryden Wheeler). Dryden was a troubadour of the colonial immigrant, the British expat who regretted his decision to leave life and love behind him in the homeland. His most famous ballad was the haunting and beautiful "The Miner's Dream of Home," which became wildly popular in 1891, a year that surely saw Hannah and her two sons living with Dryden as the boys' temporary father-figure. Surely, too, Hannah was earning both Dryden's allegiance and perhaps bed and board for herself and her sons by singing off-stage in accompaniment for Dryden as he performed this ballad. Sydney, in one account written in 1914, relates that "my first experience before the footlights was in my mother's arms, the only time I was ever impervious to a first night stage nervousness. I was oblivious of everything except the succulent attractiveness of a piece of chocolate. I don't think the audience could tell which was the chocolate and which was me."[12] Indicating that this was an instance concerning Dryden, he writes, "My father at the time was singing a descriptive miner's song, in which he tells the audience that he is leaving the gold fields of Australia and returning to England to marry the dearest and sweetest little girl in all the world"[13] — his mother.

The fact that Sydney would have been a six-year-old boy at the time of the "debut" — an age, perhaps, much too old for diminutive Hannah to have been able to hold him in her arms, should not diminish the importance of the half-truths present in this account. Dryden himself, being interviewed by the *Evening Standard* in autumn 1921, during Charlie's first trip back to London after his great film success, seems to verify at least some of Syd's earlier account and also to add to the story of his time spent as the boys' stepfather, offering that he "engaged Charlie's mother to sing the chorus of the song from the back of the stage." Of course, his reminiscences were only of Charlie, but he claims to have taught him to walk—his mother sitting on one chair and he on the other, while "the future King of Mirth toddled backwards and forwards, looking comically rueful when he fell." He also supposedly saved the boy's life in Birmingham, which, if nothing else, gives some evidence that Dryden took both the boys and their mother on tour with him. Calling at their lodgings one day, Dryden saw Charles "leaning out of the window. If I had not rushed up the stairs and caught the rascal he would have fallen many feet to the ground."[14]

Just a year after Sydney's supposed debut, he and Charlie gained a new brother, legally another George Dryden Wheeler, who later adopted the name Wheeler Dryden. Wheeler was born on August 31, 1892, and ripped from his mother's arms just a few months later, in early 1893.[15] As the Dryden-Chaplin relationship degraded, Dryden must have at some point made the difficult decision to steal his son from a mother he knew must be headed for a life of poverty and demoralization—a life he could not allow his son to experience.[16] Although Dryden's career was to lose its luster with the general downfall of English music hall, it's clear that he never experienced this sort of poverty in his own life, finding work as he did in the various far-flung colonies of the remaining British Empire.[17]

Without any male support, Hannah and her two boys soon found themselves in dire circumstances by the spring of 1893. One account relates that soon the family watched as their last table and chairs were repossessed, leaving them only with a mattress on the floor—a possession the law actually provided for at the time. Sydney, being the man of the house, was often sent to a nearby church on Waterloo Road to collect "pea soup with strands of meat in it" for the family—recorded to be one of the best soups either Chaplin ever remembered tasting.[18] As their circumstances deteriorated, so did their appearance to the world at large. Sydney related to his friend R. J. Minney, "My mother replaced the sleeves of my worn out jacket with sleeves taken from an old velvet jacket of her own. This would not have been so bad if her sleeves had not been multicoloured. I was very embarrassed, as the boys kept calling me 'Joseph with the coat of many colours.'"[19] Despite their eccentric shabbiness, the boys found that they could earn a few pence dancing to the barrel organ in the streets. While both had been taught the finer points of clog dancing by their mother, Sydney soon realized that his waif-thin, pretty brother was more apt to reap higher profits than he himself, so he began to stand by to ensure that no one relieved Charlie of his takings—a role Sydney would affect again and again over the years.[20]

About this time, Sydney found a job delivering newspapers. Brother Charlie recounts one instance of what he often referred to as Sydney's dumb luck: "Sydney had been mounting buses to sell his newspapers. On top of one bus he saw a purse on an empty seat. Quickly he dropped a newspaper over it as if by accident, then picked it up and the purse with it, and hurried off the bus." Later, alone, Sydney opened the possible treasure chest and, in fact, did discover that it held "a pile of silver and copper coins." Upon reaching home, the boon proved to provide a period of physical and mental recovery for Hannah, especially when they found a middle pocket enclosing seven gold sovereigns. Charlie remembers, "Our joy was hysterical. The purse contained no address, thank God, so Mother's religious scruples were little exercised. Although a pale cast of thought was given to the owner's misfortune, it was, however, quickly dispelled by Mother's belief that God had sent it as a blessing from Heaven." The boon resulted, not in saving for the future, but in relief for the present. Hannah took the boys to Southend-on-Sea for a holiday, outfitting them in proper clothes for the occasion: "What a day that was — the saffron beach, with its pink and blue pails and wooden spades, its colored tents and umbrellas, and sailing boats hurtling gaily over laughing little waves, and up on the beach other boats resting idly on their sides, smelling of seaweed and tar — the memory of it still lingers with enchantment."[21]

The year 1893 was not only the one which marked the little family's end of any sort of financial stability; it was the end of Grandma Hill's sanity — an illness that foreshadowed Hannah's own mental illness just two years later. Mary Ann Hill first found herself in the Newington Workhouse in February of that year, where the infirmary doctors noted, "She is incoherent. She says that she sees beetles, rats, mice and other things about the place. She thinks that the doctors at the Infy. tried to poison her. She makes a lot of rambling statements and frequently contradicts herself."[22] Dr. Williams, the examining physician, felt that her condition was due to drink and worry, but she failed to recover from these seemingly benign symptoms, dying at Barnstead Asylum two years later.[23]

Hannah's own chronic headaches first forced her to check into the Lambeth Infirmary on June 29, 1895, where she stayed about a month. Sydney, then, was taken into the Lambeth workhouse on Renfrew Road on July 1, since he was not yet old enough to fend for himself— at least legally; Charlie was given into the care of John George Hodges, a relative of the boys' grandmother's first husband. After four days, Sydney was placed in the West Norwood Schools whose purpose it was to look after such destitute children. David Robinson, Chaplin's biographer and author of *Chaplin: His Life and Art*, notes that "as Poor Law institutions went, Norwood was pleasant enough. It stood on the slope of a hill facing green fields, on the boundary of Croydon and Streatham, which were then still quite rural."[24] Sydney would have been housed in the New or Main School, situated to the north of the complex of buildings, erected in 1889. The children's barracks were three stories high, each accommodating 72 children. Each barrack had a day room on the ground floor, which was heated by an open fire. The sleeping rooms were located on the second and third floors, each containing 36 beds divided into six sections. Each child was given a wicker basket to house his clothes, his own towel, brush and comb and maybe a toothbrush. The main problem with the place was the fact that the entire building was heated by only one fireplace, this being the most likely reason for Sydney's swift dismissal by the authorities (in September rather than later when the winter chill had set in).

The Norwood Schools were not really set up to provide technical training of any sort, the emphasis instead being on finding children employment outside the premises. So most of the child's day seems to have been taken up by religious study. An excerpt from the *Chaplain's Instructions* provides some idea of the role of such ritual in the everyday life of the institution, ritual that failed to find a place in Sydney's later life:

> Family prayer to be every morning before the hour of school, and immediately after the dismissal of the monitor's class in the evening.
> 1st. A psalm or hymn to be sung, the children standing.
> 2d. The scriptures to be read.

3d. The prayers as provided by the chaplain, ending with the Lord's Prayer, the children kneeling. Reading the bible and other religious instruction, the first hour after commencement of school, except on Wednesday and Saturday; on which days it is from half-past ten till half-past eleven. The first and second classes to have the above lesson last, on Friday afternoon.[25]

Dismissed on September 17, Sydney was turned over to his stepfather, Charles Chaplin, Sr., instead of his mother, who must still have been unable to care for her children, even though they were back with her to be taken again by April 1896, at which time she again checked into Lambeth infirmary. This time, Chaplin Sr. was dragged into court (the District Relief Committee) on June 9 and ordered to pay for the maintenance of his sons, for although he testified that he would not accept responsibility for Sydney — born illegitimate — he was ordered responsible by virtue of the fact that he had married the boy's mother.[26] This decision was supported by a provision of the 1834 Poor Law Amendment Act, #57 under "Relief of the poor," that stated:

> Every Man who from and after the passing of this Act shall marry a Woman having a Child or Children at the Time of such Marriage, whether such Child or Children be legitimate or illegitimate, shall be liable to maintain such Child or Children as Part of his Family, and shall be chargeable with all Relief, or the Cost Price thereof, granted to or on account of such Child or Children until such Child or Children shall respectively attain the Age of Sixteen, or until the Death of the Mother of such Child or Children; and such Child or Children shall, for the Purposes of this Act, be deemed a Part of such Husband's Family Accordingly.

The Committee ordered both boys, then, to the Central London District Poor Law School at Hanwell June 18, 1896. Chaplin Sr. agreed to the 15-shilling-a-week maintenance fee for both boys to cover their Hanwell costs soon thereafter, but within the year had stopped his payments. Although Sydney had already had some exposure to this sort of existence at the Norwood Schools, the boys were about to embark on their first true experience in the dreaded workhouse environment — at Lambeth.

Charlie noted with candor in a 1915 interview that "English people have a great horror of the poorhouse." Indeed with the enactment of the Poor Law in 1834, such fears had some foundation. In 1877, George R. Sims published a monologue in *The Dragonet Ballads* entitled "In the Workhouse, Christmas Day," that was "recited for generations in public bars and living rooms across the country," remaining popular until at least World War II:

> It is Christmas Day in the Workhouse,
> And the cold bare walls are bright
> With garlands of green and holly,
> And the place is a pleasant sight:
> For with clear-washed hands and faces
> In a long and hungry line
> The paupers sit at the tables,
> For this is the hour they dine.
>
> And the guardians and their ladies,
> Although the wind is east,
> Have come in their furs and wrappers,

> To watch their charges feast:
> To smile and be condescending,
> Put puddings on pauper plates,
> To be hosts at the workhouse banquet
> They've paid for — with the rates.
>
> Oh, the paupers are meek and lowly
> With their "Thank'ee kindly, mum's";
> So long as they fill their stomachs
> What matters it whence it comes?
> But one of the old men mutters,
> And pushes his plate aside:
> "Great God!" he cries; "but it chokes me!
> For this is the day she died."
>
> The guardians gazed in horror
> The master's face went white;
> "Did a pauper refuse his pudding?"
> "Could their ears believe aright?"
> Then the ladies clutched their husbands,
> Thinking the man might die
> Struck by a bolt, or something
> By the outraged One on high.[27]

Given that this monologue and other such poems and stories had filtered into the common consciousness of London's poor, it's not surprising that eligible souls did everything in their power to keep from entering such places. Simon Fowler notes that the poor had a dizzying array of charities from which to seek assistance in this endeavor. Lambeth alone had at least "57 mothers' meetings, 36 temperance societies for children, 25 savings banks or penny banks, 24 Christian endeavour societies, 21 boot, coal, blanket or clothing clubs, and two maternity societies," and much, much more.[28] Still, many felt more comfortable dealing with the local pawnbroker, from whom they could receive short-term loans, sometimes pawning the items after washday on Monday in order to buy food, then redeeming them on Saturday nights, in order to have respectable clothes to wear to Church services on Sunday. Charlie remembers a similar arrangement his mother had made with a pawnbroker in regards to Sydney's blue serge suit, which he needed to wear on weekends instead of his telegraph messenger uniform in order to be able to leave the flat at all: "[The purchase] created an insolvency in our economy, so that Mother was obliged to pawn the suit every Monday after Sydney went back to work in his telegraph uniform. She got seven shillings for the suit, redeeming it every Saturday for Sydney to wear over the weekend."[29]

The Poor Law Commission operated according to the belief that workhouses had three main objectives: to "look after parishioners who could not look after themselves, that is the aged, the infirm and children; to act as a deterrent to those who would not work; and lastly, as always, to function as a means of reducing the poor rate by forcing the indigent into the workhouse."[30] One of the main "deterrents" was that family members were separated almost immediately upon admission, being forced to live in different wards. An article describing the opening of the new Lambeth workhouse on Renfrew Road, just off of Kennington Road in 1874 (the one to which the boys and Hannah were admitted) notes that "each class has its own and distinct day-rooms, dormitories, staircases, lavatories, waterclosets, airing-grounds, and workrooms; the only common-place of meeting being the chapel and the dining room, where conversational intercourse is forbidden."[31]

Upon admittance, each boy would have had his hair cut short, and his own clothes replaced with the striped shirt, jacket, trousers, cap and shoes, i.e., the basic uniform of the workhouse — a humiliation often overlooked in first-person accounts of workhouse experiences.[32] Besides its recognizable appearance (especially the striped shirt), the garments were "generally made from fairly course materials with the emphasis on them being hard-wearing"[33] rather than comfortable. Amendments to the dietary system of workhouses had been made somewhat after a certain Dr. Edward Smith's official study of the diets of 65 workhouses in the north of England in 1866, yet the Chaplin boys still would have experienced the usual staples of the workhouse kitchen: "bread, milk and gruel, supplemented by potatoes, broth, soup, cheese, pudding and pie."[34]

In comparison to the inner-city dinginess of Renfrew Road, Charlie remembers the bucolic appearance of the Hanwell property: "The country surrounding Hanwell was beautiful in those days, with lanes of horse-chestnut trees, ripening wheat fields and heavy-laden orchards; and ever since, the rich, aromatic smell after rain in the country has always reminded me of Hanwell."[35] Modifications to the Hanwell property had been made all the way back in 1857, with the dormitories affording "sleeping room for 1,500 children, allowing 300 feet cube of air to one child. They vary in length from 80 to 150 feet, by an average width of 18 feet and height of 12 feet; they are warmed by open fireplaces; fresh air is admitted by a perforated skirting at the floor, and foul air escapes through gratings at the level of the ceiling."[36] Hanwell, indeed, was a place that tried to promote a healthy lifestyle for its children, who were encouraged "with games and exercises, country walks and emphasis on hygiene."[37] Perhaps, then, this is the place that had the most influence on young Sydney in regards to his obsession with such activities and the body in general in later life. In a letter to R. J. Minney dated October 7, 1932, Sydney recollects these boyhood influences and his reactions to them: "As a boy & even now I was always fascinated by acrobats & strong men. I used to buy all the physical culture magazines & take my Sandow exercise every morning with 5lb. dumbbells. Also my cold baths & 10- and 20-mile walks." He claims he "was a fanatic in keeping fit. I worshipped the sun, what little I saw of it in England & would expose my body to its rays whenever an opportunity presented itself, being a firm believer in its curative properties."[38] In addition, "Boys were taught to play musical instruments and as early as 1865 the brass band accompanied mealtimes,"[39] a fact that provided Sydney an opportunity to pursue another of his growing passions at this venue.

The paper trail that records the Chaplin brothers' difficult childhood is also evidence of something else — Sydney's use of the "Chaplin" name. While these records show that Sydney was using his stepfather's surname subsequent to Chaplin Sr.'s marriage to his mother, he was never legally "Sydney Chaplin," a fact that is proved by the name he bears on his death certificate — Sydney John Hill.[40] The various spellings of his first name—

Syd, Sydney, Sid, Sidney — are inconsequential. Charlie's given name also took various forms over the years, in the media, on documents and in correspondence, so perhaps this was just common practice.[41]

The Hanwell School records, then, list Sydney as, "Chaplin, Sydney John, aged eleven, Protestant; entered the school on the 18th June, 1896, left on 18th November, 1896, to join the training ship *Exmouth*" (a.k.a. *T.S. Exmouth*, not to be confused with *H.M.S. Exmouth*). Unfortunately, what this meant foremost was that he was separated from his younger brother Charlie, who took the separation hard. Not only were the boys separated, but with Sydney's having been chosen for the seamanship training program, they were to be located in different cities.

The *Exmouth* was moored at Grays, Essex, at the time considered "a struggling township on the Thames,"[42] and had been commissioned for use as a training ship by the Metropolitan Asylum Board in 1878, after having served Her Majesty at Balaclava.[43] Dr. Charles H. Leibbrand described it in 1899 as a "splendid three-decker, of 3,106 tons displacement and with a measurement of 220 ft. by 59 ft."[44] While being chosen for this opportunity might seem like a stroke of luck — one which Charlie couldn't be offered due to his young age — in fact, Sydney was given the opportunity due to his physical capabilities and intelligence, for "the Board was selective about entrants," with 600 boys making up a full program.[45] In the program itself, he learned seamanship, gunnery and first aid, as well as general discipline, cleanliness, responsibility, "patriotism and citizenship."[46]

Leibbrand credited Staff-Commander W. S. Bourchier[47] with the program's success. Bourchier entered the Navy in 1840 as a navigating shipman aboard the *Impregnable*. He held command first on "the *Myrtle*, steamship tender to the flagship, for close on twelve years,"[48] following that with service as a navigating lieutenant on the *Zebra*. Prior to the appearance of this article in *The Strand* in 1899, Admiral Bosanquet, the Inspecting General of Naval Training Ships filed this report about the program: "The training ship *Exmouth* for boys is in most excellent order. The drills and instructions are exceedingly well taught, and the comfort and well-being of the lads is sedulously attended to. Captain Bourchier's arrangements are admirable and conscientiously carried out by a very able staff of officers. It is a model training ship."[49]

Leibbrand called his readers' attention first to the boys' "ablutions," believing the process to be original. "There is a huge, broad tank-bath in the lavatory," he writes, "not much smaller than a usual-sized swimming bath. Thither the lads proceed in marching order, though, of course, without any baggage, however slight; and promptly start to give themselves a wholesome shampoo with carbolic soap." Being thus lathered "they plunge head foremost into the tank. Diving straight through its full width, with wonderful agility they then bound over its anything but low side, landing — at attention — before the officer on watch, ready for inspection as to their outward cleanliness."[50]

Because the curriculum also emphasized gymnastics and band training, Sydney developed a strong basis for his future career in entertainment. "So efficiently were the boys taught [in this area], that those whom I have seen at my visit go through most difficult exercises on the horizontal and parallel bars and on the springboard, I would safely have them compete with the best model sections or Masterriegen of Germany's leading gymnastic societies,"⁵¹ wrote Leibbrand. In addition, the boys received a moral training and a practical elementary education, under W. Hollamby, the head schoolmaster on the ship.

While a large majority of the boys went on to careers in Her Majesty's navy, for the present, Sydney became a bugler. Music was also an important part of life aboard ship, and many of the young, newly trained musicians made careers in the Army. In fact, this was only one of two areas of training in which Sydney received First Class marks (specifically in "Bugle"). Over the course of his year and a third on the *Exmouth*, his record book shows that he moved from Fifth Class in all areas to Second Class in Seamanship, Fourth Class in Swimming, Third Class in Gunnery, Second Class in Signalling and First Class in Gymnastics. These marks make it clear what his strengths were from the start. It also notes that Sydney's conduct on the ship was "very good."⁵² Sydney's copy of "The Metropolitan Training Ship *Exmouth* Boys' Own Song Book" still exists as well and, of course, the first song inside its covers is "Rule Britannia." "The 'Exmouth' Song," with words by Alfred Thompson, presents a snapshot of life on board ship:

> When I was a lad, all my young days,
> Were spent in the "Exmouth" down at Grays;
> I was green at first and played the fool,
> So they bundled me into the fifth class school;
> But the fifth class school and the A B C
> Have made me a Captain in the Queen's Navee.
>
> Then I "threadled" the needle in the tailor's shop
> And pricked my fingers till it made me hop;
> Went out for a pull and whilst afloat,
> Caught a crab, and disappeared into the bottom of the boat;
> But catching the crab was a lesson to me,
> And now I'm a Captain in the Queen's Navee.
>
> My bed that night was high from the floor,
> With a number upon it like a big front door;
> And when with a spring to get in I tried,
> I nearly broke my nose on the opposite side;
> But I lashed up that hammock so carefullee,
> That now I am a Captain in the Queen's Navee.
>
> Then they bothered me with splice and knot,
> And bends and hitches, and I don't know what;
> So many I couldn't tell t'other from which,
> Nor a double Matthew Walker from a plain clove hitch;
> But I very soon passed a torn-i-key (tourniquet),
> As well as any Captain in the Queen's Navee.
>
> Well I left the ship for the Royal N.,
> And have seen a deal of the world since then;
> With its ups and downs, and freaks and frays,
> But I've never once forgotten my old "Exmouth" days;
> And I've to thank the Board, called the M. A. B.,
> That now I am a Captain in the Queen's Navee.

> Now "Exmouth" lads just list what I say,
> You all may do the same one day;
> Even Nelson once made a middy's roll,
> And was glad enough to clamber through the lubber's hole;
> So stick to your work, and get ready for sea,
> And all you may be Captains in the Queen's Navee.[53]

Due to his family's dire circumstances back home, Sydney was induced to leave the program early, being dismissed on January 20, 1898. His mother and brother needed money to survive—one thing the *Exmouth* program did not provide. And they missed the sense of security they felt when Sydney was with them. Hannah had even written Captain Bourchier on July 19, asking why he wouldn't let Sydney come home on leave in what is a very supplicant and plaintive letter: "Please pardon me for troubling you, but I am so very disappointed that my little son, Sidney, cannot come home on leave for a few days, the same as the other boys. If there is any special reason for your refusal, I should take it as a great favour if you would let me know as I feel so extremely anxious, once more apologizing for troubling you."[54] So, still the man of the "house," Sydney left the ship and Grays, Essex, soon finding a job as a telegraph messenger boy at the West Strand Post Office.[55]

By June, Sydney and his family were living at 10 Farmers Road, located just behind Kennington Park, but just a month later, they admitted themselves once again to the Lambeth Workhouse, this time staying only ten days before the boys were sent to Norwood Schools. Hannah checked them out just two weeks later, but only for the weekend. Sydney's version of this story made its way into *Motion Picture Classic* later in his film career. "Finally we hit upon a plan," he writes. "I had made ninepence doing odd jobs and had carefully hoarded it. I got word to our mother and we all checked out of the institution. They gave us back our clothes all wrinkled up from having been packed away. Hand in hand, we went out." Sydney relates that he "spent the ninepence for some cakes and cherries and we sat all day together in the park. When night came, we all went back to the workhouse and went thru all the formalities of entering again—greatly to the disgust of the officials."[56]

September 6 of that year, Hannah was committed to Cane Hill Asylum. Charlie relates that Sydney was the first to hear about it: "One day, while Sydney was playing football, two nurses called him out of the game and told him that Mother had gone insane and had been sent to Cane Hill lunatic asylum. When Sydney heard the news he showed no reaction but went back and continued playing football. But after the game he stole away by himself and wept."[57] The attending doctor scribbled the abbreviation "Syp" on her record, indicating that he had suspicions at least that Hannah was suffering from the effects of tertiary syphilis. These three letters have led to volumes of speculation on the issue, with one writer fabricating a story about Hannah's undocumented excursion to South Africa—the supposed site of Sydney's conception—where she likely contracted the disease, being unwittingly conscripted as a prostitute there. There are several problems with the theory that she had syphilis, as well as with how she may have acquired it. In regards to her having the disease, the first problem concerns the fact that Victorian doctors "remained extremely confused about the manifestations of syphilis, which could vary greatly."[58] The second concerns syphilis itself and the ramifications of the disease. While dementia does affect eight percent of patients in the tertiary stage,[59] relying simply on this information is not enough. Syphilis can also be passed and is passed congenitally, meaning that one, two or all of her sons should have contracted the disease from her as they passed through the birth canal, and there was no sign of the disease in any of them.[60] There is also a problem with Hannah's supposed flight to Cape Town and subsequent submission to prostitution. One group of scholars admits to the long history of prostitution in the area, due to its port location, but list only 213 recorded prostitutes in 1868 (when it became institutionalized[61]), with an influx of women from Europe in 1890 that plied the trade (most of whom were from Eastern Europe).[62] Philippa Levine notes the obvious priority colonial governments made to keep white proletarian women out anyway. The working class woman forced to turn to crime and prostitution to make her way, moved herself to the socio-economic level of the native races — a status considered unacceptable, even dangerous,[63] thus the passage of the various Contagious Diseases Acts (CD), one in 1864, 1866 and 1869 and later, in 1885, when syphilis was found to be a scourge upon the population (due to the gold and diamond rushes), occurring in 63 out of 67 districts in that year. This legislation "provided for the registration and periodic examination of 'common prostitutes' in scheduled areas and their 'voluntary' treatment in Lock Hospitals if they were found to be diseased."[64] Elizabeth Van Heyningen does, however, note that "many prostitutes were not members of a deviant group but formed a regular component of colonial society," a pseudo-respectable status that caused them to do perhaps the most harm in spreading the disease.[65]

The status of music hall in colonial Cape Town must also be addressed in this argument. While *The Era*, music hall's most respected tabloid, covered the colonies in some detail, no mention is made of a scandal in which booking agents (such as the alleged Sidney Hawke[s]) were caught luring innocent young soubrettes to South Africa for sexual purposes. The only theatre in Cape Town seems to have been the Theatre Royal, lessees and managers being H. C. Sidney and H. J. Fiedler, and it seems to have been a venue for more upper-echelon dramatics. The programs for late 1885 included *Lost in London, Impulse, Black-eyed Susan* (a popular burlesque — considered a real change of pace for the venue), Offenbach's operetta *Forty Winks* and *The Little Treasure*. H. C. Sidney was an actor as well, taking on the role of Captain Maydenblush in *The Little Treasure*.[66] If there was a music hall-type venue extant at this time, *The Era* fails to mention it. Still, despite all of this circumstantial evidence, the events could have occurred much as Hannah related them to her children. The same story, in fact, was passed along by half-brother Wheeler Dryden in his adulthood, and he claims to have received the information solely from his father. Therefore, if Hannah had created a fictional story around the event of Sydney's birth, she was telling it to people other than her boys.

Cane Hill Asylum's attending doctor reported further that Hannah "has been very strange in manner — at one time abusive & noisy, at another using endearing terms. Has been confined in P[added] R[oom] repeatedly on a/c of sudden violence — threw a mug at another patient. Shouting, singing and talking incoherently." He writes further that she "complains of her head and depressed and crying this morning — dazed and unable to give any reliable information. Asks if she is dying. States she belongs to Christ Church

(Congregation) which is Ch. of E. She was sent here on a mission by the Lord. Says she wants to get out of the world."⁶⁷ Still, despite this dire description of her condition, she was released by November 12 and immediately retrieved her two sons from Chaplin Sr. and his partner Louise, who were living at 289 Kennington Park Road at the time. Louise particularly disliked Sydney, on whom she could take out all her frustrations — he being no real relation to Chaplin Sr. Charlie remembered both the degraded state of Louise and of the flat itself, indicating that perhaps his father had hit upon hard times, writing also that Louise was "dissipated and morose-looking, yet attractive, tall and shapely." He describes that flat as possessing only "two rooms and although the front room had large windows, the light filtered in as if from under water. Everything looked as sad as Louise; the wallpaper looked sad, the horsehair furniture looked sad, and the stuffed pike in a glass case that had swallowed another pike as large as itself— the head sticking out of its mouth — looked gruesomely sad."⁶⁸ One account of the boys' life in this flat reported that Sydney retaliated at one point by threatening Louise with a sharpened button hook, for treatment that included being locked out of the flat at night and being denied food.⁶⁹ Back in the "care" of their mother, though, the boys moved with her into 39 Methley Street, just across the street from a pickle factory and a slaughterhouse.

Sydney was unimpressed by both the work and the pay that accompanied the position of "telegraph boy," so he decided to make the most of his seamanship training, if possible. He had to add about three years to his age, however, in order to secure jobs in the field at this point in time — his first being with the Union Castle Mail Steamship Company. He joined the crew of the S.S. *Norman* on April 6, 1901, at only 16 years of age. Charlie recalls Sydney's tentative beginning, for "before sailing, he almost lost the job when he blew the first bugle call for lunch. He was out of practice and the soldiers' board let up a chorus of howls. The chief steward came in a fury. 'What the hell do you call that?' 'Sorry, sir,' said Sydney, 'I haven't got my lip in yet.' 'Well, you'd better get your bloody lip in before the boat sails, or otherwise, you'll be put ashore.'"⁷⁰

Before the ship sailed from Southampton, Sydney relates having to spend a fretful night in town by himself beforehand. "I found that I had just money enough for a bed, but no money to eat," he related to Harry Carr in 1924 about this experience. "I went supperless to bed. The next morning when the band went to breakfast, I told them I wasn't hungry and didn't want any." Left alone, he began to cry, thinking about his helpless mother back in London and his powerlessness to assist her. Then, "A little waitress came to where I sat and asked me why I was crying. I told her about my mother. She slipped away to her room and came back with her savings which she had been hoarding. I sent the money to my mother and when I came back from the voyage," narrated Sydney, "gave the money back to the girl."⁷¹ This ship embarked on the Cape Mail run, meaning, of course, that the boy would visit the supposed site of his conception. What an existential moment that must have been as the ship pulled into the Cape to deliver its load! His position in the company was assistant steward and bandsman, and, in fact, his earliest photograph shows him to be obviously the youngest member of that particular band — by far. Overall, he made seven voyages, receiving marks of "Very Good" consistently on his Continuous Certificate of Discharge. Sydney recounted an episode to R. J. Minney detailing the work ethic that provides evidence of this. "When I first went away to sea as a steward and was seventeen years old, they put me to scrub a stairway that led down to the hold of the ship, and was used merely for the purpose of carrying down empty bottles and all waste matter used on the ship. These stairs," he recounted with pride, "were fithily black and with the aid of silver sand and holystone, I succeeded in getting these stairs so white that you could eat your meals off them. It was noticed by the captain, who sent for me, and told me he had been captain for nineteen years and had never seen those stairs look so clean." The captain subsequently congratulated Sydney and told him that if he was "always as conscientious in all my work, that I was bound to make a success in life."[72]

Sydney followed the Master of the S.S. *Norman* when he transferred to the *Kinfairns Castle*, a ship with which he was affiliated for four voyages. Of course, he was careful to send enough money to his family each time before he sailed. The last of these four voyages docked in Southampton on May 31, 1901, and with Sydney's excellent customer service and its accompanying tips — to the tune of more than three pounds — he was able to provide his family the easiest summer they had had in some time. Then when he returned to sea on September 1, he did so as a full steward on the *Haverford*, having signed on for a voyage to New York and back, on what would be his first trip to the States. However, because Sydney took ill on the voyage, his trip lasted more than the usual three weeks, a fact which threw his awaiting family into financial turmoil. The first return voyage he could acquire was on the *St. Louis*, which departed out of New York on October 5, reaching England on the 23rd of the month.

After the physical problems encountered on this voyage (physical problems that would affect him off and on throughout his life during times of stress), Sydney decided to remain in London awhile, and did so for ten months. Probably succumbing at last to the need of good stable pay and the ability to garner tips, on September 6, 1902, Sydney embarked on what would be four more Cape Mail voyages, again on the *Kinfairns Castle*. The voyages each lasted seven weeks, with two weeks' leave between them. He embarked on the last of these voyages on March 24, 1903. While he was away, his mother again became ill, checked into the Lambeth Infirmary on May 5 and was committed to Cane Hill Asylum on May 11. In the meantime, Sydney had decided to come home for good. He had saved a tidy sum and was determined to use it as a start-up fund for his stage career.

In several interviews he provided to the press over the course of his film career in America, during the teens and especially the twenties, Sydney often referred to his first experience "on the stage" as being with Miss Maggie Morton's traveling company for the show "The Two Little Drummer Boys," written by Walter Howard. The most fleshed-out of these accounts occurs in R. J. Minney's *Chaplin: The Immortal Tramp*, for which Sydney provided much of the information. As Minney tells it, Sydney found himself loitering on the London streets one day, when he should have been delivering telegrams:

> He saw in the window of a music shop the sign: "WANTED — Buglers for Touring Company." The bugle particularly appealed to him. He noted the address, applied, and was taken on by Maggie Morton's Theatrical Company at a salary of six shillings a week and his keep. Eight boys in all were engaged; they formed a bugle band and paraded the streets in uniform to advertise the show "The Two Little Drummer Boys." They did this all over the country

A 16-year-old Sydney Chaplin, far right, and his bugle corp mates (all much older) aboard one of the Castle Line ships, circa 1901 (CHACHAA).

and had also to help with the erection of the scenery and its dismantlement, to load it on to trains and unload it on arrival at their destination, collect the tickets at the door of the theatre and appear on stage in the second act. Mrs. Chaplin thought the work hard and the pay poor. Sydney, she said, ought to have remained at the post office, where in time he would have qualified for a pension.[73]

Minney places this tour post–Western Union and pre–S.S. *Norman*, which would date it in either late 1900 or early 1901, making Sydney's stage debut at age 15. Again, in a 1914 article for *Reel Life*, however, Sydney claims he was given a small stage part in this company, which played "in the town halls and exchanges." He relates in this article that "the hero [of the show] appears in the first act and is not seen again till the fourth, during that period he is supposed to be incarcerated in an Egyptian prison, which was usually the local bar-room." One night, however, the show had already started when "the dialogue was interrupted by weird sounds from a cornet blown by a would-be musician in a house close by. The noise was unearthly, the sounds penetrating the theatre, and threatening to stop the performance, when all of a sudden it ceased and the play continued peacefully, till the fourth act." When the time came for the hero's return, however, there was no hero. Sydney remembers that "the building was searched throughout, but with no signs of him. There was only one thing to do so the manager made a speech, saying, that owing to the sudden illness of the principal artist the show could not proceed and they were given tickets for another night." In the meantime, the secret of the hero's disappearance was discovered by the cast. "It appears he had gone quietly over to the house of the cornetist," Sydney remembers, "and remonstrated with him in a gentle sort of way. The musician not being amenable to argument, more forcible methods were used with the result that the cornetist spent the night in the hospital, the hero in a police cell, and the cornet in the dust hole."[74]

In the same article, Sydney talks of how proud of this part he was, even thinking he was "on the ladder," so to speak. But if he was really just a part of the bugle and baggage team, watching the members of the acting company must have been enough to eventually convince him to dump a lucrative position as a steward and try his chances once again. As the facts demonstrate, however, Sydney never had the sort of blessed luck as his brother in this area. His talents were sound — even extraordinary — but he never seemed to have the extra something he needed to make it all really work for him. In fact, his next position — really his first engagement — he acquired through Charlie's efforts on his behalf.

After leaving his position on the *Kinfairns Castle*, Sydney ended up behind the bar at the Coal Hole on the Strand, once a sort of supper club that had since become a rather run-of-the-mill public house. Still, "Out of one hundred and fifty applicants, he got the job."[75] He told one version of how he accomplished this in an interview he gave in 1927. Finding a huge line of applicants for a job advertised in the paper just that morning, Sydney hung around by the door, but away from the other men, and noticed two doors leading into a basement office. After a bobby came through that door, Sydney dove through it, dashed into a cluttered office and then bolted the door behind him: "I snatched off my cap and hurriedly explained myself to the man before me: and oh! how I lied! I got more worked up as I proceeded. Tears glistened in my eyes as I told of my mythical old mother dying of starvation and sickness in a wretched old garrett."[76] The interviewer told Sydney he would be considered, and if chosen, would receive one of five or six tickets granting another interview. He received one a short time later. Surviving that lengthy interview, he waited for another card. And the card came.

In December of that year, however, Charlie, having established himself with the Charles Frohman company in the role of Billy in *Sherlock Holmes*— a role Sydney helped him prepare for by assisting with line memorization — was able to negotiate his brother into the recently vacated role of the Count of Stalberg, which Sydney easily won and was able to retain for the rest of the 1903–4 tour, closing on June 11, 1904, at the Royal West London Theatre in Church Street, Edgware Road.[77] While they were touring the provinces, Hannah was released from Cane Hill and they arranged for her to join them. They rented a flat in Reading with the intention of installing her there. Charlie recalls: "Sydney and I waited for her at the railroad station, tense and happy; yet I could not help feeling anxious as to how she would fit into our lives again, knowing that the close ties of other days could never be recaptured." But, as Charlie remembers, "It was not long before we were fully adjusted to one another, and my dejection passed. That we had outgrown the intimacy she had known when we were children she understood better than we did, which made her all the more endearing to us." Hannah's responsibilities on tour included "the shopping and catering, bringing home fruits and delicacies and always a few flowers.

Occasionally," Charlie relates, "she was quiet and reserved, and her detachment saddened me. She acted more like a guest than our mother."[78]

Unfortunately for Sydney, his role was occupied for the next season, and so he turned back to the sea once again, signing on as assistant steward and bugler on the *Dover Castle* traveling to Natal. He sailed from the Southampton port on November 10 and did not return until January 1905. As Robinson points out, Sydney became aware of his comedic gifts on this particular voyage, ones he had most probably received from his mother. He wrote to her on December 2:

> You will be pleased to hear that I made a terrific success at the concert on board. I gave an impersonation of George Mozart as the "Dentist." They simply roared and would not let me off the platform until I had sung them "Two Eyes of Blue." There is another concert on tonight and while I am writing this they have sent down three people to ask me to oblige. They tell me the audience are shouting for the Bugler and the boy who has just got up to recite "The Boy Stood on the Burning Deck" has been hissed off. Fancy the quiet old Syd becoming a comedian. I have told him to tell the chairman I don't feel up to it tonight. The fact is I have undressed. I am lying on my bunk in my pyjamas. It is best to leave them wanting.[79]

Sydney as Count von Stalberg in the Charles Frohman production of *Sherlock Holmes* (1903–4), a part obtained for him by Charlie who was playing the role of Billy, the Page Boy. This was Sydney's debut role (CHACHAA).

George Mozart was an English music hall star who completed his career in the film business. Tony Barker notes that he rose to the top with a rather indefinable act: "George Mozart, who had such quirky material as imitating railway engines on a side drum — well, he had been a military bandsman! He was able to burlesque just about anybody, and it was once said of him 'Give him a hat and he'll entertain any house for an hour.'" He usually presented one-man sketches in which he played several characters, and a sketch called *Callers* is one of these. After an opening burst of song, he hints at other characters who would be part of the sketch later on: "A particular persistent tattered tramp is followed by the Lord of the Manor himself, tipsy Tomkins, armed with the password of sobriety, 'Crystal Palace.'"[80] Mozart and his act is an interesting and challenging choice for the aspiring stage performer, except for the fact that mimicking many characters and voices is exactly what his mother had taught Sydney and his brother to do throughout their childhoods.

On March 6, Hannah returned to the Lambeth Infirmary once again. The attending physician, Dr. Marcus Quarry, examined her and concluded his remarks by writing that she was "a Lunatic and a proper person to be taken charge of and detained under care and treatment.... She is very strange in manner and quite incoherent. She dances, sings and cries by turns. She is indecent in conduct & conversation at times and again at times praying and saying she has been born again."[81] The following week, Justice of the Peace William Andrews signed the Lunatic Reception Order and two days later Hannah entered Cane Hill Asylum, never to recover her sanity.

Chapter 2

Downstage to Marquee: Becoming a Headliner

> The top of the bill for the current week is Fred Karno's new production *Skating*, which proves to be as mirth-provoking as the other shows controlled by this experienced gentleman, and success is naturally emphatic and complete. The absurdity is written by Messrs. J. Hickory Wood, Fred Karno, and Syd Chaplin; the music is by Mr. Joe Cleeve. Certainly the amusement never flags for a moment, the second scene especially being particularly effective. The whole company are very capable exponents of the new diversion. Mr. Chaplin, whose entry was very warmly greeted, displays all his well-known powers as a comedian, and receives capital support from the rest of the company, the fall of the curtain being the signal for a great ovation. —"Islington Empire," *The Era*, July 31, 1909

DESPITE THE FACT THAT HIS MOTHER Hannah's future seemed bleak, Sydney's luck in regards to a career on the stage was changing for the better. His persistence finally paid off when he was offered a role as a knockabout comedian with the Charles Manon Company in a new production by Wal Pink called *Repairs*, in March 1906. The gist of the story consisted of bits between various inept workmen supposedly remodeling an interior — a kind of Three Stooges turn before the Three Stooges were on the scene. It was advertised in *The Era* in a one-time-only full column ad as "A New Departure — A Novel Item. WAL PINK'S WORKMEN IN *REPAIRS*. A brilliant example of 'How NOT to do it.'" The setting represented "the interior of Muddleton Villa, in the hands of those eminent house decorators, Messrs. Spoiler and Messit." This ad in *The Era* insisted that it was "not a dumb show. It is an acrobatic, knockabout, dancing interlude, plentifully besprinkled with funny dialogue and odd quips and cranks. Moreover, it hath no plot, it is NOT a stage play."[1] Fred Regina was the manager of the road company — the only company. Sydney had been given the role of "the beery, mustached agitator [shown standing on a ladder in one surviving photo], who sulks about the room, trying to get the workmen to strike."[2] One description of the sketch from the *Referee* described that "you see the Plumber, the Paperhanger, the Whitewasher, the Carpenter, and their various assistants all engaged in their respective fell tasks, breaking windows faster than they mend them, whitewashing the tenants rather than their house, painting themselves rather than the wainscots, or sleeping at their work, but very wide awake at meal-times, and especially Beer Times."[3] The only bit of the script to survive appears in the text of Minney's *Chaplin: The Immortal Tramp* and is, of course, an excerpt of dialogue attributed to Charlie's character — Charlie had reluctantly accepted the part of the plumber's assistant in the act; at this time he thought comedy well beneath him — and a bit of contextualizing description in a scene in which the plumber vocalizes his annoyance at his assistant's wearing of the green tam o'shanter:

> "Why doncher take that blarsted 'at off? 'Ang it up. 'Ang it up, I tell yer."
> "Where?" Charlie would ask mournfully.
> "Oh, any blarsted where. 'Ere! Take this 'ammer an' nail — an' 'ang it up somewhere."
> Charlie went up to the door, drove in the nail, but it only knocked the panel out. Next he tried the wall and the nail pierced a water pipe.
> This formed the bulk of the diversion, until in exasperation the plumber turned on the boy, snatched his green hat, threw it on to the floor and jumped on it again and again with angry curses.[4]

Sydney as a workman in Wal Pink's production, *Repairs* (1906). Charlie also appeared in this production for a time (CHACHAA).

The sketch opened at the Southampton Hippodrome on March 19. With Pink's name behind the show, it was expected to do well, thus the extravagant advertisement. But the ad appeared only the one time and while a long list of engagements accompanied it, it is not clear that all advertised dates were played. It listed dates at The Duchess, Balham, the Zoo Hippodrome, Glasgow, and venues at Boscombe, Belfast, Manchester, Wolverhampton, Liverpool, and Portsmouth, but reviews exist only for Balham, Glasgow, Belfast, Manchester, Hammersmith, Clapham, and Liverpool.[5] On April 14, the Zoo Hippodrome's (Glasgow) review appeared, announcing that the company "cause[d] laughter loud and long, their comedy business being funny and unforced."[6] A week later, the Palace Theatre of Varieties (Belfast) presented a similar review of the program, writing, "Wal Pink's company creates roars of laughter with the humorous sketch *Repairs*, one of the most genuine incitements to mirth and merriment that we have seen for some time."[7] Then on May 12, a report appeared stating that the company was continuing to gain admirers "adding to their reputation at Mr. Walter Gibbons' Clapham hall, where *Repairs* has been nightly received with roars by huge audiences."[8] Only the Palace Theatre (Manchester) seemed unimpressed with the group, labeling the show "an absurdity concocted solely to raise laughter."[9] Robinson notes that when the act was appearing at the Grand Palace, Clapham, Charlie left the troupe to join Casey's Court Circus.[10] Several accounts claim that Sydney's performance was seen by Fred Karno of Karno's London Comedians, who gave Sydney a contract to join him on that basis.[11] Certainly, his first contract started shortly after the completion of the *Repairs* tour, on July 9, 1906.

Fred Karno (born Frederick John Westcott) began his working life as a plumber, taught himself gymnastics and then, having an innate flair for business, soon found himself running what was to be one of the most successful music hall entertainment companies in London in the early twentieth century. The year Sydney was hired,[12] Karno constructed what came to be known as "Karno's Fun Factory," at 26, 28 & 28a Vaughan Road, Camberwell, S.E., a large theatrical multipurpose space that was announced in the trades every time new construction on the building was completed: "The magnificent NEW WING just added to the above [Karno's Theatrical Factory], comprising a Paint Room, Rehearsal Room, and Storage Dock, is now complete."[13]

Styled "Karno's London Comedians," "Karno's Komics," "Fred Karno's Pantomime Company," or other similar names, Karno came to have three grades of music hall sketches: "The rough type in pantomime such as *Early Birds* and *Jail Birds,* employing the 'Karno Boys,' adepts in tumbling, miming, and broad slap-stick comedy; the burlesques, the dialogue, song, and dance...; and a somewhat quieter type of humour in such musical farces as *Cherry Blossom, A Tragedy of Errors,* and *Yes! Papa.*[14] Sydney and later Charlie were always cast in the "rough type." In general, however, Karno's style of comedy was one that valued "tempo and rhythm, he strove for finesse and for faultless ensemble work, he originated the idea of putting a bit of sentiment right in the middle of a funny music hall turn, that a slow delivery can often be more effective than hectic speed, but that in any event pace must be varied to avoid monotony"[15] — all elements the brothers would later take with them into the American film industry. Hired as a pantomimist, Sydney initially received £3 a week, with an option of being paid £6 if he toured America, where Karno was to tour two companies at nearly the same time (one company left England about a month after the first). This Sydney did almost immediately, for he left for the States from Liverpool on the S.S. *Caronia* on July 31, arriving in New York on August 8.[16]

The second American company was headlined by Billie Reeves and managed by Alf Reeves, future manager of the Charlie Chaplin Studios. Sydney's company (the first company) was managed by Arthur Forrest. The only sketch this company performed was *Mumming Birds*, with Sydney first playing the role of the conjuror in that sketch,[17] and Billie Reeves's company performing both *Early Birds* and *The Smoking Concert.* Sydney was listed number three in the line-up of players in his company, with Harry Royston as the headliner (the Inebriate) and James Russell (Jimmy) also listed before him and probably playing the part of the spoiled child. W. Fern, Ernest Stone, Fred Bendo, Bert Clark,

Arnold McFarlane, Amy Minister (later Amy Reeves), Beatrice Barnes, and Agnes Clark made up the rest of this company.

Mumming Birds is considered Karno's most well-known, well-beloved and successful comedy sketch. It was a typical music hall show filled with this and that — "'A lot of nothing,' as Fred in one of his vivid phrases described it. He saw possibilities in it, however, and from that idea grew the sketch originally called *Twice Nightly,* or *A Stage upon a Stage.*"[18] The original title more accurately presents the gimmick of the show. The turns onstage, such as the magician, the male vocalist and the female vocalist were only a small part of the entertainment. The "stars" were the planted audience members, namely the inebriate swell and the "bad boy in the box" who reacted to each other, the turns on the stage and to the audience itself in seemingly spontaneous ways (if expert acrobatics can seem spontaneous!). None of these individuals had names. As Karno biographers Edwin Adeler and Con West suggest, "*Mumming Birds* was based on an idea as old as the immemorial hills — the essential cruelty of audiences.... Where the genius of Fred Karno came in was the engaging of accomplished professionals to portray the supposedly 'dud' performers. It purged the thing of cruelty and bad taste and made it the most riotously hilarious performance that had yet been seen."[19]

Sydney as the inebriate swell, in Karno's *Mumming Birds*, circa 1906 (CHACHAA).

Having some trouble with both his players and his sketches in the United States, Karno decided to make his first trip to America in September, 1906, along with the Billie Reeves company. Their departure from England was announced in *Variety* for September 1. Billie Ritchie, who had been touring with one of Karno's companies in the States as the headliner for *Mumming Birds*, was in the process of defecting at this time and by the time the two Karno companies and Karno himself had arrived in mid–September, Ritchie had been lured away by the same gentleman Karno took to court for plagiarism of his *Mumming Birds (A Night in an English Music Hall)* sketch, Jean Bedini.[2] The September 15 issue of *Variety* quoted Karno as saying, "I have not seen the 'copy' act, but am informed that it is an exact duplicate. I am arranging to bring over several of my companies.... My time here in New York is limited. I don't see how I can remain over ten days or two weeks at the most." But "when asked if he contemplated preferring a complaint to the International Artisten Loge, of whom both Karno and Bedini [were] members, against Bedini for 'lifting,' Mr. Karno replied: 'I have not given that a thought yet. Possibly I shall take some action in that direction. I am not jubilant over the stealing of my act; it is not encouraging, and I am greatly surprised that time could be procured for it.'[21]

Although Adeler and West claim that Karno never really received his due in many of these court cases,[22] what the courts failed to provide, the entertainment industry took upon itself, for Bedini[23] found himself an outcast in the industry and soon could not find a house to play in.[24] All this turmoil must have provided a tense and uncomfortable atmosphere for Sydney during his premiere tour, both with Karno and in America, but it had to have provided many important lessons about the entertainment business as well.

Sydney's company was listed in a local newspaper advertisement as appearing the week of August 12 at Proctor's Union Square Theatre, which would have been his first U. S. appearance, and coincidentally the venue of his stepfather Charles Chaplin, Sr.'s, only New York City appearance back in 1890. His company then remained in the New York area at various theatres, with the exception of two weeks at the Belasco Theatre in Washington, D.C. (a Karno company first), until the second week in October. With H. B. Marinelli as their booking agent, the company had been booked on the Percy Williams Circuit, which kept the company mostly on or near the East Coast, playing dates in mid–October at the Olympic in Cincinnati, the Shubert in Columbus, and the Lyric in Cleveland, then moving back east to the Colonial in New York, the Lowell Theatre in Lowell, Massachusetts, the New Bedford Theatre in New Bedford, Massachusetts, and the Poli Theatre in New Haven, Connecticut, the site of the company's final performances. In "Karno's People Return Home," which appeared in the December 10 issue of *Variety*, the reporter noted that the "ten people who came over in the first Karno company and played 'A Night in an English Music Hall' returned to England this week to take part in a new Karno act called 'A Football

Publicity photograph of a young Sydney Chaplin, circa 1906 (CHACHAA).

Match,' to be produced at Manchester for the first time December 24.... Most were disinclined to leave America. The larger salaries paid over here proved enticing and they were loath to return to the former scale."[25]

The headliner of this "new Karno act," *The Football Match,* was Harry Weldon, whom Robinson describes as "a slow-talking Lancashire comedian."[26] The aspect of this particular show that made it hugely popular was the addition of "two real first-class football teams, comprising well-known football players selected from the leading clubs of the United Kingdom, including W. C. Athersmith (late Aston Villa), Jas. W. Crabtree (ditto) Fred Spikesley (late Sheffield Wednesday)."[27] The sketch was written by Karno and Fred Kitchen,[28] probably Karno's greatest comedian headliner of such sketches written just for him as *Moses and Son, The Bailiff,* and *G. P. O.* The centerpiece of this sketch was the final cup-tie between the Middleton Pie-cans and the Midnight Wanderers. As the review in *The Era* describes it,

> The action opens in the training quarters of the Middleton Pie-cans, at "The Bull," where the members of this wonderful combination of players are seen getting fit for the coming struggle under the urgent supervision of their trainer. Athletic exercises are, of course, less in evidence than eccentric acrobatics and comic tumbling, and the general physique of the club is hardly on the side of fitness and symmetry.[29]

The plot is set in motion when an attempt to bribe certain members to lose the match is observed by a detective in disguise. Stiffy, the goalkeeper, is the most significant person on whom the bribe is attempted, but he is seen as the character with the most integrity and therefore someone who can't be tempted. The reviewer admits, however, that "to follow in detail the many comicalities which enliven the action in the grounds at 'The Bull' would be, if it were possible, to reconceive an infinite variety of spontaneous doings, such as the Karno comedians commonly employ in their embellishment of a theme."[30] In the second scene, set in the exterior of the football ground, a realistic effect was produced by the turnstiles, and a crowd of a hundred extras were employed from the Manchester streets. The third scene, the dressing-room, gave a typical glimpse into the scant few minutes before a match, and the fourth was "the scene of the struggle on which the honour of the Pie-cans and the defeat of conspirators depended, proved a spacious and lifelike picture of a football field."[31] It was in this final scene of the football match itself that the actual footballers made their appearance, playing against a team of Karno players in what appeared to be a serious game that is, in the end, rained out. Not yet a headliner, Sydney played in this particular sketch at least through the first few months of 1907. And it was this sketch that brother Charlie was later to audition with Karno, receiving great response — and a contract.

Shortly after the debut of Karno's show *London Suburbia* on June 17, 1907, Sydney signed his second contract (June 24) and received a slight raise in pay. With this signing, he effectively moved up to number two in the listings for this particular show, just behind Jimmy Russell. *London Suburbia* was a sketch, written by Karno and Leonard F. Durell, and described in a review in *The Era* for June 22:

> The delights of the outer metropolis are depicted in two scenes, the first representing a row of villas, with housemaids busy on the doorsteps. A literary gentleman in search of a secluded spot is induced to take a front parlour, but, no sooner has he started to work than

the milkman awakes the echoes with his shrill call, the coal-heaver shouts raucously up and down the street, costers cry their wares incessantly, and passers-by execute acrobatic evolutions over the housemaids' pails until the author is compelled to vacate his apartments. He seeks relief on the first floor, and a scene representing the backs of the same houses is shown. Here the disturbance increases, the neighbours carrying on an animated conversation over the walls, and husbands yelling for their wives to get their meals.[32]

Eventually there is an outbreak of fire, and the occupants of the burning buildings are forced to make their escape by the windows, resulting in a very thrilling ending for the audience.

Due to his new status in the Karno outfit, as one version tells it, Sydney "used to whisper wheedling words into the 'guv'nor's' ear, whenever he got a chance, about the superlative merits of his younger brother, Charlie."[33] Although it took much more persuading on Sydney's part to get Charlie hired, Karno finally relented in February 1908 and gave Charlie a trial. With Charlie's success in winning Karno over and soon gaining a contract, then, the brothers were bringing home £7 10S a week total (Sydney had received another raise in 1908) and so they rented their first-ever respectable flat, at 15 Glenshaw Mansions on Brixton Road. Given their new affluence, it's not surprising that they soon moved their mother, Hannah, into a more respectable nursing home, Peckham House on Peckham Road, where she was to remain until the brothers brought her to California in 1921. Karno can be thanked, really, for saving the Chaplin brothers and encouraging talents and abilities that would last a lifetime. His employment also was the first to make them feel not just solvent, but comfortable — a condition to which they would never really grow accustomed.

By late 1908, Karno was branching out. The October 31 issue of *The Era* noted, "Messrs. Fred Karno and A.H. Edwards have purchased the Royal Public Rooms, Exeter, and have nearly finished reconstructing the same in a fashion that will make the new building one of the most up-to-date vaudeville houses in the provinces."[34] This may seem inconsequential, but this business move on Karno's part was to affect Sydney's career greatly, for Karno's business inter-

Sydney Chaplin and Minnie Gilbert in Karno's *Skating*, circa 1909 (CHACHAA).

ests soon overlapped with the latest craze: roller skating. By March 13th, it was reported that Karno was interested in purchasing a rink next to the Hippodrome, Peterborough, another venue he owned and managed.[35] Whether or not he purchased it, this report provides more evidence that Karno was always in tune with what was new and potentially money-making amongst his preferred audience. It seems only natural, then, that just two months following this announcement, a new sketch premiered entitled *Skating*. What is most important about this sketch, however, was that it was the first sketch from Sydney's own pen. He is listed as co-writer with J. Hickory Wood, one of Karno's more practiced writers,[36] and generally one of the most successful and well-known writers of pantomime books—especially for the Christmas theatre season. The sketch was presented first on May 3, 1909 at the Queen's Poplar as: "A new and Original Pantomimical Absurdity on the Latest Craze." If Karno himself did not put the idea before Sydney and Wood, then one of the writers was especially adept at understanding what the boss might like—a sketch that could pay him back double! The show's review in the May 8 edition of *The Era* seems to concentrate, unfortunately, more on the scenery than the overall performance:

> Besides the unceasing fun, one of the most attractive features of the show is the scenery. This is on an elaborate scale, and has been prepared by Mr. Grimenai at Mr. Karno's factory. There are two scenes, the first representing the outside of an entrance to Olympia, with all the details of pay boxes and turnstiles, while the second scene represents the interior of the vast hall. As a background, there is a magnificent scene-cloth depicting the snowy range of the Alps, with the Matterhorn in the distance. This is, indeed, an excellent example of the scenic artist's art, and its beauty acts as a capital foil to the humorous efforts of the company.[37]

Of the plot or story, the reviewer says only that "there is, of course, nothing,"[38] but the fun in the opening scene consists of the mayhem proliferated by a volunteer doorkeeper who takes over for the regular attendant. The fun in this scene, then, centers around the parade of characters trying to gain entrance, such as "the distressed maiden who has lost her purse, the Dundreary dandy, the old lady in the crinoline, and her nephew, who desires to break her neck on the rink. The great skating professor fails to turn up, and the volunteer doorkeeper undertakes to save the situation."[39] Karno is credited for building up the comedy from here by employing both accomplished comedians and accomplished skaters to great effect. The reviewer admits that "from the start to the fall of the curtain, there is not one dull moment, and seldom an interval when the house is not convulsed with laughter. It is, perhaps, impossible to say that this latest will surpass Mr. Karno's other productions in popularity, but it certainly will quite equal any of them, and that is the equivalent to predicting for it an enthusiastic welcome alike in London and in the provinces."[40]

In the sketch, Sydney plays the Hon. Archibald Binks, a character that he will play in Karno sketches to come and even later transforms into Reginald Gussle, his Keystone film persona. One bit of dialogue from the sketch between Archibald and his friend Bertie allows some understanding of the character:

> "There we stood with our retreat cut off."
> "Our what cut off?"
> "Our retreat cut off."

"Oh, stop it."
"There we stayed for three days without food or water, think of it, not even a drop of water. What did we do?"
"We drank it neat..."
"How are your brothers getting along?"
"Do you remember my brothers?"
"I should say so. Two of 'em are bandy and the other knock-kneed."
"Do you remember when they used to go out? The two bandy ones would walk on the outside and the knock-kneed one in the centre."
"Yes, and when they walked down the street they spelt Oxo."
"How's the world been treating you?"
"Oh, up and down."
"Are you working?"
"Now and then."
"Where are you working?"
"Oh, here and there."
"Do you like it?"
"Well, yes and no."
"What do you work at?"
"Oh, this and that."
"You're always in work I suppose?"
"Well, in and out."
"Do you work hard?"
"On and off."
"How much do you earn?"
"That and half as much again."
"Who do you work for?
"Mr. So-and-so."
"Well — are you looking for work?"
"I'm afraid to, in case I find it."[41]

While the first review fails to mention much about individual performers and performances, by June and July, Sydney was receiving acclaim for his work in the sketch. The Shoreditch Olympia reported it "the essence of humour, and many a hearty laugh can be obtained from the irresistible drollery of the comedians employed."[42] The reviewer writes that Sydney "enacts the roll of Archibald with telling effect. His efforts to amuse are, without a doubt, successful to a high degree, and he is deserving of much praise."[43] About a month later, the Willesden Hippodrome reported that "special praise must be accorded to Mr. Sydney Chaplin (part author of the piece) for his representation of Archibald, whose equal for low comedy work would be difficult to find."[44] And the Islington Empire's review two weeks later suggested that Sydney had gained a following in that town: "Mr. Chaplin, whose entry was very warmly greeted, displays all his well-known powers as a comedian, and receives capital support from the rest of the company, the fall of the curtain being the signal for a great ovation."[45] Certainly, these reviews increased Sydney's estimation in the eyes of Fred Karno and, with Karno's loss of two headliners in 1909 — first Harry Weldon, who left after playing in the *Football Match* for some months, and then Fred Kitchen, who left at the end of the year, upon the expiration of his contract[46]— it seems that the time was right for Sydney to move into one of these openings and become known as an individual star, rather than just a Karno headliner. But, in fact, this never happened. Sydney's name never appeared without Karno's coming first in the mention; he found himself always and only "one" of the Karno company — an important member, but not someone whose name meant anything without "Karno" attached to it somewhere.

Also important about this particular sketch, besides the fact that Sydney gained some great experience working with J. Hickory Wood on the writing of it and some notoriety in the performing of it, was that it started a sort of precedent for Sydney's work, in that it included characters performed in drag. While Sydney's own character, the Hon. Archibald Binks, does not appear in drag, Miss Zena Flapper was often played by Jimmy Russell, and Harry Oxberry often portrayed the fat and deaf aunt. By the time *The Hydro* was first performed onstage in 1912, Sydney was performing these drag parts himself, as he does as part of the Nick Sharp characterization.

While Sydney was touring with the No. 1 *Skating* company, his brother was touring with No. 2. Sydney was also trying to enter into the thick of things by engaging in "music hall sports." On August 24 at Stamford Bridge Grounds, he is listed as having participated in the "Mile Running Championship," an indication, at least, of his continuing dedication to physical fitness.[47] But Charlie was soon to embark on his first American tour with Karno in the autumn of 1910 and again in 1912, partially because "when Karno had to find a new comedian for the 'drunk' in *Mumming Birds*, or *A Night in an English Music Hall*, as it had been rechristened in America, he decided not to send Syd Chaplin, who was valuable at home, but to take a risk on his younger brother Charlie."[48]

Robinson claims that upon his return to London in June 1912, Charlie was surprised to learn that Sydney had taken a wife, Minnie Gilbert, yet Minnie appears as part of the *Skating* company in publicity photos, meaning that she and Sydney had met and had some sort of relationship by 1909. Although by 1912, Sydney had moved on to performing in other shows. It seems odd that Charlie would not have known her, or at least known about her. The other puzzling aspect of this claim is the word "marriage." There is no traceable record that Sydney ever legally married Minnie, yet they lived as man and wife and she adopted "Chaplin" as her all-but-legal surname. The only clue to their legal status is provided by a mention in the *Moving Picture World* in February 1920 that they had just celebrated their twelfth anniversary, meaning they would have been married in February 1908.[49] Minnie Gilbert, born June 26, 1888, in Darlington, of Jewish descent,[50] probably met Sydney while he was touring the north of England, and may have been enticed to continue their acquaintance almost immediately. In fact, her picture appeared in the local newspaper as one of three finalists in a regional beauty contest, and with this information, it would not be difficult to imagine Sydney looking her up during his free time between performances, or perhaps even witnessing the beauty pageant as it occurred. Minnie, like Sydney and like the woman who was to be his second wife, Henriette, was a woman of mystery. Sydney's stories about himself, his facility in telling stories to mask inadequacies, to move himself up in the world, or simply to impress others, seems to have been a trait they shared and one that was to prove effective in keeping them together for 27 years.

The next show of importance for Sydney, but also for Charlie, was a sketch in three acts called *The Wow-Wows*. The sketch was ostensibly about secret societies, but the fact that the costumes of the society members were a play on the white hoods and capes of the American Klu Klux Klan is an interesting coincidence. Images of both Sydney and

Charlie, playing the role of Archibald Binks, and shown holding a skull à la either Rodin's "The Thinker" or Hamlet's "Alas, Poor Yorick," show the society members in the background sporting black capes and black pointed hoods, frighteningly embellished with blackface white lips on the hoods themselves, where each member's lips might be. It is not clear whether this is meant to lambast the KKK and similar societies or blacks in general. As Robinson recounts, "The first scene was set in a summer camp, where the campers resolve to get even with the tight-wadded Archie by creating a phoney secret society"[51]— after, of course, Archie had his usual scene with the object of his flirtations, here Lady Lydia, who is finally jettisoned from his lap by her repulsion at the wetness of the broken eggs in his pockets— signs of both his miserliness and his usual ineptitude. The second scene featured the aforementioned lampooning of a secret society. The dialogue and action of the sketch, however, is much more innocent and banal than the costumes would suggest. A representative passage shows Binks up to his usual hijinks:

Sydney as Archibald Binks in Karno's *The Wow-Wows,* circa 1910 (CHACHAA).

BRUNTON: Don't be afraid.
ARCHIE: All right, old boy, I say, look at that old chap up there with his legs crossed. (pointing to skull and crossbones over door)
BRUNTON: To our secret chamber?
ARCHIE: Here endeth the first lesson.
BRUNTON: Numbers one and 75.
ARCHIE: Go on! Make it two dollars.
BRUNTON: Brother nightmare.
ARCHIE: And I am good night Nurse.
BRUNTON: Archie, follow me.
(door shuts in face).
ARCHIE: I say Brunton, I'm outside, Brunton. Brunton, ah! I know I must give them the sign. (knocks)

The sketch premiered on August 8 at the Tottenham Palace,[52] with J. C. Piddock as Binks, but with Sydney in that role by the very next week at the Euston, whose reviewer noted that "there is an underlying funny idea in this sketch, but the superstructure of farce raised upon it does not argue much in favour of the ingenuity of the authors."[53] Even though this sketch failed to garner much attention or box-office, Karno did not want to kill it completely, so he soon made the decision to send it with Charlie to the United States, where it was renamed *A Night in a London Secret Society*, for clarity. It fared even worse among American audiences, but Charlie managed to distinguish himself in the role of Binks, despite the sketch's shortcomings. As one reviewer noted: "Now Charles Chaplin is so arriving a comedian that Mr. Karno will be forgiven for whatever else the act may lack. The most enthusiastic Karno-ite will surely admit, too, the act lacks a great deal that might help to make it vastly more entertaining. Still, Mr. Chaplin heads the cast, so the people laughed and were content."[54]

Perhaps Karno couldn't be bothered with the fact that one of his shows was not doing well, especially when it was all the way over in America and he was in the midst of developing one of his blockbuster shows — *The Wontdetainia*. As its name suggests, the *Wontdetainia* was a parody of travel on one of the big liners, such as the *Lusitania*, launched shortly before the show opened. Adeler and West claim "it was the most elaborate and most effective stage production yet seen. The mechanical work on it alone cost over £2000 and could not be duplicated to-day for twice the money."[55] One account explains the mastery of the set and its working parts:

> The superstructure was not the usual battens and wooden bases of stage scenery, but was of solid steel; and three hydraulic rams, made by an eminent firm of South London engineers, supplied the motion of the ship. One of these rams was placed at the back of the stage and the other two at either side, so that the ship was able to rock either from port to starboard or from aft to bow. This was a revolution in stagecraft and by its aid it was possible to get the perfect motion of a ship.[56]

The show premiered at the Paragon Theatre on Mile-end Road, one of Karno's old-faithfuls. Not surprisingly, with so much new technology to depend on, the first run had its share of problems. Co-writer of the show, Charley Baldwin, offered his recollections of the water pressure problems on that run: "A miserable little procession, consisting of the author, the scene-painter, and several of the actors, walked disconsolately to the nearest pub," because the rolling sea refused to roll and the water effects were apparently not working either. "It seemed like the sack for the working staff," Baldwin recalled, "the officers, crew, and passengers of the good ship *Wontdetainia*. What was to be done? Obviously the only thing was to drown our disappointment over the weakness of the waters by imbibing stronger fluid of the good old pre-war blends." Eventually, they returned to the theatre. Imagine their surprise, looking in through the stage door and seeing the vessel rocking gaily to and fro as if nothing had gone wrong in the first place. It turns out that Karno had called in the fire brigade, who hooked up a fire engine just outside the theatre, providing the needed pressure.[57]

In addition to these effects, the ship was equipped, through the use of railway lines, to leave the dock, an operation that required five minutes of stage time. The principal comedian, played by Sydney on occasion, in the role of the purser, was left behind as the ship pulled out and, therefore, was required to dive through a hatchway to occupy his proper place. Karno provided the setting of the departing ship with a mass of performers

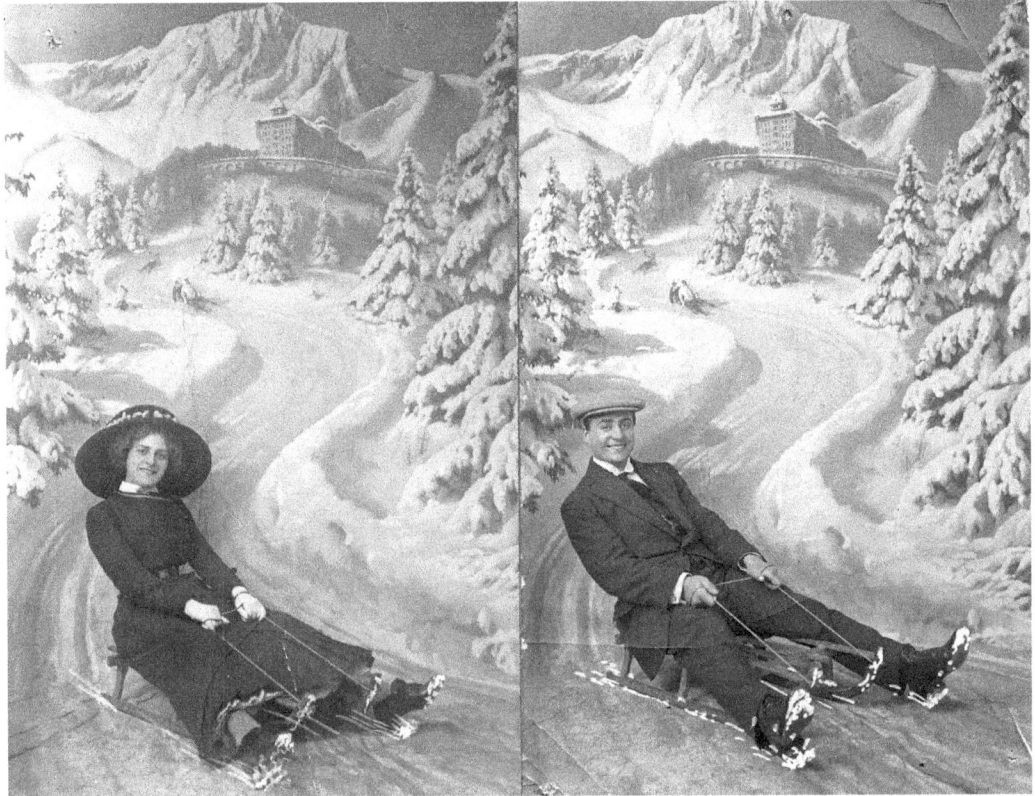

Minnie Gilbert and Sydney Chaplin at an English amusement park, enjoying some down time between Karno performances, circa 1910 (CHACHAA).

and extras who took up the deck space, shouted and waved to the crowd. This, along with the usual sounds of sirens, steam whistles, and the tolling of bells and gongs, both added authenticity to the atmosphere of the scene and worked the audience into an unrelievable frenzy.[58]

The show had its limitations, however, despite the fact that it broke records at a suitable East End theatre like the Paragon. Karno could only book it at theatres able to accommodate the huge set and all of its machinery and an audience willing and able to support higher ticket prices. Needless to say, it was not a show that he planned to take to the "provinces." So, while Sydney worked along with Karno and Frank Calvert on his next starring vehicle, he found himself spending the summer months of 1911 touring in old tried-and-true productions, such as *Mumming Birds* and *Skating*.

If Sydney's next show was any indication, Karno had become enamored with water — or at least water effects on stage. The scene was a luxury health spa, called colloquially *The Hydro*, with all of such a location's usual components. Sydney played a new character, Nick Sharp, a detective. The sketch comprised two scenes: the first in "The Pump Room at the Hydro, at Merryandbad, France," and the second, the "Interior of Bathe de Luxe at the same Hydro."[59] The set, while not as complicated in design as that for *Wontdetainia*, still had its innovations:

The stage which forms the floor of the bathroom, and below which the tank is placed, is rested on a number of trestles, or, as they are known to the company, "rostrums," each one of which is collapsible and packs up into a fat slab for convenience when traveling. The tank itself is of canvas, and the water is pumped in from a large cauldron in which it has been heated to the requisite temperature. After each performance the water is carried off by means of hose under the stage to a gully at the side of the theatre, near the gallery entrance. To see this water coming through a hole in the wall is ... intensely exciting, and so engrosses the attention of those waiting for the doors to open that they forget to go inside to see the show.[60]

While Sydney had been mentioned in the media before this particular show, having been part of Karno's company for six years by this time, as has been mentioned, he had not yet received the attention usually given to Karno's big stars, like Fred Kitchen. While he was still considered only a Karno headlining star, he at least found himself being interviewed. *The Illustrated Chronicle*, for example, not only provided a positive and enthusiastic review of the show, but went to the trouble of interviewing its star personally — and at length. The review itself couldn't have been more appreciative:

Of course, anybody can fool about in a bath (though so many take their Spring cleaning so seriously), but Syd Chaplin and his supporting comedians now appearing at the Empire do the thing with a thorough appreciation of the humour of it. I do not remember having seen audiences laugh so immoderately as they are being compelled to do at the Empire by this supremely funny sketch. "Screams," "shrieks," and "howls" are usually regarded as being comical rather than opposite adjectives to apply to laughter; but I heard some exceedingly peculiar noises emitted by those round about me when the farce was in progress, and one adipose couple quite close got themselves into a very serious state over it.[61]

Sydney's interview within this article demonstrates clearly that he had adopted the habit of embellishing and fabricating his life story very early in his career, for he claims that having last appeared in Newcastle-on-Tyne in *Sherlock Holmes* some seven years earlier, he went to work for Karno "from this very city." In addition, he claims Charles Chaplin, Sr., as his father, but Capetown as his birthplace. The interview claims, though, that Sydney, at this young age and this early in his career, already owned a car and drove it from town to town as his performance scheduled demanded. This revelation to the interviewer prompted one of Sydney's already characteristic comic yarns:

Down time with Karno's *The Hydro* troupe, with Minnie Gilbert (Chaplin) top row far left and Sydney top row center, circa 1912 (CHACHAA).

"I ran over a dog once, near Northampton," he said. "I pulled up, and crowds at once gathered round the car. They sent for the woman to whom the dog belonged, and soon she came up, weeping. Then her daughter appeared, also crying, and finally the old man turned up, and said: 'That dog has been collecting for the blind orphanage here, and I wouldn't have lost him for a couple of pounds.' So I said, 'Well, here's eighteenpence to bury him with, and the old chap sent his wife off for a sack while he took his pals and my eighteenpence into a public house.'"[62]

Another interviewer, this time from the Oldham *Standard*, described his subject as "an exceedingly pleasant-looking gentleman with a most deceivingly innocent face and an affable manner about him which quite captivated me." This time, Minnie, referred to as "a very pretty and charming young lady" and also as Sydney's wife, was present beside him. She was reported to be a member of the company as well, a report that is borne out by photographs of the company taken at the time. To this interviewer, Sydney was "the very soul of the piece. When he gets his nurse's togs on and wanders amongst the girls he is irresistibly funny."[63] Sydney was to portray this role successfully for more than two years, his importance to the role being conveyed partially by the fact that *The Hydro* toured in only one company — Sydney's — with only Sydney in the role of the protagonist, Nick Sharp.

According to Sydney, Karno's favorite part of the sketch involved a fat man who has water on the brain and the ritual of "tapping" it that results in a large geyser of water spurting from the man's head, complete with small ping-pong-like balls being supported on the stream. As with other shows, there were always bugs to be worked out. The first for this show was the fact that the cast was afraid to get into the water. That rectified, the fat man punctured his air-filled "tummy" one night, leaving Sydney on the stage without the source of most of the show's humor in that scene: "I kept on working off gags until I was afraid I was going to 'dry up,' as they say."[64] Two components of this show made it into Sydney or Charlie's future endeavors (even though Charlie never played in it). The first is the setting of the health spa, which is used in Charlie's 1917 Mutual film, *The Cure*. The second is Sydney's adopting female dress as a disguise during a portion of the performance. He was to use this technique quite ably in several of his later films, including *Charley's Aunt, The Man on the Box, Oh! What a Nurse,* and even his final film, *A Little Bit of Fluff.*

By 1913, it is clear that Karno had come to rely on Sydney and his fidelity to the Karno label. In a letter dated February 13, Karno requests Sydney to add, where he can, little bits of comic business to a new show they are working on entitled *Flats*,[65] one that exists in several drafts in manuscript form. It is a lengthy script and one which, interestingly, seems to be the first such endeavor in which Sydney was hired as a writer for a company other than his own. Unfortunately, *Flats* premiered at the Brixton Empress without fanfare on September 22.[66] No review or description of the sketch appeared in *The Era* and it seems to have run only from this date until November 24 of that year.[67] The cast consisted of Charles Kitts, Billy Matchett, Louise Zetland, and others.[68] Only the draft scripts of the first two scenes exist, and they describe a sketch that begins in a real estate agent's office, where all the characters come together, because they have some business there, and then get themselves invited to a supper party at the home of gang leader the Hon. Billy Browning, a faux aristocrat, who intends to relieve the affluent residents of their cash at the party that evening:

CLERK: Calling Mr. Browning.
BROWNING: Yes?
CLERK: Allow me to introduce you. This is Miss Fluffie de Vere. The Hon. Billy Browning.
BROWNING: Pleased to meet you. (Lady bows.)
CLERK: This lady is wanting a furnished flat & judging by her requirements, I think yours should be just the thing. Could she have permission to see it?
BROWNING: With the greatest of pleasure. I should be charmed to show you over at any time that is most convenient to yourself. I suppose you're very busy during the day?
FLUFFIE: No. I do all my browsing at night.
BROWNING: Really?
FLUFFIE: Yes, I am an actress.
BROWNING: And where did you work last?
FLUFFIE: The Strand.
BROWNING: Indeed.
FLUFFIE: Yes, it's very definitely an unlucky place. I believe they are going to change its name to the Whiting Theatre. (Browning looks relieved.)
BROWNING: Are you working at present?
FLUFFIE: No, not just at present.
BROWNING: Well, look here. Don't think me rude, but I have a little supper party on tonight & as you are not working, perhaps you would care to make one. I could show you over the flat at the same time.
FLUFFIE: Thanks. I shall be delighted. What address is it?
BROWNING: There's my card & I can count on you being there?
FLUFFIE: Without fail. (goes to exit and stops, feels in muff & looks on the floor.)
BROWNING: Anything wrong?
FLUFFIE: I've lost my purse! How annoying! I haven't even a cab fare.
BROWNING: Can I loan you a small sum?
FLUFFIE: Oh, thank you.
BROWNING: How much do you require?
FLUFFIE: Half a sovereign will do.
BROWNING: (Counting money in his hand) I'm afraid I haven't half a sovereign.
PERKS: May I suggest ...
MRS. PERKS: Sit down! (rap with umbrella.)
BROWNING: I'm afraid I have only five shillings.
FLUFFIE: Oh, that will do & that will be five shillings you owe me. Good day.
BROWNING: (under his breath) One of the nuts ...[69]

The actual party scene (scene 3) is missing, so it can only be imagined how this occurs. Scene 2, however, is concerned solely with Browning's apartment building and the elevator therein. Sydney devotes one whole page to a drawing and explanation of this device and how it will best be built for the variety stage. The gags he invents for this device are bordering on the violent, but have the important characteristic of building one upon another.

There was always a bit of down time between performances, especially for the star, and Sydney chose one of these times to visit the Wakefield Prison. He recounted the macabre experience years later to friend, journalist R. J. Minney. He simply walked to the prison gates, mentioned he wanted to meet with the governor and was shown in due to a misunderstanding: the governor thought the "chaplain" had wanted to see him. When Sydney asked the governor for a tour and explained that he was part of a theatre company only in town a few days, the governor relented, because he had just been the beneficiary of an equal kindness when another company had presented a benefit for the warders' widows. On the tour, Sydney noticed that all the halls of the prison converged at one point, like the spokes of a wheel and that the halls were deathly silent. All in all, he found the place disappointing, at least until he got to the death cell: "This was a medium-sized room with no carpet on the floor, just a table with writing materials, an iron bedstead & a screen which concealed a night commode. The door we entered by had a circular glass window in it about the size of a dollar. This was used to keep observation on the prisoner. On the other side of the room was another door & when I passed through it, I was surprised to find myself on the scaffold."[70] The prisoner, he was told, has no idea that the scaffold was right outside the door of his room. This tour began a sort of predilection for the Chaplin boys, since both Sydney and Charlie continued to visit prisons around the world for many years to come.

November 28, 1913, is the date that "all was changed, changed utterly," for that was the date Charlie Chaplin left the Karno company to remain in America and try his luck in the film business. With this bit of success, the brothers essentially switched places, with Charlie remaining "on top" for the remainder of their lives. The significance of this moment to Sydney is not known, except as it is suggested in what remains of his correspondence with his old and revered boss, Fred Karno. Shortly after this momentous date, Karno wrote to Sydney, "I am considering how and in what way I can recognize your efforts and loyalty in the past."[71] By January 23, just three short weeks later, Karno writes, "I am glad to hear that you liked the little present and are so pleased with it," then, "I thank you for sending me the letter and wire with regard to the offer you have had. I, too, do not know how they could have had the idea that you wanted a change," suggesting first that he was attempting in some small way to keep his star happy and, more importantly, that Sydney was "bargaining" with Karno by displaying other offers, real or fabricated. The timing of these communications between Sydney and Karno could not be coincidental, but rather it is a clear indication of Sydney's knowledge of his new position in the family and his struggle against the possible permanency of that change. By his letter of April 7, Karno indicates that he has either secured Sydney's fidelity once again with a raise, or that Sydney's other "offers" have since vanished. He asks him only to work up a new sketch he has in mind, entitled *Teeth*, which will allow for mayhem in a dentist's office.[72] Little did Karno know or realize that Sydney himself was about to be lured away to America.

CHAPTER 3

A Keystone Cop Aesthetic

"Gussle, burdened with coin, smote me and fled."
— Intertitle from *No One to Guide Him*, Keystone, 1915

SYDNEY'S MOTIVATION FOR COMING TO America to accept a contract with Keystone is unknown. He could have been swayed by the start of World War I and what would surely have been his imminent involuntary service therein, by the demise of his relationship with Karno, by the rise of the popularity of the film medium and its effect on other types of entertainment (like the English music hall on which he relied financially), or simply because of a sort of envy of Charlie's success in films that he felt he could either benefit from or repeat. In any event, it is clear that Charlie wished Sydney to join him in America. A rare letter from Charlie to this effect, sent from the Los Angeles Athletic Club, outlines his plan for both Sydney and himself:

> Mr. Sennett is in New York. He said he would write to you and make you an offer. I told him you would do great for pictures of course he has not seen you and he is only going by what I say. He said he would give you 150 to start with. I told him you are getting that now and would not think of coming over hear [*sic*] for that amount. If you do consider it, don't sign for any length of time, because I will want you with me when I start. I could get you 250 as easy as anything but of course you would have to sign a contract. It will be nice for you to come over for three months with the Keystone and then start for ourselves. You will hear from Sennett but don't come for *less than 175 understand?* You will like it out here it is a beautiful country and the fresh air is doing me the world of good.... Don't forget to write me before you sign any contract because there is another firm who will pay you 250. They wanted me and I told them about you, as I could not break my contract of course. Mr. Sennett is a lovely man and we are great pals but business is business.[1]

Unfortunately, no correspondence between Sennett and Syd exists, so it is not clear what sum Syd arranged before he came over (Charlie claims it was $200 a week, which would have been $25 more than he himself was making at the time),[2] but in any event, he worked out some sort of agreement, organized his affairs, and with Minnie along, left on the *S.S. Megantic* from Liverpool, on September 12, 1914, attempting to enter the U.S.

through Montreal, Québéc upon landing September 19.³ Sydney claims in "Some Reminiscences of Sid Chaplin,"⁴ that Keystone cabled an offer out of the blue, and because he had already volunteered for service (World War I), he asked if "they would let the offer stand till the termination of the war." Again, in keeping with his growing tradition of creating fictions about himself, Sydney most likely added this information to show a sense of patriotism and civic responsibility, whether he possessed these characteristics or not.

Unbelievably, the information printed in one of Sydney's first interviews with the American press of any length is corroborated by the *Megantic*'s manifest, because both his and Minnie's names are labeled with four letters, "quar," signifying that both were quarantined on arrival at Grosse Isle, Québéc. Sydney was then released from quarantine on October 6 and Minnie on October 20. In the interview mentioned above, Sydney recounts:

> I came [to the United States] via Canada but I was destined for trouble on the voyage. I was unfortunately placed in a cabin where a scarlet fever case broke out, which necessitated a fourteen days' observation in the quarantine station at Grosse Isle, Quebec, where I spent one of the most miserable periods of my life. I must say the officials were the essence of kindness and did everything for my comfort but the place was so frightfully lonely. It had just one redeeming feature, an old Irish lady, a nurse, who was the soul of wit and she kept me amused for hours. She was a character who might have stepped out of the pages of Dickens. She made the one bright spot in the whole picture.⁵

Besides the fact that his quarantine is borne out by the documentation available, other elements of this account are troubling. First, Sydney was not alone on the voyage, nor was he alone in quarantine. His "wife" Minnie (listed as single and Minnie Gilbert on the manifest) was with him, so why would he have complained of being lonely? Second, Sydney and Minnie were the only two people quarantined from that particular ship, so there could have been no outbreak in a cabin, or other passengers would have been held as well. What exactly did they have anyway? Also, the fourteen-day quarantine period was actually 17 days for Sydney and 31 days for Minnie, significantly longer than stated. Finally, who knows if the old Irish woman existed? Certainly she worked well as a vehicle for a couple of stories he wanted to relate — at least in this interview!

Figuring in a few days, then, in New York and the time necessary to travel by train to Los Angeles, Sydney and Minnie would have arrived in California

Minnie Gilbert Chaplin in Hollywood, California, July 25, 1915. Courtesy Irvine Gilbert.

sometime the first week of November. Charlie remembers that they arrived looking "fresh from England"—an understatement!—just at the moment he was to head off to film on location and that he had to be satisfied with meeting them for dinner later that night.[6] Sydney expressed his first impressions of California to a friend, many years later: "I guess you must have felt a little homesick when you first arrived. I know I did. I was so blue, I sat in Westlake Park and cried, but after a while I got to love the place."[7]

Keystone announced its new star for the first time on October 31: "Syd Chaplin, the English comedian and brother of Charles Chaplin (the funny drunk), of Keystone fame, has signed up with the Keystone company. He recently left New York for the Los Angeles studios. Mr. Chaplin is sure to be a great success with the Keystone Company, as he has been a star comedian and producer for Fred Karno, London, for the past eight years."[8] A week later, the *Motion Picture News* announced his imminent arrival, noting that he would "begin work at once"[9] and begin work he did, for his first film for Keystone was released on November 21. It was *Fatty's Wine Party*, starring Roscoe Arbuckle and Mabel Normand. Although only a small fragment of this film exists, a contemporary description of the film in *Reel Life* permits some understanding of Syd's role: "Fatty, in need of money, borrows a dollar from a friend who is waiting to take Mabel, a girl friend of his, out for a party. As Fatty walks away with his dollar, he sees Mabel in the distance. Mabel also sees him, and rushes to his side and kisses him for he is very popular with the ladies."[10] Three men (one who has lent Fatty a dollar) observe these goings-on. They also see Fatty and Mabel disappear into a restaurant, even though Fatty, due to his lack of money, was reluctant to go. "Once inside, however," the review continues, "the amusing antics of their waiter, as played by Sid Chaplin, dispel his gloom until he sees his three friends arriving. They order wine, and then leave a bill of $27.50 for Fatty to pay. Unable to do so, he is kicked out, to the amusement of his friends, but just as they are laughing hardest, Mabel takes his side and turns the tables on them."[11] Ironically playing the role of a rogue waiter in both his first and last Keystone films, Sydney received mention for this particular portrayal in one review in the sentence *before* its two main stars: "This picture is a roar from beginning to end. Syd Chaplin makes his first appearance for this company and is excruciatingly funny as a waiter. Roscoe Arbuckle and Mabel Normand also appear."[12]

A scene in the restaurant from *Fatty's Wine Party* (Keystone, 1914) showing, Sydney far left, Mabel Normand, Roscoe Arbuckle and Mack Swain. Phyllis Allen can be seen directly behind Mabel (LKSC).

The next two films in Syd's Keystone oeuvre are

fairly recent discoveries. Bo Berglund, noted silent film historian, noticed that the cop in the last scene of Charlie's *His Prehistoric Past* was indeed Sydney. It seems significant somehow that the brothers would work together in Charlie's final film for Keystone. Charlie commented in later years that he often ended a film contract by portraying a criminal trying to escape in his final film; this is true for Essanay (*Police*), Mutual (*The Adventurer*) and First National (*The Pilgrim*). What can be made then of this film in which the tramp "escapes" from his horrifying dream by being awakened by a cop — played by his brother?

Although Charlie's last film was the second film Sydney was to work on, it was the third of his films to actually be released (on December 7). The film released second and only recently attributed to Sydney by film scholar Brent Walker was *Among the Mourners* (released November 28). Surprisingly, Sydney's part is an important one in the film and allows him to show off some of his Karno-honed slapstick expertise. In it he plays a familiar part, one of the inebriate swell, who, in this case, comes along to a faked funeral in order to see what's what. Chester Conklin's character has talked Frank Opperman into testing the fidelity of his wife by pretending to be dead. Sydney's drunk, as mentioned, just happens along, but complicates the plot a bit by hitting on the supposed widow. This becomes a problem for both the "dead" husband and Chester's character who has developed this ruse only to make time with the wife himself. Competition ensues until Frank "wakes up" and order is restored by ejecting both Sydney and Chester from the premises.

This largely unnoticed film received very little press at the time of its release, with a rare review appearing in *Motion Picture News* saying only that it possessed "the usual riot of slapstick comedy which one expects in a Keystone picture, but also the usual general supply of laughs."[13] However, it is significant in Sydney's career if only for the fact that it afforded him the first opportunity to try out the character who would, two films later, become Reginald Gussle. Sydney's next, a one-reeler shot in late November and early December, directed by Walter Wright and entitled *Wild West Love*, was shot in Santa Monica Canyon. A Droppington film, it starred Chester Conklin in the title role. Droppington decides to become a highwayman in this episode, because he needs money to gain his girl, Norma Nichols. However, the money he grabs turns out to be his own. It was released December 21, 1914.[14]

* * *

Unlike the little tramp character that brother Charlie created in early 1914 for Keystone, there is no nostalgic description of the process undertaken to develop the character of Reginald Gussle that Sydney utilized in most of his Keystone films (he may appear under the label "Mr. Dash," or "the Flirt" in some films, but it is essentially the same character, and will be treated as such). In many ways, and for obvious reasons, Gussle was the opposite of Charlie's little tramp; he was obviously bourgeois middle class, a homeowner, employed, and with a wife and sometimes a dog, although no children. The British might refer to the character as a fop — a sort of pretentious and pompous individual who wears the adornments of affluence in such a way as to show their particular hilarity and who attempts to behave with an upper-class decorum that is not so much

Publicity photograph for Sydney Chaplin's Keystone character, Reginald Gussle, 1915 (LKSC).

ill-fitting but employed with a sense of rogue entitlement that results in violence, insult and outright thoughtlessness. There's no question that this character was a version of the Hon. Archibald Binks, the character Sydney played in several Karno productions, such as *Skating*, a scenario he wrote himself.

As for the name "Gussle," there are several probable reasons why this name was chosen. The most obvious was often revealed by unwary typists who misspelled the name "Guzzle" in descriptions or reviews of the films. Certainly "Gussle" is a play on the word "guzzle," to drink greedily or habitually, perhaps suggesting a pronunciation such an inebriated person would naturally give the word, if so impaired. Also important is the fact that the word rhymes with "bustle." Not only does the character have an accentuated posterior — truly a bustle, but bustles around as well. The "Reginald," of Reginald Gussle, in addition, gives the character that false sense of affluence and nobility that is so essential to its comedic possibilities.

Although Kalton C. Lahue's book *Mack Sennett's Keystone: The Man, the Myth and the Comedies* uses mostly the reminiscences of former Keystone business manager George B. Stout as support for the claims he makes in the book, his rare discussion of Sydney's Keystone experience is worth relating. Lahue argues, "Sydney Chaplin's contribution to Keystone was a mixture of headaches for all concerned."[15] His assessment that Sydney's character "Gussle," whom he describes as "the eternal errant at odds with the world around him"[16] was a reflection of Sydney's own personality is an interesting one. Lahue describes the character as:

> Garbed in the oversize loose-fitting clothes of the would-be-dude, with long hair neatly parted in the middle, combed over each side and slicked down, and with wide, upturned moustache — a comic representation of that worn by the Prussian military of the era — Syd marched through a series of comedies like a martinet, flirting with the pretty girls, insulting the others and challenging their husbands when necessary. But while he possessed a good deal of personal wit and charm, Syd was quite probably psychologically scarred far deeper than Charlie by the seemingly endless poverty of his early life and the unsettled, warped family life he had only briefly known and which had thrust him into the position of the man of the house at a tender age. This occasionally broke through the thin veneer with which he had managed to cover his memories, even though he gave every outward appearance of being better adjusted to the vagaries of life than Charlie, for whom he felt a strong sense of responsibility.[17]

Reginald Gussle first appeared fully formed in the film *Gussle the Golfer*. This is the first of five films shot in a park setting, this one probably the Midwick Country Club on Hellman Avenue in Alhambra.[18] In this film, Gussle is introduced, for the first and only time in these films as "Mr. Reggie Gussle — Expert Golfer." The film also includes what was to become Gussle's trademark pratfall, one Buster Keaton termed "the neck roll." While certainly this pratfall was a standard among vaudeville and music-hall professionals at the time, Sydney may have been the first to perform it on film. In this stunt, the performer falls down something like a staircase head first, lands directly on top of the head, does a 90-degree turn on his head and lands on his back.[19] Although the film features a great scene of Gussle mugging for the camera as he cheats at cards in the gentleman's club, the plot of the film revolves around Gussle's attempt to steal another man's wife, this time, Mack Swain's Ambrose. Gussle is able to get Ambrose arrested for cheating at cards (even though it was he himself who had cheated), talks Ambrose into allowing him to keep the wife company during his sentence, and then convinces the wife to accompany him back to the golf course for an innocent afternoon's outing. Ambrose is let out early and hunts Gussle down on the course with a shotgun, the wife is recovered and Gussle in the final frames is shown running away in silhouette with a flag from the course stuck in his behind, a veritable peacock partially plucked.

The review for the film printed in *Motion Picture News* must have been an encouraging one for the character's debut: "Sid Chaplin and Max [sic] Swain, two of the best comedians on the screen, unite their forces in this reel, with the result that there is literally almost a laugh in every foot. Syd Chaplin truly must be seen to be appreciated, as his off-hand, incidental actions which he performs with perfect seriousness cause most of the laughs."[20] After reviews like this, it's not surprising that Sydney utilized the character in all of his subsequent Keystone films except his final one.

Hushing the Scandal, the only one of Syd's films to be directed by Mack Sennett, again paired Sydney and Chester Conklin, again playing his "Droppington" character. The film also features Cecile Arnold, a pretty blonde who plays in several of the Gussle films and Phyllis Allen in a small part, the woman who will later play the inimitable Mrs. Gussle. The film involves Mary Wigg, Droppington's fiancée, and her two parents, who are giving an engagement party for the couple in a park. Gussle, though, happens along uninvited and begins to flirt with Mary (Cecile Arnold) in the opening scenes. Droppington finds out and vows "revenge," which turns out to be getting a bee into Gussle's drawers, causing him to strip to his longjohns in front of the engagement party and others in the park. The highlight here is the large polka-dotted longjohns, which appear in at least one other of Syd's films, *King, Queen, Joker*. The film ends with Gussle, who, in trying to grab Mrs. Wigg's coat to cover himself, pulls her wig off instead (thus, the name), which causes her husband to abandon her immediately.

While Phyllis Allen could have been playing Mrs. Gussle in *Hushing the Scandal*, even though it was a tiny part, she is definitely Mrs. Gussle in this next film. *Giddy, Gay and Ticklish* is significant in Syd's filmography because it exhibits the first manifestation of the many barbershop gags the Chaplin brothers were to utilize in their careers. Mr. Gussle is not the barber himself, as one of Syd's characters will be in a later film, *King, Queen, Joker,* but is still able to stir up some mischief in the barber's shop. The barber here is Edgar Kennedy, who has a second barber working for him. His young and pretty girlfriend, Dixie Chene, works as a manicurist in the shop. The film begins with what will become a sort of paradigmatic scene between Mrs. and Mr. Gussle, one which sets him up as a henpecked husband who deals with his older and larger wife through sheer persistence and guile. Allen here is much like the wife she plays in Charlie's film *Pay Day* (1922).

Having escaped the wife (as usual) with a fistful of dollars, Gussle makes his way downtown looking for diversion. He finds it in Kennedy the barber's girlfriend, whom he encounters at the fruit market. He's already had one scuffle with Kennedy outside his house earlier in the day, so the pair's history adds to the mayhem that develops in the barbershop, to which, naturally, Gussle follows the blonde. After some hijinx in the barber's chair, a gun fight and a conveniently denuded manicurist, the film ends in a water fight with a hose.

At this point in his career with Keystone, working as he was for various directors in the company, Sydney was playing the game, so to speak—going to company functions such as the Keystone Film Banquet held at Levy's Café on February 17, a restaurant located on Spring Street in downtown Los Angeles that was oft-frequented by film folk in general. Minnie accompanied him to this function attended by all the important stars in the company: Roscoe Arbuckle, Chester Conklin, Ford Sterling, Mack Swain, Alice Davenport,

3. A Keystone Cop Aesthetic

Scene from *Hushing the Scandal* (Keystone, 1915) with Chester Conklin (left) and Sydney (AMPAS).

Mabel Normand and Phyllis Allen among them, and Adam Kessel and Mack Sennett as well. It's not clear that Sydney shared his brother Charlie's affection for the boxing match, as did many of his fellow Keystoners, but certainly, having always placed importance on developing the physical body, he would have been a frequenter of Charlie's old residence, the Los Angeles Athletic Club.

His next film shot in a park setting, *Caught in a Park*, begins with an interesting title card that reads: "A Plain Wife and a Sporty Husband." Is the husband sporty because his wife is plain? Or was he sporty before he met her and ended up with her, because he easily led a plain girl astray, being sporty? Sporty, in this case, must mean "one looking for sport," probably of the female kind, because by this film in Sydney's Keystone oeuvre, the viewer must realize that this is the motivation for much of Gussle's behavior. Here, as the title suggests, the scene is a park, and the sporty objective is Cecile Arnold, here coupled with Slim Summerville. Mr. Gussle and Mrs. Gussle are visiting the park, where Mrs. Gussle is visiting Morpheus, giving her husband an opportunity for mischief. Of course, she eventually wakes, finding the mister chasing after a younger girl and joins in the antics, with Gussle himself ending up covered with ash in the final scene. Simply another film with the "antics in a park" theme — all of these films seem to be only slight variations of the other — a husband goes to a park with his older, plainer wife, the wife falls asleep and the husband gets in trouble with another man's younger, prettier girl. A review in *Motion Picture News* following its release indicated the lack of success of this formula: "A typical slapstick comedy featuring the antics of Sid Chaplin.... The picture is a little below the usual Keystone standard."[21]

That Springtime Feeling, released February 25, 1915, concerns a blonde girl (Cecile Arnold) seated on a park bench with an active one-year-old baby, Gussle the flirt who is after her, the cop (Ted Edwards), who is trying to protect her and himself and the park's resident drunk (Jack Kennedy). The missus is nowhere to be found in this one. While the plot of this short is both complicated and inconsistent, it received favorable reviews. *Motion Picture News* claimed it possessed "many laughable stunts, at least one of which seems to be entirely new,"[22] and *Moving Picture World* was especially enthusiastic, naming the film "one of the Keystone comedies that has special laugh-getting qualities. It has plenty of strenuous action, and abounds with good situations. Syd Chaplin is the funny man, supported by various other funny people."[23]

This would probably be a good moment to mention what sets Sydney's Gussle films apart from the average Keystone, elements that might have attracted some and repelled others: bits. Intricate funny bits. Many of the tricks that Sydney performed in the films require great concentration to appreciate, because they depend on the viewer's attention to each detail. For instance, in several of these films, Syd performs some very intricate tricks with eggs. Charlie, of course, made the old broken-egg-in-the-pocket gag well-known and appreciated, in such films as Essanay's *The* Tramp (1915) and Gussle performs this gag at least once, but the other egg bits that he performs are almost what could be termed close-up sleight-of-hand tricks. In *Hushing the Scandal*, for example, Sydney's Gussle character pulls a hard-boiled egg out of his pocket, does a deft hand trick in which he makes the egg disappear, then reappear. Then he performs another trick where he seemingly smashes the egg on Cecile Arnold's head, then makes it appear coming out of her

Scene from *Caught in a Park* (Keystone, 1915) with Sydney (left), Cecile Arnold and Slim Summerville (AMPAS).

nose. Gussle continues by performing a trick in which he shoots an egg out of his mouth straight up into the air and then catches it in his mouth, over and over. Finally, he acts like he swallowed the egg, but instead, pulls it from under his waistcoat, then casually throws it away, where it, of course, becomes a raw egg that splashes Chester Conklin's Droppington character in the face. Cecile then elbows Gussle in the stomach and another egg appears out of his mouth (this trick is used in Charlie's *The Idle Class* (1921). Gussle performs more egg tricks until the thing finally lands on his head and cracks open.

Meanwhile, great changes were taking place at the Keystone studios. *Moving Picture World* reported that "topsy turvey is no word for the condition of the Keystone. Ad. Kessel hardly speaks to a soul, he is so busy directing the erection of buildings, stages, dressing rooms, and a thousand other additions. Everyone is working hard and fast and the place is one bunch of debris out of which will loom up a studio, new, big, and modern in all ways."[24] Maybe this is the reason Sydney shot so many of his films around this time at Griffith Park, to be well out of the way of all the construction in Edendale.

Gussle's Day of Rest, released on March 29 and the last of the park-setting shorts for Sydney, offered a version of the same plot as *That Springtime Feeling* expanded to two reels. It was supposedly shot in both Echo Park in Glendale and Griffith Park.[25] *Motion Picture News* again wrote in support of the film, noting that "to attempt an adequate description of the riot which runs through the two reels of this picture is impossible."[26] The film begins in the midst of the action . Again, Mrs. Gussle snoozes, while the hubby is on the prowl, again for Cecile Arnold, who is with Slim Summerville. Gussle entertains Cecile in one scene with another complicated trick, this time a fruit-on-a-fork bit (similar to those seen in Charlie's *The Pawnshop* [1916] outtakes). Gussle places the fork in his collar behind his head and throws an apple over his head so that it lands directly on the fork. Grabbing it, he bites off a piece, chews it a minute, then shows through his facial expressions that it doesn't taste good, and spits it out—with it landing on the same fork that is now situated in his hand.

At least two of these park films utilize the proximity of the Selig Zoo to the shooting location, with apes, leopards and other animals appearing in the shots. In this particular film, for instance, first Gussle, then Mrs. Gussle, get locked in the leopard cage, with such scenes becoming antecedents of similar scenes in Charlie's *The Circus* (1928). The film ends with Gussle and Cecile taking off in a jitney, with disastrous results. In one of the funnier of Sydney's Keystone film endings, the two pass by a cliff that is about to be dynamited and, predictably, end up covered in a mound of dirt and ash. Gussle then reaches over to try to uncover his companion, but, instead, in what is a rather macabre turn, pulls the blonde hair he thinks is hers to find that it comes completely off. Deciding then that Cecile has been wearing a wig, he gently covers her (and it) back up with the dirt in a move that is totally consistent with the character's desire only for the beautiful, but in a move that may shock the audience nonetheless.

* * *

With his next film, Sydney began the most fruitful collaboration of his Keystone contract when he teamed up with Charles Avery. Avery and Sydney worked together to direct Sydney's last six Gussle films and, except for two, they were able to utilize ambitious locations and, in some cases, new technology in an attempt to make these films unique. Lahue relates George Stout's perspective on Sydney's relationship with his co-director and, also, with his boss, Mack Sennett: "While Syd could be a fine, sensitive comic when he felt like it, this older Chaplin seemed to delight in shocking his director, cameraman and co-workers with a comic vulgarity that no producer in his right mind would attempt to place on the screen even during 1915, a fairly raucous year for movie comedy." Stout claimed that through improvisation, Sydney would insert gestures and expressions which, though not blatantly obscene, at least had the potential of double entendre. Avery, who seemed to somehow have a good working relationship with Sydney, would patiently halt filming, call his comic aside and talk him down to standard. Stout suggested, however, that "invariably, the retake was even more vulgar in nature than the one before it had been, and poor Avery aged several years in the few months he and Chaplin worked together." Mack Sennett's reaction to what he usually saw in the rushes was far more violent, for he "would explode in righteous indignation and anger, leaping out of his seat and heading for the door to find Syd and Avery." This process was repeated a sufficient number of times in the course of filming a single routine that it sort of became a routine in itself, with Sydney becoming the reputed "bad boy" of the Keystone lot. Stout claimed that

> no one seemed able to reason with him after Charlie departed, for the simple reason that Syd chose not to argue but merely accepted the verbal admonition to "clean up the routines" with a simple shrug of the shoulders. The next day during retakes, he seemed delightedly bent on topping the previous day's vulgarity before the camera (and often did), with only clever cutting and matching of these various takes allowing Avery to turn in a completed film on schedule. Even at that, Avery was usually far over the limited budget allowed at the time.[27]

Interestingly, Keystone was not publicizing Sydney's position as a co-director at first. Even as late as June 5, well after Sydney and Charlie Avery had completed four films together, the *Moving Picture World* listed only Avery as one of a group of directors currently working under Mack Sennett.[28] It wasn't until July 10 that Sydney was mentioned as co-director with Avery in another article on the Keystone Company submitted to the press.[29] Perhaps Sydney's relationship with Sennett, as Lahue suggests, was a tentative one and better left unrecognized or unheralded. Sennett himself seems to suggest this himself in his autobiography, *King of Comedy*, when his only mention of Sydney's tenure at Keystone is encapsulated in the comment that he gave "us nothing but pains in the neck."[30]

The first of the Chaplin-Avery films was *Gussle's Wayward Path*, released April 10. The difference working with Avery as a co-director on the film is clearly evident. First, the film has an easy-to-follow plot that is able to remain consistent with the characterization of Gussle as already developed. The action begins with Gussle returning home from "the hunt" with a very large gun and a very small dog. Second, there are some brilliant comedic moments in the film that are not so complicated as to be off-putting. One of the best bits of the first few scenes, for example, is created when Gussle hangs the little dog on his coat rack and Mrs. Gussle, finding the dog in that condition, decides to allow her husband to see how he likes it — whereupon she hangs him on the rack as well. What makes this gag even more effective is Gussle's reaction. While suspended from the coat rack, he makes a glass of water appear to be a glass of wine, through his deft handling of it. Given his leisure here, he lights up a cigarette, grabs his cane and hat and acts like he's going for a walk, all while hanging from a coat hook.

In the second reel, Gussle has escaped the wife once again and heads for the train station. She has equipped him this time, however, with a photo of herself, which he is supposed to consult "when tempted." Of course, Gussle is tempted immediately. The first time he consults the photo, despite the flies that seem to be interested in it, he is able to resist. However, an attractive blonde (Joy Lewis, who will appear in several Gussle films)[31] he soon meets causes him to simply tear up the photo and discard it. But the plot twists yet again. In this ending, instead of Mrs. Gussle beating her husband into tomorrow, Gussle finds her on the same train as the blonde, but because she is enjoying herself with another man, he becomes jealous and retaliates violently!

Reviews from several sources were very positive. The *Motion Picture News* reported that "from [its] start, the picture proceeds with a highly entertaining series of mishaps in which Gussle springs the startling stunts which are always to be expected of him. A very good piece of slapstick throughout."[32] The *Moving Picture World* went even farther, noting that "some novel innovations have been introduced in the course of the picture."[33] And, the small-town press simply touted it as "a screamingly funny single-reeler."[34]

Gussle Rivals Jonah was the first "exotic location" film for the Gussle character. It involved renting a boat and sailing to Catalina. Because such an operation was a bit of a departure for the usually low-budget Keystone Company, the *Moving Picture World* reported on it: "The Keystonian Players have boated over to Catalina to get some fun scenes on the sea. Syd Chaplin and his followers made the perilous trip across the channel to the famous island of scenic beauty."[35] Grace Kingsley, in her column "At the Stage Door," noted, "Syd Chaplin and Charlie Avery have returned from their two weeks' vacation at Santa Catalina, with a record of two excellent one-reel pictures, and several reels of fishes."[36] A group photo of the company on location appeared in her column about a week later.[37] Obviously, this was not business as usual for a Keystone production company, but perhaps, once again, the location shooting was at least partially justified by the continued construction on the Keystone lot. One report dated May 22 stated that "a $35,000 building is under course of construction and several other small buildings have been started just across the street on a plot of ground just signed for. There will be a large stage housed in a big frame building, equipped with powerful electric lights so that the rain will not hamper work anymore. The stage is 155 by 70. A garage is being built to house the Keystone cars, and additional dressing rooms and other operating rooms are being provided."[38] It sounds as though the "topsy turvey" conditions first reported in March continued unabated.

Although this was Syd's first film on a boat, it would not prove to be his most well-remembered. That was yet to come. What the film did prove to be, however, was Minnie Chaplin's film debut. Playing one of the boat's female passengers, she appears in a dark, rather Victorian outfit, suggesting a prudishness, which seems to be borne out by her character's later behavior. Seated next to the "heavy" in the cast, played by Frank "Fatty" Alexander,[39] Minnie, Alexander and Gussle's flirtation interest in the film fall asleep on deck chairs. When he wakes up, Alexander arbitrarily finds his arm around Minnie, who then also wakes up, slapping his arm away, yelling and then running off. Then in the final scene, she is one of the female bathing beauties involved in Gussle's rescue.

Sydney in costume as Reginald Gussle, on the Avalon docks, Santa Catalina Island, California, filming *Gussle Rivals Jonah* (Keystone, 1915) (LKSC).

Sydney was to include her in the cast of the three other location films as well: *Gussle's Backward Way*, *Gussle Tied to Trouble* and *A Submarine Pirate*, as well as one studio film, *Lovers Lost Control*.

As hinted at above, this film concerns a holiday cruise embarked upon by Mr. and Mrs. Gussle. As per her usual behavior, Mrs. Gussle falls asleep and Mr. Gussle goes a-flirting, again with Joy Lewis, who is attached in some manner (as either wife or daughter) to Frank Alexander. The local fauna of Catalina Island is highlighted in one scene in which Gussle and Lewis are looking through an eyepiece given to them by the captain. When Mrs. Gussle and Alexander awaken, however, mayhem ensues. Alexander goes overboard, Gussle is chased by first a seal and then a shark (he also goes overboard) and upon his rescue, the missus steps on his stomach to release what seems to be a large, unending geyser of water. The enthusiastic reviews for the film seem to indicate that the outlay of funds required to film it was warranted. *Motion Picture News* gushed,

> It is difficult to comment either at great length or with much dignity on so hilarious a comedy as this one, but it seems hard to refrain from a few words of praise for the marvelously fertile imagination which made the picture possible. Seldom has more fun of the slapstick sort been crowded into the space of two reels. From the first flash on the screen to the last there is a constant succession of laughs. One of the most original scenes is towards the end, when the hero is pulled from the water, and a husky shark is seen hanging from the western part of his trousers.[40]

Moving Picture World agreed, stating simply that the film was "a two-reel Syd Chaplin picture which has no lack of action and would be considered one of the best of the Keystone farce comedies."[41]

Sydney's next film, entitled *Gussle's Backward Way*, was also a location film. In fact, the next two films were shot on Mount Baldy (technically Mt. St. Antonio), part of the San Gabriel Mountains, which has an altitude of 10,064 feet at its summit. Phyllis Allen again plays opposite Sydney's Gussle, although it isn't clear that they are husband and wife here. Wesley Ruggles plays a young man in Malvolio-esque, alpine drawers, which are adorned with colorful stripes. Gussle arrives at the "Mountain Inn" riding backwards on a mule, thus the title. The justification for this is provided by the fact that a couple of crooks tried to rob him in the forest, so, if he faces backwards, he will see danger creeping up on him. In fact, both of Sydney's Mount Baldy films seem to suggest that the woods are a dangerous place. Once at the Mountain Inn, he causes problems by flirting with the barmaids and drinking Phyllis Allen's beer through a meerschaum pipe. Unlike the first and second of the Chaplin/Avery films, this one seems to be plagued with the old problem of too many complicated gags. But, although there is little plot to this film (while its mate, *Gussle Tied to Trouble*, has a plot that is too complicated), it, too, was well-received. *Motion Picture News* reported that "there is a wealth of humor in the reel, Chaplin effecting some incidental and original antics which are very funny. The scenes in which his trusty steed, a mule, is galloping along the road backwards, is a sidesplitter. There is nothing that is vulgar in this and much that is comical."[42] The publication's reviewer, however, was not as enthusiastic about the other film shot at the same time, *Gussle Tied to Trouble*, commenting only that the film "is a very good comedy containing several scenes which take away the breath, as well as many more that mostly amuse."[43] *Moving Picture World*, called *Gussle's Backward Way* "well photographed," "the snow scenes good and the humor abundant."[44]

The gist of *Gussle Tied to Trouble* is that the folks at the Mountain Inn decide to go skiing and must hike up the mountain to do so. Frank Alexander and Gussle get tied together—obviously a typical strategy for inexperienced alpine hikers—and must flee through the woods from Phyllis Allen, who may or may not be Mrs. Gussle in this film. However, she spends most of the film looking at the two men through a scope and taking pot shots at them with a rifle when she can, from whatever bizarre distance. Gussle finally frees himself of Alexander and decides to rip off the other group of skiers by adorning a fake nose and pulling a revolver on them. They get wise to him, however, and allow him to plummet over a cliff. He miraculously survives this fall and a long journey down a roaring mountain stream, only to be snatched from safety by a final blow dealt by Allen, this time in the shape of a boulder. The plunging-from-the-cliff scene was witnessed by some unsuspecting tourists to the area. Kalton C. Lahue and Terry Brewer recount the encounter in *Kops and Custards: The Legend of Keystone Films*:

> While on location at Mount Baldy with Syd Chaplin, Charles Avery scared the living daylights out of three tourists. These people had been taking in the scenic views and had stopped at the foot of a cliff to eat their picnic lunch. Imagine their horror when a loud scream pierced the mountain air! Looking up, they saw a body sailing over the cliff, to land with a sickening thud a few yards from their chosen spot of rest. Hurrying to the mangled piece of humanity crumpled on the hard ground, they paused and turned ill. The broken body before them could not possibly have survived such a fall. While staring at the remains, one man noticed something peculiar. Approaching closer to the still form, he bent down to read a label, "THIS DUMMY BELONGS TO THE KEYSTONE FILM

COMPANY. RETURN AND RECEIVE A REWARD." The badly shaken tourists trudged up the cliffside with the dummy and were treated to a royal time watching Syd Chaplin and the cast go through their paces.[45]

Because of the comparative uniqueness of a Keystone company filming for such an extended period in such an exotic location, the group received more than its fair share of media coverage. The first piece appeared on April 24 upon their return: "Syd Chaplin and his Keystoners are back from a little ascension to Mount Baldy where they did a week's work in the snow.... Here is the contrast of locations in this part of the country. Some shoot snow, others do mountain stuff, while water scenes are done, and on the side they do most everything from big city, desert, foreign, down to the lowliest interior. Great, yes!"[46] Then on May 8 appeared the news that Charlie Avery and his party had shot a mountain lion and other wild beasts on their sojourn,[47] but with some sacrifice, because in the same publication was the following announcement: "'Army' Armstrong, cameraman with the Chaplin Keystone company, which returned from Mount Baldy this week, was shot twice by bullets which glanced from the face of a rock near which he was standing. The first wound was close to one eye, and the second was in the abdomen. Medical attention was quickly given the suffering man and a fatality was averted."[48]

In fact, chaotic and violent as this film's plot was, it paled in comparison to the real-life drama that was unfolding during and following this location shoot. A string of misfortunes now seemed to haunt the group. In addition to Armstrong's accidental shooting, it was reported on June 5: "Syd Chaplin, of the Keystone powerhouse, has been on the sick list for the past half week, suffering from an attack of nerves."[49] In the July 3 issue of *Moving Picture World*, it was reported that "out at the Keystone studios, where so many people are working on fun pictures, they have diversion in the form of swimming. The Keystone plunge is always full of fresh cool water and at the end of a hot day's work the players all jump into bathing suits and plunge for half an hour. The other day there were about twenty filmers in and it was fun to watch the boys and girls enjoying the water."[50] Always enamored of such sun and water fun, perhaps Sydney was able to take part in some of these amusements. What is certain, though, is that by June 19, he was on the beach with Roscoe Arbuckle, an on-again, off-again companion:

> Last Sunday was a scorcher in town and many filmers came to the beach for the week end, that is, those who did not have to work. Roscoe Arbuckle, Syd Chaplin, and many others were on deck at the beach wearing white clothes and enjoying the strand. Some picture men were on the beach doing stunts with a phoney camera for amusement of themselves and the throngs of visitors. Roscoe and Syd were soon enmeshed in the "shop" stunts, and soon a great crowd had gathered to see the stars "work." But it was only their play.[51]

Although this would indicate he was on the mend, by July 11, it was reported that he had "entirely recovered from the accident he sustained a week or so ago,"[52] but by July 19, he had supposedly been once again "ill at his home for the past week, but [was] expected to be about in a few days. Mr. Chaplin has been working unusually hard for several weeks and suffered a nervous breakdown."[53]

The bad luck continued unabated. *The Ogden* (Utah) *Standard* reported in an article entitled "Jinx Still Follows Chaplin" on August 28 that, although preliminary production had begun on the submarine picture, more accidents and misfortunes were occurring:

All the hard luck that has visited the Keystone studio for the past two or three months has seemed to center itself on Syd Chaplin and his company. Syd was shot in the eye with a piece of fireworks; his director, Chas. Avery, is in the hospital and will remain there for several weeks more as the result of an accident that took place recently while the Chaplin company was putting on a scene. Last week the company went to San Diego and while there, Chaplin, his new director Chas. Parrott, Wesley Ruggles and Glen Cavender were all stricken with ptomaine poisoning and were seriously ill for nearly a week after.[54]

Until this report in late August, the industry weeklies were pretty much lacking in Syd mentions, suggesting that problems continued throughout that period. Meanwhile, Kessel and Baumann were changing things at the New York Motion Picture Company, first reducing Keystone releases from two a week to one by June 19 and later working with Sennett to hire some well-known stars to work under the Keystone banner[55]: Eddie Foy and family, Joe Jackson and Bert Levy, Weber and Fields, Raymond Hitchcock, and Fred Mace.[56] Charles Baumann had even suggested to Sennett in a letter dated June 4 to "be sure to make a new contract with Sydney Chaplin if you believe him to be of a value that will fill the bill for the big scheme, and use your own judgment in getting him at the best figure, but at any rate get him, especially if it will help you get Charley back at the expiration of his contract [with Essanay]."[57] Of course, Sydney and Charlie had other plans and the $3,000 a week Keystone was prepared to offer came to seem like a drop in the bucket.

All of these new stars were expensive and proved to be ill-suited to working in film, mostly due to their larger-than-life stage personae. But at least one of these stars, Joe Jackson, became a good friend of Sydney's. A postcard from Jackson to Sydney suggests the type of relationship they had and its longevity, since it's dated March 12, 1926, many years following the end of Sydney's Keystone contract. On the front is a photo of a naked baby lying belly down on an animal pelt, with Jackson's character's face[58] replacing the baby's head and the words above it, "'Still Young in the Business.' Joe. Jackson."[59] Sydney formed at least one other important connection with an individual at Keystone that he cashed in on later in his career. Charles "Chuck" Reisner (Riesner) was listed as a member of the Keystone scenario department in an article dated September 18.[60] One account relates his particular method of formulating gags that caused him to be both noticed and rewarded by Sennett. Certainly, had Sydney witnessed this behavior, he would have at least admired the technique and made a mental note of it for safe keeping and future use:

> The source of [Chuck's] happy inspirations was the five-and-ten-cent store. Reisner would stand in front of this bazaar each Monday when the window-dresser changed the display. Chuck would have a note-book and pencil in his hands and jot down the names of all the articles. Then he would ask himself: "What can be done with a knife? With a spool of thread? A fire shovel? Napkins? Plates? Dolls? Candy?" And so on, endlessly. After figuring out the things which could be accomplished with these props, Reisner filed his memoranda in drawers labeled: "Kitchen," "Bathroom," "Bedroom," "Farm," etc.[61]

Not surprisingly, Reisner would become Sydney's director in four of his five Warner Bros. films in the late 1920s (notably the four most successful of these films), thereby proving the importance of this relationship to Sydney's career.

Sydney's next film after *Gussle Tied to Trouble* was *Lovers Lost Control*, released on

August 2 under the old New York Films (Kessel and Baumann) banner, even though Harry Aitken's Triangle Films was about to take over. It utilized virtually the same cast as the other three Chaplin/Avery films, but is distinctive in that it gives Minnie Chaplin her longest on-film scene and allows the audience to see, for the only time, her acting skills, skills probably gained while working for Karno. The film also features Wayland Trask, a new big-guy actor for a Gussle film. It is really a good one to pair up next to Charlie's first film for Mutual, *The Floorwalker* (1916), in that it takes place in a department store and utilizes many gags later utilized in Charlie's film. Here again, Gussle looks for his chance of dumping the wife in order to chase a younger chicken, again played by Joy Lewis. He manages to leave Mrs. Gussle in lingerie, while he goes to the shoe department to try his luck. A fat older gentleman (Frank Alexander) and blonde woman (Joy Lewis) arrive there. This couple is advertised as Mr. and Mrs. Lewis in printed descriptions of the film.[62] After causing his usual mischief in the shoe department with Joy Lewis's character, Gussle and girl take off out of the store and jump into the Gussle-mobile, beginning what is the only iconic Keystone Cops chase in a Gussle film, complete with too many cops in the paddy wagon, hanging out the sides with their nightsticks waving. After Mrs. Gussle, Mr. Lewis, and the cops go off a cliff in the wagon, they give chase on foot, but before they can meet up with the fleeing couple, the car has arrived at the beach and slams into the surf, with both Gussle and the girl in the final shot, shown trying to remove themselves from the sinking car.

Motion Picture World was brief and non–committal on the film, writing only that the comedy was "particularly gay" and that it was "a good example of Keystone ingenuity." The release of this, the seemingly final Gussle short, combined with the misfortunes and the length of time needed to film the four-reel *The Submarine Pirate*, caused Keystone to pull the two-reel *No One to Guide Him* off the shelf, dust it off, fix it up and release it. Directed by F. Richard Jones, this film was "completed" on January 14 and had been shelved since that time. It is indeed the poorest of the Gussle films and this may be because it started life as a three-reeler, being received in New York initially in that form on April 22. The film was subsequently returned to Edendale on August 16 and reshipped as a two-reeler on August 24. It was then released in this shorter version on August 30. This bought Sydney and Avery some time to work on the submarine film, but even so, that film was not ready to go until October and wasn't given a wide release until the very end of the year. *No One to Guide Him*, in the meantime, proved to be another episode in the unhappy marriage of Gussle and Gussle.

Like many of the other Gussle films, it begins with a scene of marital misery between the Gussles. Mr. Gussle then goes to work at a tavern and tries to figure out a way to rob the cash register, but is witnessed in the act by a shady character. The two decide to work together to effect the robbery and then meet up afterwards at an exclusive club. Here Gussle can try to achieve his other usual goal, that of trying to find a woman. Mrs. Gussle and the cops, though, somehow find the club and what follows is much mischief with a trapdoor and a chute. The final moment shows Mr. Gussle sliding down the chute once again, getting bopped on the head at the bottom, but then Mrs. Gussle wraps her arms around him in a comforting/caring move in what has to be an unexpected ending for a typical Gussle film. Reviews for this film are scarce and the newspapers obviously were trying very hard to introduce the film to viewers in the most positive way they could, without really committing to it. *The Portsmouth* (OH) *Daily Times*, having not received the film for viewing until November, calls it "rich, hilarious fun and frolic," and its stars "three of the greatest comedians before the camera."[63]

Mack Sennett had known since July 1 that Keystone's Mutual Films contract (Keystone's current distribution company), which expired on September 1, would not be renewed, so it was with this knowledge and his ambiguity about forming SIG (Sennett, Ince, Griffith) Films that he boarded a train to La Junta, Colorado, with Tom Ince and D. W. Griffith to meet Harry Aitken. That meeting resulted in the formation of Triangle Films on July 20 by Aitken, a firm that picked up contracts for all three film heavyweights on that very September 1 deadline.[64] Triangle was to release films in the first run through its own theaters, located in most major cities. The first Triangle ad then appeared in the September 4 issue of *Moving Picture World*, an article appears in the September 11 issue, with the debut program occurring on September 23 at the Knickerbocker Theatre on Broadway in New York. That program featured Douglas Fairbanks in *The Lamb*, Ince's *The Iron Strain* and Keystone's *My Valet* with Raymond Hitchcock.[65] Strangely enough, although Sennett and the New York Film Company had just remodeled the Keystone Studios on Alessandro Street in the spring and early summer, modifications that were described in the July 10 issue of *Moving Picture World* in great detail,[66] Triangle undertook what was purported to be a $100,000 renovation of that studio in late September.[67]

Sydney's first and only film for Triangle was *The Submarine Pirate*,[68] released on December 26. The story leading up to this date is a long and complicated one. Although it is unclear whose idea the film was initially, the *New York Times* reported on November 14 that "on the last day of April Mack Sennett telegraphed to Secretary Daniels and requested the use of a submarine for the picture, which is now completed. The Secretary at once notified the commander of the Pacific submarine flotilla that one of the undersea boats was to be placed at the Keystone director's disposal."[69] But, as has already been noted, the production schedule did not go according to plan, being encumbered as it was with accidents, sicknesses and other misfortunes. Secretary Daniels had ordered the date of October 16 as that on which the filming would be completed and the submarine re-instated for duty. Sennett was then compelled to ask for an extension and easily received one for ten days from that date.

In the film, Glen Cavender ("a shrewd inventor") and Wesley Ruggles ("his accomplice") plan the destruction of a government battleship. The film opens in a ritzy hotel. Sydney's character is fairly Gussle-esque, except for his garb, in that he likes "to mingle flirtation with pretty guests with the juggling of plates and edibles."[70] Phyllis Allen, however, does not play the missus in this film, but a difficult patron of the establishment, lying in wait for Sydney (the waiter) in one scene.

Inside the hotel restaurant, Cavender and Ruggles discuss their plan, which Sydney overhears by means of a telephone receiver disguised as a flower arrangement that he has been placed on their table. Sydney, noticing that Miss Allen's bag nearly matches that of the inventors, effects a switch between the two, then steals the one containing the plans and the submerging key. The *Moving Picture World* describes several subsequent scenes missing from the film as it exists today: "They run for their room with her and all the guests in pursuit. They get into their apartment and one of them puts a bomb in the box containing their plans and models and in which Syd has hidden himself. There is a great explosion and Syd and the inventors escape injury. There is a pursuit in which Syd jumps from one building to another."[71] After buying an admiral's uniform at a second-hand store and arriving at the submarine, the commander turns the craft over to Sydney. The interior with all its levers and cogs is shown to him and he is instructed on how to submerge. What follows is a mistaken attack by the sub on a passenger ship in a quest for gold, the sinking of the submarine, then by a U.S. gunboat, and Sydney, the waiter, being attacked by a shark.

A scene inside the submarine showing Billy Gilbert (far left), Al Hill (second from left) and Sydney from *A Submarine Pirate* (Keystone, 1915) (LKSC).

Continuity documents still in existence provide evidence of some of the scenes that were attempted and later omitted from the final film. The scene in which Sydney and his lifeboat containing six men, whose mission it is to board the *Harvard*, the passenger ship believed to be carrying a cargo of gold, is fairly short and straightforward in the completed film. In this scene, the lifeboat reaches the passenger ship, which Sydney and his men immediately board. They then greet the captain and first mate a little too cordially, and state their business, after which the sailors line up briefly in formation. After finally being threatened with weapons, the first mate leads the sailors to the gold room while the captain sneaks off to wire for help. In one continuity document, this scene was envisioned as far more complicated and elaborate:

369 Deck of sub — Syd on, talking to Harvard
370 Wheel house — Cap and Rug on — talk biz — drop megaphone
371 Harvard on — sub pulls alongside
372 Wheel room — sailors on — biz of getting gun and exiting
373 Side of Harvard — Syd comes up over side and ex
374 Life boat — Syd enters and x

375	Side of Harvard — sailors up and x
376	Life boat #2 — Syd enters and turns around
377	Life boat No. 1 — sailors enter and line up
378	Life boat #2 — Syd on — gives orders
379	Life boat #1 — sailors on — biz of drill
380	Life boat No. 2 — Syd on — gives orders
381	Lifeboat No. 1 — sailors on — biz of drill
381½	Lifeboat #1 — Passengers on watching drill
382	Lifeboat #2 — Passengers Syd on — biz — exits
383	Lifeboat #1 — sailors on — Syd enters — instructs sailors in drill — takes fall
384	Passengers on — biz — laugh at fall
385	Lifeboat #1 — Syd and sailors on — biz — Syd exits
386	Lifeboat #2 — Syd enters — biz
387	Wheel house — Cap and Rug on — biz — exits
388	Ext wheel house — Cap and Rug enter and exit
389	Lifeboat #2 — Syd on — Cap and Rug enter
390	Lifeboat #1 — talk biz — sailors lined up
391	Lifeboat #2 — Syd — Cap and Rug on — talk biz — Syd
392	Lifeboat #1 — Sailors on — bring guns to aim
393	Lifeboat#2 — Syd-Cap and Rug on — talk biz
394	Lifeboat #1 — Flash of sailors aiming
395	Lifeboat #2 — Syd, Cap and Rug on — biz — Syd — talks to sailors
396	Lifeboat #1 — Sailors on — bring guns down
397	Lifeboat #2 — Syd-Cap and Rug on — biz — Syd talks to sailors all exit
398	Lifeboat #1 — Sailors on — biz — 3 sailors x
399	Engine room hatch — Syd — Cap and Rug enter — Rug opens door — 3 sailors enter — Biz to sailors exit
400	Goldroom — Rug and 2 sailors enter — biz
401	Lifeboat #1 — sailors on — biz — 2 sailors exit
402	Goldroom — biz of sailors throwing up boxes, etc.
403	Hatch — Syd — sailor and Cap on — sailor catches box and throws it off
404	Lifeboat — sailors on — catches box and throws it off
405	Lifeboat — sailors on — catches box and throws it off
406	Goldroom — sailors throwing up box
407	Hatch — sailor catching box and throwing it
408	Lifeboat — sailor talking — box hits him — biz — to throwing box
409	Hatch — Syd and sailor and cap on — biz — Syd gets hit
410	Goldroom — sailors throw up box
411	Hatch — Syd gets box and falls
412	Goldroom — sailors throw up box
413	Hatch — Syd gets hit with box — biz
414	Goldroom — Sailors throw up box
415	Hatch — Syd gets box in face
416	Goldroom — biz of sailors
417	Hatch — Syd bawling out sailors — Cap sneaks off [72]

If these scenes were actually filmed before they were deleted, this might partially explain why, in addition to the spate of bad luck, the film took so long to complete.

While it was originally planned that the week of November 14 would be the general release date of the film, initial showings at the Knickerbocker Theater in New York, for instance, suggested that more forethought was needed in regards to publicity. As the *Waterloo Times-Tribune* reported on December 5, *A Submarine Pirate* "will not be placed in the regular releases for some weeks. Great plans are in preparation for the proper promotion for what, it has been agreed, is one of the most remarkable films ever produced, and when these have been perfected, an announcement will be made."[73] However, the *New York Times* review of the film appeared the day after the Knickerbocker showing, perhaps in order to whet the audience's appetite, for it related that "the film does give a good idea of the workings of a submersible craft. The submarine is shown above water, submerging and firing a torpedo. The interior is pictured when the boat is up and as she goes down, and the use of the periscope is also illustrated."[74] These characteristics of the film caused Secretary Daniels to decide that he wanted the right to use the film as a recruiting device, before its general nationwide release in the theaters,[75] which turned out to be the real reason for the delay.[76] The studio's own periodical, *The Triangle*, reported the process that resulted in the Navy's enthusiasm: "John McKeon, one of the Triangle executives, submitted the novel film to the Navy Department in Washington last week. Secretary Daniels saw it at a private exhibition there Thursday Morning.... The officials decided that not a foot of film needed to be cut out of the picture. In fact, they were so pleased with it that they regarded it as a splendid advance agent for recruiting."[77]

In addition to its obvious qualities as a recruiting vehicle, the subject matter of the film was just plain timely and prescient, a feature also duly noted by the *New York Times* reviewer. In a more recent study of the Keystone product, film scholar Rob King develops this perspective of the film's significance: "At the time when *A Submarine Pirate* was released, there was indeed exceptional public interest in 'submersibles,' albeit not for reasons that had much to do with comedy. The sinking of the Cunard ocean liner RMS *Lusitania* by a German U-boat on May 7, 1915, had provoked a widespread outcry that, while it did not precipitate American entry into the war, nevertheless fostered U.S. government support for new defense programs and boosted public anxiety about military preparedness."[78] Although he suggests that this is not especially fit subject matter for slapstick comedy, such it proved to be, for, as King later argues, the emphasis of the film must be on the technology, not the recent actual tragedies involving that technology: "The film's progress, stated broadly, is to invert a menacing imagery of technological mastery with a more comic imagining of out–of-control machinery."[79]

The November 20 edition of *The Triangle* reported that the film would be released for general distribution on December 19, but by the December 4 edition, it was delayed yet another week. Meanwhile, William Randolph Hearst gave a party for the 400 on Thanksgiving Day, showing, for the night's entertainment, Syd's film in conjunction with *The Coward* (1915) with Charles Ray and Frank Keenan. His guests included "Former Governor and Mrs. John Marshall Slaton of Georgia, E. L. Doheny, the California oil man, and Mrs. Doheny and others."[80] By December 4 as well, some of the reviews were in and *The Triangle* happily reported the cream of the crop of reviews the film had received. The *New York Herald* reported that the film was "not only amusing but also instructive," and the *New York Sun* that it was "a combination of thrills and laughs." The *Chicago Examiner* called it "a serious comedy." The *Philadelphia Press* was more verbose, reporting that "uproarious comedy was furnished by 'A Submarine Pirate,' in which the leading roles engaged the hilarious services of Syd Chaplin and Phyllis Allen. Some wonderful submarine effects were produced."[81] Louis Reeves Harrison reviewed the film for *Moving Picture World*:

Sennett has masked some fascinating and vitally interesting pictures of a real submarine in action behind a bright farce comedy called "A Submarine Pirate," has pretended to submerge the live question of submarine attack in a roaring force, and he has produced a winner, one of the best examples of his art yet shown. The movements of the vessel in a sham attack on a passenger steamer are taken from aboard of her part of the time, part of the time from a third boat, a swift series of operations such as have never been before been shown on the screen, the company performers playing their parts on what has every sign of being a genuine coast submarine from the United States Navy.

The company scenes are not confined to the studio-built interior of the submarine; they take place on the needle-like vessel while she is running on the surface, diving and emerging from hidden depths. Syd Chaplin, in a second-hand Admiral's suit, is in charge having seized the vessel by a stratagem, and there is apparently nothing faked about his exploits on the deck when he is shut out of the manhole as the vessel is about to dive. The realistic touch, brought constantly into contrast with a running farce in the imaginary hold of the boat sets the whole story apart as a noteworthy achievement in that difficult, if delightful, art of making people laugh.[82]

Business was good, even at just the Triangle flagship venues. By December 18, *The Triangle* reported that the film had been renewed yet again for a fifth week, despite theater policy "to only show the plays at this model theatre for one week, but so sweeping and irresistible was the success of 'A Submarine Pirate,' and so many people were insistent on getting a chance to see it, that the management decided on its revival."[83] The same issue announced that the film would *finally* be released nationwide on December 26,[84] and with that in mind, offered information on its box office success so far, as well as helpful hints for expanding that success. In an article entitled "Bally-Hoo Display for Syd Chaplin Comedy, 'A Submarine Pirate,'" *The Triangle* offered up a half-page graphic showing one possible way to prepare a theater lobby properly for the film, admonishing its readers that being a "special" comedy release "it should be treated in a *special* way." The graphic shows a typical theater lobby, adorned with a camouflage netting on the ceiling, a torpedo displayed on one side of the ticket booth, a periscope on the other and American flags emanating from the opening of the lobby out towards the street. The ticket taker is dressed as a sailor. How to accomplish this cheaply? The writer suggests that "sailors' costumes may be gotten from any costuming establishment (or pawnbroker's) and the periscope may be made with ordinary pipe and mirrors placed at proper angles. In order to see the reflection of a scene through the periscope a photographer's hood should be placed over the head to cut out lights. Blank torpedoes and other marine implements may be had from the National Security League, 31 Pine Street, NYC."[85]

Despite the great success of this film, as Lahue notes, "This was Syd's last appearance for Sennett and marked the end of his career at Keystone. His one-year contract had expired and Sennett, tired of the constant haggling necessary to wring a suitable comedy subject from Syd, had no overwhelming desire to renew it."[86] In an article in the *Waterloo Times Tribune* entitled "Syd Chaplin Quits Keystone," the writer notes the irony of what seems like an untimely parting between the comedian and his studio: "It's a curious world. A few weeks ago, we laughed so hard at Syd Chaplin in 'The Submarine Pirate' that we thot [sic] he was one of the funniest comedians on record and a prize possession to the possessing company. Then comes the chill news from Keystone: 'He is no longer connected with this company.'"[87] But, regardless of Sydney's future film career or his imminent plans, *A Submarine Pirate* proved to have some endurance beyond his other Keystone efforts. It was still being widely shown on into 1916, and *The Triangle* for February 5 devotes nearly a page to a big event featuring the film held in Oakland, California. Meant as a showcase for the new $100,000 Franklin Theatre, as well as for the film itself, 500 Marine cadets from Yerba Buena Island were invited to town to view the film:

> Commandant Phillips Andrews and his five hundred bold lads from the U.S. naval training station appeared in a body in Oakland and marched up the main street with banners and bands, to the Franklin Theatre.... The procession was led by a long line of automobiles and the city made of it a gala occasion, giving the visitors conspicuous welcome all along the line of march. Captain Andrews, Mayor Davie and city officials were saluted by the men with "caps off," while the five hundred passed into the theatre. Outside the section reserved for the marines and their officers, every seat in the house was sold and filled. The orchestra greeted the guests with "The Star-Spangled Banner" and the audience cheered.[88]

Forty-seven years later, Robert Youngson released a film entitled *30 Years of Fun* that featured excerpts from this film, thereby passively acknowledging the film's overall importance in the pantheon of silent film comedy. Even Charlie tipped his hat to his brother's achievement with a few lines in his 1964 *My Autobiography*, despite failing to remember the film's correct title: "One that broke records throughout the world was *The Submarine Pilot* [*sic*], in which Sydney contrived all sorts of camera tricks."[89] And so, Sydney left the limelight for the shadows in January, 1916, one article suggesting that he had "'no regular job,' dividing his time between running an advertising service and helping brother Charley direct at the Essanay studio."[90] He had ended his Keystone career in a way that would become a bad habit and would come to haunt him in years to come — in bitterness. Not only had Sennett had enough of him, but Sydney severed whatever tentative ties existed between himself and Roscoe Arbuckle when he noted to the trade press and later in a letter to a friend that Arbuckle had stolen his (Syd's) idea when he came out with his film *He Did and He Didn't* on January 30, 1916:

> When I worked for Mack Sennett, I got a great idea for a story with a very original angle & something entirely different to what the Keystone comedians had ever done. I was anxious to do it & told Mack Sennett the story. Roscoe Arbuckle was in the room at the time. Roscoe left shortly after to make a story in New York & some time after that I also went to New York & arrived there just in time to see the first night's showing of Roscoe's new picture. Imagine my surprise and disgust when I saw he had done my story. When I taxed him with it, he told me Mack Sennett had instructed him to do it. That is film world ethics.[91]

Maybe such behavior seems self-destructive and self-sabotaging, which it was, but what Sydney failed to do for his own film career, he made up for in Charlie's. Reading Charlie's lines to him to help him learn his *Sherlock Holmes* part and paving the way for him with Karno would be considered minor efforts in comparison with Sydney's achievements for his brother in the first few months of 1916.

Chapter 4

Surviving Hollywood, 1916–1921

Sydney suddenly burst into laughter. "This goes into my memoirs: you with that towel around your hips, playing the violin, and your reaction to the news that I've signed you up for a million and a quarter!" — Charles Chaplin, My Autobiography (203)

People who three years ago thought of aviation as an interesting form of suicide are today trampling all over one another for the privilege of making the first trip to Catalina in a flying boat. — William N. Henry, "Southern California Soon to See Commercial Aircraft," Los Angeles Times (April 20, 1919): V13.

SYDNEY CHAPLIN IS BEST KNOWN FOR THE WORK that he accomplished on Charlie's behalf over the course of 1916–1918, three short years, really, in what was a very long life. This is either suggestive of his wizardry as a businessman or critical commentary on the rest of his life's accomplishments. Regardless, when Sydney made the decision not to pursue other film contracts after the one with Keystone ended, he took over his brother's business dealings with relish and wasted no time in doing so. As 1915 came to a close, Sydney found Charlie embroiled in a contract dispute with Essanay, in which Charlie failed to complete five of the ten films he had promised. Essanay took him to court over the matter, and in the meantime, created a longer version of his *Burlesque on Carmen* which included reels of footage filmed after his departure from the company. Into the first months of 1916, just as Charlie and Sydney were negotiating the Mutual contract, Essanay was in court asking for half a million dollars in restitution for their loss, and were willing to go to any lengths to get it, including pressing the brothers' aunt, Kate Mowbray, for a repayment of funds advanced to her by George K. Spoor's brother to pay for Hannah Chaplin's care at Peckham House in London, where she had been placed on September 9, 1912. World War I had placed this arrangement in jeopardy, because, although Sydney and Charlie were diligent about sending payments, these payments often didn't make it to their destination in time. One such time placed Aunt Kate — the only relative nearby who could handle such matters — in the position of asking Spoor for an advance on Charlie's salary to cover the costs.[1]

One of Sydney's earliest accomplishments involved his setting up the Charlie Chaplin Advertising Service Company,[2] a short-lived company at the time, but one that was a progenitor of Chaplin licensing as it exists today (under the label Bubbles, Inc., S.A.), protecting as it does Charlie's image from unauthorized reproduction. With this company's creation, Sydney immediately took Arts Novelty Company to court, suing them for producing unlicensed Charlie Chaplin statuettes. Sydney also started The Charlie Chaplin Music Corporation at about the same time, with even less success; during its brief lifespan, it published exactly three songs, all ostensibly written by Charlie, but none of which became very popular. In his next business effort, however, Sydney would more than make up for these unimportant failures.

After helping his brother to create a sort of fervor in the film industry about who would be lucky enough to sign the golden boy (Charlie), Sydney left for New York via Chicago in February 1916, to prepare the way for Charlie's arrival a short time later. Sydney found that he had plenty of offers to choose from and took his time in negotiating, in order to get what Charlie wanted — essentially a million-dollar contract, if possible. John Freuler,[3] of the Mutual Film Corporation, won in the end with a contract that provided Charlie $10,000 a week with a bonus of $150,000 on signing. Freuler told columnist Louella Parsons, "I went after Chaplin last July. I was negotiating with Sid Chaplin before Charlie ever reached New York. Sid has the business brain of the two, and Charlie has sense enough to be guided by his brother's advice."[4] Much was made of this signing event, which was covered heavily by the press and offered the opportunity for a little hammy acting. After Freuler handed Charlie the bonus check for $150,000, he "looked over the check critically then gingerly passed it on. 'Take it, Sidney. Take it away from me, please. It hurts my eyes.'"

Charlie's new studio (to be called the "Lone Star" studio and located at the corner of Lillian Way and Eleanor Avenue in Los Angeles), was managed by Henry P. Caulfield, who joined the brothers on their journey back to California on the *Twentieth Century Limited*.[6] They left New York on March 10, stopping off at Chicago to satiate the press. The *Chicago Daily News* reported Sydney's part in the drama: " Syd Chaplin stood by his little brother beaming upon him and occasionally interjecting a few remarks about his own future. He expects to appear on the same program with Charlie, although plans have not been definitely arranged." Meanwhile, the *New York Review* reported that Sydney's efforts had not gone unrewarded: he had received $75,000 as a bonus for his negotiating prowess, fully half of Charlie's Mutual bonus.[8]

When they returned home, however, it was to the unhappy news that their mother's only sister, Kate Mowbray, had died suddenly while alone in her apartment.[9] Sad as this was simply for the loss it meant, the news also left Hannah without a person nearby to see to her needs, financial and otherwise. This duty would soon fall to Aubrey Chaplin, Charlie's cousin (son of his father's brother Spencer), a publican by trade, who always had some interest in getting into the entertainment business himself. It was Sydney, however (really no relation to Aubrey), that set up this connection and continued it, using Aubrey first in dealings with his mother (he would be instrumental in getting her to America), then with Charlie's first homecoming visit to England in 1921, with Sydney's coming back to London to work from British International Pictures in 1927, and especially with his charity event involving the *Exmouth* training ship boys, and finally, Charlie's world trip in 1931–2. Aubrey never even made it over to America to visit the Chaplin studios, although his oldest daughter, Betty, would do so in his place many years later.

The Lone Star Studio opened on March 27. Charlie had chosen a cast of players, many of whom remained with him for years, including his leading lady Edna Purviance, Albert Austin (another ex–Karno player), John Rand, Charlotte Mineau, Lloyd Bacon, James T. Kelley, Frank J. Coleman and the all-important "Goliath," Scotsman Eric Campbell. Sydney acted in none of the Mutual films, at least that have been identified, but he was ever-present behind the scenes. The Mutual outtakes in the British Film Institute collection show him training the company actors in all sorts of stage business, from pratfalls to juggling tricks. And, most importantly, Charlie counted on him for brainstorming gags and scenario possibilities. How much he counted on him is evident in letters and cables that passed between the brothers when Sydney was away. Wiring him at the Hotel Bonta in New York City, July 31, while he would have been filming *The Count*, Charlie pleaded: "Have you any suggestions for scenes? Have dining room and ballroom. I am playing a count but an imposter to win heiress but cannot get story straight. Wire me some gags if possible. Playing in Chaplin make-up in fancy dress ball." Charlie's problems with this story continued, however, causing him to film the mostly one-man-show *One A.M.* in the meantime. By August, the situation was so dire that Charlie's butler and Man Friday, Tom Harrington, wired Sydney again:

> Charlie is very depressed condition for past two weeks. Doesn't seem able to get mind around to his story. He wishes nearly every other day you were here. Unless he pulls up within next couple of days am afraid he will miss release on this picture. Think it very important for his future success for you to drop everything in New York and come here immediately spending at least three or four weeks. Charlie hasn't been sick but whenever he gets into difficult situation, which doesn't work out satisfactorily, he always wishes Syd were here. Don't let Charlie know I wired this as it might make him feel badly, but it is my honest opinion he needs you and that you should take next train for coast. Have shown Caulfield this wire and he thinks the same as I do. Wire answer immediately.[10]

Five days later, Charlie wired his brother himself: "The last two pictures have given me great worry and I need you here to help me. Drop everything and arrange to be in Los Angeles by Saturday August 12 to help me in directing next picture. Wire answer immediately." Why was Sydney leaving his brother in such misery? In fact, why was he in the East to begin with? An article that appeared in the *Chicago Morning Telegraph* (and elsewhere) June 17 provides part of the answer. Its headline reads, "Chaplins 'Split,' Is Western Rumor: Los Angeles Claims Famous Film Funny Man and Brother Are Quits." The report asserts that the brothers have quarreled a few days prior "both professionally and personally." Charlie refused to be interviewed on the subject; the studio manager Henry Caulfield refused to acknowledge the existence of a quarrel. Sydney was already talking about a venture that wouldn't come to fruition until three years later: the forming of the "Sid Chaplin Film Company." A subsequent report on the quarrel that summer, quoted Charlie's reply to further questions on the subject as "Deny it flat. Somebody's foolish." Sydney, also now speaking on the topic, simply commented, "Not only is there no split, but we never have had a serious difference."[11] Ostensibly in New York on Charlie's

4. Surviving Hollywood, 1916–1921

business at this time suggests that Sydney was simply being his recalcitrant self. A cable sent to Charlie on August 8 suggests that Sydney was feeling himself "used" by Mutual without proper remuneration, and Sydney was simply holding out for more money: "If Caufield or Freuler think that there is possible chance of me coming to coast and directing you for nothing I will not get contract I am after. I value my services at twenty five hundred week." The next line of the cable, "Why should I give them benefit of my brains for nothing although would do anything to help you," clearly indicates a lack of animosity between the brothers. Sydney told Charlie that Freuler was supposed to offer him a contract for review the following Tuesday: "If satisfactory will sign same and leave for coast immediately. If they don't meet my terms I will know they are using you as bait to get me out there for nothing. Don't worry."[12] That a settlement was reached is indicated only by the fact that Sydney eventually returned to California.

The year 1916 meant other trials for the brothers: problems with the unauthorized publication of Rose Wilder Lane's *Charlie Chaplin's Own Story* by Bobbs-Merrill Publishing, the rise in number and diversity of Charlie Chaplin imitators, and conscription. About a year and a half into World War I, Great Britain began to take notice of the fact that the Chaplin boys had not signed up. Robinson reports that one of the first such notices — one probably started up by a disgruntled Lord Northcliffe — appeared in the *Daily Mail* and mentioned the war-risks clause of Charlie's Mutual contract, one that stated he was not permitted to return to Britain for the duration of the war in fear of being conscripted into service.[13] Less was made of Sydney's similar failure to serve, except that eventually the California Draft Board received anonymous reports that he had falsified his age so as not to be eligible. Although he was not 31 in 1914 when the war started, he had no trouble testifying his true age when called before the board in June, 1917, being then a whole year older than the legal ineligible age.[14]

As 1917 dawned, Sydney helped his brother to begin appreciating the finer things in life. On Sydney's recommendation, Charlie purchased a Locomobile and engaged a Japanese driver for it, Torachai Kono. He also hired a valet-secretary, the aforementioned Tom Harrington, a New Yorker, who had performed many of the same duties for Bert Clark, a former Keystone player. Harrington was to be the first in a long line of caring men and women to occupy this post, individuals who often went above and beyond the call of duty in order to secure Charlie's happiness and peace. Despite his growing desire for a similar status in Hollywood and in the film business in general, Sydney never engaged a personal assistant, perhaps because he was married, but it could have been that he would never have trusted anyone with the responsibility. He did trust his wife Minnie, however, and in the early months of the year found himself launching into the women's clothing business purely on her recommendation.

The Sassy Jane Manufacturing Company, incorporated on March 22, 1917, was the first of the boom-and-bust endeavors he was to engage in and not the last that caused him to bring down the fortunes of complete strangers while remaining seemingly unscathed himself. Sassy Jane was the brainchild of a Missouri-born single woman, June B. Rand (no relation to John Rand, of Charlie's Mutual company of players), a seamstress who had moved out to California much like many other young people at the time, to try her hand in the land of milk and honey. The mythology around Rand was that

Sydney (center) surrounded by the Sassy Jane Clothing Company girls modeling the company's wares, circa 1917 (LKSC).

she found herself in Los Angeles with only $4.90 left in her pocket before she decided to use her handiwork to support herself. She began with a simple product: gingham aprons that came in all colors of the rainbow. Successful at that, she soon added gingham dresses and it was for this product that she became most famous and caught the attention of the Hollywood fashionistas of the time, of which Minnie Chaplin was surely one. As one report described, finding herself in need of capital to both continue the business and expand it, Rand "decided to sell an interest in her business, and hunted up Sydney Chaplin, whose wife she knew to be the owner of a number of 'Sassy Jane' frocks and a booster." Sydney negotiated to become treasurer of the company and brought his colleague, Victor H. Levy, an importer from San Francisco, into the deal as secretary. The media suggested that Charlie was one of the company's stockholders as well, having invested some $10,000 in the company.[15] One article claimed that the 200 employees of the Sassy Jane Company had been added to Charlie's Christmas list, with each employee later receiving a turkey from him for their holiday repasts.[16] While Rand had only 200 employees in 1917 when she first incorporated, by 1920 (when she had added items of apparel such as the lady's pajama[17] to her repertoire), she was able to acquire "spacious quarters in the M.J. Connell buildings, Los Angeles, operate 500 power machines, employ over 600 persons, and is growing weekly," according to a several-page profile of her that appeared in the business journal *System*.[18] Unfortunately, the company was bankrupt by 1923, with the name being resold to other investors that year and again in 1926. Sydney and his partner, Victor Levy, claimed themselves investors in the enterprise, due to the fact that they had invested $40,000 apiece upon its initial incorporation. These loans were then repaid to them out of the company's assets upon liquidation. Although the story for June Rand is a sad one by this point, Levy and Sydney would soon find themselves in trouble as well, trouble with the Internal Revenue Service, the first such in Sydney's long career of dodging the tax man.

Indicating the company's tax returns for 1918 and 1919, the IRS felt the two had underpaid. Judge Littleton of the U.S. Board of Tax Appeals offered the government's position:

> Among the deductions claimed in such returns were items of $3,600 for a salary to Victor H. Levy for each year. The salary for 1918 was stated to have been for his services as secretary, to which, it was stated, he devoted one-half of his time. The salary for 1919 was stated to be for his services as secretary-buyer, and it was further stated that he devoted one-third of his time to his duties as secretary-buyer. Victor H. Levy did not perform any services for the Sassy Jane Manufacturing Co. other than the little time necessary to attend to his duties as secretary, and the deduction of $3,600 in each of the returns was claimed for the sole purpose of evading the just tax due from such corporation. That the salary deducted by the corporation was in order to evade tax was well known to all the stockholders of the corporation. June Rand and Sydney Chaplin passed the resolution authorizing the salary.[19]

As David Ort explains in his unpublished essay on Sydney's life, the case resulted in fines repayment of taxes plus penalties of $6,117.97 for 1918 and $4,098.56 for 1919. The case wasn't settled until early 1930, and in favor of the defendants, who ended up paying no tax or penalties.[20]

By May, Sydney had also bought a new car — a Mitchell convertible sedan — really for wife Minnie, or at least that's what he told the press: "Mrs. Chaplin was not familiar with operating a machine so her husband was particularly careful to pick out one which did not have a lot of complicated devices unknown and hard to operate by a woman."[21] This new model was a striking dark blue with white wire wheels — and one of many top-of-the-line automobiles Sydney was to purchase over the years.

Reports were that Charlie had refused a new Mutual contract[22] by June 12. In fact, Sydney had made his way to New York in April to consider offers. In Chicago (halfway there), he told the press that as he carefully negotiated Charlie's next contract, he would be considering Charlie's wish for time — time to perfect quality films with well-fleshed-out stories. In addition, Sydney promised, "I myself will play with Charlie" in the coming series of films: "I have a great many things that are new and will go big, and the two of us, with a strong supporting cast, good stories and good directing and scenery, will be unbeatable."[23]

Sydney had written to John Freuler suggesting to him that Mutual was the company with which Charlie most wanted to stay, but that he would need $10,000 a week and a $50,000 bonus upon signing. Sydney himself would need to receive $3,000 a week.[24] Freuler answered these demands in an undated letter addressed to Sydney at the Lone

Sydney displaying his directorial capabilities with Hans Koenekamp (far left) and an unidentified cameraman, Lone Star studios, circa 1917 (CHACHAA).

Star Studios, using careful wording, perhaps to get Sydney in the right frame of mind: "As I turn the matter over in my mind now I am constantly reminding myself of your important services in connection with the Charles Chaplin contract. I realize too that there is an important influence from Syd Chaplin in the Charles Chaplin product."[25] He offers Sydney the $3,000 a week and Charlie the same $10,000, but without the bonus, making no real explanation for the reduced amount. Neither man accepted the offer. In fact, the deal with First National[26] was announced only ten days later. On the east coast Sydney worked with Charlie's lawyer, Nathan Burkan, on the negotiations with First National's J. D. Williams (the initial deal was supposedly agreed upon "over coffee and cigars with Thomas L. Tally at the Los Angeles Athletic Club"[27]) and chatted to Charlie in a rare brotherly letter about the contract details, including his demanding the $200,000 bonus being paid to Charlie up front (First National wanted to put it in escrow), and his dreaming up the idea to make First National pay extra for film footage over the amount the contract required.[28] For himself he had won the position of general manager of Charlie's new film company. John Jasper was to remain business manager (he had just taken over for Henry Caulfield in this capacity in June and brought Carlyle Robinson into the company at the same time as publicity agent),[29] but Sydney was working to change that, for he had been in contact with his and Charlie's old Karno manager, Alf Reeves, and expected him to be stateside at any time.[30] Betwixt and between these achievements, Sydney's wife found herself in Stearns Hospital in New York in great pain from an ectopic pregnancy. Sydney reported that "the doctor was compelled to cut open the stomach from the outside. He cut away a large growth, also took away a six-weeks child. He said she will be all right and will be able to have children in the future," but she never did. Her recovery took several weeks,[31] part of which was spent at Lake Placid, New York.

While Sydney was away, Charlie became lazy. Jasper wrote him in New York, pleading for him to "do whatever you could in spurring Charlie on to a quick finish.... Mr. Freuler is beginning to become very disagreeable."[32] He also mentioned to Sydney an attractive possibility of picking up "a very neat bag of change," as he put it. Jasper felt sure that Sydney could achieve the lucrative position of acting as William S. Hart's agent. Several companies were interested in signing him and Jasper felt that Sydney could easily "step in and pull the wires in the direction of the new corporation [First National] your reward would come as well as another large feather in your already envious crown."[33] Charlie's valet, Tom Harrington, in a strongly-worded letter to Sydney,[34] had first suggested this opportunity ten days previously, but Sydney never took this advice.

In September, Hannah's youngest son re-entered the lives of his half brothers. Having had no success in achieving a response from either Sydney or Charlie, the persistent Wheeler Dryden, presently located in India, wrote to Edna Purviance: "Kindly excuse the liberty I take in writing to you, but I am sending you this letter in the hope that you will assist me in my hitherto futile attempts to obtain recognition and acknowledgement from my half-brother, Charles Chaplin." In this desperate effort on Wheeler's part for said recognition, he used the ploy of explaining to Edna the fact that Sydney was just as much a half-brother as he: "In this way you see, Miss Purviance, Charlie Chaplin is my mother's only legitimate son, and that Sid and myself are both illegitimate.... If Charlie has seen it fit to publicly acknowledge Sid as not only his half-brother, but his BROTHER, and allowed him to use his name, too, then surely he can at least ACKNOWLEDGE me, his other half-brother?" Wheeler demanded that his goal was not money, only "friendship and brotherly interest and encouragement."[35] Such filial attention was not to occur for Wheeler any time soon, however, and when it did, it turned out to be Sydney who capitulated and later became as close to Wheeler as any full-blood brother. After Wheeler came to New York for the first time in early 1919, he received an announcement and photo in *Motion Picture News* in April that reported he was at work on his first Gray Seal Production comedy at Estee Studios in New York City.[36] Later that decade, when he made his way to Hollywood and was re-introduced to his mother for the first time there, Sydney brought him into his side of the business, hiring him as a director on his only British International Pictures film, *A Little Bit of Fluff.* He did not become a part of the Charles Chaplin Film Company until 1939, when Sydney was back working for Charlie in Hollywood himself and brought Wheeler on board, where he remained until Charlie left the country.

Charlie finally finished up the films required to complete his Mutual contract in early fall, took off for Honolulu with Edna and Rob Wagner, and the studio at the corner of Lillian and Eleanor became a ghost town for a time.[37] With Charlie's new contract came the opportunity to own his own studio. Choosing the old R. S. McKlellan estate, on the southeast corner of Sunset and La Brea in Hollywood, the brothers began promoting the place in late October. Sydney had the pleasure of announcing the plans for the new studio to the press on October 28, stating that the five-acre lot, for the most part covered at that point with orange trees, would be both workshop and home for Charlie (there was a 10-room house on the property!). The brothers planned to build six buildings in an English architectural style (i.e., Tudor) and in an arrangement that suggested an English village. Charlie's total investment would be about $100,000.[38] While local authorities were skeptical about having the studio in the neighborhood at first, once they had viewed the plans, it was approved by a vote of eight to one.[39] Sydney belabored this point to cousin Aubrey Chaplin for effect: "We had a great difficulty in getting the site and were opposed by our surrounding neighbors. We had to fight the matter out in the Council Chamber, and only succeeded in winning out after bringing the influence of bankers and other influential people to bear upon the case."[40] As for the colonial-style dwelling on the property, it was soon announced that Sydney and Minnie would be its sole occupants.[41] Sydney explained that although the house had been beautifully cleaned up and furnished, Charlie preferred to continue living at the Los Angeles Athletic Club, and so, having three vacant bedrooms, Sydney planned to reserve them for the use of "Mother and two nurses."[42]

Given the loss in June 1916 of Aunt Kate, Hannah's only caretaker in England, Sydney and Charlie spent the ensuing time fostering their relationship with Aubrey. As mentioned before, Aubrey really wanted to be asked to come to Hollywood to be a part of the studio and film business, but found himself serving as a sort of Britain-based liaison to the brothers on personal matters. By mid–1917, Sydney had written a long letter to Aubrey, explaining that he had acquired permission from the United States government to allow Hannah to enter the country. The letter was full of detailed instructions about how to prepare her for the journey, what clothes to pack, and how to deal with her money. Then, by July 20, Sydney had decided it was not wise, given the situation with submarines, that Hannah come over at that point. Still, he wanted Aubrey to attend to Hannah, demonstrating in the letter his growing anxiety about her treatment at Peckham House:

> Now I think it would be a good idea to give her a change & transfer her to some other place, more select and nicer surroundings. Never mind about the price. If you think she is getting value, it would be better if she was further out from the heart of London, especially during these air raids. Another idea Charlie and I had was to take a nice furnished cottage & keep her there with a couple of trained nurses. Then she could have everything she needed, in the way of food and drivers & it would not convey the impression that she was under restraint.[43]

In the June 12, 1918 letter, Sydney waffled again. Obviously still very anxious about his mother's safety, he wrote Aubrey, "After giving the matter due consideration, I have decided to try and get my mother here immediately." Aubrey had, given the tenor of the letter, not fulfilled Sydney's wish of a year ago that Aubrey both visit Hannah *and* get her moved to better accommodations: "I don't suppose you get much chance to run down to see her. I quite understand that it is very difficult for you to go so far very often."[44] As it happened, Hannah would have to wait a bit longer to make her journey, but Aubrey did try to come through on finding Hannah a seaside residence — at Cliftonville — but this arrangement never came to fruition.[45]

* * *

The brothers are shown in existing photos breaking ground for the new studio in November, an event the press seems to have missed, but one that cameraman Rollie Totheroh filmed for posterity. Three months later, on January 15, it was labeled officially open and the first production, *A Dog's Life*, was begun. Biographer David Robinson's description of the film is one of the best in its conservative elegance:

> Chaplin's battle with other applicants for the few available jobs at the Employment Office is compared with Scraps' furious struggle over a bone with a horde of bigger and fiercer dogs. The two strays adopt each other and prove an effective partnership in filching a meal from Syd Chaplin's lunch-wagon. They chance into The Green Lantern ... [and] it is there that they meet Edna, and become rich by outwitting a couple of crooks who have stolen the wallet of a passing drunk.[46]

Sydney in costume as the cart-owner in *A Dog's Life* (Chaplin–First National, 1918) (CHACHAA).

As mentioned in this description, Sydney played the cart-owner in the film; his wife Minnie can be glimpsed in a floppy light-colored hat with a band on it, dancing in the Green Lantern scenes. It wasn't long after the studio opened that it became a sort of Mecca for entertainment and other celebrities. Harry Lauder, a Scotsman who had long been a successful comedy star on the British music hall stage, was one of the first, stopping by for a tour and a bit of entertainment on January 22. Charlie and Harry made a short film of the visit that day, one later used to aid the Million Pound War fund, to which Lauder was dedicated.[47] While not all filmed celebrity visits were used quite as lucratively, Lauder's started a tradition of filming such visits at the Chaplin studios that was to continue for years.

Still in the midst of filming, Sydney received a letter from the British-Canadian Recruiting Committee on February 5, stating that he had been appointed a member of the General committee, Los Angeles Branch.[48] Of course, given his prior troubles in this area, he immediately assented.[49] Of more importance, Grace Kingsley announced in the press that Charlie had incorporated on February 25, under the name of the Chaplin Studios. Sydney and Tom Harrington were named as members of the organization, its capital stock being $200,000. Kingsley, obviously informed by Sydney, included the information that Sydney himself would soon go into the production of films, with himself in the leading role.[50] The many times he mentioned this to the press emphasizes the fact that the idea was never far from his mind, regardless of his other responsibilities at the time.

Filming was completed on March 22 and, with the help of five assistants, Charlie completed the editing late on March 31, directly before he was expected to leave on the Third Liberty Bond tour with Mary Pickford, Douglas Fairbanks and Rob Wagner. He charged his company to spend the ensuing weeks coming up with ideas for the next project. The film was released on April 14 and as Sydney remembered, "It has made an enormous success over here, and has been breaking records everywhere." Still, he worried about a seeming lack of financial caution in filmmaking, commenting candidly to cousin Aubrey, "Charlie is not turning out pictures as fast as I would like. He takes about ten weeks for a picture now, which of course runs the cost of production very high, but no one in the world can hurry him. He is striving very hard for quality, and the monetary part has become a secondary consideration."[51] Charlie's casual relationship to money at this time would result in a casualty as well. John Jasper, his business manager, put in his resignation during Charlie's absence, an act that allowed Alf Reeves, who had arrived to work at the studio in early January, to smoothly step into the position—one he would occupy until his death in 1946.

By the end of May, Charlie had been back in Hollywood a month and was ready to start his next production, tentatively titled "Production No. 2 *Camouflage*." Sydney reported that Charlie was intent on showing the humorous side of war—the humorous side demonstrated by commentators such as Captain Bruce Bairnsfather, creator of a cartoon series based on World War I Tommies and later called *The Better 'Ole, or the Romance of Old Bill:* "Charlie will handle the subject very delicately and will strive his utmost not to offend. We have not published the fact as we do not care to acquaint the public with the subject of his picture until it is finished."[52] But, Charlie's initial vision for the film—one which provided an uncharacteristic back-story for the Little Tramp character—was totally scrapped after a month's shooting. Early July was spent in revising the story and building new sets. As filming began anew, Los Angeles found itself experiencing a heat wave. Sydney, playing both Charlie the soldier's sergeant *and* Kaiser Wilhelm in the film,

Sydney in costume as the Kaiser in *Shoulder Arms* (Chaplin–First National, 1918) (CHACHAA.).

experienced the deadly heat right along with the rest of the cast. The realistic trenches constructed as part of the set for the film, while accurately depicting the ever-present menace of water on the actual battlefields, must have served as welcome relief from the temperature outside them during the four weeks it took to shoot these scenes.

Still filming in August, Charlie and company were obliged to change direction on the 15th and put together a short film for the Liberty Bond effort, to be entitled *The Bond*. It was completed in six days and is the only Chaplin film to utilize "simple stylized white properties against a plain black back-drop,"[53] settings that gave it an Expressionistic look well before the Germans. Sydney had only to dress up in his Kaiser Wilhelm costume for his sole appearance in the final scene of the film. Although Charlie, upon returning to the *Shoulder Arms* set, claimed himself now tired and no longer interested in the production, it was finished on September 16 and released on October 20, just 22 days before the Armistice was signed, yet it became one of Charlie's most successful and important films. With two successful films under his belt on his new contract, Charlie became diverted by a young actress named Mildred Harris, soon to become his first wife. And, with this diversion came near derailment; beginning with his first post–Mildred production, *Sunnyside*. His creativity seemed to have dried up — or perhaps this condition had something to do with the fact that noticeable by his absence from the cast was one Sydney Chaplin, although Sydney was reported to have delivered the finished film to First National in New York.[54] Skeptical of the Chaplin-Harris marriage, as he must have been, Sydney began to court and consider offers for his own film career in the fall of 1918. In addition, he and his brother were soon to step out on another matter, making the separation a good move at the time: the immigration of Hannah Chaplin to America.

After the Armistice, Sydney had lost no time in arranging for cousin Aubrey to make arrangements for Hannah to come to America and Peckham House received due notice of her imminent departure in a letter from Sydney dated November 30.[55] But yet his efforts were once again to be thwarted, for in April, Charlie sent him a telegram: "Second thoughts. Consider will be best mother remain in England. Some good seaside resort. Afraid presence here might depress and affect my work."[56]

* * *

By early 1919, after helping Charlie to sign a lucrative contract with First National *and* open a new studio on La Brea and De Longpre in Hollywood, Sydney must have been itching to try his hand at making a better career for himself. He had worked for Charlie three years, securing him contracts, playing bit parts in his films and helping with scenarios and in any other capacity where he could. Now it was his turn. Unfortunately, Sydney could never think conservatively on these matters and was to take on more responsibility than any normal human being could be expected to. Still, it is certain that his loved ones — Charlie and wife Minnie, for instance — did their best to support Sydney in these new business ventures, all the while knowing in their hearts that his anxiety disorder would never allow him to succeed.

Perhaps the $75,000 boost Sydney received from Charlie as a bonus for helping him to acquire the Mutual Films contract, way back in 1916, started the chain of events in some small way. By early 1919, after *Shoulder Arms* was completed and released, Sydney made the decision to return to films himself *and* to solidify his importance in Hollywood by developing and launching a new idea in film distribution — one that came to be called United Artists. In addition (and this was probably what helped to taint his other endeavors during the year), he decided to start the first domestically owned airline service in the United States, aptly titled the Syd Chaplin Aircraft Corporation. The palpable failure surrounding both his new film contract and his airline worked together to secure Sydney's fall from grace and temporary hiatus from the film business by late 1920.

But at the start of 1919, the film industry was about to burst apart, never to be the same. Adolph Zukor, having merged Famous Players, Lasky and Paramount into one company in 1916, was now about to join up with his only competition — First National — a move that would mean the end of the star system as it had existed in Hollywood thus far. Even though Thomas Tally was denying such rumors, Charlie believed them — mostly due to the fact that First National had recently turned down his request for an increase in his production budget. Of course, if Charlie was slightly worried, Sydney would have been a thousand-times so and decided to meet with Mary Pickford and Douglas Fairbanks about the situation. Both stars were on edge as well, because their contracts (with First National and Famous Players–Lasky, respectively) were about to run out and thus far neither had received his/her customary offer to renew. This coupled with some unfavorable information uncovered by a detective the group hired led to a revolt, one for which Sydney claimed responsibility on more than one occasion. He called a meeting on Tuesday,

Scene from an unknown film, circa 1918, showing Adolphe Menjou (left), an unknown actress, and Sydney (CHACHAA).

January 14 at his house on the Chaplin studio property, inviting Charlie, Charlotte Pickford (Mary was ill), Doug Fairbanks, Bill Hart and D. W. Griffith to discuss their options in a meeting that lasted until the wee hours of the next morning. A. H. Giebler recounted the events for the *Moving Picture World* after things blew apart the next day. He found Doug Fairbanks at his studio "sizzling around like a bottle of old-fashioned soda pop.... Sydney Chaplin came in just then with an important looking paper in his hand. Three signatures were already on the document, the names of Fairbanks, Griffith and Hart." Within minutes and a car ride later, Sydney, Giebler and Fairbanks added the names of Charlie Chaplin and Mary Pickford "at 2:45 P.M. on Wednesday, January 15, 1919,"[57] five signatures had been signed to the articles of agreement entered into by the United Artists Association. The articles of agreement contained the following statement: "We believe this step necessary to protect ourselves, as well as the exhibitors who play our pictures, from injurious combinations between the various producing concerns now operating and to protect the exhibitor from having poor pictures forced upon him." Giebler also reported that Sydney had signed with First National at this time for two five-reel light comedies,[58] although he himself denied the claim: "I have not signed up with First National, nor do I intend to."[59]

It was only in late 1932 that Sydney finally returned to the events surrounding his airline venture and was able to recount and reflect on some of them for close friend Jim Minney. Minney had promised to print an article on the subject in *Everybody's News,* a British periodical for which he served as editor at the time. Sydney remembered that he had "always been extremely interested in aviation; from its earliest inception I have collected newspaper cuttings[60] and have some very interesting articles dating from the time of the Wright Bros.' first attempt, also the Air Races at Reims and the conquering of the British Channel.[61] I was even so enthusiastic as to dash into Selfridge's where Bleriot's machine was on exhibit, and wrote my name in bold letters on the fuselage. Such is the craving for fame!" He explained that the airline he established ran "between Los Angeles Harbor and Catalina Island — twenty-two miles away. The boat takes more than two hours, but we did the journey in twenty minutes. I obtained a ten-year franchise from Wrigley, the Chewing Gum King, who owned the Island, and had the exclusive rights of a small bay on the beach adjoining the St. Catherine Hotel, which is the largest hotel there." It wasn't long before they realized that the warming of airplane engines at 6 A.M. disturbed the hotel guests, so Sydney was asked to change the airline's location to a more remote part of the island. He noted that Wrigley was duly appreciative of his willingness to be accommodating. At the time, Sydney had "the largest commercial flying-field in California. I could have bought this field for several hundred thousand dollars, but I made the greatest mistake of my life by not doing so. The field is now one of the most exclusive residential districts of Los Angeles; right in the center of my take-off stands one of the finest moving picture theatres in California — the Carthay Circle." Had he bought this field he could have made several million dollars. At the height of the business, Sydney recounted that he "had twenty planes flying and a large downtown showroom with three planes upon a floor, similar to our automobile showrooms of today. We were the California representatives for the Curtiss Co. and sold over two hundred and fifty thousand dollars worth of planes the first year." The planes were new and second-hand "Jennies"

Aerial shot of the Chaplin Airdrome, Los Angeles, 1919 (CHACHAA).

purchased from the American Government and used by them for the training of their pilots for the World War I. Most of his sales were made to Army pilots who had been let out after the termination of the war. After this trade was exhausted, there was very little doing in the way of sales, because the private public were not sufficiently interested. Sydney soon found it "most difficult to make a go of it as, unlike British Airlines, we were not subsidized by the American Government." Being a novelty at the time, the airline attracted many celebrities and Sydney's pressbook on the venture was filled with the subsequent articles that appeared. One such celebrity was His Majesty the King of Belgium. Sydney remembered an amusing anecdote about the King's experience: "We had a young girl who was about to make a parachute jump for His Majesty's pleasure. Before going up, she requested that I should give the King a small memento; it consisted of a little nude cupid doll with the usual protruding stomach and her name written across the centre. I did not wish to disappoint the poor kid and as I handed it over to His Majesty, the expression on his face was a study. I only wish the camera had been there to have recorded it."[62]

It's probably not ironic that an article appeared on April 16, 1919 (Charlie's 30th birthday), announcing that Sydney was leaving for the East Coast in order to secure a deal with airplane maker Curtiss to buy several airplanes for his new business venture that would fly tourists, vacationers and others back and forth between Santa Catalina Island

and Los Angeles Harbor. Sydney had secured the first-ever agreement[63] with Mr. Wrigley (real estate mogul on the island and chewing gum wizard) to land planes there for this purpose just the week prior, so was eager to secure a favorable deal with Curtiss for planes that had seen some service in World War I and, as such, came with a more reasonable price-tag. Sydney hoped to secure two flying boats, better known as Curtiss Seagulls, for the task, because these hydroplanes would easily accommodate five passengers plus a pilot.[64] He himself had signed a contract with Al Wilson (of Al Wilson Aviation) on March 6 for instruction in flying planes himself. For the $3,500 he expended, he was to receive 600 hours of flying time and "a ground course to consist of care and upkeep of airplane and motor."[65] Whether or not he completed this course is unknown, however, it is clear that he wished to validate his seriousness about this venture with such a contract. He planned to have the venture up and running within three months — that would place it at about mid–July 1919 — an interesting date, indeed, because this would be the month Sydney would choose to depart America for France, where he hoped to begin production on the first of his Famous Players–Lasky efforts.

By April 20, Sydney had warranted a nearly full-page article in the *Los Angeles Times*, complete with a photo of himself aboard one of the planes and a detailed discussion of the venture. At this date, Sydney hoped to beat competing companies in the eastern United States for the honor of being the first domestic airline company in the nation and he was, at least, able to meet this particular goal — and, in fact, best it. Sydney was truly at the forefront of the developments in this industry; while Packard had begun taking orders for a speedy, sporty model of plane, it failed to meet its deadline. Other companies were hot on its heels — one of these being Curtiss and another Aeromarine Corporation. Boeing of Seattle was not far behind. Sydney had settled on Curtiss, however, and was able to procure two seaplanes and three or four land planes (Curtiss "Jennies") during the trip as a start-up battalion for his service. All planes were capable of carrying six people (five passengers and the pilot) and sported double engines to ensure the safety of all. In addition to its 20-minute flights between Los Angeles harbor and Santa Catalina Island, Sydney's company hoped to provide flights between Los Angeles and Coronado or San Diego in the south and Santa Barbara or Del Monte in the north.[66] By May 3, two articles appeared in the film industry press, one noting that Sydney was testing the winds above New York and Atlantic City in an airplane, and the other noting his intention to start a ferry service (via airplane) to Catalina *and* a flying school.[67]

The contract with Curtiss Aeroplane and Motor Corporation was not signed, however, until May 29. Sydney had partnered with World War I pilot and scion of the Rogers silver family, Emery H. Rogers,[68] in the venture and so both men had to be equally satisfied with the contract terms. It is not known the state of their relationship at the start of the business venture, but Rogers was to bail out well before the end — in disgust. His son, Emery Rogers, Jr., was not quite born at this point,[69] but remembers clearly the dislike his mother bore Sydney Chaplin, such that it became the stuff of family legend. The initial contract with Curtiss named it as exclusive supplier of aircraft for the Syd Chaplin Aircraft Corporation, with the Corporation receiving a 20 percent discount off of Curtiss's list price for such vehicles. A yearly payment schedule was set up, with an option on the part of Curtiss to apply by registered mail, to regain the money believed to be in default, which, if not rectified within 15 days of receipt, would terminate the contract, with all previous payments to be kept by Curtiss. The agreement would end on the first day of July 1924, if not canceled by either party beforehand.

The principal office was set up as being located in Wilmington, Delaware, a location that would save the investors considerable money in taxes. Two thousand five hundred shares were authorized initially, with the wives of Rogers and Chaplin owning the largest amounts (the Chaplins were listed as owning 1,500 shares and the Rogers couple as only 1,000). Fifty thousand dollars was the initial investment. The initial board of directors consisted of A. Sween, J. A. Gans and Henri Behoteguy, with Gans and Behoteguy being replaced by Sydney's disreputable business associate Victor H. Levy and Rogers respectively on July 21. Rogers was also made general manager at this time.[70]

Syd Chaplin Aircraft Corporation began operations on June 10, 1919, a full month before the date Sydney had proposed to the press and well before any East Coast airline was to get underway. The incorporation of the company was to be capitalized at $250,000, naming Sydney as president and Lieutenant Emery H. Rogers, R.M.A. of Santa Monica vice-president and general manager. Its main office was located in the Wright & Callendar Building in downtown Los Angeles. Sydney's corporation was provided with 200 J. N. 4 Curtiss airplanes (known as "Jennies") recently used to train military personnel at March Field in Riverside, California, by the government. Most of these were intended for sale to the general public, with a few to be held back for use in the planned flying school. By this date, Sydney had purchased three seaplanes for use on the 26-mile route between Los Angeles and Santa Catalina Island. The route was to be in operation no later than July 1. For planned routes over land, such as between Los Angeles and San Diego, Sydney purchased a three-passenger plane called "The Oriole," which, at the time, was the latest thing in air travel. Pilots of these vehicles were pledged to all be qualified aviators with more than 1,500 hours of flying experience and licensed by the American government.[71] Finally, Sydney purchased two speedboats constructed by the Consolidated Shipbuilding Corporation for use as an added precaution on flights between the mainland and Catalina. Each of these vessels was capable of speeds of at least 35 mph.[72]

Inauguration of the Los Angeles-to-Catalina service began on time, with one plane beginning the hourly service on July 4 and two additional planes to begin the route by July 10. The fare was $25 one way and $40 round trip. More than 100 applications had been received for seats on the first trip over.[73] The first hangar in Chaplin field was to go up June 29 and would house the battalion of Curtiss Orioles Sydney was planning to use for overland service. This service was scheduled to begin July 15.

The Catalina service had a problematic start, one that would probably work well as a metaphor for the entire venture, in that the "Seagull" given a test run the day before the inaugural run "got so much brine in the carburetor that the engine could not be started."[74] In essence, the seaplane was going under — drowning — much as Sydney would be within the year. The inaugural flight occurred a full week later than planned and Charlie's leading lady, Edna Purviance, served as the honored guest, breaking a bottle of grape juice on the body of the craft in imitation of the christening of any seaworthy vessel. She, Emery Rogers and pilot A. C. Burns then flew to Catalina, taking off at 9 A.M.[75] The same day (July 12) an article appeared announcing that Sydney was expecting delivery of

400 new planes from Curtiss and that he had purchased an additional $100,000 worth of speed boats as well making this, "by far the largest number of airplanes ever controlled by a private citizen."[76] But where was he getting the money? Every new expenditure announced in the press seemed to emphasize what could only seem like reckless, foolhardy behavior, yet it continued. The next day, more bad news appeared in the paper. It didn't take long for Uncle Sam to stick his hand out for a share, for it was announced that passengers would be subject to a tax on their rides "according to regulations under the transportation feature of the internal revenue law."[77] This would amount to approximately $2 on a one-way ticket and $3.20 on a round-trip ticket. Sydney had probably hoped to get the business started before the various taxes and licenses required for air travel arose, which he did to some degree, but within the year of the Syd Chaplin Aircraft Corporation's existence, it's remarkable how many of them came to be the law of the land—adding safety for passengers, of course, but also great expense for the entrepreneur. And then, of course, came along the insurance companies with their hands extended for a piece of the action. By late October 1919, Traveler's Insurance Company became the first to insure Syd Chaplin Aircraft Corporation passengers. Passengers were insured against all accidents and received their trip insurance tickets as they boarded the conveyance—another service Sydney's company soon had to provide.[78]

The showroom was up and running by late November and R. L. Crozier was hired to manage it and to act as sales representative. This airplane showroom, the first of its kind, was located at the corner of Seventh Street at Lake in Los Angeles and was leased for five years. Five thousand dollars was spent just on decorating the place.[79] Crozier lost no time advertising his product, sponsoring many open houses (10,000 people attended the showroom's opening day[80]), and advertising in the papers essentially that time meant money. Fast, fast, fast, was the company's promise and enticement strategy. "Use One for Your Business," one ad suggests, because "stores are delivering merchandise, publishers are delivering papers to suburban towns, doctors and surgeons are making hurry-up calls—every day adds to the list."[81] And, of course, cost could not be a consideration, because a used Curtiss Jenny, priced between $2,000 and $3,500, would pay for itself in a week or two, because "you can make from $500 to $1,500 a day carrying passengers."[82] One article reported on their success, which seemed astounding. Crozier and his colleagues sold 47 airplanes of different types in the first 90 days of business.[83] Unfortunately, even the choice of Crozier for this position turned out to be a bad idea. He and associate S. C. Parr had the distinction of being brought up on charges of embezzlement in what was one of the first court cases involving a stolen airplane tried in this country. Both men were acquitted of the charges, but the damage had been done.[84]

The flying school aspect of the business (the Chaplin-Curtiss Flying School) was up and running by early September 1919. An ad that ran in the newspaper promised that an "Aero Club of America Pilots license" would be provided on graduation and that former Army instructors were in charge of all instruction.[85] Sydney's company joined forces with the YMCA Auto School in this endeavor. The idea was to provide all aspects of flying, maintenance and safety—a program that would guarantee the 600 hours of flying time needed, for instance, but to do so at a much-reduced cost from other schools (much less than Sydney's $3,500 price tag for his own training at least). Small clubs of five men at

One of Sydney's celebrity passengers on the Syd Chaplin Airline, music hall comedian Harry Lauder (left) (CHACHAA).

a time would undertake the training in order to save on costs. The school believed the program to be "the most complete of its kind in the United States and includes every detail of gas engine construction, repair, operation, as well as thorough training in the handling of aircraft."[86]

Of course, Sydney and his team were interested in receiving as much free press coverage for this endeavor as possible. This was partially accomplished by flying celebrities around. Of course, Charlie's leading lady of many years, Edna Purviance, helped the company out on its inaugural flight, but after her came dignitaries from all corners, including such figures as Albert, the King of Belgium and Harry Lauder (already mentioned), Charlie's first wife Mildred Harris (who presented the Belgian queen with a bouquet), violinist Jascha Heifetz, the daughter of Arthur Conan Doyle (creator of Sherlock Holmes) and the renowned journalist/writer Mary Roberts Rinehart. Rinehart's comments appeared in the press in November,[87] after a trip into the skies over Los Angeles with company vice president Emery Rogers: "The most amazing thing about flying to me was not that I was actually flying. It was that I was not afraid. Not for a moment. I was curious, interested, just a little bit proud of myself and inclined to patronize shore plodders down below who make such slow progress along the thread-like roads. But afraid — no."

Speaking of Rogers, she wrote, "I had, immediately, a real feeling of confidence in that young man. After all, he liked himself as much as I did myself, and he seemed to look at the whole thing as a mere incident, something sandwiched in between breakfast and luncheon, like a marcel wave or buying a pair of gloves." Rinehart came away from the experience with the feeling that she had just experienced that which soon would be commonplace for many: "I am convinced that not only is flying a gentleman's sport, but that we will all soon have an aeroplane in the back yard, or on the roof, and what is more, that women will drive them as they do motor cars now."[88]

Over on Santa Catalina Island, the local newspaper often carried thrilling stories of what had come to be called "joy rides" of the air. Alma Sierks wrote frankly of her first ride aloft, ostensibly to cover the maiden flight of Admiral Rodman, the commander-in-chief of the Pacific Armada. In an attempt to dismiss her own reactions to the flight, Sierks was interested in finding out the Admiral's reactions, but found herself stymied by her inability to communicate with him in the air:

> I could not ask him the million and one questions I wanted to — the law of the air is cruel to members of our sex — speech is impossible and signals are the only means of communication. The Admiral and I had not rehearsed a wig-wag system before ascending, so the merry twinkle in his eyes and his big, broad smile were the only symptoms from which I could diagnose another case of aero fever.[89]

The Chaplin Air Field soon became the home of many community-minded events and Sydney often took part or made an appearance if he was in town. One of these was the Rickenbacker Air Day, at which he arrived in a military uniform that was one of the costumes for the Famous Players film he was in the midst of shooting. For this event, he presented "a handsome silver cup"[90] to the boy or girl chosen as the winner of the contest — one that required the child to construct a flight-worthy balsa wood plane. Another was called a "Smart Set Day" — a charity event held to raise funds to build a hospital for the Crippled Children's Guild to which many screen celebrities were invited to participate. Among these "was the thrilling exhibition by 'Buck' Jones and his cowboys and cowgirls from the Fox studios." Many other airplane stunt fliers took part and offered quite a show to the crowd in attendance.[91]

In addition to the voluminous coverage Sydney's airline received in the press, his team was busy promoting the different facets of the business with ads, in the newspapers, in brochures and posters, many of which are full-color works of art. One ad coaxed aviation enthusiasts to "View the Pacific Squadron from the Air in Chaplin Air Line Curtiss Flying Boats: The Sight of a Lifetime,"[92] another to "Fly to the Mainland in Chaplin Air Line Curtiss Flying Boats: Short Observation Trips 10 A.M. to 2:30 P.M." A brochure simply reads "Fly" on its full-color cover, but the word is enhanced by what makes it look as if it is speeding by. Inside are photos and text that make up a complete catalogue of the operation — the planes in operation, the services, the Chaplin Air Field, the flying school, the showroom and everything in between. Perhaps most important is the narrative the brochure contains, one that seems to work hard to convince the most reluctant customer:

> Contact! Calls your pilot, the mechanism twirls the propeller and with a growing rush of air and gathering speed, off you start gliding smoothly down the field, or if in a flying boat, slipping along the surface of the water, on your first venture in the wake of the eagle.

Sydney Chaplin, in costume for *King, Queen, Joker* presents an award to the most able balsa airplane builder during "Rickenbacker Air Day" at the Chaplin Airdrome, Los Angeles, 1920 (CHACHAA).

Settling back in your comfortable armchair seat, you note with surprise that with scarcely perceptible change your ship has left the ground and with long easy circles is climbing into the blue, sunny sky. Again you are surprised that you experience no effect of height or dizziness and that you feel as secure and as steady as though in your own car waiting you below.[93]

Most likely, this brochure came out at the height of the company's success and popularity — in August and September 1919. Interestingly, Emery Rogers would have been in full command at this time, because Sydney was in France on his Famous Players production. Yet, there was no sign at this point that the business was in trouble, at least not to the average person. In fact, from the period of July 1 to September 15, the company made 1,067 successful flights, numbers that at least make the business seem successful.[94] By November, Sydney's business had competitors, even within the ranks of his film business colleagues. An article entitled "Movies up in the Air over Aviation" named three such businesses, just in the Los Angeles area: Sydney's, Thomas Ince's and Cecil B. DeMille's (Mercury Aviation).[95] These aviation companies were making Los Angeles a center of the aviation business in general — and quickly. But Sydney's company was soon to bow out of the competition permanently.

While the problems didn't start with the departure of Emery Rogers as director and secretary (and general manager), this event was certainly the bellwether of its subsequent demise. The corporation records indicate some problems beginning in December 1919, when a resolution was passed that "no contract, debt or obligation should be incurred in excess of $250 by the general manager without the written approval of one other director."[96] The tenor of this resolution would suggest that the general manager, Rogers, was incurring reckless debts for the company, although this is not certain — and not probable, given his fortune. At the same meeting, Rogers was awarded a $250-a-month salary in another resolution — a savvy move on his part that presaged his upcoming resignation. As a salaried employee, Rogers could not be held responsible for the company's debts, whatever they were or would become. The first meeting of the new year (1920) resulted in a resolution to allow the president and secretary to borrow amounts not to exceed $5,000 against the company assets[97] and then by February 20 a resolution was passed to borrow $60,000 to pay its obligations (especially to the Curtiss Company). Sydney wanted to advance the money to the corporation against the stocks owned by Minnie and himself. Emery Rogers refused to do the same.[98] By March 26, Rogers submitted his resignation ("effective immediately").[99] This followed hard on the heels of a legal notice of debt from the Curtiss Company, received on March 12, claiming Syd Chaplin Aircraft Corporation was $89,000 in arrears at that time. Curtiss demanded payment in full by April 1.

Yet, in May, Sydney was spotted back east at the New York Aeronautical Show in the company of Roscoe Arbuckle, indicating to the press his plans for expansion of the business.[100]: "Larger aircraft, for one thing, will figure in the future activities of the Chaplin company. Of the enclosed type, which provide a maximum of comfort and convenience to passengers, the new big flying machines will be used in handling intercity and sightseeing traffic, which has now reached a volume of big proportions."[101] He also attended the Third Pan-American Aeronautic Congress and Exposition there at about the same time, as an invited representative.[102] Although there is no entry in the Syd Chaplin Aircraft Corporation meeting minutes book after February 12 (and so, no official date of the company's death), press coverage of the company ceased by June 1920. The company had fallen after its meteoric rise in less than a year. But Sydney himself would not be rid of it so easily. In October, while recovering from an appendicitis operation at the Sisters' Hospital, Sydney was served "some papers in a civil action brought against Chaplin by the Curtiss Aeroplane Company," an act which, supposedly, had caused a reaction from the patient that placed him in critical condition. Clearly, the debt to Curtiss had not been paid. What is not clear is whether Sydney was in the hospital to avoid paying (via the usual "act of God" loophole in every contract he signed) or if he ever paid. Minnie, who spoke with reporters about the incident, was well prepared for the usual narrative of subterfuge she needed to deliver, declaring that she had "instructed her attorney, Arthur Wright, to bring damage proceedings against the Curtiss Company" due to her husband's decline in health. Even the hospital spokesperson advanced this narrative, stating to the press that "his condition was critical and that there were some doubts as to his recovery."[103] The story's coda is that Emery Rogers bought the Chaplin Airdrome from Sydney, naming it Rogers Field, only to die in a plane crash near there in 1921.[104]

* * *

Jesse Lasky fails to mention his experiences working with Sydney beginning in 1919, choosing instead to focus on two other Hollywood greats who fell from grace at about this time — both of whom were on his payroll: Roscoe Arbuckle and William Desmond Taylor[105] — perhaps only because it was Adolph Zukor who signed Sydney. Arbuckle was accused of murdering actress Virginia Rappe at a party in San Francisco in September 1921 (and was acquitted of the crime much later) and Taylor was found dead under mysterious circumstances in February 1922. Obviously, Hollywood and the growing film industry were operating increasingly outside the expected system of moral conduct, or at least they were finally getting caught doing so. These scandals and others like them would lead to the laughable first attempt at film censorship the industry would soon undertake, with the installation of then–Postmaster General Will Hays as a sort of figure-head censorship czar in 1924, who was pretty much on the payroll of several of the major studios. Sydney's problems with his Famous Players–Lasky contract predated these scandals a bit, so they can be considered either a preamble to this behavior or simply too watered-down to make the list, depending upon perspective. They were not less serious or less important to Sydney himself, however.

Reading Sydney's Famous Players–Lasky contract, which was, upon signing, Sydney's own million-dollar film deal [106] — one designed to assuage the continuing barrage of punches to his ego Charlie's career was landing — it is easy to discern the web of loopholes he created for himself therein, loopholes that were to allow him too much freedom and not enough impetus for responsibility later on. Signed on May 14, 1919, the contract required Sydney to complete two new photoplays, under his direction, and in which he would personally star as the lead comedian. Famous Players–Lasky had just changed its policy of how films would be distributed (a plan called "selective booking" in which "every picture will be produced, distributed and exploited as if it were the only picture made or distributed by the Famous Players–Lasky Corporation, and each picture will be a financial success or loss according to its own quality"[107]). Therefore, the film and all publicity for each film would name "Sydney Chaplin Productions" as the company producing it. Just this much description of the deal illustrates clearly that Sydney had taken on too much — too much for his personality and his continuing problems with anxiety and melancholia. It was already a recipe for failure. And, in fact, this is exactly what it ended up to be. His first photoplay was required to be delivered to Famous Players–

Cast and crew of *King, Queen, Joker* (Paramount-Artcraft, 1921). Sydney is front and center and Al Garcia (with big mustache) is next to him (CHACHAA).

Lasky within nine months of the contract signing, which would have been in February of 1920. Perhaps it was Article Seven of the contract that provided a too-tempting loophole for Sydney and, in some way, guaranteed his failure in this venture. Article Seven stated that

> in the event that Chaplin shall be delayed in or prevented from the performance of any of the agreements which he has herein agreed to perform, by reason of labor troubles, riots, war, acts of God, the public enemy, casualty, unavoidable accidents, any unforeseen occurrence, not due to his act or omission, illness or physical disability of Chaplin, injury or construction of any of the negatives or the working positive prints of any of the aforementioned motion picture photoplays by any of the aforesaid causes, delays or failure of performance by common carriers or any other cause beyond his control, including the restraint or interference by any legal authority, such delay or failure of performance shall be excused and all claims, demands or causes of action for damage therefore, or arising there from, are hereby expressly waived, and in such event the time of Chaplin to fulfill this contract shall be extended for a period equal to the time of such delay, but not exceeding six months. If cause, after such time, shall prevent performance by Chaplin, he shall refund all advances made to the Corporation, and the agreement shall terminate without further liability to either party.[108]

Sydney's first production, released as *King, Queen, Joker* on May 15, 1921, was the only Famous Players–Lasky production he was to complete, and this a full sixteen months overdue. In addition, it failed miserably at the box office with, therefore, the "selective booking" program both working against it *and* perhaps providing it a sort of critical review that it could not escape.

This proved an ironic ending to a business endeavor that had such a promising start. With the signing of the contract in May, Sydney was finally beginning to claim for himself some of the media coverage and publicity that his ego had sorely been craving. The June 7, 1919, issue of *Motion Picture News* announced the happy business deal, indicating (falsely) that Sydney would be required to complete four films over the course of two years, which would have made the deal a true million-dollar contract (Sydney was to receive $225,000 per film). The article also made the claim that Sydney would be filming the interior scenes at his brother's studio, a claim that failed to hold true. Interviewed briefly for this piece (obviously already well-versed in doing his own publicity), Sydney graciously explains his departure from Charlie's employ: "My business activities as business manager for my brother have been particularly pleasant but the call of the screen proved resistless."[109] Paramount–Artcraft Pictures placed a full-page ad announcing the deal and its tenets, including the fact that all films would be "roaring five-reel comedies, produced with elaborate attention to detail and with plenty of time necessary to achieve something really worthwhile in the screen comedy line."[110]

By July, Sydney had decided to move production to Europe (specifically Paris) and Famous Players gave him a send-off befitting his new status.[111] The luncheon event was held at the Hotel Claridge in New York on Friday, July 18 and Carl Pierce was the toastmaster for the occasion. Guests included Carlyle Robinson, who had joined Sydney as publicity agent — having worked for Charlie in this endeavor since 1917 — Minnie Chaplin, Henry Clive, art director for Sydney Chaplin Productions, Alexander De Bray, scenario writer (well-known from the Society of Authors, France[112]), Sam Palmer, representative from Paramount's trade papers, J. A. Creelman for the newspapers and Emel Shaner for the foreign press. In his speech, Sydney concurred with the opinions later expressed by a reporter for the *Moving Picture World* that "the foreign settings will add the charm of variety and the fascination of viewing scenes associated with the romances of yesterday"[113] and explained his own particular desire for the expensive locations: "My first film calls for a number of scenes in the various quarters of Paris. Although it would be possible to construct the sets in Los Angeles and take the exteriors in and around there, still it is my desire to give the public genuine color and therefore I am going to the logical place."[114] Sydney explained further that he very much wished to see his mother, whom he had not seen in six long years.[115] Following this speech, guests were handed what they thought was a preliminary scenario for the upcoming production. The cover was labeled "Remarks of Mr. Sydney Chaplin, July 18, 1919." Inside turned out to be all "Greek" to the readers — literally — in a practical joke that had Sydney's name written all over it. It was a good way to cap off a perfect evening.[116] By the August 16 issue of *Motion Picture News*, Famous Players was running a full-page ad featuring Sydney's portrait and the text: "Sydney Chaplin says (by wireless, *enroute* to Paris, where his first feature comedy will be made): 'Four days of extra heavy going. I feel funny, I act funny. But

Sydney in costume as the King of Coronia for *King, Queen, Joker* (Paramount-Artcraft, 1921), on location in France (CHACHAA).

it's no laughing matter. It's a tragedy in six reels. Regards to exhibitors waiting for the first of the SYDNEY CHAPLIN PRODUCTIONS. Tell 'em I'll make my comedy on land. The sea puts the roll in drollery.'"[117] The *Moving Picture World* countered, in its August 23 issue with another such ad, this one depicting a supposed cable from Sydney to Famous Players: "Arrived safe. Met at dock by Shah of Persia who sends this greeting to exhibitors of America: 'Lamoo, Lamoo, Rantivet Gewaltmeer! (Those American exhibitors are lamoo, lamoo lucky who book!)'"[118] With all this publicity, it seems clear that Famous Players was dedicated to making this deal a financially successful one.

This publicity promoted the narrative that Sydney had set himself up in a studio six miles outside Paris "on the bank of the Seine." The *Moving Picture World* reported "the studio has never been occupied, having been completed just as the war broke out. The plant is modern in every respect."[119] In fact, Sydney had leased the Éclair Studios, housed in the Chateau de Lacepède in Epinay-sur-Seine and in existence since its founding in 1907 by two Parisian lawyers, Charles Jourjon and Marcel Vandal. By 1919, the studio had fallen on hard times especially due to the war (this fact probably appealed to Sydney) and was to move most of its energies to the production of cameras by the early 1920s.[120] Sydney's party was to arrive by boat, the S.S. *Celtic,* at Liverpool on July 31, where they were to part company while he and Minnie traveled directly to London to visit his mother for two weeks (he would stay in the Berkeley Hotel in Picadilly during this visit[121]), having already engaged an airplane to take him to her side every week thereafter (one he would supposedly fly himself). Minnie took the opportunity to visit her own family, spread throughout England and Scotland — some living in Leeds, some in Glasgow and other places (she was born in Darlington) and from these visits much family folklore arose. Jack Green, Minnie's grandnephew and the grandson of her sister Laura, offered this amusing tale: "My grandparents were living in a Glasgow tenement in the Gorbals, probably the least salubrious address in Scotland. On seeing an old lady scrubbing the stone steps (a chore which everyone in a tenement would take turns doing), Minnie [who had come alone in a chauffeur-driven limousine] immediately [sent the chauffeur] out [who] bought her a black maid's outfit, complete with little white hat and apron. This, of course, caused a great deal of mirth and was still talked about, even when I was a child."[122] Jack's brother Ricky added, "The real reason that Minnie was in town was to try to convince her sister Laura to let her take her oldest child, Beckie (Rebecca), back to America with her and bring her up as her own daughter. This may seem a strange thing to ask, but this was quite common practice among the working class. When one sister had more children than [she] could afford to keep and raise, it was considered a better option for all parties concerned. In any event, my grandmother who had three children, Beck (the oldest), Maurice (my father) and Cissie (Cecelia) refused the offer."[123] Clearly, Minnie had realized by this time that motherhood was not on her biological horizon. She was 31 years old.

The others in Sydney's production company went on to Éclair. Work in the studio was to begin officially on August 15, where his studio manager and other members of the production company were to have been working in his absence. Sydney was also reported to have taken over a 60-acre estate within a short distance of the studio as his residence. By all appearances, he was finally beginning to live the life of the lord's son that was the stuff of the stories his mother had fabricated in his youth. Sydney offered to the same reporter that he had been approached by the managers of vaudeville star Elsie Janis to co-star with her in a stage play in Paris. Another female musical comedy star (unnamed) was being considered as his co-star in the film.

Despite the fact that he assured reporters that he had investigated conditions in Europe prior to moving his production there, Sydney returned to the States only a month after he was to begin production in France, leaving on the S.S. *Adriatic* on September 3 and arriving in New York about ten days later. He accomplished only exterior shots on this trip, taken at a castle or castles, seemingly somewhere in the French countryside. It must not be forgotten that this endeavor fell hard on the heels of World War I and, while certainly Sydney's first impetus for the trip was to see that his mother had survived the war in good condition back in England, he most certainly had not counted on the inability of Europe to provide all the requirements of film production at that time, regardless of his research on the subject. He reported some of the devastation he witnessed to an American reporter:

The most impressive thing I ever saw in my life was the leveled city of Rheims at sunset. I happened along by what used to be the town's opera-house. The ceiling was shot away, only the walls remaining.... The sun was very red and flooded what was left of the old place. It was deathly still, until a little boy came down the street, his heavy shoes making a clumpety-clump that echoed long after he passed. Then, again, everything was still. I stood there a long while.[124]

Although he claimed to have returned with a useful 30,000 feet of film, he reported his dissatisfaction with the fact that it was not complete and he would have to continue filming back in Los Angeles, largely due to the fact that winter was fast approaching and Europe was suffering badly from a coal shortage: "Coal is one of the greatest essentials being used for the electrical apparatus. Just now coal is at a premium and it is a speculation as to whether there will even be a sufficient supply to meet domestic demands in Paris."[125] Without a nod to the criticism he had endured for going to Europe in the first place, Sydney wrote frankly to brother Charlie (in a wire reported verbatim by columnist Grace Kingsley), "Hereafter Los Angeles is good enough for me."[126] By this point, reporting from his arrival in New York and heading back to Los Angeles to continue filming immediately, Sydney planned to have the picture wrapped in just two months and at Charlie's studio. But that was to change.

By November 1, *Motion Picture News* was reporting that Sydney and company were ensconced in the Jasper Studios in Hollywood, shooting interiors and looking for a leading lady. It seems odd that he wouldn't have had one on the payroll by this time, given all the footage he was to have shot in Europe, for instance. Still he claimed for the article to have auditioned more than 200 actresses, without locating just the right one: "If I have to search every department store, shop, factory and even go into the high schools, I will not stop until I find the girl suited for this part. There is such a girl and I am going to locate her."[127] The part called for a girl about 17, blonde and with a pretty face, but a "country-looking individual, with the look that signifies nothing above the neck."[128] He finally chose unknown actress Lottie MacPherson for the part, because she assured him "I'm sure that I'll be the exact type for that part by acting natural, for I am just that in everyday life."[129] Outtakes from the film in the British Film Institute collection show some of the audition footage and show clearly the probable reason for Sydney's deliberations. If the existing film is any indication of his usual procedure, he subjected each actress to a lengthy series of lascivious poses in a sheer nightgown-type covering (if you can call it that) and nothing else. Clearly, Sydney was already getting bogged down in the "details" of film production and slowly sinking into a quicksand that would soon claim him. The article also states that he envisioned another six to eight weeks before production would be completed, a claim that again extends his completion date. Remaining with him in this venture is his crew, listed in this article for the first time: Carlyle Robinson (now studio manager); Henry Clive, art director; John Meighan, purchasing department; Dick Johnson, master of properties and Danny Hall, technical director.

In order to keep his mind and body fit and in shape for the long days of filming, Sydney engaged in nine holes of golf each morning before production began at the studios at approximately 9 A.M.[130] Reports of his routine seemed to suggest that he had much more of an organized schedule for filming than his brother was known for (he rose each day at 5:30 A.M.), but by mid–November, footage was still being shot and Sydney seemed to be sparing no expense in order to get it. One industry publication noted that he had flown his entire crew to a location near Santa Barbara, 140 miles from the Jasper Studios, in order to shoot some exteriors. Sydney's publicity makes the argument here that significant time had been saved in the endeavor (despite expense): "The trip and the shooting of the scenes would have taken several days," but instead "was accomplished in only eight hours from the time the company left the studio."[131] However, the fact that one of his planes was stolen during this location shoot seems to run counter to this argument: "Leaving the airplane unguarded, the company went about its duties, Syd intending to return shortly to the plane and fly back to the studio. Instead, Syd walked to the nearest farm house and telephoned for other means of transportation, for the 'ship' had disappeared." Several days later, Sydney received information that one of his airplanes had been found on the Morrow ranch, just north of Los Angeles. The bandits had simply run out of fuel. Sydney commented nonchalantly, "Hereafter, when I use an airplane for location work, I'll have to use a safety lock. Airplanes and pilots are getting almost as common as motor cars and we'll soon have with us the professional airplane thief to add to the 'joy' of life."[132]

The Sassy Jane Manufacturing Company was put into overdrive in an attempt to supply the lavish costumes for the production that Sydney desired: "Due to the rush of business at the plant, it was necessary for the operators to work overtime in getting out the costume order, but the results justified the extra trouble and expenses,"[133] or so it was reported at the time. Another extravagance came in the form of the special speed camera Sydney had picked up in Europe for the production. Publicity for the film claimed he had spent $5,000 on this camera, which was used to capture just one exterior shot — and then an additional $5,000 for camera appliances to shoot some particular interior shots back in the United States.[134] Perhaps these two extravagances are especially ironic, considering the fact that much of the film's negative criticism — at least for one reviewer — lay in its poor camera-work. But it was a pair of French handcuffs that may have caused the most commotion on the *King, Queen, Joker* set. Another of the expensive baubles Sydney had purchased in Europe, the actor required to wear them in the film got into a bit of trouble when the key could not be found with which to release him after the shot was completed. The handcuffed actor was sent over to the Lasky studios, where Harry Houdini kindly obliged to work his magic — which he did in under thirty seconds — thereby providing Sydney a nifty snippet for his film publicity pack.[135]

By December 6, Famous Players was still optimistic that the production would be completed soon, announcing the film's title at this point as *One Hundred Million* and that Sydney was engaged in filming the barbershop scenes at the Jasper Studios on Santa Monica Boulevard.[136] Syd and Minnie spent New Year's Eve in San Francisco, having arrived there by plane.[137] Then, on January 19, 1920, a lengthy article by Reed Heustis (with illustrations by Wyn Barden) appeared in the *Los Angeles Evening Herald,* promising that "the first of the stories [Sydney's films for Famous Players] is rapidly nearing completion." The several-paged article deals mainly with Sydney's business acumen and the particular companies he had started and deals he had made, among them the Sassy Jane Clothing Company and Syd Chaplin Aircraft Corporation. Heustis was sworn not to cover the details of the film in order to keep the gags confidential. However, in the article Sydney's film company is all in attendance and individually introduced. Carlyle Robinson is noticeably absent from the line-up, Cliff Eifelt having taken his place as studio manager (notably, Eifelt is mentioned as the new general manager of Syd Chaplin Aircraft Corporation following Rogers's departure). John Meighan is still the purchasing agent. The actresses (there are now three) are all in attendance and include the brunette Fontaine La Rue, a "custard-pie comedy" graduate, playing the part according to negative stereotypes: "She sings a nasty dirk. As a queen of the Apaches she canters hither and thither, blasting and blighting and putting Sydney, as we fear, over the hurdles of a certain amount of domesticity."[138] The two blondes were Lottie MacPherson (a film neophyte) and Sylvia Grey. Among the male actors mentioned in the cast is one important to the Charlie Chaplin oeuvre—Al Garcia, who later will appear in Charlie's *The Idle Class*, *The Circus*, and, most memorably, as the factory boss in *Modern Times*. In Sydney's film he plays a master crook of sorts—a supposed barber working both sides of that operation. Other of the films crooks are played by Ivor McFadden and Harry Griffith. Sydney's cameraman the day of Heustis's visit was Murphy Darling. Despite the fact that the article failed to give up much info regarding the plot or subject matter of the film, it served another perhaps more important function—that of reassuring the film-viewing public that Sydney's film production was continuing strong and thereby seemed to suggest completion of the job within a few weeks or months. Shortly thereafter, however, Sydney's Famous Players film fell from the soon-to-be-released listings, from Famous Players–Lasky advertising and any other mention in the press.

Sydney and Minnie were reported to have thrown a party to celebrate their 12th wedding anniversary February 14,[139] in what should have been a happy occasion. At this point in the story, though, the looming failure of the Syd Chaplin Aircraft Corporation and the deterioration of Sydney's first film production endeavor swooped and swarmed around each other, infecting and infiltrating seemingly all the days of the year. And Sydney was not the only one affected. Mildred filed suit against Charlie for divorce on April 4, 1920, a move that left Charlie and all his assets in jeopardy, including the first film that showed some promise of success since his marriage to her: *The Kid*. The first strategic move, however, was to sell the Chaplin Studios to Sydney and Minnie, which Charlie did April 14, just before his 31st birthday. A cable sent to Sydney in New York by Tom Harrington the next day suggested that all the involved parties were determined to make the deal look as authentic as possible: "Who do you wish elected as director? Wright says Minnie can sign your notes. What rental do you want charged?"[140] Later, Mildred, through the advice of her lawyers, tried to have the footage of *The Kid* seized, a threat that caused him to steal it away under the cover of night to cut it together in a hotel room in Salt Lake City—a Hollywood story that is now the stuff of legend. Sydney acted first as advisor to Charlie on what action to take, then worked with him, Tom Harrington and two cameramen in a room at the Hotel Utah in Salt Lake.[141] October 8, Sydney had successfully negotiated with Carter De Haven's manager for De Haven's rental of the Chaplin Studios for $1,250 a week during Charlie's extended period of residence in New York,[142] where he was spending his time editing *The Kid* and visiting with his new close friends, Max Eastman and Florence Deshon. *The Kid* was released to great acclaim on February 6, 1921, and quickly

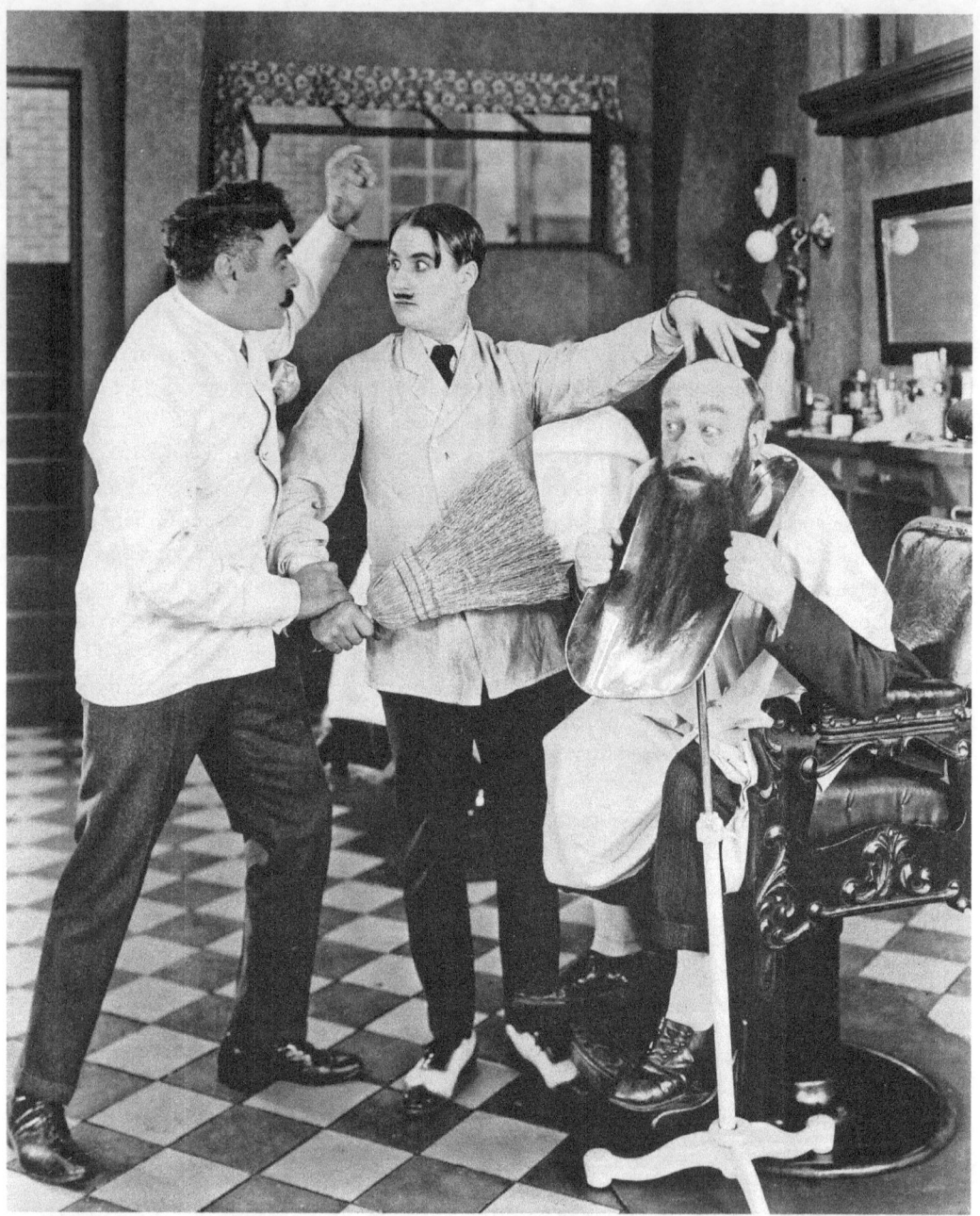

Scene in the barbershop, *King, Queen, Joker* (Paramount-Artcraft, 1921) with Al Garcia, far left, and Sydney in the center (CHACHAA).

trumped the other films in Charlie's oeuvre in terms of artistry and popularity. Sydney's yet-to-be-released *King, Queen, Joker*, in comparison, would be Sydney's greatest flop.

On October 14, Sydney and Emery Rogers were made defendants in a suit by the Curtiss Aeroplane and Motor Corporation for merchandise purchased, but not paid for. Rogers's debt came to $29,210.46 and Sydney's to $43,815.69.[143] As has been mentioned, Sydney received his summons while he lay in St. Vincent's Hospital, recovering from an appendectomy and what was being reported in the press by November as pneumonia as well.[144] But, despite reports that announced he was near death, he left the hospital on November 13, arriving back at 7132 Sunset Boulevard to continue his recuperation.[145]

Although some reports claimed Sydney's film was completed in December 1919,[146] others clearly demonstrate that filming continued at least into the first three months of 1920. Although the film only exists today in pieces in the British Film Institute collection, much evidence remains of the final version of its story. The story, set in the kingdom of Coronia, revolves around a plot against the king. A simple barber is found who is very like the king in appearance and so is bribed to take the monarch's place, after he is kidnapped and placed in a dungeon. The switch is so effective that even the queen doesn't suspect until the true king escapes from his prison and reveals the crime. Still, in his compassion for the rebels who incarcerated him, the king grants their demands for social change. The barber is allowed to return to his old job.[147] A press release for the film included the following synopsis:

> The little kingdom is on the point of a revolution. The common people have tired of their profiteering king. So they use a barber to double for the king while the latter is spirited away. The barber fools the court attachés, and the rest of the entourage. But his actions at the banquet are positively disgraceful. But the court attendants dismiss the breach of etiquette because the king is drunk. In time the real king is rescued from his plight. And the barber is ordered to be shot at sunrise, but escapes to become the king of the razor and strop again.[148]

"School for Criminals" scene from *King, Queen, Joker* (Paramount-Artcraft, 1921) with Sydney seated left center (CHACHAA).

Add to this description the fact that the chief conspirator in the plot is the prime minister, the king is saved by Sonia, the manicurist, and that it is the queen who saves the barber by having the bullets removed from the guns of the firing squad, and the story becomes easier to understand.[149]

Frank Scheide, a scholar who has been working on this film for many years, was the first to notice that an untitled scenario in the Chaplin archive, written for Charlie during the Mutual period by Sydney, had found its way into the plot of *King, Queen, Joker*. An important part of the story has to do with the criminal element of Coronia, the film's fictional kingdom. As Scheide also has pointed out, Sydney includes a scene in the film common to the music hall stage: the school for criminals. Publicity for the film suggested that Sydney created his "Apache den" according to one he visited in Paris during his weeks shooting exteriors there, one that included "mysterious entrances, getaway exits, unique devices, periscope lookouts," and other utilitarian innovations. In this real-life outlaw hangout, an intricate system of passageways opened out into a larger room in which the criminals held their sessions — the school for criminals, as Scheide has termed it. And, the leader of the gang possessed a luxurious suite somewhere in the building, one adorned with secret traps, bells, buzzers and every modern convenience available.[150] Much of this real-life inspiration must have hearkened Sydney back to the Mutual scenario he had already written, one that Charlie never used, for it contained both a plucky barber and a band of criminals — this time, counterfeiters. Scheide's description for the British Film Institute of one of the extant sections of the film provides a close correlation: "Syd standing behind bald-headed impatient customer in barber's chair. Other barber brings in list of numbers and Syd calculates on bald head. Barber upset. Syd wipes them off frantically, customer upset with activity. Syd rubs hand lightly over head at end of take."[151] The corresponding segment of the Mutual scenario reads: "Charlie's wife calls at shop and asks Charlie for money to settle some bills. Charlie tells her [he] hasn't any and disputes figures on bills. He takes lead pencil and starts adding up figures on customer's bald head; he also sets customer's whiskers alight with taper."[152] But this little scenario, just seven pages long, had an even longer life than the one Sydney's film provided, for it proved to be another in a series of barbershop scenes that eventually culminated in the character of the little barber in Charlie's *The Great Dictator*, a film that also uses a case of mistaken identity as its premise.[153]

When Sydney actually finished *King, Queen, Joker* and whether or not he took part in the editing end of it is uncertain. What is certain is that its release was delayed again and again. In January 1920, Jesse Lasky announced: "Sydney Chaplin has a surprise in store in his picture 'One Hundred Million.' Mr. Chaplin has shown me some of the picture and has told me of things that have been done in the production of it. Some of it was made in France, some in England and some of it on shipboard. In fact, it is an international picture and will have an international success."[154] Yet, the film's next mention occurred the following January when it was finally listed for a May release — its name change to *King, Queen, Joker* having gone completely unheralded.[155] On March 5 and then again on April 16, on his brother's 32nd birthday, a half-page ad for the film appeared in *Motion Picture News*, complete with a photo of Sydney in costume and the following text: "The great comedian's greatest picture. The *Ben Hur* of screen comedy. A titanic laugh sensation, packed with giggles, gurgles and gasps.... Filmed in two continents, on earth, air and water."[156] Just a week before its scheduled release on May 15, the film was still listed for that date in *Motion Picture New*'s "Advance Information on All Film Releases,"[157] and again in the May 14 issue, in an article entitled, "Many Paramounts in May."[158] Sydney's film was released on the date scheduled, but was almost completely overshadowed by another big production, Ernst Lubitsch's *Deception*, a European import that was held over at New York's Rivoli Theatre for four weeks.[159] Evidence of *King, Queen, Joker*'s less-than-favorable reception may be indicated by the fact that reviews of the film didn't appear in the trade press until the second week in June, and even then, they were very bad. The review in *Motion Picture News* began menacingly with the title, "Fails to Come up to Expectations":

> "King-Queen-Joker" comes to the screen as out-dated material with its burlesque of court life and the revolution of the common "pee-pul."... Probably had he put it out sooner it would stand some kind of chance. But, as it is now, it seems a futile attempt to make entertainment out of weak material. In watching the expressions of an audience in a neighborhood house where the offering was shown, the impression we gained was that the spectators wondered what it was all about.[160]

Laurence Reid, the author of the review, is detailed in his criticism of the film — all of which falls squarely on Sydney's shoulders: "Chaplin tries to play straight at times here, then when he suddenly switches to the baldest kind of slapstick, it tends to make the picture confusing. He has arranged his scenes so that long shots are mostly conspicuous and this is fatal for farcical pretentions. Then again he has permitted himself to overact in most of the situations." Reid gives Sydney credit for one good scene, the banquet scene, in which slapstick "with a capital 'S'" is well employed. Perhaps the most cutting of Reid's critiques, however, comes with its constant comparison of the film to Charlie's work — a critique that always finds Sydney lacking, of course: "Compressed into two reels, with the camera at close range, and with Charlie Chaplin, or some other gifted comedian, it might get over."[161]

Sydney may have been able to recover from one such review, but similar reviews came from all quarters. West Coast exhibitors reported: "Full week, but not to a full house. Great sets, photography and scenes. Material for a great comedy, but not with Sidney, who did nothing but overact and kill any possibility he might have had of being accepted by the public as a comedian. Poor business all week."[162] The East Coast reported simply: "Picture and business both bad."[163] Only the *Moving Picture World*'s Edward Weitzel softened his critique a bit with such lines as "Sydney Chaplin is to be commended for the vast amount of energy he must have expended in getting his Paramount picture, 'King, Queen, Joker' onto the screen," and, "The interior scenes and all the 'pomp and circumstance' which surround the uneasy head which wears a crown have been faithfully produced, and there are times when the story has the genuine atmosphere of an Anthony Hope romance." As Weitzel explained, however, the film was a comedy and it was in this area that he found it most lacking: "Sydney ... has delivered everything demanded ... except the requisite amount of laughs."[164] Although the film's run in the larger houses was short, a fact that is not surprising, given these reviews, it was still playing the smaller houses on into 1922. Whether or not Sydney lost his contract, then, due to his inability to finish the first film on time or due to the film's miserable reception is not known. The humiliation that he must have experienced, however, set his own career back a bit, but not really for very long. His next appearances onscreen were again due to the graciousness and support of brother Charlie, appearances that worked in Sydney's favor, showing as they did, his excellence in portraying carefully crafted character roles. The character part, as Sydney perfected it, would lead him back to the screen as a headlining star, but he would have to pay his dues first. Meanwhile, by late June, when most of his bad reviews appeared, Sydney was helping to make his mother comfortable in her new home — at last.

CHAPTER 5

Rebuilding a Film Career, 1922–1925

> We are celebrating the return of Sydney Chaplin to the screen this week on Broadway. After a long, long absence, he has suddenly arrived in two of our biggest film theaters. At the Strand he appears in "Her Temporary Husband" and at the Capitol in Marshall Neilan's "The Rendezvous." Both are playing to capacity houses. —Helen Klumph, "Likes Syd Chaplin," Los Angeles Times (June 6, 1924): B13.

ON MARCH 3, 1921, THE CHAPLIN BROTHERS finally acquired approval for their mother's visa from the U.S. State Department. The ever-helpful Tom Harrington was now chosen to travel to England and retrieve Hannah from Peckham House and bring her back to California. Aubrey Chaplin and his new wife handled affairs on the opposite end, helping Harrington to shop for Hannah's wardrobe for both the trip and for her new life in America.[1] They then sailed together March 16 (appropriately on Sydney's birthday) out of Liverpool on the S.S. *Celtic,* arriving in New York on March 26. Harrington had a difficult moment when they reached Immigration, however, for Hannah chose that point in time to declare that the particular officer interviewing her (Inspector Leonard) was Jesus Christ.

Back in Hollywood, some reports suggest she was settled in a bungalow by the sea, and others in a small house in the Hollywood Hills. Her location was kept somewhat secret, for obvious reasons, although carefully prepared profiles of her appeared in the press, especially shortly after her arrival. Joan Jordan's "Mother Mine," appearing in *Photoplay* in July, was one such profile. She created a romantic narrative that would have surely touched every reader:

> In the wide bay window of a charming house on a hill in Hollywood, sits a little, gray-haired woman, with delicate old hands folded upon the open pages of her bible.... Often the little gray-haired woman rises from her seat in the window and takes a few faltering steps to meet the man on the doorway of her drawing room. On the evenings when she does not, he slips quietly in and sits down beside her in the window, holding her hand in his. Because then he knows that her gentle mind has strangely slipped back to the horrors of a Zeppelin raid, to the shock of bursting shells and crashing buildings, death screams and imminent destruction. And she does not even know he is there! But either way—Charlie Chaplin and his mother are together again.[2]

Sydney suggested to one reporter that his mother's influence and tutelage were the real reason for Charlie's talent and resulting success: "Mother is the one who made Charlie a successful mimic. When we were little boys living in bitter poverty in London, Mother used to brighten the drab days for us. She would point out, for instance, the incongruous manners of the old chap who worked in a laundry and who took his best suit out of pawn on Saturday night to meet his 'Moll,' and bright and early Monday morning would pledge it again." Sydney recounted that his mother would then offer her commentary on the man's activities: "'Look at him,' Mother would say. 'He's walking way out near the curb for fear of getting the suit dirty and losing a shilling on the value of the pledge. Now watch him. He's not used to gloves and he wants to put his hands in his pockets.'"[3] The very next day, then, as Sydney remembered, Charlie would have an imitation of the man and his behavior for his mother's approval.

Hannah's presence in the United States seemed to cause the federal government some anxiety. Just a year after her initial arrival, her sons were compelled to engage in a letter-campaign to the Secretary of Labor to get her visa renewed. Charlie eventually sent his lawyer to Washington, hoping to use his financial clout to guarantee her support and safety, claiming that Hannah's health had "materially improved" during her stay.[4] The problem was, according to one report, that the decision would create a precedent if made in Hannah's favor, which of course, it eventually was. Then again in 1925, Immigration actually attempted to have her deported, demanding that she leave by March 26. Charlie's Washington attorneys presented affidavits from two doctors, Homer S. Wilson and T.T. Aaxline, that presented Hannah as suffering only from shock, a condition that had improved for her during her years of residence in the States. Charlie and Sydney also presented affidavits detailing their belief in her continued improvement over the same time period.[5] Sydney took it upon himself to then announce that he would make his appeal before President Calvin Coolidge himself if his mother was deported: "We think Mother should be where we can see her. I don't know whether it would do any good for me to see the President, but I am going to make the effort if the matter cannot be arranged with the immigration authorities."[6] But the matter was arranged and Hannah stayed on. During Hannah's seven years of residence in California, she received frequent visits from Sydney and Minnie, Amy Reeves (wife of the Chaplin Studios manager, Alf), Win Ritchie (widow of comedian Billie Ritchie) and, sometimes, even Charlie himself. She was characterized as spending her days happily, but never really recognizing the fame and achievements of either Sydney or Charlie.

Meanwhile, *King, Queen, Joker* continued to make the rounds of the "provinces," so to speak, playing small-town cinemas and theatres throughout America and the rest of the world well into 1922. A letter to Sydney from Chaplin studios manager Alf Reeves indicated that Sydney was hiding his property here and there about town; his Cadillac and his $5,000 movie camera, for instance, were being housed at Charlie's studio.[7] All were in danger of being attached — information that suggests that Sydney was running from his creditors, aeroplane manufacturers and film studio executives among them. Charlie traveled back to London for his first homecoming visit there in September, following the release of *The Idle Class*. Sydney figured into this venture in only two known ways: his comment at the station in Los Angeles upon Charlie's departure, "For God's sake don't let him get married!" and his arrangements with cousin Aubrey Chaplin to facilitate Charlie's visit once his brother reached London. After Charlie's return to America a month later, he began shooting his next film in late November, with Sydney in the company. *Pay Day*, Charlie's last-ever short film, was shot in just 30 working days. As Robinson explains, the second part was filmed first, at the studio "in the last five days of November and most of December."[8] Production started up again the second week of January, with the first part of the film being shot on the building site in four working weeks. It was edited and sent to First National February 23 and released April 2. In it, Sydney plays one of the workmen on the building site, who later appears in the bar during Charlie's night of carousing. He also plays the cart-owner in a brief scene. In the First National press book for the film, one of Sydney's scenes outside the bar at night is highlighted:

> Ever since the passing of "the poor man's clubs," back-yard quartets have been at a premium; but Charles Chaplin revives this historic custom in "Pay Day," his latest comedy for First National in which he and his companions engage in a tremulous rendition of sentimental ballads outside the door of the pub. The sweet music continues long enough to arouse the neighbors, but no longer. Typical means are employed to bring the melodies to an end and a sudden downpour of rain completes the defeat of the Midnight Rounders.[9]

Charlie's final film for First National was also Sydney's final film with his brother, at least in the acting capacity. Known initially as *Western*, *The Pilgrim* began shooting on April 10 with the scenario already well worked out, probably due to the fact that journalist Monta Bell (later a director in his own right) had come into Charlie's employ after ghosting Charlie's first book, the travel narrative, *My Trip Abroad*, a few months before. Because the scenario was so well-planned beforehand — a strategy new to Charlie's way of working, the film turned out to be one of the most economically produced of his films, even though he utilized many locations in and around the San Bernadino Mountains. Sydney plays several characters once again. The first is the male half of the eloping couple in the first scene who are chased by the girl's father and generally make Charlie the preacher nervous. Sydney also takes Charlie's long string of tickets as the latter boards the train, signaling to him that his tickets allow him a seat inside, instead of under the conveyance. Finally, Sydney plays the weaker half of the couple with the devil child who come to visit Charlie the preacher at his residence Sunday afternoon after his first service. Sydney, Charlie and the child, Dinky Dean Reisner (son of actor/director Chuck Reisner, also a member of the film's cast) work so well off of each other in the tea party scene at the manse that the viewer would never guess the effort that was necessary to achieve these results. Dean, who became an acclaimed writer in Hollywood much later, recalled late in life that it was hard for him (as a four year old) to wrap his mind around the fact that he was being asked to hit and slap two men he knew and cared for as "Uncle Sydney and Uncle Charlie." The two men convinced the boy by beating on each other (with smiles on their faces) until Dean came to understand that it was all meant to be a game.

This film, being four reels long when finished, caused some controversy on many fronts. First, it became the subject of a misunderstanding (even an out-and-out conflict) between Harry Schwalbe, the head of First National, and Charlie regarding the fulfillment of his contract. Being twice as long as one of the two-reelers the contract required, naturally Charlie wanted more for the film and sent Sydney to New York to negotiate

In makeup for and on the set of Charlie's *The Pilgrim* at the Charlie Chaplin studios with vaudeville star Elsie Janis, center. Sydney is standing with hat in hand (CHACHAA).

with Schwalbe on the issue. Essentially, Charlie wished Sydney to either acquire credit for *The Pilgrim* as a feature, similar in length and scope as *The Kid*, or to accept a two-reeler titled *The Professor* as the eighth and final film of the contract. Sydney cabled Charlie that Schwalbe came to the negotiations amicably and desiring a quick and suitable agreement, but wanted to see the two films first. Schwalbe also suggested that Charlie offer both films to First National, with *The Pilgrim* to be treated as an independent production. Charlie refused to offer both films and to show *The Professor* at all, but did allow a showing of the feature film. Negotiations continued into December 1922 with much hostility on both sides. Still, First National finally released *The Pilgrim* February 26, 1923.[10] The second of the film's controversies involved the opinion of church authorities and film censors that the film's humor was defamatory. Extremist groups either demanded its withdrawal or the editing out of key scenes. Luckily, Charlie had his fans even among the clergy, because most felt that the film was a satire of the church but not a harsh critique of it.

Back in April, Charlie sent Sydney and Tom Harrington to Salt Lake City to testify in court regarding contested lawyer's fees Charlie incurred during the kidnapping of the negative of *The Kid*. King & Schulder filed the suit, claiming that Charlie owed the firm $25,000 for advice provided at the time of his impending divorce from Mildred.[11] Held in the U.S. District Court in Salt Lake City on April 27 the firm had agreed upon a fee of only $10,000 at the time the advice was given, because they believed the film to be worth much less than the $800,000 it eventually made.[12] These initial fee negotiations were handled by Sydney in his brother's stead. Charlie lost the suit, but King & Schulder only received $4,000 from him, instead of the original amount demanded.[13] Well before the release of *The Pilgrim*, however, Sydney was working on his own behalf to get back into films — outside of the Chaplin Studios. The time was coming on fast when he would no longer make such errands for his brother's interests — a role that he never found very fulfilling anyway. His self-publicity started in October 1922, when his portrait appeared in the papers along with the recipe for his favorite dish, as part of a series called "Food for Stars." Sydney's favorite was supposedly Chicken Curry: "Cut a chicken into small pieces and stew until tender. Mix two tablespoons of flour and two tablespoons of tomato catsup and one teaspoon of Worcestershire sauce with one tablespoon of curry flour. Mince four onions with four tomatoes. Cover the chicken with the mixture and stew all for fifteen minutes, seasoning with salt and pepper to taste. Serve with boiled rice and Indian chutney."[14] Since this dish was not particularly a common one in America at the time, it did its work in amplifying Sydney's cultured Englishman persona.

In early 1923, Sydney stood to make $100,000 from an under-the-table deal with an individual, called by the alias "Joe Goddard" in Sydney's correspondence and "Godsol" in lawyer Nathan Burkan's, for creating a working agreement between the individual's company and United Artists. Obviously, Nathan Burkan and Loyd Wright, initially Charlie's lawyers, had earned the rare honor of achieving Sydney's trust as well, because he was to utilize their services often in the coming years. Sydney was keen on getting a contract written and signed by Goddard/Godsol for the $100,000 and had engaged Burkan, this time, for that purpose.[15] The wording of the contract Goddard/Godsol then signs names four times the company in question as being Goldwyn Pictures Corporation and lists an expiration date for the agreement (between Goddard/Godsol and Sydney) as being July 1, 1923.[16] Unfortunately for Sydney, while Sam Goldwyn was signed to an exclusive deal with United Artists, as Tino Balio explains, this didn't happen until August 25, 1925. Goldwyn was a bit of a rebel, and Mary Pickford and Douglas Fairbanks were hesitant about the deal, even though Charlie — probably through Sydney's advice — was for it. Joseph Schenck, United Artists Chairman of the Board at the time, finally talked them into it,[17] but not in time for Sydney.

At some point in time, probably during the trip to England in 1919 during the filming for *King, Queen, Joker*, Sydney made the acquaintance of Sidney Garrett, General Manager of Inter-Globe Export Corporation, a film distribution company specializing in foreign distributions, based in New York. Their correspondence suggests that Sydney applied his usual strategy here, that of using his ability to be gregarious and affable in order to win "friends" in business who might someday be useful to him. A letter dated August 23, 1921 from Garrett seems to be a sort of plea for him to "go with" Associated Exhibitors, Inc. (for which he was the foreign distributor) rather than with United Artists in his future filmmaking considerations: "Your activities with United Artists would be very limited, whereas with us they would not."[18] Garrett is more revealing in his letters to Sydney about Sydney's promiscuity than any other correspondent. In late 1921, for instance, he suggests that Sydney had made a pass at his secretary: "I would like to know what chance you have of stealing her away, not that I do not think that your eloquence and magnetism plus your personality is not in your favor, but since you have become an actor I am afraid you have lost whatever chance you had."[19] In October 1922, though, he was trying to help Sydney get back into the film business . Sydney's cable to Garrett demonstrates his contract hopes: "I propose to make six two reelers a year. I want a guarantee of seventy-five thousand per picture net to me. Fifty thousand on signing of contract to be applied on last picture. Distribution on a sixty-five/thirty-five basis."[20] This cable reveals much. First, it suggests that Sydney was held in breach of the Famous Players Lasky contract and was fined $50,000 (the exact amount he would have received for the second film he never made), an amount he refused to pay out of pocket (a policy he would apply to his British International Pictures contract as well)—probably, he was already hiding his assets in Minnie's bank account, a strategy that would get him into trouble later. Second, he had perhaps learned from his last film experience, inasmuch as his goal of two-reelers for the new contract suggests he now knew his limitations. Third, the distribution percentage he proposed was the same one he had just negotiated for Charlie with First National, so in some sense, he was still chasing his brother's success, or at least measuring his own success or lack thereof by comparing it to Charlie's.

Garrett advised Sydney to take advantage of the fact that Arthur Kane would be in Hollywood, visiting the Charles Ray Studios and present his proposition to him there (Garrett wrote, "Confidentially, he likes you very much and would not mince matters with you and will give straight dope."[21]). Arthur Kane, who had resigned as president of Realart Pictures in late 1919, organized the Arthur Kane Pictures Corp. in January 1920,[22] which then fathered Charles Ray Productions. In 1921, he became the president of Associated Exhibitors, Inc. Garrett's Inter-Globe Export Corporation was his exclusive foreign distributor. It's clear that Sydney hoped to make films of a similar standard as Ray, with Kane's backing. Sydney's other idea seemed to be to approach Pathé, which was in crisis due to Paul Brunet's recent departure:

> Had a long talk with Kane. He was very nice and presented a good distributor's argument which was only to be expected from a business point of view. He finished up intending to wire Pathé for a counter proposition to mine. I hope they will submit something worthy of consideration. It would be foolish for me to attempt anything cheap. You cannot hook a race horse to a plough or start a good workman with bad tools and good tools cost money.[23]

Garrett explained to Sydney that Pathé was "all fixed up for this year, they are not entertaining anything for the coming year until the place of Mr. Brunet has been filled, therefore nothing can be done with them." Garrett then suggested trying elsewhere, with the Metro Corp. as one possibility.[24]

Sydney's first film contract outside the Chaplin Studios since his *King, Queen, Joker* debacle turned out to be with Marshall Neilan Productions at the Goldwyn Studios to make a film entitled *The Rendezvous*, from a short story by Madeleine Ruthven. It's likely that Sydney's winning this part had everything to do with the deal Sam Goldwyn was hoping to make with United Artists—Sydney, acting as he was, as paid intermediary at the time. Perhaps Sydney knew that all he really needed was a chance to show his talent once again and his career would take off, despite his failure with Famous Players–Lasky. In fact, *The Rendezvous* proved to be all the chance he needed. The report announcing his signing with Neilan the last week of April 1923 also mentioned two other projects he would be involved in—*Her Temporary Husband*, a First National production, and *Charley's Aunt*, for which it was being announced that he would travel to England. However the *Charley's Aunt* deal was not yet signed at the time of this report. Mary Pickford's frequent director, Marshall (Mickey) Neilan tested Sydney "in different make-ups in order to get the correct comedy characterization" he had in mind.[25] Sydney would be playing an English Tommy (World War I soldier) named Winkie Harrington. Other members of the cast included Conrad Nagel, Kathleen Key, and "Wampas Baby Star" Lucille Ricksen. This was Nagel's first part in a Goldwyn Studios film and he played the lead here, the part of an American soldier, Lieutenant Stanford.[26] Lucille Ricksen, given her first leading role in a film with this project, received rave reviews for her portrayal of a Russian peasant girl: "Fifteen years old, she gives a performance which, for emotional expression, is a singularly agreeable combination of professional maturity and youthful naiveté."[27] More importantly, she was to figure significantly in Sydney's life over the next few years as he got re-established in a film career, beyond the character roles he was presently playing.

The Rendezvous was shot in Culver City, where an entire Russian village, nicknamed "Little Siberia," was erected to serve as the film's setting.[28] Harry Oliver,[29] noted artist and architect, lead the construction crew, which built "log houses with double windows and doors, and banked with dirt," two fine houses constructed of cement blocks and "painted dark Russian red," and the government building, adorned with two black-and-white-striped guard boxes and a nearby sentinel.[30] At one point in the film, the "Russian-ness" of the setting was enhanced by a scene in which the principal players witness the performance of a typical Russian circus that has come to town—one that included a Wooden Soldiers' Parade, similar to one featured in the Chauve Souris on Broadway at the time (a Russian Art Theatre production).[31] Other locations included San Francisco, where Fort Mason and the troops stationed there utilized "400 soldiers from the 30th infantry and heavy artillery, obtained through Corporal Morton, in command of the Presidio will be seen in the picture.... Doughboys from the Presidio and Fort Winfield Scott, loaded with the regular 66-pound overseas packs worked under the direction of Neilan for twenty hours." Transports, such as the *Cambrai* were visible in scenes showing the loading and unloading of soldiers. Also, the S.S. *Harvard* was used in some shots, but filming was interrupted by a southeaster that caused all company members to become ill except Sydney, who was noted for having his "sea legs" due to his experience on the high seas as a child.[32]

The story opens in the czar's palace in St. Petersburg, Russia. The czar doesn't approve of the woman with whom his son Sergei has fallen in love and places the son in exile at a military post in Siberia. The son marries the woman, Varvarra, and takes her with him. After Sergei reaches the post, he finds that the revolutionaries have assumed control. Meanwhile, Varvarra has his child there, but soon dies. Sergei flees, leaving his child in the care of a general. Years later, after the child, Vera, has grown, the Bolsheviks come into power, and order the execution of the general, Vera's guardian. The Bolshevik leader,

Cast plus director of *The Rendezvous* (Goldwyn-Cosmopolitan, 1923): Lucille Ricksen and Conrad Nagel (front row); Emmett Corrigan, Marshall Neilan, Sydney and Richard Travers (CHACHAA).

Godunoff, falls in love with Vera and, due to this fact, becomes especially vindictive in regards to the general, securing his execution, confiscating his possessions, etc. Meanwhile, a young American officer, Lieutenant Stanford, has also fallen for the girl and, upon leaving the post, promises to return for her. In his absence, Godunoff tries to force Vera to marry him and, when defied in this attempt, beats her until she is deaf. Stanford returns. Godunoff goes to hide in the girl's mother's tomb, suspecting that it is the couple's rendezvous. Vera, not knowing his presence there, simply locks the tomb before she prepares to leave the village forever with Stanford and life in America. Being deaf, she fails to hear Godunoff's cries for help and he dies a torturous death inside the tomb. Vera and Stanford travel to America, where they live happily ever after.[33]

    This adaptation of Ruthven's story uses only a few elements of Ruthven's original tale[34] — the knocked-about young deaf wife who visits a tomb for solace and an abusive husband who ends up imprisoned there, facing death. The Russian setting, the American and English soldier — in fact, all the soldiers in the film — were additions implemented by the screenwriter, Josephine Lovett. Sydney's part, although perhaps not created specifically for him was an invention — a decision on someone's part to include comic relief into the story. Having chosen Sydney to portray that character then, it would not be difficult to see his unique mark on the character, in terms of personality and gags employed. His character is introduced in Reel 3: "Sergeant Winkie Harrington, the pride of the British army—Sidney Chaplin." And his first gag employs the low comedy he knew so well—this one a foot-odor gag:

> M C U doorway, Winkie enters and exits
> L S Winkie comes down to table in f. g.
> M C U English soldier at table waxing moustache
> C U Winkie watching him, waxes moustache with tallow
> M C U English soldier
> C U Winkie, looks at feet
> C U Winkie
> INSERT C U feet
> C U Winkie
> M C U Winkie hands pan with mushrooms to girl, stoops down
> INSERT FEET, hand picks daisy
> M C U Winkie and girl, Winkie hands daisy to girl, she exits
> INSERT FEET, hand picks last daisy
> L S Vodka shop FADE OUT[35]

Described by critics as "a typically Russian, morbid melodrama,"[36] or in Laurence Reid's view, "A dull and dreary picture [in which] the heavy hand of Obviousness guides the monotonous tale," the film's bright moments centered on Sydney and his characterization of this comedic character, Winkie. In many ways, this character presaged his starring role as Old Bill in Bruce Bairnsfather's *The Better 'Ole*, which he was to film for Warner's in about two years' time—a character that was also a Tommy and one that Sydney would portray in very similar makeup.[37] It's clear that Sydney had been thinking about Bairnsfather's cartoons since 1918, when Charlie made *Shoulder Arms*, because Bairnsfather had been successful in finding the humorous in what was a dire and deadly situation—the trench warfare surrounding World War I. Sydney's reviews for his role in *The Rendezvous* were excellent. One critic called him "one of the most skillful actors on the screen, both for pantomime and facial expression."[38] Another raved that Sydney "gives a performance rich in the qualities that stand out in brother Charlie's work."[39] Daisy Dean, writer of the Hollywood gossip column "News Notes from Movieland" commented, "As Sergeant Winkie of the British army in 'The Rendezvous,' [Sydney] indulges in a little of the broader type of humor, but the touches of pathos that he manages to insinuate into the last scene when 'Vera' the girl [Ricksen] he has protected sails away with her lover—the quiver of his lips under the grotesque moustache—reveals the artist."[40] A review appearing in the *Los Angeles Times* mentions that "he very nearly steals the picture. The scene in which he comes into the girl's house and nonchalantly interrupts the villain [Elmo Lincoln] by juggling three hand grenades is a bear."[41] Another reviewer predicted the characterization would "result in a deluge of offers to the star."[42] Since Sydney had signed on for *Her Temporary Husband* at about the same time as *The Rendezvous*, really only two more films resulted from this acclaim. However, it is clear that though it took a couple of years, his contract for *Charley's Aunt*—his first starring role after *King, Queen, Joker*—represented an offer nearly equivalent to a deluge of offers for smaller parts.

By May 13, the papers were announcing that Sydney would be filming *Her Temporary Husband* and that John W. McDermott would be directing.[43] Originally a play by

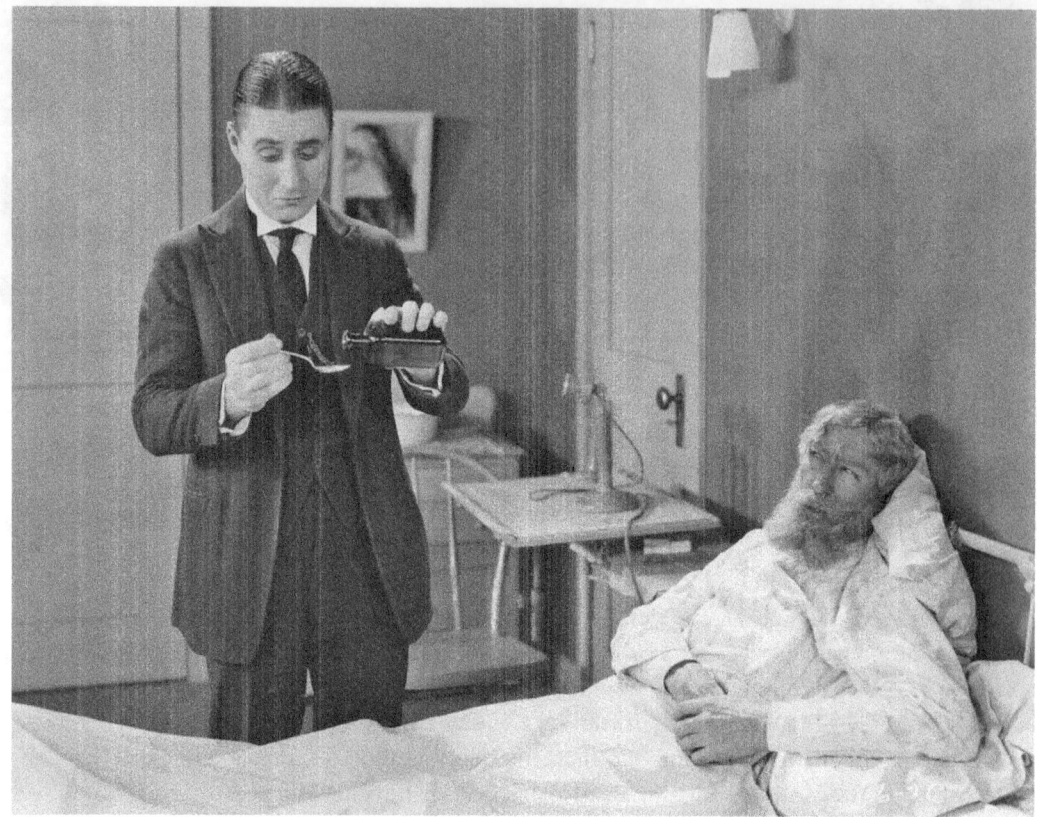

Sydney (left) as Judd and Tully Marshall in a scene from *Her Temporary Husband* (Associated First National, 1923) (LKSC).

Edward Paulton, the farce pitted a young girl against the terms of her aunt's will — that she marry within 24 hours and not to her fiancé. She determines to marry an old invalid instead, believing that he hasn't long to live.[44] Of course, events don't go according to plan. When wedding bells finally ring out, Sylvia Breamer's Blanche Ingram "finds herself firmly wedded to a hale and hearty young stranger named Tom Burton (Owen Moore), who looks as though he will live forever and ever."[45] Sydney plays the role of Judd the butler who works as a sort of comic intermediary between the scheming characters. George Landy offered his critique of the portrayal:

> The comedy nuances of Syd Chaplin's characterization are of a more delicate refined nature. In this story, he plays an over-timid, middle-aged butler who is forced into melodramatic situations in an attempt to help his impoverished master. While all the other principal persons in the story are rushing madly about in wild pursuit of one another, and during several actually gory battles, the apparently imperturbable butler, who is really scared sick, manages to save the day principally by pantomimically informing his master of conspiracies directed against him.[46]

The film marks the second of his films acting alongside Chuck Reisner, who would work as an assistant director on Charlie's *The Gold Rush* and later work in collaboration with Sydney on most of his Warner Bros. films.

Long Beach, California, reportedly turned out en masse to take part in some of the film's location shots. First National placed a sort of call to its citizens, suggesting that due to the grand scale of the film, there would be many available positions as extras for one or two exterior scenes. Although only 3,000 people were actually employed, nearly 125,000 turned out for the opportunity. In addition to the extras, director McDermott utilized the city's police department, letter carriers and members of various military organizations. This "huge mob" can be seen "rushing to relieve the inmates of a home who are at the mercy of a band of roughnecks and cut-throats" led by Reisner's character. The crowds rush to the house in response to a call for help — and an S.O.S. sent over the radio waves by Sydney's butler character.⁴⁷

Sydney trying out Mexican character makeup, circa 1924 (CHACHAA).

Neilan's film, *The Rendezvous*, was not released until November 11, 1923, but due to its immediate success for Sydney, by the release of *Her Temporary Husband* on December 23, his name was headlining ads for the film, despite the fact that Owen Moore and Sylvia Breamer were the film's protagonists. *The Film Daily*, in fact, ran a full-page ad congratulating Sydney on his continued success: "You're wonderful, Sydney Chaplin, and we congratulate you on the part you played in making 'Her Temporary Husband,' the greatest container of side-splitting laughs of any comedy ever produced and you know that means Big Business in any theatre."⁴⁸ Sydney himself was surprised by the film's success, writing to friend Arthur Kelly,

> I was very much surprised to hear that "The [*sic*] Temporary Husband" is a big success as you know I was very pessimistic about it & lost heart in my work right from the beginning & if it has turned out successful, it must be due to the situations and the cutting, because very little time was spent on the acting or characterization. I know I could have improved my part 100% if I had had the right cooperation from the director. I never saw a fellow who was so unanimously voted by the whole company incompetent, but he muddled through & the picture is a success, which only goes to show what a gamble this game is & the more you know about it, the harder it is to be proprietary.⁴⁹

By the date of this film's release, he would have already shot his next film, with Thomas Ince Productions, a contract he signed on October 5.⁵⁰ This film, *The Galloping Fish*, would be an ensemble piece, starring a group of established comedians that included Ford Sterling, Louise Fazenda and Chester Conklin. Sydney wrote to Sidney Garrett that he expected to finish the film in just six weeks' time, which would allow him to be free to film *Charley's Aunt* (which he still expected to film in England) no later than early December. But, as of the first of October, he was still negotiating this potential contract with Ideal Films, a British film company that started in 1912 and was known more for serious dramas than for comedies. Sydney's requirements by this point seem to have decreased somewhat: "Would want twenty thousand dollars minimum and transportation. Payable five thousand advance and two thousand weekly. Would work eight weeks. Want two thousand weekly beyond eight weeks. I could leave Monday. Must know immediately as Mary Pickford and Tom Ince want me but prefer English trip."[51] *Charley's Aunt* would be known as "the first Anglo-American co-production"[52] between the aforementioned Ideal Films and Al Christie's Studios in Hollywood. This film would finally make him the screen star he desired to be, but, clearly, he would have to pay his dues first.

* * *

The Galloping Fish seemed to offer some chance for a movement towards autonomy again for Sydney. He would be one of three stars this time, which was a definite move up from his recent character roles. The story, an original one by Frank Adams, was translated to the screen by Will Lambert. Sydney played the first of his many roles as an ineffectual husband or lover. Just married, Freddie Wetherill "is suspected by his wife of flirting with a group of bathing beauties near her mother's beach bungalow, where they are visiting. A quarrel results, and Freddie is bundled off back to the city, his wife [played by Lucille Ricksen] refusing even to kiss him goodbye."[53] Freddie decides to try to forget his worries by attending a performance at a vaudeville theatre, where the star attraction is Undine, "The Diving Venus" (played by Louise Fazenda), her trained seal (also named Freddie) and a supporting cast of bathing beauties. During the performance, a process server tries desperately to attach Freddie the seal, but is initially unsuccessful. George Fitzgerald (Ford Sterling), Undine's fiancé, tries to figure out a way to secure the seal and fool the process server at the same time, so comes up with a plan to steal the animal away in an ambulance. In the process, he sees Freddie Wetherill, a friend, in the audience and recruits him to help. Wetherill is persuaded to ride along in the ambulance with the animal, while George and Undine escape in a taxi. The process server, not to be outdone, crawls into the seal's abandoned box and in that manner is delivered to Undine's hotel with her other baggage.

The driver of the ambulance becomes suspicious and dumps Wetherill and the seal out into a park, where Freddie wriggles from his sheet and escapes. Wetherill finally catches the seal in the lobby of a fashionable hotel, from which they are both ejected. They make their way to Wetherill's home via taxi driven by Chester Conklin as Jonah. At the Wetherill home, the seal takes up residence in the bathtub. Meanwhile, George and Undine are unable to locate the seal, but bump into the process server, who is unceremoniously ousted from the seal's box by the baggage handlers. The couple takes off.

Enter Cato Dodd (John Steppling), who is Wetherill's uncle. He has also just had an argument with his wife and decides to reconcile with Wetherill, because Dodd needs Wetherill's wife, a woman he's never met, to take charge of his house to spite Mrs. Dodd. Wetherill tries to reach his wife, Hyla, at the beach, but is unsuccessful, so Undine is

Flood scene from *The Galloping Fish* (Thomas Ince/First National, 1924), with Louise Fazenda (far left), Ford Sterling, Sydney and Lucille Ricksen (AMPAS).

substituted for her in this part of the plot. George plays Blithers, Wetherill's valet, in this scene. So, while these three characters are masquerading at the Dodd mansion, Hyla returns home, discovers evidence of Undine's presence there and, finding out the group's whereabouts, soon arrives on the scene. George thinks quickly and claims she is his wife, which fools Uncle Cato for a time. At this point in the film, it is made clear that the rain is falling in torrents outside and that the nearby dam is threatened by it.

Though they are shown to separate lodgings in the house — Wetherill and Undine and George and Hyla — Hyla breaks out and finds the room her husband is occupying with this other woman. There is a scene: "Hyla, after a torrent of words, dashes from the room, runs down the hall and plunges into the flood water, which, by this time has risen almost level with the second floor of the house. Her screams bring everyone into the hall.... Seeing that Hyla cannot swim and realizing her plight in several feet of water, Undine dives into the murky water and rescues her."[54]

The flood scene is a complicated one. Mrs. Dodd's home floats alongside her husband's, circus animals are stranded here and there about the scene, scaring everyone, and Freddie the seal becomes a hero, towing several characters to safety on Mrs. Dodd's roof — a location that proves not to be safe when it goes over the dam with everyone on it. Of course, all survive, everything is explained and all is forgiven. The film ends with Freddie the seal coming through a skylight on the roof with Jonah the taxi-driver hanging onto his tail "still howling for his fare."[55]

In a letter to friend and United Artists representative Arthur Kelly (brother of Charlie's first love, Hetty Kelly), Sydney, having just returned from shooting scenes for the film in Yuma, Arizona, offers some frank commentary on it:

> I am having a tough time — this picture. Ince made the mistake of putting too many comedians in it & no straight foils.[56] The result is that no one will work up to the other & each is trying to hog the lens. You would laugh at some of the things they pull to grab or steal the scene. But don't worry, this baby will be right in at the finish, unless the director [Del Andrews] spoils me in the cutting which is possible as he has a violent crush on Louise Fazenda & spends a great deal of time inserting her from every angle & getting her full face, while he shows the backs of other people's heads. It's a good job, I have a sense of the humorous. It makes all this byplay amusing.[57]

Fazenda does seem to be the focus of advertising for the film over the other actors. Louise Fazenda, born in LaFayette, Indiana, and raised in Los Angeles, had her debut in a Universal film, but she cut her comedy teeth in the Mack Sennett comedies, as had most of the other comedians in this film. One of the articles in which she was featured, "Poor Fish Fell Hard for Louise," uses a catchy subtitle, "Partiality of Leading Actor for Comedienne New Hollywood Scandal," to draw the reader into what is simply the tale of Fazenda's relationship with Freddie the seal: "During the action of 'Galloping Fish,' Freddie and Louise had many scenes together and while the seal doesn't like petting or being 'made over,' he invited such attentions from her. The cast declared, jealously, that he hardly noticed anyone else in the picture and many little jokes resulted from this partiality."[58] In "Understudying Venus," an article that claims Fazenda was, in fact, the lead of the film, it is explained that she had to drop some weight in order to feel confident about playing a "diving Venus."[59] The set for this vaudeville act was described as "a jewel box of a theatre with a deep glass-encased tank and two high-spring boards projecting from rocky craigs."[60] Many of the water scenes with Freddie the seal were filmed in a special "mammoth" tank created for the occasion. For the flood scenes, a nearby waterfall was utilized, making the actors bad insurance risks for the duration of that part of the filming.[61]

But Fazenda wasn't the actress Sydney needed to worry about. This was his second film with Lucille Ricksen, the young Wampas Baby Star that Sydney first starred opposite in *The Rendezvous*. Although publicity for that film claimed the actress was 15, she was born in 1909 and so, would have been only 13 at that time. By the time *The Galloping Fish* was being shot, in the latter weeks of 1923, Ricksen was just 14 years old. Her role as Freddie Wetherill's wife Hyla and her premature death a year and half later on March 13, 1925, set gossips' tongues wagging from that day to this that Sydney, notorious for his infidelities and predilection for young actresses (much like his brother), had gotten young Ricksen pregnant sometime in 1924. In 1924, this aspect of his reputation made the papers on more than one occasion. In the column "Chatter of the Make-believers," it was reported that Sydney was witnessed trying to pull a "Lew Cody"[62] "Syd Chaplin is often seen about town dining with sweet young things — quite young. In fact, Syd says he finds mental relaxation in vapid chatter, the younger the better.... Syd wishes us to deny the rumor that he is engaged to Baby Peggy."[63] He made no pretense of hiding his behavior as one report found him at the Montmartre club, right on Hollywood Boulevard, dancing with a "snuggling little girl" called Shannon Day.[64] The gossips, therefore, believed that Lucille Ricksen died prematurely from a botched abortion that Sydney arranged. Adding to this gossip is the knowledge that Sydney and Minnie were separated for the only time in their marriage. It was reported in one column that Sydney had been living at the Hollywood Athletic Club, but "there is to be no divorce in Syd's family after all, as formerly rumored."[65] Still, the evidence against Sydney in this case is circumstantial. Ricksen's death certificate reports that her death was due to pulmonary tuberculosis, a disease that took her mother just three weeks prior on February 21.

Despite his bad feelings about *The Galloping Fish*, Sydney was not completely overlooked in the publicity for it. In "New Film Star and Chaperone," Sydney is interviewed about his experiences with Freddie: "It took weeks for me to gain Freddie's confidence — the first requisite for any chaperone — and then it was at the expense of all human society.... Fish was what Freddie craved and fish was what I had to carry about me every minute under penalty of losing his confidence and affection." However, he explained, this cost him the companionship of others in the cast, who "began to shun my company more and more as their olfactory nerves weakened under the strain of the continuous attack."[66] The film was received positively by its reviewers and audiences after its March 10, 1924, release. Helen Klumph noted that "the delicious humor of 'The Galloping Fish' is more than anyone has a right to expect."[67] Louella Parsons wrote that the film "is pictured so deftly that we sit first in wonder at Thomas Ince's daring and then at the excellent technique employed.... I dare anyone to go to the Broadway this week and not laugh."[68] Thomas C. Kennedy of *Motion Picture News* wrote, "The laugh is the largest in this case and the producers have taken aim with a shotgun.... The action travels at a break-neck speed and knows no limit in its whirlwind onslaught upon the risibles. There is everything from slap-stick to a dash of bedroom farce included in the material given the players, who, on their own part have been permitted to ad lib to their heart's content."[69] Kennedy noted that while the gags had been polished up and fleshed out to provide the feeling of fresh comedy, the plot was weak and might act as a deterrent to viewers. While reactions from theater-owners was mostly positive, their comments indicated that business created by the film wasn't as good as they might have expected. M. G. Kirkham of the Strand Theatre in Hays, Kansas, reported: "Didn't do much on this picture owing to rather strong competition. This was not the fault of the picture, however. It is all there. The tape is in good condition and the advertising accessories are snappy. The crowd was very well pleased. More power to the comedies."[70] Sydney himself indicated that Ince was pleased with the film and wanted to sign him on for more work: "Ince is exceptionally pleased with it & wants to sign me up to make a series of pictures in the same character. But I do not intend to bind myself down until I know the outcome of the Hearst & First National propositions."[71] The Hearst contract never materialized. The one for First National, however, did.

At the end of 1923, two other schemes were afoot, the formation of the Regent Finance Company, and Sydney's attempt to achieve a film contract that would allow him to complete it using old footage he had already shot — two two-reelers that he hoped to cobble together into one three-reeler. Regent Finance Corporation, incorporated in Delaware, of course, was to be a company that allowed both Charlie and Sydney to benefit from that state's lack of income tax on their revenues. In other words, it was one of Sydney's usual schemes to evade the tax man, one he now brought his brother into and one for which both paid dearly later on. As regards the mysterious two-reelers, Arthur Kelly wrote, in a letter dated November 30, "Do you think that I could be of any assistance to you in trying to dispose of your two comedies? If you care to send them to me, I could show them to the United Artists crowd and see what they think of them before trying to sell them to outsiders."[72] But Sydney had other plans. Shortly thereafter he wrote Kelly on the subject:

> I think that as the Educational already know what I have got, we should leave them alone. Pathé, I think, would be the first people. I would want $40,000–$20,000 on signing contract & $20,000 on delivery of negative. We could not give any options for further pictures or contract for any beyond the one. It would have to be sold on the basis that I was about to sign a big contract as a salaried artist to make big feature comedies & that before I commenced that contract, I wanted to make a three-reel comedy that I had in mind and contract for it with another company, as the company I had signed with did not handle short subjects, etc. If you think you can put this one over, Arthur, I will pay you a ten percent commission, but don't do anything about it until I have signed with First National or Hearst.[73]

Kelly told Sydney a week later that Hearst was rumored to be closing down.[74] Sydney had already met with First National's Earl Hudson anyway and was very near a deal — one that he would sign within a week or two of this correspondence.

Before the release of this third effort *après* Charlie, Sydney began to be interviewed by the press. His career was taking off and people wanted to hear from him and about him. One important interview appeared on January 12 in *"Camera!" The Digest of the Motion Picture Industry*—important because it asked Sydney to talk about his philosophies of acting. Perhaps he was trying to portray himself as a cerebral individual as well as someone blessed with the physical and athletic prowess necessary for the successful slapstick comedian. He suggested to the interviewer that the actor could not be a businessman at the same time: "The actor is the subjective mind; he develops it at the expense of his objective mind, which becomes atrophied, as it were, and that is why the actor is a notoriously bad businessman." He defended his vocation as a film comedian by providing a thoughtful history of the beast, arguing that "the actor who supplies the comedy relief in the present-day picture, brings laughter that is not forced, not dependent on far-fetched gags, slapstick or the custard-pie school of thought. It is based on logical character development, and thus in satisfying the best in the actor, it permits him to give that best to the audience."[75] This, Sydney noted, was the type of part he was devoted to playing as his career moved forward — the provider of comedy relief in a straight drama, arguably, as he had done so well in Neilan's *The Rendezvous*. Actually, Neilan's film turned out to be the *only* film in which he played such a role. But, in February, he was reciting the same refrain, telling Grace Kingsley that he was considering two offers, one from Ideal Films and one from Vita, located in Vienna, Austria: "I want to do character work. I don't wish to identify myself with any sort of type or make-up, however, as I think that is limiting."[76]

Another interview started its rounds a bit later, one that, in its creepiness, probably contained more truth than most of his others to date. Writer Jack Jungmeyer's recording captures Sydney's state of mind at one of the most successful moments of his film career.

Sydney began the interview with an arresting confession, "For years I contemplated suicide almost daily." He worked this out in his mind, he said, as a lifelong desire for adventure. And then another hyperbolic statement was recorded: "I used constantly to carry a vial with poison enough to kill ten men. During somber moods, it became almost an irresistible dare." But then one especially sunny, happy day, he threw the thing into the Thames. At the point in time of this interview, he declared he was now able to satisfy his hunger for adventure, now had the *money* to do so. He was in the film business for money, after all, not for fame or to be an artist of sorts. He admitted the only thing he dreaded now was old age and its limitations on physical activity and the pursuit of such adventure.[77]

In between times, Sydney made a cameo appearance in a little film directed by Slim Summerville, his old co-star from the Keystone days, called *Hello, 'Frisco*. The one-reeler starred Summerville and Bobby Dunn. The premise was that Slim and Bobby, being unable to find camerawork on the Universal lot, got hired to shoot some footage of the Wampas Baby pageant in San Francisco, one attended by many stars each year. Among the other stars were Bryant Washburn, Antonio Moreno, Hoot Gibson, Bebe Daniels, William S. Hart, William Desmond and Elliot Dexter, among others. Slim and Bobby discover their camera isn't even loaded and in attempting to correct that problem, drop the film, which proceeds to roll downhill, as does the camera behind it. Needless to say, they return to Universal without any evidence of their hard day's work.[78] It was released on September 29.

His next film, First National's *The Perfect Flapper*, directed by John Dillon, with actress Colleen Moore in the title role, provided Sydney a character role, but not a dramatic one. Perhaps he was already entertaining some hopes of becoming a headlining star again, however, what with the hopes of filming *Charley's Aunt* still viable and his continuing notice for the smaller roles he was accepting, for Sydney began modeling as a sort of sideline during this period. A week after the release of *The Galloping Fish*, he could be seen in full-page advertisements for Stetson hats, wearing a particular snap-brim model called "The Craig."[79] By December, he was modeling for Crown Army Shirts. In this ad, he is pictured on page one of the newspaper from the waist up in what is described as a serge flannel shirt. His sleeves are rolled up and he has an axe thrown over one shoulder, a pose which enhances the text that reads: "MANLY! Built for strenuous action, yet fashion-designed and tailored."[80] The caption "Syd Chaplin wears a Crown Army Shirt on his ranch" highlights the fact that, despite folklore that he never owned property nor ever wanted to, Sydney purchased a "ranch" in Encinitas, California, 25 miles north of San Diego, overlooking the Pacific Ocean, sometime in 1923: "Chaplin recently completed a home for himself on Victor Avenue, and has given a contract for a store building on the boulevard. The business structure, which will be of the Spanish type of architecture, will be occupied by a café, barbershop and dancing floor."[81] He paid $5,000 for the property and, by the end of the year, was trying to ensure that it appeared only on the books of the Regent Film Corporation, not on his own tally of assets. This and the fact that Regent had been set up at all points to the probability that Sydney was avidly trying to find places to hide his newly earned money and property. Sassy Jane Manufacturing Company folded in 1923 and perhaps he knew he might be called to trial for tax evasion on that front — a fear that may have motivated him to continually look for film opportunities abroad, like with Ideal Films, or Vita Films. The ranch, however, became both a macho getaway, a place to hold brainstorming conferences and a venue for parties. The house on Charlie's studio lot, while he still occupied it as a residence with wife Minnie, was not really his, so this new experience of property ownership must have been an interesting one for him. Sydney nicknamed the place "the gag ranch," because he reported that day-to-day chores worked as sources of inspiration for humorous bits of business: " Syd says that fixing the fence, superintending the drilling of the well and road construction give him just the right mental relaxation and he declares that he will bring back enough brand new gags for his next part to fill a seven-reel feature with laughs at the rate of one per minute."[82]

The filming of *The Perfect Flapper* had not gone without incident. Sydney succumbed to a foot injury when falling from a ladder in the Romeo and Juliet scene.[83] During his recuperation, he entertained three female journalists, all the while dressed in "a pair of tussore silk pajamas and a fetching silk brocaded dressing gown." The topic was sex-appeal and expert vamping: "It was all delightfully scientific. This matter of sex attraction, opined Syd, is made of vibrations, electrons, perfumes, color and harmony of aura. Thus, even the most beautiful of women may be devoid of the essential harmonious vibration with never an electron to call to electron from out the vastly sphere." Quoting to the women from Lord Chesterfield and Byron, he admitted to an appreciation of fine perfumes and the ladies deemed him "an artistic soul, replete with appreciation of music, color, and all artistry, even unto epicurean cooking."[84] But he would get no similar attentions

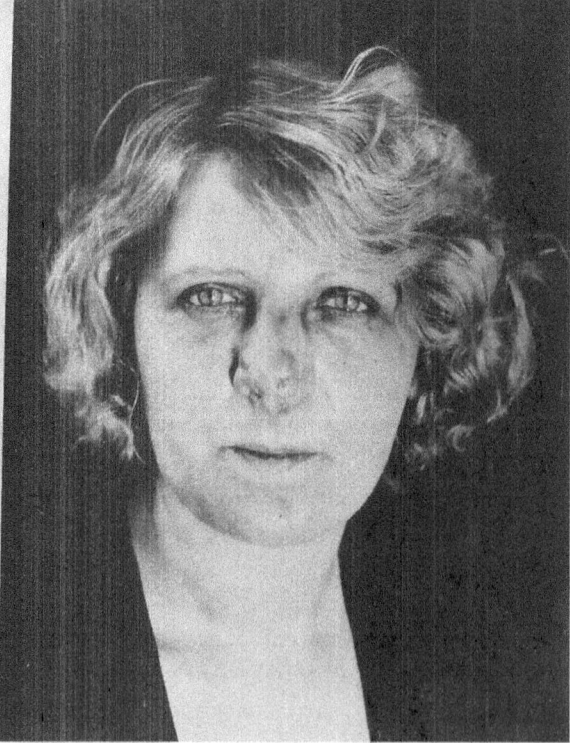

Minnie Chaplin, before and after her botched nose procedure, 1924 (LKSC).

from Minnie at this time, however, for she had just suffered one of the first botched nose-jobs in the history of cosmetic surgery. Minnie had decided to have her nose remodeled and engaged Dr. Robert Griffith to do the procedure. She had operations on January 7, 29 and February 23, all of which resulted in complete deformity of the feature. By April 4, she had the doctor in court, suing him for $100,000 in damages, possibly the first such case in the American court system.[85] Minnie told reporters that the procedure was to have required only one operation, yet she was still both deformed and suffering from terrible pain after the third.[86] More bad news arrived in the Sydney Chaplin household April 6 when it was reported that the brokerage firm of E. W. Wagner & Co. out of New York folded, leaving investors Sydney (and Tom Harrington as well) several thousand dollars in the hole.[87] In May, Sydney may have recouped some of these losses, however, when he cleaned up big at the track in Tijuana, Mexico, on a horse named Hilarity: "Syd's visit to Tijuana came as a week-end interlude to his stay at the newly acquired ranch at Encinitas, in San Diego county.... It was logical for a comedian to bet on a horse named for just the thing the fun-maker tries to arouse in his audiences."[88]

The Perfect Flapper, as the title indicates, tries to help Colleen Moore's character, Tommie Lou, determine: "What kind of girl must I be to be the kind of girl boys want me to be?" Wallflower Tommie gives her first party and it is a flop, because all the boys suspect it will be like her — quiet and conservative. Then, by accident, a mishap with alcohol finds Tommie embroiled in a trumped-up affair with a married man, Sydney's character, Dick Trayle (another ineffectual husband), who offers her drink after drink only to quiet her self-indulgent tears, but somehow ends up at the Laurel Inn with her in the same inebriated condition with a party blower in his mouth. This situation gives Tommie the kind of reputation she has never had and so works as a sort of tonic on the male population around her. She becomes a male magnet. But Dick finds himself in trouble with his wife, Gertrude (Phyllis Haver) over the deal, because his escapades with Tommie have made the papers. Gertrude's lawyer, Reed Andrews, played by Frank Mayo, decides to find out the truth and, when he does, decides to engage Tommie in a ploy to help Dick and Gertrude reconcile by pretending he and Tommie have a relationship of their own. Over the course of this performance, Reed finds that he can't be attracted to Tommie because she seems to project none of the purity and sophistication a wife should possess. Frustrated, Tommie retorts, "You demand tinsel girls for playmates, pure gold for wives." The two are married anyway when Tommie's aunt explains her current behavior as a pose and Dick and Gertrude are reconciled as well, in a typical happy ending.[89] The film was completed by late April and released May 25.

Colleen Moore, best known for her signature bob haircut and flapper characterizations, made her Hollywood debut in a film called *The Bad Boy* (1917) with Robert Harron and Mildred Harris. Just the year before her film with Sydney, the film *Flaming Youth* had finally made her a star.[90] Interviewed later in life, Moore remembered working with him:

> I thought Syd Chaplin was as great a comedian as Charlie. He was very funny in all our scenes together. But I'll never forget his telling me the whole story of their mother. It seems that she was mentally incompetent in a home in England. There was some kind of law that you can't bring mentally incompetent people into the United States, so they had a special law passed in Congress to bring her in.[91]

Of note in the film are two scenes. One features Babe London, Christie Studios' comedienne, who also had a part in Charlie's *A Day's Pleasure* as the tramp's unfortunate dancing partner in the scene in which he is suffering from seasickness. Here she finds Sydney's character attractive at the jazz party and makes her advances known. His attempts to escape her and her continuing advances demonstrate the comedic skills of both. One reviewer took special note of London, writing, "The coy, kittenish performance of fat Babe London ... merits more than a line of praise."[92] The other scene is the mock Romeo and Juliet scene enacted between Moore and Sydney's characters in typical Elizabethan dress. After Moore and Sydney arrive at a fancy dress party in fancy dress, an empty table is brought into the room and Sydney's character is placed upon it. Initially he recites from *Richard III*: "A horse, a horse, my kingdom for a horse!" but quickly switches to *Hamlet*, using a man's head as the prop he needs: "Alas, poor Yorick!" Immediately he begins again: "Juliet, Juliet, wherefore art thou, Juliet?" He falls off the table, looks for her under it, then sees her one floor above, stuck out on a balcony, because she's locked herself out. "You jump and I'll catch you," he says and holds out a little pocket scarf. Moore looks frightened. Sydney holds the scarf out wider: "Remember, my life is in your hands."

Sydney and Babe London in scene from *The Perfect Flapper* (Associated First National, 1924) (CHACHAA).

5. Rebuilding a Film Career, 1922–1925

Moore chooses to climb down the trellis instead, but gets caught due her garments. Sydney also becomes fastened. Meanwhile a crowd has gathered in the yard and a camera is set up and pictures taken. A decrepit old sheriff with a goatee arrives and tries to pull the couple off the trellis. The result is that the whole thing topples over with everyone on it. Sydney lands with his face in the dirt, Moore holds her head, and the sheriff tests the viability of his cigar before hauling them off to jail.

After the huge success of *Flaming Youth*, the reviews for *The Perfect Flapper* were wanting. Because Colleen Moore was such a bankable star at the time, Sydney was not featured in advertising for the film, but did receive good reviews. One noted, "Sydney Chaplin in an important role gives the picture its greatest comedy moments. He is acclaimed and rightly one of the screen's greatest comedians, and if his work in 'The Perfect Flapper' does not land him on the very top of the ladder of comedy, we miss our guess."[93] Of the four films he made before *Charley's Aunt*, however, this one provided his growing reputation as a comedian the least energy.

Sydney, ever the guardian of America's youth — in one way or another — had an essay on the creation of a separate category of movies for children published in the newspapers in late August, exclusively by the International News Service. The crux of his argument was that censorship of film could only be abolished by creating two categories of film: one for children and the other for adults. The rest of his essay seems to stray off course to discuss the absolute necessity of allowing directors full creative authority: "The truly great directors of today are those permitted full latitude in the selection of the story, choosing of cast, filming and editing."[94] This argument seems to, in some way, support his brother Charlie's method of making films *and* to hearken painfully back to his own attempt to operate in the same manner with Famous Players–Lasky, a failed venture. Perhaps Sydney was wishing himself, once again, more in control of his own output, having worked for other people now in six films and about to begin the seventh.

Meanwhile, Charlie was in female trouble again, this time with young Lita Grey, an actress who first appeared in a few scenes in his *The Kid* and *The Idle Class* and was now under consideration for the role later played by Georgia Hale in *The Gold Rush*. Forced to marry her due to her pregnancy, Charlie left the country for Mexico and left behind much conjecture as to whether the marriage would take place there or anywhere. Sydney commented to the American press: "I tried to get in touch with Charlie yesterday but failed. I don't know whether he's going to do it or not."[95] Lita never liked Sydney and made her feelings well known in a book written late in life, in which she claimed Sydney made a pass at her on the beach at Catalina Island during the summer of 1925, when she was still married to Charlie.[96]

With this film, the press began to pit Charlie's success against Sydney's in a sort of brotherly rivalry for the best comedian that was to act as a sort of refrain over the next few years. In "Chaplin Brother to Compete," the writer posed the question as to whether Sydney's recent film successes coaxed Charlie back into his little tramp costume in advance of his next film — *The Gold Rush*.[97] Of course, rarely was Sydney's name mentioned without reference to Charlie. Unfortunately, this extended to the deal eventually landed with Ideal Films and Al Christie to play Babs Babberley in *Charley's Aunt*. Sydney had been working on this deal since mid–1923, yet Charlie received full credit for it in the papers,

Sydney the hunter, California, circa 1924 (CHACHAA).

in articles claiming that as soon as he read that Ideal Films had secured the film rights for the story from Brandon Thomas's widow, "Charlie Chaplin cabled that in his opinion his brother, Syd, was the man who could best play the part, and as a result of this recommendation Ideal Films chose him to do the work."[98] Although it can be asserted that Charlie, given the opportunity to help his brother in this manner, would not have hesitated, given the significant paper trail on this deal, it seems unlikely that it all occurred solely from his recommendation. In fact, in an interview Sydney claimed it was he who kept track of the sale of film rights of the story to Ideal Films and then he who immediately sent a cable recommending himself for the role, commenting that "for years I have yearned for the part of Babs."[99] Grace Kingsley, in her report on the deal, states that it was Al Christie who chose Sydney for the role, without any mention of the part the Ideal Films folks played in the negotiations.[100] Nonetheless, by June 5, 1924, it was duly announced in the press that Sydney had been signed and would begin filming later that year. This film and the role of Babs Babberley was to finally make him a star of Charlie's caliber.

CHAPTER 6

Stardom and a Tenuous Homecoming

> To my mind it is much more satisfactory to play a character that the audience will remember because they hate him than to do heroic stuff. I haven't the least desire to play that sort of lead.—Syd Chaplin, quoted in "The Screen 'Charley's Aunt,'" *Picture Show* (24 October 1925):6.

FILMING OF *CHARLEY'S AUNT* BEGAN IN early October 1924, when it was announced that Sydney had moved into the city from the Encinitas ranch to begin work. Initially, he was concerned mostly with the costume he would wear, because Al Christie was still casting the company of players who would be his co-stars. Even the director, Scott Sidney, was brought on board *after* Sydney was chosen for the lead. Affectionately called "Al. E.," Al Christie, owner of the Christie Studios, a man well over six feet tall and known for his ready laughter, had made his first big success by producing the *Mutt and Jeff* series of films.[1] He produced mostly comedy two-reelers, and in the fall of 1924 had notably hired on both Bobby Vernon and Walter Hiers to complete their films under his umbrella.[2] A feature comedy, especially one with the stage history *Charley's Aunt* had, would be a rare and ambitious experiment, and possibly the reason that Christie went into collaboration with Ideal Films on the project. The widow of the playwright Brandon Thomas released the film rights to the story very carefully, it being a play that had been successful on the English stage since 1892. Ideal Films reportedly paid $100,000[3] and a percentage of its earnings to her for these rights.[4]

Mrs. Thomas had graciously sent over the original costume for Sydney's role and he spent the intervening time getting it fitted to him and trying out "corkscrew curls and lace mitts" and other trappings unique to the character.[5] Two weeks later, Christie had chosen most of his other cast members for the film. English actor James E. Page was selected to play Spettigue, having triumphed in that characterization on the English stage for many years. In fact, Christie managed to steal him away from his commitments for the part in England. It was reported that he played the role "in York, England on a Saturday night, and made up for work in the Christie studio in Hollywood exactly two weeks later."[6] Other members of the cast included Phillips Smalley, Eulalie Jensen, Ethel

Al Christie, right, shows Sydney the original Babbs Babberley costume just sent to Hollywood by Mr. Brandon Thomas for use in the film *Charley's Aunt* (Christie-Ideal/Producers Distributing Corp., 1925) (CHACHAA).

Shannon, Priscilla Bonner, James Harrison, Daird James, and Lucien Littlefield.[7] The last week of November, brother Charles Christie and Harry Rowson of Ideal Films settled all bets on who would distribute the film, choosing Producers' Distributing Corporation for the United States and Canada. Being Christie's "biggest attraction to date"—i.e., longest comedy film at six reels—this aspect of the endeavor was of great importance.[8]

The film was shot largely on a interior sets, with little or no use of exteriors. Al Christie traveled over to England before production began and took many photographs of the Oxford University campus there with his Graflex camera, to be used in constructing the sets for the film back home in Hollywood. At the studio, then, the quadrangles, gardens and chapels of a seemingly typical English university setting took shape. Because of the difficulty in lighting this big set, an elevator was constructed and what was termed a "stage kitchen" was built up on the second level to store additional lighting. In addition, "The interior sets, showing the college boys' rooms, were built immediately next to the gardens, and the exterior walls of the classic old buildings were removable, so that long shots could be made from almost any angle desired."[9] Shooting on the film was complete by the first week in January 1925,[10] but Mrs. Thomas had to give her approval before it could be released. So, a print was sent over to England before it ever reached the offices of Producers' Distributing Corporation. Christie was still able to release it in New York as planned, on February 8.

Charley's Aunt concerns the story of two Oxford University undergraduates who, in their determination to get married, must recruit a friend, Sir Fancourt Babberley, to masquerade as one of the boy's aunts in order to first supply the girls with a chaperone and then to secure the hand of one of them from her irascible guardian, Spettigue, who meant to take her with him to Scotland. Babbs Babberley, in his guise as Charley's aunt, creates such a reaction in old Spettigue that "she" finds herself the subject of a marriage proposal and much mayhem and hijinx ensue. Babberley's "antics take in slapstick as he scampers about on walls, turns somersaults and tries to steal a drink or three."[11]

Both critical and viewer acclaim for the film was instantaneous and overwhelmingly positive. Laurence Reid, decidedly difficult to please at times, reported that "there are sixty minutes of solid laughter here, judging from the response by the audience at the New York Colony Theatre. The famous old stage farce releases a rich volume of gags and incident — none of which are repeated, thanks to the skillful characterization of Syd Chaplin and the clever director of Scott Sidney."[12] Ben Shlyen, writing in *The Reel Journal*, a periodical whose policy is *not* to review films stated, "It rings the bell, loud and long, as one of the season's biggest laugh-provoking features and puts Syd Chaplin near the top of the list of screen comedians."[13] W.W. also gave Sydney the most credit for the film's success, but also praised James E. Page who played Spettigue, remarking that "his sudden matrimonial inclinations when he learns that Charley's 'aunt' is both widowed and wealthy and the subsequent pursuit form a large share of the laughs."[14] The general filmgoer was equally appreciative, as can be gauged by his attendance and responses. The film's New York premiere, held at the Colony Theatre, surpassed all expectations of the Christie Brothers and theatre management: "From two o'clock in the afternoon until nine at night, the line at the box office remained unbroken while inside the audience proclaimed the production a huge success by almost continuous roars of laughter."[15] Another box-office report, this one from the Midwest, announced, "Still going strong on the fifth week of the run. Some claim it the best comedy of the year."[16] Of course, Christie publicity capitalized on such press in its advertising, persuading theatres to print what appeared to be an insurance document that guarded their audiences for the film against the possibility of laughing themselves sick.[17] The idea that the film caused not just laughter, but laughter of an usual type — strength, length, severity — came to be central to all aspects of the film's publicity. A feline mascot from the story's old stage days was reincarnated with its particular motto: "Funny enough to make a cat laugh." Since the cat traveled around England with the play and its players, acting as a lucky mascot, if nothing else, the film adaptation's director, Scott Sidney, decided to put it back into commission: "There was never a scene shot without the black cat on the stage at the Christie studio. The studio cat was taken to the first preview of the picture in South Pasadena and the audience yelled with mirth."[18]

By about April 1, Grauman's Million Dollar Theatre in Los Angeles was still running the film. Ever the showman, Sid Grauman turned one of the evening performances into an orphan benefit and invited Sydney to attend in drag — in the *Charley's Aunt* costume, of course.[19] Although news photos show his attendance, he was never very comfortable with these affairs, although he readily gave his time and money to such causes over the coming years. He also was not comfortable viewing himself on the screen. Writer Alma Whitaker, however, convinced Sydney to join her at the Million Dollar one evening for a showing: "Syd looked weighed down with responsibility. A mighty serious business, this, making laughter for the masses." Sydney's initial reactions to the show were negative: "'I think the prologue ought to have shown Oxford undergraduates in mortar boards and gowns. And maybe we made the first half too hurriedly — takes too long to get to the laughs.'" But, when the audience started laughing, Whitaker pressed him, "Now thank me for a delightful entertainment."[20]

Sydney began, more and more, to appear at public functions and to actually participate in openings and gala events like the annual Wampas Frolic — an announcement of the Wampas Baby each year (of which Lucille Ricksen had been one in 1924). This event was held on February 9 in the Ambassador Ballroom.[21] As part of the Studioland Revue, Sydney performed a comedy piece called simply "In and Out."[22] The announcement in January that the Hollywood Sixty Club, a new club "composed of members interested in the motion-picture industry," would construct "a handsome clubhouse at the corner of Hollywood Boulevard and McCadden Place [that would] contain four large ballrooms and several private dining rooms."[23] This was followed in March by a dance party for the club held at the Biltmore, which Sydney attended, along with other actors, including Leatrice Joy, Raymond Griffith, Constance Talmadge and Dorothy Devore (notable for the fact that she is linked with Sydney in at least one other bit of press at the time[24]). Sydney was named as being on the club's board of directors.[25] He attended the opening of a new "confectaurant" in Hollywood named Paulais, dressed in chef's attire, and sampled the fancy goodies and listened to the Venetian Players right along with other stars, such as Bryant Washburn, Clara Bow, Priscilla Dean and others.[26] In each case neither Minnie's presence is mentioned nor that of the particular girl he was escorting, although it's improbable that he would have attended such functions alone, as uncomfortable as they made him.

The first week of March, Sydney was announcing his view that the next big paycheck would go to a radio star: "Only a few years and radio concert artists will be drawing down $50,000 for a single broadcasting performance." He claimed all this would take was one star's willingness to ask for it. He believed that there would soon be synchronized receiving sets that allowed a listener to insert a quarter to hear a broadcast of a great artist, much like they would use a pay phone. Such sets would award the broadcasting companies millions of dollars in revenue, thus making a paltry $50,000 performance fee seem like a small price to pay.[27] Sydney was always well-versed in the technological advancements of the day, particularly when it came to the entertainment business and modes of transportation. He was often right in such predictions.

Sydney was signed by Warner Bros. on March 11,[28] but the death of Lucille Ricksen due to tuberculosis must have put a temporary pall on the deal. Ricksen died on March 13 and was laid to rest on March 15, just a day before the birthday of the man Hollywood believed had some hand in her demise. Both Sydney and Charlie are listed as having sent their condolences via flower arrangement, most probably in lieu of attendance. Her service was performed by the Reverend Neal Dodd of the Little Church around the Corner, a part of the Forest Lawn cemetery.[29]

Warner Bros. was expanding. The big gambles the brothers made during this period were to pay off in a big way. At about the same time as they signed on Sydney and elusive star John Barrymore, they merged with Vitagraph "in one of the greatest mergers ever effected in the industry."[30] And they were signing more and more stars, many of whom, like Sydney, had heretofore been considered freelancers in the business. Warners announced in the press that they would be scheduling the release of 40 films for the year instead of the usual 26, with added costs of $3.5 million.[31] After an eight-hour conference with the Warner executives, Sydney was signed to a five-feature-film deal in which he was to play the starring roles: "The contract is said to involve the greatest sum of money paid to motion picture artists in the past year. He is to head his own company. A special director and crew of gag men are to be turned over to him and everything set for a regular independent company."[32] Just five years after his miserable Famous Players–Lasky debacle, Sydney seemed to have restored himself to a similar apex in filmdom. But would he succeed this time?

By the end of March, Warners had chosen Fred C. Newmeyer, of the Harold Lloyd Corporation, to direct Sydney's first picture, *The Man on the Box*, from a novel by Harold McGrath.[33] The film rights to the story had been purchased from Alma Kenyon McGrath on March 19 for $11,250.00.[34] Chuck Reisner[35] was hired on to adapt the story to the screen, with help from Charlie Logue. But Newmeyer was out by mid–May and replaced by Reisner as director. Surprisingly, it was Jack Warner who forced the departure: "I was dissatisfied with the progress of the picture. Mr. Newmeyer is an able director, but we couldn't agree. So, when he asked to be taken off the picture, I let him go."[36] Newmeyer had already shot 10,000 feet of film in the three weeks of his tenure and Warner insisted this footage would be kept intact. He, of course, expected Reisner to place the production back on schedule.

In the film, as the character Bob Warburton, Sydney is called upon to shape-shift from a millionaire into a cab driver, a groom, a butler and, finally, a lady's maid in order

Opposite: **Alice Calhoun and Sydney Chaplin outside the Warner Brothers' studios, Hollywood, during the filming of *The Man on the Box* (Warner Bros., 1925) (LKSC).**

Advertising for *The Man on the Box* (Warner Bros., 1926) (LKSC).

to get both the girl and the plans for a helicopter away from the Russian enemy, Karloff. Warburton, a millionaire, decides to back an inventor of the helicopter. This inventor becomes jealous of Warburton's attentions to his wife and chases him out of the house. In the mêlée, a burglar is able to steal the plans for the Russians. Warburton then falls in love with Colonel Annesley's daughter, played by Alice Calhoun, and decides to work for her as a groom in order to be near her. But his predicament requires him to assume the role of butler, then lady's maid in his quest — the latter placing him in intimate situations with Miss Annesley that lead to occasions for humor. In the end, of course, the plans are retrieved, the lady won, and the inventor placated, for the usual happy ending.

Critics hated the film, but audiences seemed to love it, or at least, they patronized it in droves. Charlie offered his two cents with a cable that simply said, "Wonderful!" and was displayed at the Warner's Theatre in New York where the film opened. Jack Jungmeyer, the writer who had obtained an uncharacteristically confessional interview from Sydney the previous year wrote one of the few positive reviews: "In this piece there is some rare pantomiming, and Syd shows himself on a par with brother Charlie in this gentle art. His effort, at a crucial moment in the story, to signal his adopted name 'Goldfish' to a fellow conspirator, all in dumb mimicry, is masterly. So is his impersonation of Roosevelt, with candy minis for teeth and a couple of wafers for eyeglasses — a startlingly effective caricature."[37] Mordaunt Hall, Quinn Martin and Helen Klumph, however, found little to compliment in the film. Hall remarked, "Sydney Chaplin's portrayal in 'Charley's Aunt' suited Brandon Thomas's well-knit farce, but Sydney has no such clever vehicle in 'The Man on the Box,' and perhaps for that reason he slumps into acting that would make a pantomime clown's gyrations with a string of sausages look like high-class comedy."[38] Martin claimed the film was "ninety-nine and one half percent turkey."[39] Klumph, not to be outdone, described the film as "hackneyed and tiresome," with Sydney's performance "deplorably exaggerated."[40] British reviewers were equally torn, but most seemed to appreciate the Roosevelt impression at the very least.[41] The public, however, showed their approval by attending. The Forum Theatre in Los Angeles played the film to packed houses the first week and even reported turning many viewers away at the evening show times. Despite their policy of a new feature each week, the theatre decided to hold over Sydney's film.[42] New York theatres reported similar numbers of attendees.

Although critics were quick to mention the old-fashioned-ness of Sydney's acting in this film and the gags he tried to put over — blaming most on the "vehicle," i.e., the story as much as the comedian, the script for the film leaves much room throughout for ad libs and improvisations. In the scene in which Warburton transforms into a maid to remain in the Annesley house undiscovered, the script reads, "Gags to be worked here." When Chuck Reisner as Karloff's butler encounters Warburton as the maid, it reads, "Gags where Syd sees Chuck for the first time and then routine of gags and business where we show being waited on by Syd and Chuck."[43] This evidence from the shooting script, then, seems to place the blame squarely on the actor's — Sydney's — shoulders. Sydney's next film, *Oh, What a Nurse!* was better received, though certainly not to the extent he had experienced with *Charley's Aunt*. This and his constant comparison to Charlie's work by critics and film viewers (Charlie's masterpiece, *The Gold Rush*, had preceded Sydney's first Warners' film at the box office by more than three months) must have caused him more than a little anxiety. Perhaps the atmosphere of his working environment, one that allowed him full access to the hedonistic and anti-authoritarian lifestyle he so desired, made up for these insecurities.

The year 1925 presented Sydney with his first nephew, Charlie Chaplin, Jr., born to his brother and wife, Lita, on May 5. Their second child, his namesake, would be born less than a year later on March 30. Not much is known about his relationship to these two boys, although considering Lita's negative feelings for Sydney following her divorce

Sydney and Alice Calhoun in a scene from *The Man on the Box* (Warner Bros., 1925) (LKSC).

from Charlie, it is likely that they were not close. Sydney's social life, however, continued to thrive at this time. He was pictured at a banquet at the Biltmore Hotel honoring United Artists chief Joseph Schenck in April—a rare occasion when he and Charlie attended an event together (Arthur Kelly was also there).[44] In early June, he took part— as did almost everyone in Hollywood—in the Shriner's Parade led by Doug Fairbanks and Mary Pickford from Hollywood Boulevard to the Hollywood Bowl where a pageant of sorts was then performed.[45] But perhaps the most important event in June that year was the big premiere of Charlie's long-awaited *The Gold Rush*, feted by Sid Grauman in a grand premiere event at the Grauman's Egyptian Theatre on June 26. Sydney attended the event with his wife for a change, showing full support for his brother, right alongside Edna Purviance, Georgia Hale, Lita Grey (still Charlie's wife), and Marion Davies— in other words, Charlie's women.[46]

It was announced on July 23 that Sydney's next vehicle would be a story by film critic Robert E. Sherwood entitled "Goodnight Nurse."[47] Sherwood was paid $7,500 for the film rights.[48] The film did not retain this title and, in fact, was announced as *Nightie Night Nurse* before the final *Oh! What a Nurse!* was finally chosen. Most likely, the word "night" in relation to "nurse" had to be removed in order to please the censors. The two former titles also belie a bawdiness to the film that simply didn't exist in the final product.

The story not only changed titles three times over the course of its metamorphosis, but changed characterization — in Sherwood's story, the protagonist is a lawyer; in Sydney's, he is a newspaper hack. In fact, there are at least two scripts in the Chaplin archive with this title that bear little if any resemblance to the plot that occurs in the final film. Clearly, the aforementioned anxiety was having its effect on Sydney at this time, although distractions of the female persuasion, provided by the studio atmosphere, probably didn't help matters. Chuck Reisner would again direct and also worked on the scenario with Sydney over the next month or so.[49] This time, they would not congregate at Sydney's ranch for story conferences, but chose to travel to Yosemite and inhabit the lodge there for the time it took (Charlie was known to have engaged in similar "work trips" over the course of his career). With them this time was a young Darryl Francis Zanuck. Zanuck did not sign up full time with Warner Bros. until the end of October, but he was known to be freelancing on this particular film and, in fact, remained writing for Sydney on his next three films.

Of Sydney's collaborators, only Zanuck remembered him in print and it is his recollections that offer a window into the goings-on of the Warner Bros. environment that might provide some evidence of Sydney's slippery slope. Zanuck remembered to biographer Leonard Mosely that Sydney was "better read and handsomer than his younger half brother." He felt strongly that "if a shrewd director had only taken him in hand, probed his real character, soothed his resentments, calmed his phobias, he might have developed a quality in him that could have changed his career." These frank observations indicate Zanuck's close connection to Sydney — one that had originated at the Mack Sennett Studios back in 1915. It seems to explain Sydney's personality better than anything else in print. Because no one took the time to "take him in hand," however, he had developed into what Zanuck termed an "outwardly confident and cocksure, and inwardly embittered" personality, one whose motto at this time Zanuck recalled: "Fucking is the best revenge."[50] A dedicated womanizer, Sydney "was a predator, a hunter of vulnerable females, and his appetite was practically insatiable." Back in the Sennett days, he would troll the neighborhoods around Hollywood High school for likely victims and once he found a willing individual (usually using his own name as bait), he would perform the sex act right there in the car, often with Zanuck either in the front seat or walking around the car uncomfortably. Sydney justified his actions with his belief that mothers — women — were fallible creatures, all of them nothing but a bunch of whores, so women deserved what they asked for.[51] If any of this account is true, it points to Sydney — admittedly one of young Zanuck's early influences — as the impetus behind what came to be called the Hollywood "casting couch," since Zanuck is credited as having invented the concept. An epigraph attributed to Zanuck and now well-known is "Sydney Chaplin was the greatest cocksman that ever lived, greater even than Errol Flynn."[52] Still, by the time Zanuck was interviewed — late in life — there was no longer any love lost between the two men. Zanuck had turned a blind eye to Sydney's plight in the 1930s in one of his many quests to return to the business. While it's certain there is some truth to Zanuck's claims, it is also certain they contain some embellishment, if only due to the passage of time.

Sydney, Zanuck and Reisner wrote the script for *Oh! What a Nurse!* at Camp Curry in the Yosemite National Park, arriving there August 17, to the great excitement of the female contingent of the place.⁵³ Filming started back at the Warner Bros. studio about September 24.⁵⁴ Patsy Ruth Miller,⁵⁵ Sydney's leading lady, was one of Warners' starlets and as such subject to placement in whatever production the company desired, but she felt working with a low comedian was beneath her. She recalled to William Drew,

> I did *Oh, What a Nurse!* with Syd Chaplin in 1926, but I never got to know him. That was a mistake. I should never have been put in that picture. That's one of the few times I was angry at the studio. It was silly. They were using my name because Syd Chaplin really didn't mean a thing. So I was forced to do it simply because they thought my name on it would make the picture amount to something. I didn't enjoy making it. I thought it was a stupid film, and I didn't think Mr. Chaplin had any personality. I thought he was rather common — sort of a music-hall type of comic — and we had nothing in common.⁵⁶

Perhaps for this reason, she succumbed to the flu within the first week of production, thereby causing a delay. Reisner wanted to begin the film shooting the water scenes in San Diego.⁵⁷ The San Diego shoot was plagued with another problem at this time. On September 25, Sydney injured himself. In an attempt to dive off a Coronado ferry boat, he struck a submerged pile, necessitating a recuperation period of several days.⁵⁸

A reporter for *Girl's Cinema* visited Sydney on the Warners' set for this film and found it a lively place, with little groups of people standing around laughing and cutting up — a scene that stood in stark contrast to Charlie's reputed way of working. Sydney's dressing room looked like a luxurious drawing room in someone's house, decorated as it was with bright cretonne coverings on the furniture "and curtains of the same material. There are numbers of pictures on the wall and a gramophone is often playing while the star puts on his make-up."⁵⁹ A bookshelf filled with tomes, such as the eight-volume set *Opus Sadicum,* a collection of pre-revolutionary French dialectics, adorned one wall. And, taking up more than a bit of room was a period piece, "A massive appurtenance, all bound in brass, containing little doors and numer-

Sydney in disguise as a nurse in *Oh! What a Nurse!* (Warner Bros., 1926) (LKSC).

ous recesses with sliding panels, all of which are kept locked as a matter of precaution."[60] What secrets this piece must have held! Offering his own particular theory of comedy, Sydney commented, "I can, of course, make myself look quite silly by affecting a mannerism or a disguise, but that is not the essence of fun-making. It may draw a laugh the first time I appear on the screen, but gives no lasting touch to the picture, whereas a logical coherent plot that permits of grotesque, ridiculous incidents that fit into places as smoothly as a jig-saw puzzle door, appeals to the public."[61]

In the version of Sherwood's story presented on the screen, Sydney as Jerry Clark, who, by day is substituting for an advice columnist for the lovelorn called "Dolly Whipple," discovers a plot afoot that involves a young rich girl, June Harrison, played by Miller, in which her treacherous uncle, Tim Harrison, wants to force her to marry a man, Clive Hunt, against her will. Clark, then, decides to go to her rescue, and must dress as a woman at different points in order to do so. He escapes a rumrunner, whose ship he boards by accident, and rescues the girl, whom he finally marries himself.

This was one of Sydney's cross-dressing films — in fact, it turned out to be his last cross-dressing film for a while, a fact which he made emphatic in the advertisements for his next production, *The Better 'Ole*, in which he plays Old Bill, an aging World War I "Tommy." Perhaps it was the fear of being typecast, or just the cross-dressing overload that caused this change for Sydney, but — as would be expected — the publicity for the film seemed to suggest that Sydney really didn't mind donning women's clothes, except for the fact that he had to shed ten pounds for the role in order to wear the required corsets without doing damage to himself. Alma Whitaker went to the Warners' studio to interview the film's star: "She smiled archly under highly luxurious, incredibly lengthy eyelashes and wiggled her sizeable toes in her stockinged feet. 'I can't eat a morsel while I have the things on,' she gasped. 'Excuse me while I fix the little thing that holds my stockings up, so I can sit comfortably.... I had to take off ten pounds for this picture and these tarnation corsets,' she sighed sadly."[62] The film required Sydney to play two women, instead of the usual one: a widow and a nurse. The designer of his feminine togs was Margaret Whistler, who remembered finding it very difficult to fit a man in women's clothing, despite Sydney's seemingly unending patience with the task.[63] Critic Mordaunt Hall offered his assessment of the costuming: "In several of the sequences he is garbed in widow's weeds, the masquerading attire of a burly bootlegger who is known as the veiled runner. When he is kicked over the traces enough in these skirts, he tackles the costume of a nurse, who through ignorance of clinical implements uses an ordinary thermometer, a hot spoon and a hammer on a poor man to ascertain whether he has a temperature."[64]

Again, after its March 7 release in New York, reviewers wrote negatively about the film, saying that it was filled with too much comic business and gags and strayed too far from what promised to be an interesting plot.[65] Hall concurred in the *New York Times*: "The present offering is an improvement on 'The Man on the Box,' but is far from being as wildly funny as 'Charley's Aunt,' in which Sydney Chaplin first appeared in skirts.... Mr. Chaplin errs in using his so-called gags too frequently in this obstreperous mileage of slapstick, in which it is true that not a single lemon meringue pie is thrown. There are, however, two hats that are crushed, and on four occasions Sydney Chaplin tosses a liqueur into the fire with explosive results."⁶⁶ Edwin Schallert was more positive, calling the film "breezy and bright.... It is such a shot-gun prescription of mirth that it will arouse a laugh, a chuckle, and even an occasionally great old-fashioned hilarious roar from practically every person who happens to see it."⁶⁷ And with Schallert the film-going public seemed to agree. In Los Angeles, it was held over three weeks at the Figueroa Theatre, instead of the two *The Man on the Box* enjoyed.⁶⁸ So, while the critics and the public were not entirely in agreement about this film, they would be about the next — one which Sydney had been working toward in his mind since the days of World War I.

* * *

The boys went to Palm Springs this time to develop the adaptation of Sydney's next film, *The Better 'Ole*, an event lasting about three weeks that made the papers with a photo of the group "in conference."⁶⁹ They returned to Hollywood to begin production about March 7. With the start of production, the press concentrated on the fact that Sydney would swap his skirt for army togs in this film: "Syd departs abruptly from the types of roles he has been portraying for the last year or more. No longer is he hampered by clinging skirts, flaming garters and high-heel pumps, for the humorous Warner Brothers' star again assumes his breeches."⁷⁰ This wasn't the only thing new about the production.

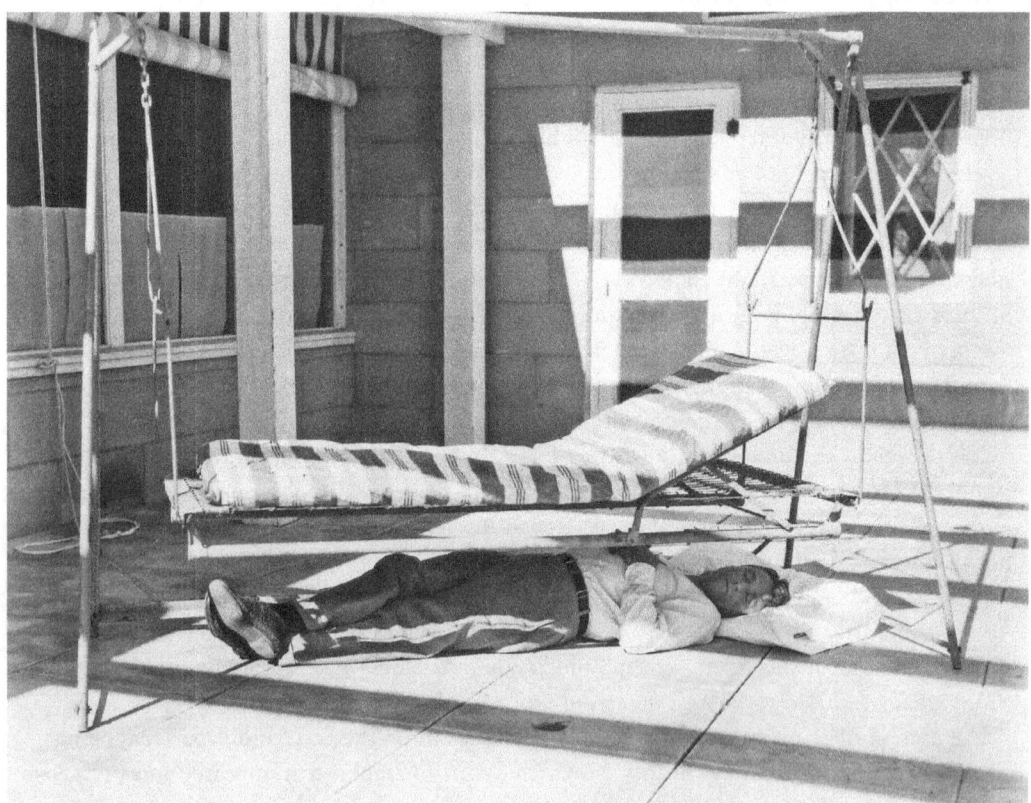

Taking a nap between story conferences for *The Better 'Ole*, the Desert Inn, Palm Springs, California, 1925 (AMPAS).

According to Zanuck, Sydney was to step up his assault on women at the studio, his fellow employees taking note of the fact by hanging a clapper board to his dressing room door with "Take 4" written on it, announcing the number of "female scalps" he had taken that day.[71] Also new was the fact that six of the original eight Keystone Cops found themselves working on the production, creating a sort of "good old days" reunion. They were Hank Mann, Edgar Kennedy, Bill Hauber, Grover Ligon, Billy Gilbert and Tom Kennedy.[72] Then, of course, Sydney, Reisner and Zanuck were also graduates of the Mack Sennett school.

The Warner Bros. archive records show that the company gained rights for the Bairnsfather and Eliot story — but only the silent rights — on March 4, 1926.[73] Previous to this, on January 21, a reading of a synopsis of the original play was performed for significant Warner's personnel by Burl Ives.[74] Bairnsfather himself was reportedly pleased with the choice of Sydney for the Old Bill characterization: "I think it is particularly fitting that Syd Chaplin, who is an Englishman, should play Old Bill. Syd's experience in the music halls of England gives him exactly the right perspective. He has instinctively the British sense of humor."[75] Sydney himself seemed able to quantify his motivation for the role: "I knew just what sort of chap he was, this Old Bill. A pothouse politician. I know that kind. So I understood not only how he would act and what he would say, but what he thought, too. During the picture we often planned a gag and then stopped and decided that Bill wouldn't do that. So, I think he is real."[76]

In an editorial entitled, coincidentally, "The Better 'Ole" that appeared in the *Oakland Tribune* shortly before the Warner Brothers' 1926 release of its new film adaptation of the play by the same name, the writer comments on a recent article from the *Atlantic Monthly,* whose author, "A Returning American," promoted the claim that "in every important respect, America was inferior to England.... The editorial writer argues, however, that "there is another and larger class of returning Americans who have a different reaction. They regard residence abroad as a sort of prison sentence, and rejoice to be back in a country that has ice water, steam heat, bathrooms, beefsteaks, decent tobacco and readable sporting pages."[77] America as "The Better 'Ole" was fast becoming the majority opinion of residents here, as its World War I achievements, followed by a booming 1920s economy, allowed its citizens to mentally separate themselves from the old world of their forefathers — especially that of the British Isles — and wallow in a new, fresh-faced American optimism and sense of American-ness. But this growing sensibility in America must have given the film industry pause, especially when a company like Warner Bros. made the decision to purchase an old worn-out story about British Tommies in World War I for its new successful comedy star, Syd Chaplin, for there wasn't an American character in that script — and what was a "Tommy" anyway? How would they put it over?

A "tommie" (sometimes "Tommy Atkins") is simply a common nickname for a British foot soldier. In use since at least 1815, many a song and poem utilized this appellation, much as Rudyard Kipling did in his 1892 poem, "Tommy," of which this is the first stanza:

> I went into a public-'ouse to get a pint o' beer,
> The publican 'e up an' sez, "We serve no red-coats here."
> The girls be'ind the bar they laughed an' giggled fit to die,

Cast and crew of *The Better 'Ole* (Warner Bros., 1926) with Sydney front and center (in Old Bill makeup), Hank Mann, second row far left, Chuck Reisner, second row fourth from left, and Darryl F. Zanuck, to Chuck's right (CHACHAA).

> I outs into the street again an' to myself sez I:
> *O it's Tommy this, an' Tommy that, an' "Tommy, go away";*
> *But it's "Thank you, Mister Atkins," when the band begins to play,*
> *The band begins to play, my boys, the band begins to play,*
> *O it's "Thank you, Mister Atkins," when the band begins to play.*

Because of the gravity of World War I, however, the term is now mostly used to refer to the rank-and-file British soldiers of only this war, much as Americans used the term "doughboys." The Tommy of World War I was probably no better portrayed in literature or art than in the caricatures and cartoons of Captain (Charles) Bruce Bairnsfather, who survived the war to relate his exploits to the world. In other words, Bairnfather's play about these experiences, entitled *The Better 'Ole*, was immediately successful in 1917 when it was first produced.

Bairnsfather developed a humorous series for the *Bystander* life in the trenches, which later appeared in book form as *Fragments from France* (1917). This series featured the "Old Bill" character, a curmudgeonly soldier with trademark walrus moustache and balaclava, later the protagonist of *The Better 'Ole*, which developed out of a cartoon with the caption, "If you know of a better 'ole, go to it." Considered "vulgar caricature" by some, Bairnsfather's work was very popular with the troops, a fact which Sydney himself had noted when searching for justification for Charlie's filming *Shoulder Arms* during wartime. In about 1916, Bairnsfather developed a sketch for the stage out of a drawing called "The Johnson 'Ole," which was literally a black, smoke-filled shell-hole that resulted after a German fusillade of shrapnel and gas-filled bombs. Andre Charlot, of "Charlot's Revue," saw the skit and suggested he expand it to a full-length play.[78] So, by the end of summer 1917, Bairnsfather had partnered with Captain Bruce Eliot to turn his "Old Bill" series into a stage play entitled *The Better 'Ole, or The Romance of Old Bill*. It premiered on August 4 at the Oxford Theatre in London, eventually playing for 811 performances in five traveling companies over the next few years. Arthur Bourchier, an established Shakespearean actor born in 1863, played Old Bill, which became the most successful role of his career. For this production, Bairnsfather is noted to have also designed the sets. This British production ran successfully for more than a year before it made its way to the United States.

Charles Coburn and his wife, Ivah, successfully won the American rights and took over the Greenwich Village Theatre in mid–September 1918 to begin rehearsals. Coburn, along with his wife, had formed a production company called the Coburn Shakespearean Players in 1905, but only counted two Broadway productions to their credit by the time they took on *The Better 'Ole, or The Romance of Old Bill* (as it was properly called) in 1918. It was to make both of their careers. Opening on October 19, the *New York Times*'s reviewer claimed that the play itself was "as artless and unsophisticated as were the original drawings. The plot is childlike in its simplicity. The music, composed, selected and arranged by Herman Darewski and Percival Knight is mostly selected and arranged."[79] What stood out for this reviewer, however, was Coburn's "Old Bill" and Bairnsfather and Eliot's finesse in putting him on the stage: "This 'Bill' of the theatre is a work of the broadest sympathy combined with the most delicate art. He is the Old Walrus of the cartoons, with his pendant-mud-guard of a mustache, his impregnable ignorance, and his racy, basic humanity; but he is also Mr. Coburn's Bill, with a thousand indefinable touches of character and humor that mark an authentic creation."[80] Coburn's production ran 353 performances, closing only because of an Actor's Guild strike on October 4, 1919.

Meanwhile, over in England, the Welsh, Pearson & Company, Ltd. was readying a seven-reel version of the play for the silent screen at Twickenham Studios. Thomas A. Welsh and George Pearson had signed a contract on October 31, 1917, granting them exclusive films rights to *The Better 'Ole* five years from the date of its first public screening. Production began in January 1918 with actor Charles Rock in the role of Old Bill. Rock had been in films since 1901 and was to die shortly after *The Better 'Ole*'s release, in July 1919. This version was released April 22, 1918, in England and February 23, 1919, in America, where it played concurrently with the seven road companies engaged to perform the stage version (an entertainment first). In fact, in advertisements for this film, the suggestion was that this screen version was simply a filming of the play, which could be viewed by audiences at a much cheaper ticket price. With a total production budget of only £5000, Welsh & Pearson's adaptation "was much more symbolic than the Bairnsfather-Eliot play."[81] A reviewer for the *Oakland Tribune* made the Britishness of the film palpable for potential viewers when he described the portrayal of Old Bill as "Old Bill, he of the walrus mustache, who stands as a mighty symbol of the smiling courage that characterized Tommy Atkins in the world war."[82] The *Lethbridge Daily Herald* describes him as symbolizing "British pluck, tenacity and resourcefulness," relating also that *The Better 'Ole* itself is "brimful of humor, but it also contains a moral and its message will certainly not be overlooked by the public." The reviewer suggests that Bill, in his heart of hearts, actually takes the war quite seriously, therefore what the viewer should take away from the film is the knowledge of the humor of *our* brave boys, who display the lighter vein of human nature under most tragic, appalling circumstances."[83] His use of "our," rather than "their" in this final line perhaps offers some foreshadowing of the direction the next film version of the story will try to take. In fact, advertisements for the American trade press, like the one shown here, attempted to interest theatre owners by linking Old Bill with Charlie's Little Tramp character, who had been featured in *Shoulder Arms*, just the year before.

Even this 1919 version broke records, despite it being in competition with the stage version. The film premiered at the Strand Theatre in New York City. The manager of the theatre, Joseph L. Plunkett, reported in the *Moving Picture World* that he was initially instructed to consider the film simply a comedy that happened to have a war-era setting. "I was advised to subdue the war element and the British soldier element entirely in my advertising and in the show surrounding the picture," he reported. "I did nothing of the kind."[84] Instead, Plunkett worked to get past any reticence on the part of his American audience by playing up the exoticness of this story and its characters. "The very nature of the picture," he said, "made it a novelty to a public that witnesses only American stories and American atmosphere."[85] Bookings for the film worldwide grossed £40,000. Unfortunately, no copy of it exists today.

Each of these versions, though presumably different in some elements, portrayed essentially the same story — a story of British Tommies fighting in and surviving World War I. Bairnsfather and Eliot's play centered on Britain — British patriotism, citizenship, and philosophy. As America entered the 1920s, however, she began to turn her back on her long-estranged mother country, trying less to emulate her and more to diverge from her. Soon, American English would drop its "re" vs. "er" as in "centre" and its "our" as in "colour" and other British-inspired spellings. Congress would pass into law America's first immigration quota in 1924, known as the Johnson-Reed Act that limited the granting of immigration visas to 2 percent of the total number of people of each nationality in the United States, and completely excluded immigrants from Asia. America, with these and other developments, following on the heels of her successful aid of the Allied Nations in World War I, began to define herself differently — not yet as a world power, perhaps, but certainly as a new player on the world stage. Given these and similar developments, when Warner Bros. negotiated for the rights to Bairnsfather and Eliot's play for development into a project for Sydney, perhaps Reisner and Zanuck — the writers chosen to do the screen adaptation and Americans themselves — naturally modified Bairnsfather and Eliot's original script with an American audience in mind. Reisner and Zanuck's star was British, but even he had been trying to please American audiences as an American comedy star on and off for ten years.

Because the Welsh-Pearson film no longer exists and the script of the original play seems to be non-existent, this synopsis is used here to measure the significant differences between the 1919 and 1926 film productions, or, in other words, the original and the Warners' version. And they are significant. Warners' *The Better 'Ole* reportedly cost the studio $392,331 to make. It ran ten reels and employed the use of authentic military technology such as jeeps, motorcycles, planes and artillery as a backdrop to the story it set about to tell. Most of the supporting actors were scheduled to begin shooting near the end of February 1926, the script in the Warners' collection marked "Final" and dated February 20, 1926, presumably heralded the start of the production.[86] Zanuck and Reisner were the credited scriptwriters, but there is no question that Sydney, as always, had significant input on the final script, despite his lack of credit.

By focusing on three significant differences that exist between the original Bairnsfather and Eliot play and the Warners' 1926 version it can be demonstrated that these differences allow the story to better accommodate an American audience: the introductory scenes, the role of espionage in the film, and the animosity developed between Corporal Quint and Old Bill in the film, a relationship that didn't even exist in the original play. Besides the elaborate gags included in the Warners' version, other differences include the role of women, which is almost non-existent in the Warners' version, despite playing a significant role in the original, and the differences in the endings. In the original version, Bill, Alf and Bert are shown back in Old Blighty (England) taking up their previous roles in the local community, except that Bill's wife, Maggie, has invested her husband's wages in a new business for him — as proprietor of a public house.

The original play opens in a French village schoolroom, behind the front, that has been converted into some sort of bar/dance hall in which both French and English soldiers and a couple of dozen local French girls are passing the time. Old Bill becomes the life of the party when he launches into a rendition of "Tipperary" here, which he is allowed to finish before the colonel and captain make their announcement to the troops that they must move up to the front on the following day. In fact, the original play was a musical, having the performance of nine songs as enhancement for the spoken dialogue. The farewell moments between the troops and the girls allow for a bit of display of both music and dance, allowing the play to present the feeling of a variety show. In the Warners' version, however, the first moments of the film take place in the German headquarters, setting up the importance of espionage in the film as a whole. Unbeknownst to the audience, in this scene we are introduced to Major Russet, who will later reveal himself as a German spy, disguised as a British officer. The next few moments show Bill and Alf stranded in "No Man's Land" and the last of the Bairnsfather trio, Bert, having arrived back at the British trenches anxious about their fate. Unlike the play, Bert is immediately introduced in the film as an intelligence officer investigating espionage. In the play he is merely a lothario, making his rounds among the female population, in both France and back home in England.

While espionage and Bill's unfortunate involvement in it is important to the original play, it becomes the central focus of Warners' version. In Act I of the original, Bill is clued into the fact that a character named DuBois is in possession of a blue sheet of paper that seems to carry a secret message. As the Warners' synopsis indicates,

> Old Bill snatches the paper from Dubois who makes an effort to recover it. DuBois pretends and protests the paper is nothing of importance. However, Old Bill's suspicions are aroused when he sees the map drawn upon it. DuBois offers money to Bill for the return of the paper

and Bill accepts, but instead of giving him the real paper, substitutes a piece of music, which he finds on the piano, then, taking the money, blows the light before Dubois knows he has been duped ... and trapped. Then Bill saunters out with the information tucked snugly in his tunic.[87]

Old Bill discovers the presence of espionage in the French village of Boucaret by happening upon a system of carrier pigeons, which only later becomes linked to the German spy, this time named Russet. Far more military action occurs in this version because of the information transmitted by spies: Boucaret is forcibly taken by the Germans in one scene and when the information is received that the Brits intend to retake the village the next day, a bridge is rigged to explode and kill these returning forces. No French troops either appear in the film or are referred to in it. In the original version, it is only when Bill encounters a French girl, Victoire (Doris Hill), who is able to decipher DuBois's blue note that he finds out the impending threat to his fellow soldiers. Victoire tells him that the Germans know that the French intend to attack the enemy along the river. To counter this attack, the bridge has been mined and must be fired ten minutes after it, thereby cutting off the French troops (or British) and trapping them. In both versions, Bill acts alone on the bridge, with somewhat different results, but in the original version, Alf, Bert and Victoire at least have knowledge of what he plans to do.

In the original version, there is certainly the usual pecking order set up between enlisted and commissioned men. However, there is no one-on-one animosity evident between Bill and his comrades and the next in command. In the Warners' version, however, everything is made of the army class system. The character of Corporal Quint (Edgar Kennedy) is created seemingly to get Bill's goat. Much comedy springs from the interaction of the two — none of which appears in the original version. In some ways, this interaction simply works well for slapstick comedy, which, of course, is at the heart of the Warners' version, if only because it has chosen Sydney for the central role. But in other ways, it works to set up an adversarial relationship between the rank-and-file soldier and the next-in-command, which leads naturally to the altered ending of the film. In this version, Old Bill ends up in trouble for bombing the bridge, not because he disobeyed orders, but because he is not supported by the higher-ups — including Russet and Corporal Quint. It is this adversarial relationship and the importance of the individual military hero over the military team that seems important here. Sydney's Bill faces the firing squad, while Bairnsfather and Eliot's, only a court-martial.

Warners' Old Bill fails to return home to England in the final scenes to his new life as publican, perhaps because America was in the bloody throes of Prohibition in 1926. Sydney's Old Bill remains on the battlefield, having just won the most important battle of his life. The scenes of the Brits returning to take back Boucare, show off to the filmgoer their military might in troop numbers, in weaponry and in mastery of both land and air, must have reminded the mid–1920s moviegoer of America's effective last-minute role vanquishing the Allies through similar means. Old Bill and his compatriots are British, with his caterwauling diction, and his Anglo-centric dug-out decorations, but he feels more American in this film, a least to some extent.

Warners' film managed to take an old story, with old, nearly forgotten characters, and make it a new hit. It premiered on October 7 in New York and November 18 in L.A.

at Grauman's Egyptian Theatre,[88] where Sid Grauman presented the film on opening night in his usual extravagant fashion. Sydney failed to attend. Several years later he wrote to friend Jim Minney about his fear of seeing himself onscreen and of attending such events:

> You will be surprised to know that I have never seen "Charley's Aunt" in a theatre & only once on the screen in the cutting room. The same with "The Better 'Ole." This picture had it premiere at Sid Grauman's theatre in Hollywood, which is an event in that burg.... You can imagine Grauman's feelings when I failed to turn up. I was the only star that had ever let him down. I did not do it to be different, but because I was too d—d nervous. I walked around the theatre several times, took a look at the crowds outside & went straight home to bed, so that I could have a plausible excuse of illness if he sent someone home for me. I am afraid I made an enemy for life. He has never been the same to me since.[89]

Celebrities that did show up included William Randolph Hearst, Marcus Loew, William Gibbs McAdoo, Mayor Cryer of Los Angeles and Mayor James Rolph of San Francisco.[90]

Premiere night program at the Grauman's Egyptian Theatre, Hollywood, for *The Better 'Ole* (Warner Bros., 1926) (CHACHAA).

Perhaps part of this version's success was due to the fact that *The Better 'Ole* was only the second film to feature a Vitaphone soundtrack, and in fact, many believe that the series of talking Vitaphone shorts, including one featuring Al Jolson singing "Red, Red Robin" and a few other popular songs, were the draw of the evening.[91] But, Vitaphone soundtrack or not, Sydney and his cohorts received rave reviews for their efforts. Mordaunt Hall was truly won over this time, noting that the film was "truly a Hollywood notice of 'The Better 'Ole.'"[92] *Picture Play* magazine commented, "Syd surpasses his own record, and one trembles for fear his later pictures may not live up to his present one. Incidentally, this is one of the rare instances when a film is better than the play from which it was taken."[93] Other reviewers noted that the film was "a tornado of such excellent and sustained entertainment as is all too rarely swept into Broadway" and "without a doubt the most sensational laughter-making production of the year."[94] It ran for 24 weeks in New York City before packing them in and turning folks away around the rest of the country. Representative of "the rest of the country" is the review in the Fitchburg (MA) *Sentinel,* which noted that the film's capacity crowd offered up "a spontaneous and hefty applause at the end."[95] Many of the smaller venues only received the film in April or May of 1927 and were still holding it over an extra week or two in order to satisfy demand. Whatever Zanuck and Reisner did to that script appeared to have worked.

Back in July, shortly before the title of his next film was announced, but during the weeks he spent in Catalina with Reisner and Zanuck working on the scenario, Sydney was engaged in serious correspondence with his old friend Arthur Kelly about possibilities for his next film contract. Kelly was promoting First National to Sydney initially, alerting him on July 8 that Earl Hudson, who was probably negotiating his own future as a manager for that company, was to be in Hollywood, providing Sydney a good opportunity to discuss a deal.[96] It seems that Sydney had some promise from Charlie for financing his future films, however, as Kelly mentions this in his cable and Sydney himself reiterates the fact two weeks later: "Charlie is very anxious that I do not renew my contract with Warner Brothers and has offered to finance me without any cost to me — even without charging any interest for the money, as he is desirous that I release thru United Artists." According to Sydney, Jack Warner had already approached him with a deal — another three-year contract — except that Sydney wanted an additional $2,000 a week over what his original contract provided and Warner only wanted to offer $1,000.[97] If true, this claim contradicts the mythology surrounding Sydney's Warners contract — that being that Warners had had enough of his escapades offscreen and refused to consider renewing it. A week later, Kelly countered with his usual candid advice — advice only an old and trusted friend could risk giving Sydney: "I make one suggestion, however, that if you do consent to have Charlie finance you, you get all the money you want for your production before you start. Otherwise, you are apt to have trouble because if he finances you week by week as he does with his own pictures, there will be too many people telling you that you are spending too much money and you do not want to put yourself in this position." Releasing through United Artists, Kelly wrote, had its own challenges, mainly that Sydney would have to begin financing his second picture before he received any revenues on the first, because UA did not make any advance on the negative. All of this advice on Kelly's part was really provided to convince Sydney that he needed to be on salary with someone, that he didn't want to take on too much again (as he had done with Famous Players–Lasky): "But you must remember, Sid, that nothing big was ever gained without taking some responsibility and I believe that you could organize yourself in such a way that no more responsibility will be placed on your shoulders than you now have with Warner Bros."[98]

The title of his next project was announced August 12 as being *The Missing Link*.[99] After working on the scenario with Reisner and Zanuck over on Catalina for several weeks, Sydney had met and enjoyed a game of golf with Earl Hudson one day, took him fishing the next, played more golf each of two successive days thereafter and then took Hudson and his wife to dinner and a show. This is a good description of the way Sydney worked best. Although he never really trusted anyone completely and everyone in his life probably expected to be either rejected or abandoned by him at some point in their relationship, he was certainly good at "courtship." He knew how to entertain, was witty and a great conversationalist, and had a great sense of humor. He was able to project a gregarious amicability that was really only bait he used to reel a person in. Once cap-

Sydney's "health nut" publicity campaign, 1927 (LKSC).

tured, however, Sydney seldom discovered a fish that didn't stink in some way and then promptly wanted to throw it back. The stinky fish in August 1926 became Warner Bros. Less than a month after they had tried to sign him up again, he became rankled — paranoid and distrustful of their dealings with him. First, he had found out that Warners had tried to cut *The Better 'Ole* to eight reels without consulting him (it remained at nine after previewed to audiences, however). Second, he blamed Warners then for the bad reviews he had received from critics, because he claimed that all of his Warners films had suffered in the cutting: "I have found that the trouble with Warner Brothers is that they have nothing on their minds but getting belly-laughs and the first thing to be cut in a picture is the story and the finer acting scenes. No wonder the critics say that the pictures are merely a potpourri of slapstick gags." Third, he was beginning to discover that since he had not renewed his contract, publicity for his films was gradually diminishing: "I am receiving practically nothing, and it was very little before."[100] And finally, Warners was supposedly screwing him on returns. This last complaint would resurface again and again, until it's certain that Warners finally did look forward to seeing Sydney's backside after the completion of his last film a few months later. Kelly tried his best, in the meantime, to convince Sydney that he must consider his salary the end of his compensation for a picture and consider any small percentage he received as mad money, but to no avail.[101] By the end of October, Kelly still believed that Sydney would soon be producing his own films at Charlie's studios, but, of course, this never happened, probably due to two important crises just on the horizon: one involving Lita Grey and one involving the tax man.

Meanwhile, as *The Missing Link* production began, Sydney was enjoying life at the bachelor's table at the Montmartre restaurant on Hollywood Boulevard.[102] A married man, he was living the bachelor-est of bachelor existences and it is unclear when and if he spent time with or co-habitated a residence with his wife, Minnie. She lived her own life, filled with friends and family and travel — to New York whenever she wanted or anywhere in America. It seems certain that she was given *carte blanche* terms of her expenditures, probably as compensation for the open marriage arrangement she had with Sydney, for it could only have been that, given Sydney's comportment.

The Missing Link, a story written entirely by the Chaplin-Reisner-Zanuck team is, in some ways, Sydney's return to the supposed land of his conception, Africa, in a characterization that allows him to face all the fears and insecurities that location and its baggage had caused him over the years. The original story treatment was simply titled "Syd Chaplin in Africa."[103] The setting is not just Africa, but Cape Town, South Africa, the specific location of his mother's folktale of the experience. The Great White Hunter character of the story is named Lord Dryden — a figure for the wealthy sire the original folktale contained, but also one named after Leo Dryden, father of his half-brother Wheeler and one of the first male figures in his life who had some impact. Sydney's character — in the film version a timid poet named Arthur Wells — is in the original story treatment "a derelict, homeless and hungry, munching a salvaged sandwich." He is "alone and lost in the world, spirited with ambitions, but lacking the courage to see them thru,"[104] and possesses a phobia of all animals. He decides to stow away on a ship he thinks is bound for America, the land of opportunity, but ends up in Africa instead. Over the course of the film, however, suffering through the many trials and tribulations confronting him, the character becomes the Great White Hunter, winning the girl in the bargain. In the treatment especially, the plot is nearly his life, or at least of his vision of that life.

Lord Dryden, the original Great White Hunter in the film, (Crauford Kent), is invited to Africa by Colonel Braden (Tom McGuire) to enjoy a celebration there of his

6. Stardom and a Tenuous Homecoming

Ruth Hiatt and Sydney in costume for *The Missing Link* (Warner Bros., 1927) (LKSC).

exploits to be given by his daughter Beatrice (Ruth Hiatt). Arthur Wells, a poet, has been hired by Dryden as a sort of luggage handler, but he gets stuck on board as the ship sails and hides in Dryden's cabin. Discovering him there, Dryden decides to play a hoax on his African hosts (who've never seen him) and dress Wells in his clothes as The Great White Hunter. Once in Africa, Wells falls hard for Beatrice. Meanwhile, the Missing Link — a sometime threat to the residents of the area — goes on one of its rampages. Of course, the Great White Hunter is called upon to rid the village of this menace. Akka, the chimp, a Braden family pet, is mistaken by Wells for this missing link and so he goes armed with Akka's favorite food — chocolate fudge — to try to capture him. While the real missing link (not Akka) attacks Beatrice, Wells realizes his mistake and then recruits Akka to help in the counterattack. Wells places Akka on his shoulders and covers them over with drapery, making what appears to be a giant "thing" that is now aiming its hostile attentions right at the beast. Distracted with fudge, the beast is backed into a post and lassoed there by Wells and Akka. Beatrice is revived, proposed to and consequently married.

Although this film featured a number of animal stars, Akka was one of the best known. His best scene in the film was considered to be the kitchen scene in the African camp:

> Coming into the room and jumping on a chair, the chimpanzee spies a plate filled with eggs. Looking slyly around, Akka is assured no one is watching him. Picking up one of the eggs,

he lets it fall to the floor in an experimental manner. After regarding the results for a moment, he throws the next. Then with increasing force, he throws the remainder of the eggs, jumping higher and higher and laughing harder and harder at the results.[105]

The chimp also had a penchant for fat bald-headed men. He liked to slink up to the fat man and sneak his hat off his head, then kiss the bald spot! Numa, the lion from Gay's lion farm that also was to appear with Charlie in *The Circus*, was also featured and Sydney had a turn or two with this old guy. With Numa on top of him, Charlie Gay, the trainer, was just offstage, doing what he needed to do to get the lion to growl and spit. Then he became deadly quiet, as if he had just noticed Sydney's presence, and Gay couldn't regain the lion's attention. Finally, in desperation, Gay took out a revolver and shot into the air. This seemed to break the spell, for Numa got up and walked back to his cage, Gay shouting expletives at him in French all the while. He later told Sydney: "If I hadn't gotten his attention when I did, he would have slapped you silly!"[106]

Although he had blamed Warners' cutting techniques for making his films a sort of collection of gags in a bag, without any real characterization or plot, in November he spoke to the press about the value of the slapstick gag in comedy films, as if hinting that this film would be more of the same: "Slapstick in pictures is no more dead than pictures themselves. The only difference between slapstick today and yesterday is that slapstick which is broad then is dressed up today."[107] Due to the growing appreciation of the moviegoer's mentality, the director today might introduce slapstick into a film subtly, i.e., instead of hitting an actor in the face with a pie, he might only suggest such an act, by placing a custard pie in the vicinity of an arguing couple. The meaning is understood — the joke goes over — but the pie is never really thrown. But, as he predicted, such little articles in the press started to diminish. Warners was no longer spending much money on publicizing his work. So, Sydney spent his own money on a publicity campaign at this time, in which he appeared in very little clothing — essentially a tank top and boxer shorts — performing every kind of sporting activity, from boxing, to acrobatics, tennis and even horseback riding. In mid–October, the photos were being published in the press, showing him "keeping fit for picture work."[108] Perhaps the irony of this endeavor is that the salubrious Sydney succumbed to the flu in late December around the holidays before production was complete,[109] thereby causing the first delay in his Warners' tenure and one that may have been a tactic to remain under the Warner banner, completing his last two films, for as long as possible. Did he have a plan for the future at this point? Did he have a new contract in the works?

The Missing Link was not released then until May 6, 1927, in New York at the Colony Theater and on June 18 in Los Angeles at the Forum Theater, where it was held over for a second week.[110] The New York premiere was a benefit for the Hebrew Orphan Asylum of New York. Mordaunt Hall actually liked the film, writing that "there are sequences in this comic contraption that are almost certain to appeal to anybody." His focus on Akka, the chimpanzee, however, suggests that the animal stole the show from its star: "Akka ... gives a sterling account of himself, manifesting an uncanny talent for acting before the camera."[111] Quinn Martin deemed the film "a fairly funny picture," but also noted that he felt it a well-timed burlesque of the popular wild animal adventure picture.[112] These reviews are fairly lukewarm and don't particularly belie the huge amount of money Warners' made on the film. In the period 1926–27, *The Missing Link* made the most of any silent film produced by Warners.[113] It cost $313,000 to make and earned $608,000: "The other twenty-five silent films had costs between $57,000 and $214,000 and earnings between $184,000 and $373,000."[114] Sydney clearly still had a following, but he was almost out of time — and luck.

Meanwhile, Charlie's second marriage was nearing its end and with it, Sydney's hopes for having Charlie finance his upcoming film productions. But, his continuing correspondence with Sidney Garrett of Inter-globe Export Corp., and by November, many other concerns (according to his letterhead), shows that Charlie had long been out of the picture anyway. Garrett wanted so badly in this letter to tell Sydney exactly the story he had ready for him to film, in order to entice him to sign, however, given the insecurity of such correspondence, he never named it or the company involved — couldn't name them, he claimed: "We have the TITLE, and we are going to have a story written around same by the best possible author we can find, and we presume with this TITLE we shall be able to get the English, French and Belgian Governments greatly interested in this proposition, and it has occurred to me that a great part, in fact *the biggest part* in your career could be found in this story."[115] Garrett suggested that Sydney send along a modest proposal regarding his salary requirements to keep the momentum going on the project. A month later, Garrett had received Sydney's "modest" proposal of $200,000 per picture, a sum he claims to have been offered in America. Garrett tried to explain, however, that the present state of the British filmmaking business couldn't bear such costs. Garrett was not put off by Sydney's demands, however, and seems to have had a personal stake in the whole deal, a fact that comes to light in later communications between the two men. He proposed meeting Sydney in Kansas City, Indianapolis or Chicago the first week in February 1927 to talk further and more candidly about the deal.[116] Although it is not known whether or not the meeting ever took place, Sydney did not leave for Palm Springs to work on *The Fortune Hunter* until mid–February, so the meeting was at least a possibility for him. What is certain is that the film — even the story — Garrett spoke of never materialized. Whether or not the company Garrett was negotiating in that instance was British International Pictures, the company with whom Sydney eventually signed is unclear, however, Garrett does serve as intermediary in the British International deal signed sometime in June 1927, so it is highly likely they are one and the same.

Meanwhile, Lita left Charlie's house in Beverly Hills with her two children on November 30 and filed for divorce on January 10.[117] The tax man followed close on her heels, after Charlie's studio safes were opened to receivers on January 18. Charlie had gone to New York to consult with his lawyer, Nathan Burkan, in an attempt to stay out of the public eye, thereby leaving Sydney back in Hollywood to try to watch over the studio. Sydney himself was completely flabbergasted at the whole situation: "It was like a bombshell to me. I did not believe that she could be so vindictive as to actually try to ruin you." Finishing up *The Missing Link* at that time, it was easy for him to keep one eye over on La Brea and Sunset and he usually didn't like what he was observing there. He wrote a poignant letter to his brother in New York with his concerns: "I noticed that several people are still walking around the studio — such as publicity men, etc. and I am wondering if you know they are still on salary and if you want to keep up this big expense as your future actions are so indefinite."[118] Charlie settled his income tax debt with a payment of $1 million. Sydney was luckier, for the Bureau of Internal Revenue report shows that he had actually overpaid taxes for 1925 by about $4,000. It also showed he had only earned $57,498.55 in 1925 and $20,308.61 in 1926—figures that seem modest given the fact that he was to have achieved one of the highest-paying contracts in the business with his Warners' deal.

There was much confusion in the press about what exactly Sydney's last film for Warners would be. In early December 1926 it was announced that his next story would be *The New Boy,* an English comedy by Arthur Law that was first staged in 1894. Sydney would have played the role of Archibald Rennick in this farce. The story centered on an aging teacher, Horace Candy, who was trying to decide whom to settle his estate upon, being childless. He at first chose his first cousin, Martha, with whom he had been estranged for years, but who he knew to be a widow and to have a son. Unbeknownst to him, she had remarried and to Rennick, a man of small stature and small success in life. Arriving for a visit with only the new husband, Martha discovered that Candy's will stipulated that she could not remarry if she planned to inherit. Within seconds, she converted her new husband into her 14-year-old son and the rest of the play involved the ludicrous situations surrounding that deception and its discovery. Rex Taylor was supposedly adapting the story for Sydney.[119] Into 1927, however, as promising as *The New Boy* sounded, a story called "The Race Track Tout" was announced, with director Chuck Reisner still at the helm.[120] The story finally chosen was *The Fortune Hunter* by Winchell Smith, written in 1909. This had already been presented in two film adaptations, one by Lubin in 1914 and one by Vitagraph in 1920, starring Earle Williams in the title role of Nat Duncan. John Barrymore had gained much acclaim playing that role on the stage. With this choice, it is clear that Sydney had not dropped the bar in terms of his own performance ambitions, but as the reviews for this film would suggest, the Warners adaptation did not live up to the reputation this play had already built in the minds of its audience.

On February 13, Robert Dillon was hired to help Reisner and Brian Foy, son of Eddie Foy, in writing the scenario for the film.[121] The story conferences again took place in Palm Springs at the Desert Inn. Darryl Zanuck had abandoned Sydney's ship at this point, but Reisner stayed on. Writing to Kelly from the desert, Sydney noted John Barrymore's success with the story as it existed, but suggested his writing team would be "jazzing it up a bit to get the laughs." Palm Springs was experiencing torrential rains and flooding at the time: "At present we are cut off from all outside communication—no mail—telephone wires down and all roads washed out—with only three days' supply of food in the town, but we are not worrying as the rain has let up a bit today and if the worst came to worst, we would have to depend on aeroplanes for our supplies. We used to go horseback riding in the morning, telling ourselves we needed the exercise to keep our brains from getting fagged.... In the afternoon we sat down at our typewriters and banged off our ideas. Thus we constructed what we call a straight-line story."[122] Gags were something to worry about back at the studio, where props would often inspire comedy. These concerns, however, barely scratched the surface of his present worries, most of which centered around his brother Charlie and how he must have been feeling post-divorce. Sydney was engaging in a sort of campaign with Kelly to send Charlie as much evidence as possible of his well-wishers around the world. He writes Kelly, "I think that complaint swung the public sympathy in his favour."[123] Still working in his brother's behalf in Charlie's absence, he had managed to get both Charlie's Rolls Royce and any money left in a studio bank account away and in safe-keeping while the receivers did their work. In addition, he and wife Minnie were working hard to collect as much damning evidence against Lita as they could, hoping Charlie's lawyers could use it in court.[124]

In the film resulting from the Palm Springs conferences, Nat Duncan, a bouncer at a café, spots his old colleague, Harry West, on the arm of a sugar mommy, and is advised to get one of his own. West offers to tutor Duncan in the finer aspects of the art, for half the money he acquires upon marriage. Duncan agrees. West outfits Duncan in style, then sends him off to seek his fortune in the small town of Radville, where he quickly becomes recognized as a man of leisure, a churchgoer, and subsequently, a lady-killer: "Chief among Nat's admirers is Josie Lockwood (Helene Costello), daughter of the richest, and one of the meanest, men in the district."[125] Duncan gets a job at the pharmacy, which he finds is near bankruptcy. He promptly pays off the pharmacist's debts and in his position as part owner, decides to make the place a successful prospect. Instead of falling for Lockwood, however, he falls in love with the pharmacist's granddaughter, Betty Graham (Clara Horton), a girl with no fortune attached to her. West shows up, having lost the sugar mommy, and proceeds to hurry along a match between Duncan and the rich girl instead.

Scene from *The Fortune Hunter* (Warner Bros., 1928) with Sydney and Clara Horton (LKSC).

The engagement of Duncan and Lockwood is announced by her father, who thinks that Duncan is only just too shy to announce it himself. Graham is bereft at the news. Duncan decides to undo this work by staging a violent love scene with a dressmaker's dummy, one witnessed by Lockwood's father, who thereby calls off the engagement. Graham and Duncan become man and wife instead, for love is always more important than money.

Press for the film, despite Sydney's criticisms, was not completely lacking. Grace Kingsley wrote an interview featuring Sydney for *Picture-Play* at the time that characterized him as the happy-go-lucky comedian, one that was in stark contrast to his unfortunate upbringing. He told Kingsley one of his typical jokes, to promote this fun-loving nature: "The mother-in-law had died but on the way to the burying ground a thorn on a bush by the wayside had accidentally scratched her body, drawing blood and causing her to come to life. She died again ten years later. Her son-in-law exclaimed as they were carrying her away, 'For Heaven's sake, keep away from that thorn bush this time!'"[126] Photos of Sydney and Helene Costello, his co-star, accompanied by a he-said she-said discussion entitled: "For & Against — Movie Stars on Marriage" ran in the newspapers in Australia as well (a place Sydney's films were wildly popular). Sydney's half of this discussion bears repeating, especially given his reputation on the subject:

> Women are like the breakfast egg — you never know what's coming to you till you break the shell — some are "hard-boiled" — others just plain "soft," but very often the "soft" ones are deceiving. The state of the modern man's man is like the States of N. S. W. and Victoria in Australia (if what I'm told is true). Forever at war. When he is with one woman he wants the "other." The man who strikes the happy combination of a woman who can inspire and amuse at the same time is a lucky man indeed and if anyone does so, I'd like them to get in touch with me right away. [127]

In addition, his birthday (altered to March 17, St. Patrick's Day, by this time) was celebrated in the press with Sydney serving as an example of a typical Pisces, thought to be "an emotional and sensitive sign." "Your Birthday," by Stella, featured in London's *Evening Graphic* displayed his astrological chart, noting his particular strengths as falling in the areas of dramatic ability, rhythm, artistic talent, success in motion pictures, business ability, executive power, humor, public success, and eventful career. Persons born on this day (not really Sydney's birthday anyway), were "charitable, sympathetic and hospitable but they do not let emotion take the place of common sense and justice."[128]

Finished with the film by May 1927, it wasn't released until the following January by Warners. It premiered in New York at the Hippodrome Theater on January 9 and was immediately panned by Mordaunt Hall, who claimed the film was "more obstreperous than imaginative." Hall continued his habit of negatively comparing Sydney's work to Charlie's, this time in two ways. In the review for Sydney's film, he refers to Sydney as "the brother of the film star comedian,"[129] thereby making the comparison palpable. Then, in a separate and longer article entitled "A Clown Is an Artist," about Charlie's new film *The Circus*, he tacks on a coda about Sydney: "Still another idea about humor was presented by Sydney Chaplin, Charlie's half-brother, in a film called 'The Fortune Hunter.' This is a slapstick comedy with old reliables turned to use."[130] Irene Thirer, writing in the New York *Daily News* concurred in her review of the film: "Maybe it's pretty mean to suggest that Syd, the elder Chaplin brother whose 'Fortune Hunter' now occupies the

French novelization for Warners' *The Fortune Hunter*, circa 1928, showing Sydney Chaplin and Clara Horton (CHACHAA).

Hippodrome's screen should take a squint at brother Charlie's 'Circus,' now at the Mark Strand, to discover what constitutes a good movie."[131] Premiering in Los Angeles about two weeks later, the film doesn't seem to have merited a feature review, yet it was still held over a second week at the Broadway Palace where it opened.[132] This being Sydney's last Warners' film, his fall from grace, so to speak, is evident even in the venues chosen to play the film — the New York Hippodrome and the Broadway Palace being far lesser venues than the Colony or the Forum.

By the time of the film's premiere, Sydney had been in England seven months and had completed his first film for British International Pictures. His departure for New York in May caused him to miss the inaugural dinner of the Academy of Motion Picture Arts and Sciences at the Biltmore Hotel in downtown Los Angeles, to which he was formally invited[133] and at which his brother would receive his first Oscar statue. Arriving in Southampton on the S.S. *Aquitania* on June 7, 1927, Sydney claimed he had three tasks to accomplish while in England: to visit his old training ship, *Exmouth*; to see some old friends from his pantomime days; and to "help the British films be as financially successful as American films," or, better stated, to help himself be as successful financially in Britain as he had been in America. His new film contract reportedly gained him $150,000 for a ten weeks' stay in the British film business.[134]

In July of 1926, shortly after *The Better 'Ole*'s success, Sydney began planning a charity event back in England for his alma mater, the T.S. *Exmouth*, the Metropolitan Asylums Board's training ship for young destitute boys. He had benefited greatly from his experiences on board in the early 1890s, the training, providing as it did, skills that helped him to earn a living for himself, his ailing mother and little brother, Charlie, when there was no other income at their disposal. He wrote to Aubrey, "It has always been my wish to provide some pleasure for these kids, in memory of my boyhood days and I think it would be a great idea if we could arrange with Warner Brothers and the theatre owner or the exhibitor in London to bring the whole ship's crew up to town, give them a free show previous to the public showing."[135] Through the assistance of Charlie's cousin Aubrey Chaplin, residing in London at the time, Sydney began to work out his plans for an event of some kind. Of course, it couldn't be *just* a film screening, because this wasn't *just* charity. In mid-October, Sydney's plans were to arrange a showing of *The Better 'Ole* for the boys, defraying all expenses himself, but as the film had not yet reached Britain, no other plans could be made.[136] By mid-November, the film had arrived in London and Aubrey set about making plans, announcing to Sydney that there were 600 boys aboard ship at the time, of which 300 would enjoy the day out on November 26 at the Hippodrome Theatre and the rest in February when the film was to begin its run there. Aubrey visited the ship in order to solidify the arrangements, and found the man in charge, Captain Currey, to be an affable guy. Aubrey was shown Sydney's records of having been a boy there from 1896 to 1897, and seemed duly impressed that he had received high marks, especially in conduct.

The boys were motored to London, shown the film then taken to Lyons Restaurant on Coventry Street W. for tea, where they each received a packet of chocolate. The boy, Richard Care, now bearing Sydney's number from his days aboard — the number 151— received an engraved silver watch as a prize especially from him. Sydney was adamant

Sydney (center) visiting the boys aboard the T. S. *Exmouth*, Grays, Essex, his alma mater, July 1927. Sydney had just previously entertained all 600 boys by providing them a day out to see *The Better 'Ole* and enjoy high tea (CHACHAA).

about the fact that he wanted the ship's band to play at the event, even if it was only the National Anthem, because indeed it was with this group that he received his earliest training in the entertainment business. In fact, Aubrey had the parade of boys marching down Charing Cross Road to the theatre headed by that very band. He remembered the tea party following the show in great detail:

> They sat down to a jolly tea and did themselves right well having loads of pastries, sausage rolls, tea, etc., until they could eat no more. Lyons provided a nice orchestra who played the whole time and in a friendly manner. Captain Currey challenged them with his band of boys, who followed with a few selections as good as any military band.... The boys gave hearty cheers in the theatre and again after tea. I said a few words for you and read your last cable and told them as I should have some cash left and they wanted a new projector for their ship's cinema, that you would be pleased to give it to them.[137]

In December, following the first outing, he received a long letter of thanks from Captain Currey, one which revealed an additional gift he had provided the boys — "2 shillings per head which has been placed in their banking accounts and will be given out in the form of new coin when they proceed on leave this month."[138] The recipient of the silver watch, Richard Care, also sent a letter (in notably outstanding penmanship) to Sydney in which he included his heartfelt thanks: "You may be sure that I shall treasure the watch more for the giver than for the gift and it will always bring back to mind a most pleasing incident."[139] The whole thing—for both sets of boys—was to cost £300 and afforded Sydney some of the best publicity of his career. Notably Warners could not be bothered to contribute much of anything to the event.[140] "I have only one regret," wrote Aubrey, "that you were not able to be present and enjoy seeing them so happy. Sydney, it would have been ample reward for your kindly thought." Although he would miss the second outing by about two months (it occurred on March 25), Sydney did visit the *Exmouth* shortly after his arrival back in England to begin work for British International (in early July), and, as a result of that visit, extended his generosity by a further donation of £400 to start an Old Boys' Association.[141]

As romantic as all this sounds, Sydney was really in London to sign a one-picture contract with British International Pictures, one that company head, John Maxwell, would only agree to after MGM agreed to distribute the film in America. In fact, Maxwell was wary of the big salary Sydney wanted for the film and, frankly, didn't have the ready cash to pay it, and even with the MGM collaboration, which had increased the capital for his company another $250,000 with complete approval of his shareholders in November 1927, in order to keep things a float at Elstree.[142] In August, an article entitled "British Picture Loan Made" appeared in the *Los Angeles Times* removed some of the mystery behind this deal. It seemed that California banker Dr. A. H. Giannini of the Bank of Italy had made Maxwell a significant loan to back Sydney's production costs: "The loan, he explained, is to the British National Picture Company, which will produce a Syd Chaplin picture for distribution for Metro-Goldwyn-Mayer in this country. British banks are not particularly interested in or familiar with this business, and are in about the same position as the American banks were fifteen years ago," when Giannini provided a similar service to companies "then regarded as poor risks."[143] In July, Garrett was trying to turn the deal into a multi-picture arrangement for Sydney, but, even before he started shooting on the first one, Sydney was asking Maxwell for a million-dollar contract on a subsequent deal. Maxwell wanted a 21-day option attached to the proposed salary in order to think it over, which Sydney would not provide, because he wanted to "know exactly what I am going to do immediately upon the expiration of my present contract." Still, he offered to Garrett that he had a proposal that Maxwell need take no time in considering: a contract for three pictures only at $175,000 per picture, with $75,000 to be paid in advance.[144] Although Sydney was to sign with Maxwell again, it was not according to these terms, and Maxwell kept him in suspense for some time about the matter. So in the summer of 1927, Garrett went over to British-Gaumont with a deal, but reported to Sydney that they weren't interested either.

A lot of speculation has been made over the years about why Sydney went back to England to make films in the first place. He claimed to have been made an offer of renewal by Warners in the States, but turned it down. Taxes and his perpetual attempts to escape from them, some have suggested, may have been the reason, except that any money he earned went straight into the Regent Finance Corporation and so, never appeared on his own accounts. The receivers who investigated Charlie's finances in 1927, for instance, found only that the United States owed Sydney money. As for the Sassy Jane Manufacturing Company and Sydney's tax evasion tactics therein, he addressed this issue clearly in a letter to Kelly, dated February 8, 1929 (Sydney had heard from Victor [Vic] Levy a day or so earlier): "I have just received your letter stating that the Income Tax matter is being taken up, and I trust that you will let me know the results as quickly as possible, as there is very little time left before I sail [he was in Canada ready to head back to England]. I shall be very glad to pay the fee, and I certainly hope that your expert will see a way of saving me money, and still remaining within the letter of the law, as you know there are so many legal loopholes if you look for them."[145] Levy and Sydney's petition was denied at the time, but later settled in the favor of both, for neither had to pay anything.[146] Running away and going into exile would be strategies he would adopt a bit later in response to another concern. More likely is the fact that Sydney was both burning too many bridges and asking too much money for his services. By 1929, it was revealed that he took Warners to court because of the fact that he believed he had been cheated on his percentage of film revenues for all his Warners' films, but for *The Better 'Ole* especially. The picture played at the Colony Theatre in New York for more than 25 weeks and took in nearly $30,000 in revenues per week, at least according to Sydney's accounting. "You can imagine my surprise when I received the Warner Brothers statement to find that they had debited me and showed a loss on this engagement," he wrote to Kelly. When he asked Nathan Burkan to investigate their books, Warners took umbrage and stopped sending any royalty checks to him after that. Sydney charged Burkan with filing a suit against Warners to try to recoup some of the money, which he did, and Warners then made an offer to Sydney of $100,000 to settle out of court. Burkan advised him to take the money. "I was not a bit enthusiastic about it," he remembered, but he took the money, despite the fact that he believed himself to be owed much more.[147] In this way, Sydney exited from film contracts. So, by 1927, with the firestorm Warners had created with its introduction of talking pictures, it is likely that an actor who had crossed the company would be an actor who had made himself unwelcome in Hollywood. Besides, he was a silent star untried in the talking film world to come, and he was asking $200,000 per picture.

* * *

After Sydney had made his visit to Grays, Essex, to the training ship *Exmouth* had had secured a perfect photo-op for himself with the boys there, he went on vacation. Production on his new film, a screen adaptation of Walter Ellis's play *A Little Bit of Fluff* would not begin until late September 1928. Prior to that he would be meeting up with brother Wheeler Dryden and old pal Jess Robbins, the co-directors on the film, in Montreux, Switzerland, for a confabulation on the scenario. Sydney chose Montreux after happening upon it during what sounded like a wild road-trip out of something like *The Sun Also Rises*—a trip so impromptu that Garrett, Robbins, Dryden and even Minnie didn't know where he was for some time and waited anxiously to hear from him (they had arrived in London unexpectedly on July 19). Sydney had been joined in Montreux, Switzerland, on July 28 by Robbins and Dryden, from where he wrote to Garrett that he had stayed in Paris only two days, then traveled on to Nice. There he spent some time being taken through Rex Ingram's studio, which he found very impressive: "It was an agreeable surprise for me to find that Ingram had practically everything he needed for production purposes right there at his disposal, and after carefully perusing the cost sheets he showed me, I found that prices of materials, labor, and hire of 'extra' people were extremely reasonable." His conclusion was that he would demand filming his next picture there as part of any subsequent film deal — despite the fact that MGM and Ingram were at odds (this was to come to nothing, however). After two days in Nice chez Ingram, he traveled onto Lucerne, Switzerland, but met an American woman on the train who invited him along on a road trip she would be taking with her husband and one of his Hindu friends from college. Sydney and the woman spent the night in Milan, then traveled to meet the husband in Munich, whom he found to be a great fellow, as was his friend. The plan was to motor through Monte Carlo, the Austrian Tyrol, stopping at St. Moritz and then continuing onto Lake Como, returning to Milan the day after. After this adventure, he made his way to Montreux, where he had holed up at the posh Montreux Palace Hotel, a spot that was to become a frequent residence. But presently, he was impressed not just with the scenery, but with the favorable cost of his accommodations: "I have a fine room, also commanding an excellent view of Lake Leman, and surrounded with large flower gardens, flowered tea terraces, beautiful tennis courts, etc. For this I am only paying the equivalent of four dollars per day, and my view of the lake and the mountains is probably the best in the whole hotel!"[148] Liking it so well, Sydney had made it his location for his film's scenario work. His colleagues were pleased with the venue as well, making it "an ideal place for the type of work we are doing and the result is that we are all in the right frame of mind for concentrating on our story — which by the way, is working out in great shape."[149] Sydney was trimming down for his part, taking only one meal a day in order to keep very physically fit for the work ahead.

Sydney Chaplin, tanned and lean, enjoying some time on the French Riviera waiting for production to begin on *A Little Bit of Fluff* (BIF/MGM, 1928) (CHACHAA).

Back in London, Minnie was keeping busy looking for a place for the couple to live and visiting family. She looked over someone called George Graves's flat, but Sydney vetoed the idea,[150] and the couple ended up staying at the Mayfair Hotel on Berkeley Square for the duration of the filming—about three months. Sydney and his team arrived back in London on September 1 and Sydney seemed very pleased at first with the production facilities and general demeanor of people working there.[151] The same day, he wrote a rare letter to Charlie, offering him some consoling words concerning the outcome of his divorce, now settled.[152] It's strange that there is no mention of his mother's passing in this letter, or indication of any depression that it may have been causing him. Hannah Chaplin had died on August 28 from an infected gallbladder. She had been hospitalized with this ailment a full week before her demise, so it seems unlikely that, as newspapers were reporting following her death, "As a score of cabled messages to Sydney Chaplin went unanswered, it was believed he was unaware of her passing."[153] In fact, no evidence of his reaction to this news exists. By the end of the month, though, he was worried about his own concerns, until a check containing the amount of three British International payments was finally sent to him on September 23, with the final payment promised the next day.[154]

For Sydney's film, British International had engaged actress Betty Balfour, voted by the *Daily Mail* in 1927 as Britain's favorite world star. Her choice for his film continues a narrative Maxwell was creating about the production — that it was a big investment and that he expected to reap big profits from it. Balfour was best known from her success in George Pearson's *Squibs* series of films, and, as Wheeler Dryden later reported to Sydney, she was barely able to catch her breath from the *A Little Bit of Fluff* production before she started work on Alfred Hitchcock's *Champagne*.[155] Victor McLaglen's brother, Clifford, plays the heavy in Sydney's film.

A reporter from the Australian film magazine, *The Photoplayer*, visited the set of *A Little Bit of Fluff* in October and submitted a feature on Sydney as a result. The reporter's "hook" was the old female impersonator game that Sydney had successfully played in films like *Charley's Aunt*, one he returned to briefly in this new film in one short scene in which he has to put on some of Mamie Scott's clothes in order to get out of her apartment safely. The scene in which he puts on "woman's make-up" at Mamie's dressing table was one he spent hours rehearsing. The writer described a scene she witnessed between Betty Balfour and Clifford McLaglen: "All in a moment, we glimpse a pretty, persuasive girl and a very angry looking young man seated on a sofa, with several cameras and more lights trained upon them. The room is quite full of people, all looking extremely sea-sick in the funny light." Sydney, when he comes to greet this reporter is described much as he always is in such circumstances: "The soft courteous voice; the rather serious eyes;— even the pipe, clasped in a strong expressive hand,"— indicative of the affluent, cultured, aristocratic Englishman persona he had developed to perfection by this time. His eyes are described as "mauvish," neither blue, brown or hazel, but "undeniably kind, with a deal of humour beneath their deep-thinking look." His accent had a decidedly American tinge. The writer then witnessed Sydney in his uncredited role, as that of the film's director — doing what he terms is his producing work: "Mr. Chaplin starts to his feet. The cameras are silent; he crosses to the actors;— a few soft, well-chosen words; a gesture or two of that expressive hand (still clasping the pipe) and they commence to click again. The scene doesn't just *seem* good now; it is good. With unfailing accuracy he has picked the weak points and strengthened the good ones."[156] In what is to be his last-ever film production, it is clear that Sydney is completely in control.

Bertram Tully (Sydney Chaplin) is ripped from the arms of his new bride, Violet (Nancy Rigg), by her overbearing mother, who insists on taking her to London. Left alone, Bertram (another of Sydney's ineffectual husband characters) gets into heaps of trouble in her absence, which amounts to the span of just one afternoon. He determines to spend it practicing for the evening's flute recital, but is interrupted by his new neighbor, Mamie Scott (Betty Balfour), an actress whose phone seems to be out of order. While Mamie uses the phone, Bertram's friend John (Edmond Breon) arrives. The two men discover they are both sans wife for the afternoon, so decide to go to the Five Hundred Club, a popular cabaret, to hear Mamie perform. At the club, Mamie's old boyfriend, Henry Hudson (McLaglen), a prizefighter, and his new girl take a seat at the table next to the gentlemen. Mamie plays up to Bertie during her number in order to make Henry jealous and soon the two—John and Bertie—are involved in a sort of barroom brawl that lands them in jail.

Back at John's apartment after successfully explaining their way out of jail, John's wife comes home early and begins to make a scene, so Bertie sneaks out and tries to achieve his own apartment via the outside of the building. In error, he enters Mamie's apartment instead of his own, and discovers Henry inside trying to retrieve a diamond necklace he once gave her as a present. Bertie is able to secure the necklace but arrives back in his apartment dressed as a woman, having resorted to this disguise to elude Henry (and Mamie). Finding his wife and mother-in-law home, his explanation for the disguise is simply that the costume is a gift for Violet, and, when Mamie's necklace falls from one of its pockets, it becomes a gift, too. But Mamie wants her necklace back and threatens to call the police. Henry, too, still wants the necklace. So, while Bertie and John devise a plan by which John will masquerade as a thief in order to "steal" the necklace, Henry enacts the same performance. In the end, both Henry and John are arrested, the necklace is retrieved and Bertie is happy to be simply lying on his own rug, dizzy from a slight bump on his noggin.

One of the most-touted scenes in the film was the Five Hundred Club cabaret scene, which was supposedly based on a real establishment, the Kit Kat Club, a place oft-frequented by the Prince of Wales. Sketches were made of the place so that it could be

The cabaret scene featuring Sydney and the Tiller Girls in *A Little Bit of Fluff* (BIF/MGM, 1928) (LKSC).

successfully reproduced on screen. The Tiller Girls, a popular London dancing troupe, grace this scene directly before the entrance of the star, Mamie Scott, who comes onstage in a "striking costume made entirely of white ostrich plumes." Perhaps the most innovative shot, however, comes in the film's introduction to the scene. It involves a unique shot in which the camera focuses on a full champagne glass: "Reflected in the glass as the camera comes into full focus is a party of people seated around a long table. Then the glass itself disappears from the picture, leaving only the people and the table in the scene."[157]

From the moment production was completed in late 1927 (Jess Robbins was back in the States by December 27), Sydney began to worry about how the film would do — not just in Britain, but in the States as well, so much so that he reported to Wheeler that he had been ill most of May. They were both disappointed by the fact that "many of our neat little gags and so forth were cut." Also, British International had not yet signed Sydney for another film and he was probably in quite a panic about it. It premiered in London on May 24, 1928, where it had been "extremely well-received by practically every critic who has written anything about the film." The *Daily News* reported it "a veritable harlequinade of slap-stick fun," and *Faulkner's Film Review* that it was "a rollicking farce with potential box-office values."[158] A reporter for *The Daily Mirror* found the Duke of Wellington sitting in those comfortable royal circle seats at the Plaza laughing at the 'Little Bit of Fluff' film, which has Betty Balfour and Syd Chaplin as the stars. This film survived the acid test of presentation at a West End super-cinema, and the bursts of laughter which greeted it are proof that the British film studios at Elstree are turning out the right stuff."[159] Wheeler reported that Sydney's devoted Australian fans — his most loyal in the world — also enjoyed it. But there was little good to report about America's view of the film. MGM renamed it *Skirts* for its American release on July 26 and "the critics in America did not receive it particularly well." Wheeler's letter, dated June 8, suggested that Sydney's future plans had not been made: "Like yourself, Sydney, I have many possibilities in the offing, but nothing definite."[160] Sydney was to request Wheeler be brought on board his next British International Films production, but failed to make this happen.

In April, Garrett reported to Sydney that he still had no confirmed deal for him. Since MGM still had the print, he figured that their positive reaction to it, if they had one, would speed things along.[161] Sydney and Minnie had taken the opportunity to do some sightseeing together while they waited. By May, their Lincoln Town Car arrived,[162] and so began the long road-tours of continental Europe that Sydney would take on and off for the rest of his life.[163] Kelly wrote at this time that he had pushed the Sydney Chaplin cause to Joseph Schenck, who pretty much balked at Sydney's salary requirements and Mack Sennett, who was very interested and simply dismissed those same requirements as any sort of barrier to working with his old colleague: "He wants to pay you a minimum amount for the entire picture, including helping him on the story, starring and assisting generally in the direction where you can against a percentage of the profits." Kelly then suggested a new man to the motion picture game, one Howard Hughes "who has a lot of money." Again, being an old family friend, only Arthur Kelly had the fortitude to broach uncomfortable subjects in his letters to Sydney. His first was that Sydney should immediately return to America to work: "If you are away too long people forget you." Reassuring Sydney not to be disheartened, he calmly stated,

Sydney (center) in costume as Bertram Tully entertaining Fred Karno (left center) on the cabaret set of *A Little Bit of Fluff* (BIF/MGM, 1928). Clifford McLaglen is standing front right (LKSC).

> There may not be just as much [money] as you want [in this business], but when you take into consideration that there is a darn fine salary in it for you, there is no reason why you should not have it.... Don't be foolish as to hold out for too much, but try to permanently establish yourself in some studio where you can get a contract for the year, and have some money coming in regularly every week.... Why try to hit a producer for one picture for a big sum of money, and then have the trouble of hawking yourself around for another picture.[164]

"The motion picture game, Syd," Kelly remonstrated, "is getting a little harder [and] no one is getting the grosses they formerly made."[165] But, as with most good advice he was given — and Kelly gave him some of the best — he failed to take it.

At the end of September, Garrett was negotiating a contract for Sydney with Maxwell once again, but was running up against Sydney's (and probably to some extent, Maxwell's) personalities. Garrett had written Sydney on September 14 that Maxwell would sign a two-picture deal for $200,000 for the two, meaning Sydney would only get $100,000 per picture. Garrett had also stipulated that he expected Inter-Globe Corp. to be paid at least 5 percent (10 percent was standard) for acting as negotiator, for, after all "as you say, friendship is one thing and business is another." By September 28, Sydney had not responded in any way to either the offer or to Garrett: "I am wondering why you haven't answered my letter.... There is no reason in the world, Sydney, why you shouldn't answer it."[166] Although no record exits of when the deal was finally signed, it is likely that Sydney had something definite in hand by the end of the year, for he traveled back to North America for three months beginning January 20, having taken the S.S. *Aurania* from Southampton to Halifax, Nova Scotia, the week before. He never left Canada for the duration of his visit, claiming to Garrett that he was in the area to do business: "I have spent a week here, but mostly confined to my hotel, because outside it is thick snow, and cold enough to freeze the balls off a pawnbroker's sign!" He was to return to London on the S.S. *Regina* on February 25, his new contract stipulating that he must begin work March 11, 1929. His new story was an old one — Fred Karno's *Mumming Birds*. Karno remembered how the whole thing came about. After Sydney arrived back in London and began work in early March, he called his old boss: "I've told 'em that the first film is to include the *Mumming Birds* sketch. I've worked out a sort of adaptation for the cinema, and I'd like you to help."[167] Karno was enthusiastic as he had been trying to break into the business for years. Later Karno took Sydney for a walk around London's East End, to gather information for the film. After Petticoat Lane, they crossed over the Thames to Lambeth Walk, both in high hopes for the film to be made. But it never would be.

CHAPTER 7

"An Incident at Elstree"

> I have no desire to return to England. It is only a place of tragedy for me. My early days there were nothing but starvation, backrooms and workhouses. It has never given me anything and now finishes by wrecking my future. I hate the sight of the place.—Sydney Chaplin, letter to R. J. Minney, August 1930

MANY SILENT FILM STARS FOUND THEIR careers ending with the onset of talking pictures in 1927. The great irony is that Sydney's film career also ended around this period, but not because he was opposed to the new technology (unlike Charlie who was notorious for resisting talking technology for as long as he possibly could). Nerina Shute interviewed Sydney on this topic in *Film Weekly* in 1928. He argued, "England is bound to go 'Talkie' as America has done, and what is going to happen to us wretched comedians is more than I can say. Until now people like my brother, Harold Lloyd, and myself have worked almost entirely without script, depending on the inspiration of the moment for our greatest 'gags.'" But despite his persistent attempts to break into talkies throughout the 1930s, his last film would be a silent one: *A Little Bit of Fluff* (1928).

Sydney's film career was not cashiered by an ill-suited or cacophonous speaking voice, his inability to act without pantomime, nor by any of the countless reasons cited by the many actors and actresses who disappeared after Jolson's first spoken words onscreen in *The Jazz Singer*. It was halted seemingly by the suit of a 22-year-old actress named Molly Wright, who took out a writ against Sydney for assault, libel and slander, after what he himself came to term his "alleged cannibalistic attack"[1] on her, in which he was supposed to have bitten off one of her nipples in an overzealous sexual encounter. The press only took notice of the whole affair later, reporting on August 3, 1929 that Sydney had departed Elstree five weeks prior and that "neither the company nor Mr. Chaplin's agent [Sidney Garrett] has succeeded in locating him," with British International Pictures (BIP), subsequently suspending the production of *Mumming Birds*, his current film production.[2] Where BIP and Garrett failed, however, the press soon succeeded. Karl K. Kitchen, writing in an August 24 column entitled "A Broadwayite Abroad," recounted meeting up with Sydney in the Chateau Basque restaurant in Biarritz, France, but, unaware that he was "missing," asked Sydney only, "Are you Charlie Chaplin's brother?"[3] Of course there are two sides to this story: Sydney's version and that promoted by the media and BIP. Matthew Sweet in his article, "A Life in Full: The Other Chaplin," offers the argument that Sydney was guilty of Wright's charges:

> The company's lawyer, J D Rayner Goddard, KC, issued a statement conceding the truth of Wright's claims. "I have only to say," he announced, "that the defendants hold, and have held the view that the lady plaintiff is, and always has been a lady of irreproachable character. They much regret an incident complained of in the statement of claim, which took place on their premises, but for which they were in no way responsible."[4]

It does seem likely that Sydney was mostly responsible for the events of June 1929, that led to the suits (his bankruptcy) and eventually, the permanent end of his film career. But Sydney himself would have the world think otherwise. A detailed discussion of the case in letters Sydney he wrote to close friend and confidante, R. J. (Jim) Minney, English journalist (especially for *Everybody's Weekly* during this time period), novelist and playwright, asserts that his career came to a close because he himself neglected to sue BIP and its owner, John Maxwell, for breach of contract. According to Sydney, BIP failed to have talking picture technology in place in time for the scheduled production date for what would have been Sydney's first talking film, an adaptation of Fred Karno's skit, *Mumming Birds*, in which Sydney had garnered much success through his portrayal of the inebriate swell during his music hall days.[5] Molly Wright's suit, then, made as it was against BIP (for negligence)[6] and settled out of court by them in late July 1930,[7] could have been simply a trumped-up affair designed to take the focus off of BIP's inability to have talking technology in place for Sydney's film, as his contract stipulated.[8] In an undated letter (probably October 1930) sent from Ambassador Hotel, Paris, Sydney outlines his version clearly to Minney, in a section of the letter prefaced by, "Let's get down to logic." He writes, "Maxwell is a shrewd Scotsman. He has paid out £60,000 for which he has got nothing but a script. He had made a bad contract & knew it. Now he tries to wriggle out of it by this charge." Weeks go by and Sydney does not sue him for breach of contract. "In fact, all the way through," Sydney writes, "we have acted on the defensive, so have not forced him to this issue, but he has forced us to fight every inch of the way. At first, he thought he might get his money back by threatened publicity but we won & forced it into Arbitration. Weeks elapsed & we did not press the case, but played a waiting game, until at last he applied to the courts to appoint an arbitrator." Sydney believed Maxwell was determined to fight the case to the finish:

> If he had not got the cards stacked against me — either the witnesses are bought, or he has secured some information that he thinks will damn my character or he is pigheaded, which he is, and as stubborn as a mule, or he is playing a high class poker hand of bluff, thinking I will not fight on account of publicity & my brother's name, especially as Charlie is coming out shortly with a new picture. You can see he is still playing upon the fear of publicity by this trick suit of the girl's against him — or he may be hoping that there will be a compromise before the case is heard.[9]

Sydney also writes, "I will always maintain my innocence of these charges, even on my death bed. I have been made the goat & sacrificed & I certainly would not slink back to the studio like a whipped cur, taking with thankfulness anything that might be offered me."[10] He claims he did no more than make an immoral proposal to Wright,[11] a small-time bit part actress working for BIP.[12] The charge of slander he was especially opposed to, writing to Minney that "the girl's charges of slander are ridiculous. She said that two newspaper men called upon her and said that I said she was a blackmailer. I don't know who the men were from Adam. I have done everything in my power to keep it out of the papers."[13] Using a strategy similar to one that resulted in Charlie's first two "shotgun marriages," Wright teamed with her mother in the scheme, such that Sydney hired a private investigator named Walter West to dig up some information on them.[14]

What Minnie Chaplin, Sydney's wife, thought of all this is unknown. He hints at the situation in a letter to Jim Minney written in October 1930 when he writes, "It is just as well not to tell them how much my wife knows," in reference to BIP and Wright. How much did she know, then? In June of 1930, shortly before Wright's hearing, Minnie met with her solicitors in London.[15] They, too, probably wanted to know how much she knew. Sydney mentioned in a letter written in August 1930 from Ostende, "Minnie is still taking this matter very seriously, but I hope I eventually get her to shake it off."[16] A surviving letter between Minnie and Jim Minney offers absolutely no information, except that it seems to suggest that she has come around to Sydney's side once again:

> I am going to put up a proposition to my darling & ask him to adopt you and the family & we can all tour the world in a comfy caravan, as he will never be able to get away from the Minnies from now on, as they are his only mascots. I am anxiously waiting for the result today, as Syd said he thought the case would end today. I feel sure he will come out on top when the arbitrator realizes the kind of people Syd has been dealing with. I have been terribly lonesome without him, but I have had one consolation, that he had someone around him that has shown his true colours, a sincere faithful friend [Minney] that we shall never forget, as they are so few and far between when in need.[17]

Arriving back in Paris after the Wright hearing in London, Sydney also suggests that his marital relationship continues to be strong: "Minnie was out to dinner when it [Minney's letter] arrived & on her return to the hotel, they told her I was here. You would think I had been in jail for years the reception she gave me. She cried & laughed and wouldn't stop kissing me. We are both very happy & Paris looks good & seems like home."[18]

In presenting his side of the story to Jim Minney and others, Sydney insisted that a secretary, probably one working for BIP at the time, and his director for *Mumming Birds* (Monty Banks[19]) would have been able to give important testimony on his behalf. This, however, proved impossible as they had allowed the director to return to America: "He was the one that could prove the secretary's story in case she lies. Now I impressed them how important it was to obtain his evidence. They never even told her [the secretary] what efforts they had made to secure it. It could not have been much, as he was very friendly towards me & would have done anything to have helped me."[20] Indeed, this testimony by Monty Banks, a popular movie comedian and future husband to BIP star Gracie Fields, who was also experiencing what Sydney referred to as "contract trouble," might have been helpful (at least Sydney believed so).[21] Perhaps allowing Banks to give evidence would have not been the smartest move, however, as Sydney's lawyer, Mr. Oliver, may have known. Aubrey Chaplin's[22] eldest daughter, May (better known later as Betty Chaplin Tetrick), revealed in an interview in 2003[23] that she understood that Banks was, in fact, involved in the assault. In fact, a ship manifest for the S.S. *France*, sailing from Plymouth, England, on June 6, 1929, had Banks on board, claiming that he had no intention of leaving the States again and would become a United States citizen — all information that suggests he was possibly in some kind of trouble and running away from someone or something. However, because Banks was scheduled in the cast for E. A. Dupont's *Atlantic* due to start filming back at Elstree just as he landed in New York City on June 12, Banks's stay in the States, as well as his estrangement from BIP, was short-lived. Obviously, he was convinced his role in the affair would not be investigated further.

Still other opportunities for helpful testimony were missed, according to Sydney. In another letter to Jim Minney, Sydney claims, just after Molly Wright's initial hearing (which had taken place approximately July 7–15, 1929), "I ran into a fellow over here who was the chief engineer at the British International studios when I was there."[24] He was also in sole charge of the installation of the Talkie apparatus that [John] Thorpe [Elstree Studios Manager] brought over with him from America in June [1929]. "As you know," Sydney continued, "Thorpe swore that this apparatus was installed in the new stage & that they started to shoot a picture with it at the end of June. He also sent down to the arbitrator documents to prove this true. The documents were purely technical & of course meant nothing to Oliver [Sydney's solicitor] or the Arbitrator." The chief engineer, however, came along and claimed, "Thorpe is a d — d liar, that the apparatus was not installed until September & that *no* picture was shot with it before that month. This would fit in with information you got over the telephone from those two directors, regarding the time it takes to install talkie apparatuses."[25] If this information had been true, it would have given Sydney the evidence he needed that not only was he innocent of all charges, but had been set up as well. Unfortunately, while the early days of sound production at Elstree were fraught with problems,[26] Hitchcock's *Blackmail* and J. B. Williams's *White Cargo* were complete (in their sound versions) by early July — just days after Sydney's incident was to have taken place.[27] *To-day's Cinema*, in fact, reported that BIP had four fully operating sound production studios by July 24, all with full filming schedules.[28]

It is clear, however, that the Elstree under Maxwell and Walter Mycroft was not a warm and friendly place, especially for a person of Sydney's temperament. By nature, as has already been suggested, he was often paranoid and distrustful of people.[29] By late 1930, he even suspected his solicitors of being against him, writing that "they maneuvered me into a position of agreeing that any damages awarded against the Swiss Corporation[30] should apply to myself. They gave this undertaking without consulting me & then prevailed upon me to agree to it as the only way in which the case could be heard in arbitration."[31] Sydney seems to have made it hard for others to please him and gain his trust, as these sorts of comments indicate. Perhaps such an attitude and the behavior towards Wright made him into a creature that was impossible to support, especially given the hard economic times the studio itself encountered in 1929.

John Maxwell is best known as the chairman and managing director of the Associated British Picture Corporation, Ltd., and British International Pictures. Starting out as a local lawyer in Glasgow, Scotland, with a loyal clientele, Maxwell eased into the film business by first purchasing a Glasgow cinema, then by forming Waverley Films of Scotland in 1918 and soon, through his effective partnership with Arthur Dent, by accomplishing a fruitful takeover of Wardour Films of London. In 1926, Maxwell acquired the failing Elstree studios and made the move to London. British International Pictures was then formed in 1927, with Sydney and his entourage making one of the earliest of the silent films produced there—*A Little Bit of Fluff*, with co-star Betty Balfour, based on the stage play by Walter Ellis. Maxwell's vision for Elstree was that it become the titular "home" of British pictures in general, and through what the *London Times* referred to as "sound financial insight" achieved by his "[employment] of conservative and prudent methods" and the avoidance of excess, his goal was mostly realized.[32] Sydney, however, referred to these same characteristics derogatorily, especially because he considered Maxwell's Scottish ancestry to be at the heart of his thrift—a thrift Sydney claimed was not above dishonesty and deceit in order to guarantee its success. To Jim Minney, he referred to Maxwell at different times as "miserly Scotsman," "pigheaded," and even that "d----d shrewd Scotsman." These epithets, at first, can be taken as the ravings of a bitter and egocentric individual, but when compared to the "endearments" Walter Mycroft uses in his autobiography to refer to a boss he both admired and worshipped, they don't seem so far-fetched: "He was the instinctive complete and absolute dictator, John Maxwell—yet he hated dictators and all dictatorships, except his own. He was a patriarchal Hitler, human, humane, kindly, and at the same time he was ruthless, inflexible and even callous where it was a question of his will or someone else's."[33] Later, Mycroft alludes to problems with, perhaps, Sydney,[34] but certainly with director Adrian Brunel and even Hitchcock, both of whom were summarily fired,[35] when he states, "Mr. John Maxwell had made strides in the world of films, and when he strode there were echoes. There had been crises. He had overcome them, not without travail."[36]

Maxwell and Mycroft saw the opportunity for British sound pictures as a milestone in their endeavor to "[establish] BIP as an internationally oriented production operation"[37] and seemed to view actors as expendable in an effort to achieve that goal. Film scholars Rachel Low[38] and Vincent Porter report that BIP typically engaged its actors much as was common in the theater: "There would be no roster of well-paid stars that were kept under contract, and no place for people to write original screenplays."[39] In fact, Sydney had to negotiate his contract for *Mumming Birds after* his first BIP film was released. Interestingly, though, this second BIP contract was for two talking pictures instead of just one.[40] Although a later letter to Jim Minney illustrates that Sydney returned to London and began work as scheduled, according to his BIP contract on March 11, 1929, the first film of the contract was never completed beyond the writing of the script, which he worked on with former music hall star George Carney.[41]

While Maxwell's early press for the launching of BIP in 1927 used only Sydney's name as an example of its "signing up of several prominent film makers and players,"[42] after the great success of Alfred Hitchcock's *The Ring* later that same year, it would seem reasonable that the tide had turned, then, in Hitchcock's favor, with Maxwell giving *Blackmail* access to the temporary sound studios over Sydney's film. However, the *London Times* for March 13, 1929 reported that Benn Levy's *Tambourine* (to be directed by Hitchcock), *Under the Greenwood Tree* (directed by Harry Lachman) and "*Mumming Birds*, the music-hall sketch, in which Mr. Syd Chaplin will play the principal part," were to be the earliest "all-talking" films BIP would be producing in their sound studios—

evidence that by the start of Syd's contract in early March, and despite the success of *The Ring*, Syd's film project had remained a priority. And, on May 31 Sydney had a lengthy article published in *The Daily Express* entitled, "Charlie Chaplin's Brother Says:—'Anyway, *I* Am Making a Talkie'" in which he writes mostly about why Charlie *wasn't* making one and not about the progress on his own, but the article's existence at this date proves, at least, that the project was still on—and a good two months after Hitchcock had started filming the sound version of *Blackmail*.[43] Unfortunately, this evidence strongly suggests that something happened between June and August 1929 to change everything. That something could easily have been the assault of Molly Wright.

Hitchcock, for his part, seemed to know that his film was going to be a sound production. He revealed in his interview with François Truffaut that he was shooting "separate takes of each shot in order to prepare a negative for the sound version of the film" along with the silent version sanctioned by Maxwell "since [he] suspected the producers might change their minds and might eventually want an all-sound picture."[44] Also, Hitchcock had enlisted young Oxford playwright Benn Levy to begin working on dialogue for the film in the spring, early enough that the dialogue pages were ready for production in mid–April, shortly after the film's sound production began.[45] In fact, *Kine Weekly* for June 27, 1929, reported that "last autumn the directors redesigned the new studios at Elstree then in construction with a view to making them sound-proof studios for the production of talking pictures. In January, the necessary plant for making of talking pictures was installed and in March the recording of full-length talking pictures started for the first time in this country at the company's studios."[46] According to reports in a later edition of *Kine Weekly* and *The Bioscope* for April 10, "The temporary studio—which was constructed inside another building—was small, with one stage about 40 by 70 feet with a 20-foot ceiling. The walls were hung with heavy flannelette material and the ceiling and floor treated with sound-absorbing materials." Although the reporter suggested that the studio was not entirely sound-proof, "The company installed American sound equipment—RCA's Photophone system—and there were adjacent rooms for monitoring and recording sound." In addition, another temporary studio was planned and Maxwell had hired two sound experts from the BBC, R. E. Jeffrey and D. F. Scanlan, to make it a reality.[47]

Both Hitchcock and scriptwriter Rodney Ackland disclosed that the filming for *Blackmail* was done in partial secrecy, with the crew using signals and cameras to hide certain parts of filming from company executives, lest they "would be wary of the complicated process involved in achieving [certain] shots" of the film, though the official reason later announced was the use of the Schüfftan Process of filming.[48]

Sydney's letters reveal no knowledge that any of this was going on at Elstree. In fact, Hitchcock's name was never mentioned. It seems possible then that although the production history does not support the argument that Elstree had no sound technology in place and so wanted to renege on Sydney's contract for that reason, the absence of commentary on either Hitchcock or the *Blackmail* production in Sydney's letters makes his sincerity in the matter more credible and less defamatory.

Simple economics may have also played an important role in Sydney's demise. Low points out that "in May 1929 the authorized capital of ABC was put to £2 million. A public issue was made in July but as it was a time of economic depression only 20 per cent of the issue was taken up, despite estimated profits of £280,000 for ABC and £194,651 for BIP."[49] This caused a requisite pause in production as other funding sources were located. John Maxwell explained simply, "We have been working for a considerable time past under great pressure in order to bring our silent pictures up to date as 'talkies.' Our output, consequently, has been far higher than usual for some time. We have, therefore, a great many pictures in hand — enough to keep our distribution organization very busy for several months to come."[50] This pause occurred the third week of August 1929,[51] but it is probable that BIP may have begun to feel an economic pinch much earlier in the year, due to the great expense necessary to create sound studios from scratch. After all, the Wall Street crash was to hit America just a few short months later, and the economic stability of the world was already an issue. Low reports, "BIP was profitable from the beginning, although at a declining rate. Profits of £170,000 in 1929/30 had fallen to £110,426 in 1932/3."[52] Just as long-time employees are often offered either early retirement or immediate dismissal by economically challenged companies, in order to free up the money necessary to pay their large salaries, it seems possible that Sydney's large salary could have easily been the focus of attack in such tenuous financial times, especially if he continued to be an irritant due to bad or irrational behavior.

Finally, there is some evidence that Sydney's scandal was highlighted in the press by outspoken BBC and *Daily Express* film critic G. A. Atkinson. In a column entitled "British Film News" in the industry paper *To-day's Cinema*, the reporter comments on a broadside that had appeared in the *Sunday Express* just prior to publication in which Atkinson "attacked the studios on the grounds of immorality."[53] He emphasizes the seriousness of such charges, especially in light of the worldwide coverage Atkinson's claims would surely receive. And, while other papers had attempted to paint studio life similar to convent life, this reporter admits "it would be puerile to suggest that Mr. Atkinson is wholly incorrect. Everyone knows that is not so, and nothing is to be gained by pretending it is. Indeed, one would not have much difficulty in adding to his incriminating list." Had Sydney Chaplin's name appeared on this list? Several pieces of evidence make this probable. First, the *To-day's Cinema* reporter mentions that "there have been a number of scandals drifting round the studios of late. One of them is such a bedtime story that the really fashionable young men refrain from mentioning it for fear of being thought a little *démodé*.... The company concerned in the latest one did well in taking firm steps against the guilty party." If this guilty party was indeed Sydney Chaplin, then much becomes clear as to why this run-of-the-mill scandal claimed, once and for all, his film career. Perhaps more damning is the second piece of evidence: Sydney's own correspondence to Jim Minney. Two October 1930 letters to Minney mention Atkinson by name in reference to "the girl," i.e., Molly Wright, one from the Ambassador Hotel in Paris begins: "Just received your letter relating to Atkinson." This letter suggests that Jim Minney and Sydney have worked out that Atkinson's article may have been meant "to scare me from coming back it may be that the girl has got a genuine suit against the B.I. & he [Maxwell] is afraid that if I come over & win, it will miss her, whereas if I stay away, she will defer to him." In other words, the letter suggests that Atkinson's diatribe on studio morality and its accompanying list were commissioned by John Maxwell himself.[54]

Despite this overwhelming evidence, Jim Minney seemed to believe in Sydney's innocence so strongly that he spent the years 1930 to 1939 working on Sydney's behalf in London, seemingly with no remuneration or other benefit to be gained, although Minney did pen a biography of Charlie much later, in 1954, entitled *Chaplin: The Immortal Tramp*.[55] In Minney's only surviving letter on this issue, his description of a recent encounter with John Maxwell on Sydney's behalf is compelling: "I did not like Maxwell's attitude at all. On the occasion of our first meeting, he kept me waiting quite a time, and ordinarily I am damned if I should wait for anyone beyond a reasonable few minutes. But he kept me hanging about for half an hour, although, in the interval, I had told the attendant to inform him again that I was still waiting." Maxwell finally came into the room, stretching his limbs and yawning as if he had been asleep. He then became apologetic and said he had not been informed that Minney was there. "He was very woolly for the first few minutes and after that disposed to be accommodating," Minney wrote. "He gave me the impression that he was very eager that everything should be patched up satisfactorily, but could not make up his mind about the percentages. He was vague and up in the air. I handed him the contract saying 'Glance through this in case there are one or two points you wish to raise.' But he would not."[56] The letter confirms Sydney's evaluation of Maxwell's personality and business tactics, if nothing else.

At their next meeting, Minney reported that Maxwell continued this tack: "He was by turns sarcastic and offensive; but although it would be easy for me to answer him in his own coin, as an intermediary, I did not take advantage of the position — for it is also easy for anyone to be rude on behalf of someone else. I was tolerant, patient, tactful, yet firm."[57] Later in this letter, in a move that may be due only to the dramatist inside Minney, but one that lends slightly less authenticity to the contents, he provides a "verbatim" dialogue to Sydney of a conversation he had the next day following this second meeting, with Maxwell's solicitor, Robert Clark. Even if slightly enhanced by Minney for dramatic effect, the conversation demonstrates his own stalwart belief in Syd's innocence:

> I said: "In plainer language, after Mr. Maxwell's previous behaviour, after his despicable trumped-up case, after his harassing and browbeating and blustering over this affair for four years, you cannot blame me, at any rate, from wondering whether he may not pick a quarrel just to cash in on the money on deposit at the bank."
> He said: "Mr. Minney! Mr. Minney!"
> I said: "Well, think it over calmly. Put yourself in Syd Chaplin's shoes."
> He said: "I see — there are two sides to every question."
> "Exactly," I said.[58]

Despite Minney's efforts, Wright's hearing came up in court on July 7, 1930 and Sydney was present. According to a letter Sydney's wife, Minnie, wrote to Jim Minney, it lasted about a week. The criminal charges never materialized (Sydney believed that "the only reason she [Wright] did not make police charges was because of my wife, as she had met her & my wife was very kind to her"),[59] but, nevertheless, he continued to worry about the possibility of "the girl" suing him further throughout the 1930s. The damage, though, had been done. Instead of suing BIP, BIP sued Sydney for breach of contract. He had been paid £60,000 in advance of filming *Mumming Birds* and BIP would get neither a film nor a return on its investment. Although the company took its time about it, BIP sued through an arbitrator to make Sydney bankrupt, a procedure that had its first hearing on November 14, 1930, when the receiving order was made. On December 12, an order of adjudication in bankruptcy was created. Sydney's public examination, then, was held on January 14, but adjourned *sine die*, because he was not present and believed to be in California (he was successfully hiding out in Nice). Sydney was finally made bankrupt then on March 18, 1931,[60] almost exactly two years after the start of his second BIP contract. When he received the news, his only recorded remark was, "In future when I sign the Hotel Police forms, in the place where it says 'occupation,' I shall put 'Retired Bankrupt.'"[61]

Brother Charlie, at the time, was just getting started on a 17-month world tour to promote *City Lights*—a trip during which he was to be fêted, coddled and caressed by the public at nearly every stop he made. Sydney wrote poignantly to Jim Minney in November, with a self-reflexivity uncharacteristic of him, "When I read of Charlie's wonderful reception, I cannot help but feel my position. However, my time will come. 'It is always darkest before the dawn.'"[62]

* * *

Although Sydney seemed to make a pretense to Jim Minney and other correspondents about keeping his whereabouts confidential, no one was ever really chasing him. His presence at the hearing in July 1930 turned out to be his last-ever trip to England, because, given the outcome of that hearing, he felt he had to either move around a lot or hide, so that he wouldn't have to pay. His "exile," as he came to term it, started on July 16, 1930, when he arrived in Paris after the end of the Wright hearing. It began with a bang, too, because "the trip over was excellent & very interesting, as I had never been in a large plane before."[63] His journey moved him from Paris to "the Low Countries" (the Netherlands and Belgium) by August 1930, but this was only a brief vacation for himself and Minnie, one in which they visited Ostende and Antwerp, Belgium, exploring the Exposition there, and experiencing both crowds and cold rainy weather.[64] Rotterdam seemed to raise their spirits slightly, because Syd reported that "we had the good fortune to run into some old friends of ours that we had not seen for ten years—the Riggoletto Brothers and their wives. They were headlining at the Arena Theatre, so we had quite a talk about old times."[65] The couple traveled on to Germany in September, stopping first in Baden Baden, where Sydney enjoyed "the most wonderful Turkish baths" that make "you feel ten years younger and pounds lighter."[66] By the end of September, it was being reported back in Hollywood that Sydney was gravely ill with a pulmonary ailment, that he had traveled to Algiers to seek a recovery in the desert conditions, and that he would return to America soon thereafter.[67] Of course, it is certain that much of this story was designed to throw newsmen off the track.

Sydney's paranoia about being found had no basis in fact until an article appeared in the *Daily Express* and then, subsequently, a barrage of reporters discovered his whereabouts at the Hotel Westminster in Nice. As Sydney related to Jim Minney, "One of them traced me to a very small hotel & because I would not see him, wrote a piece in the *Chicago Tribune* that I had disappeared from the 'fashionable' Hotel Westminster & was living in an obscure hotel Monty & had fifteen trunks with me. Of course," he wrote, "the trunk story was all d—d his. Also the 'fashionable Westminster.' Had he said I had left a third rate hotel for a cheap fifth class, the story would have suited me down to the ground, but he twists what I said to hurt me. Anyhow, I have left that hotel before the other hounds arrived."[68] Even so, he appears to have been in little danger after such sightings, except, of course, for the damage they did to his nerves. As a result, from early January 1931, when this article appeared, until early June, Sydney took off in earnest. His recounting of his movements during this period is equivalent to any slapstick scenario in terms of "bits" and humor. Two episodes are worthy of inclusion here: his chilly refuge at the Hotel de Paris in Monte Carlo in February (where the above letter was written) and his brush with civil rebellion in Lisbon, Portugal, in late May. Having fled from Nice altogether for a time, Sydney writes about "living alone in a *very obscure hotel* on the high Cornish, perched on a rock one thousand feet above Monty Carlo. I am the only guest there and have been for days. The hotel has no heating system and I am gradually freezing to death. It has redeeming features — the view is wonderful. I see all Monty Carlo & the coast of Italy and at night I look down on a blaze of lights." He believed that while he sat having dinner, he could imagine himself flying over some city in a zeppelin: "I get a little French practice, as no one speaks English & we are all in bed at 9:30. Except for the view and food, which is excellent, it is the nearest thing to a prison I can imagine."[69]

Certainly, the irony of his location — and the metaphoric quality of it, in terms of his life and current situation — could not have been lost on him. Sydney Chaplin, lover of sunshine and society — the life of the consummate hedonist — finds himself unceremoniously perched atop a cliff alone, looking down on the life he once had and very much desires to have again. He is cold and must communicate in a language foreign to him. His brother is currently being lauded by the citizens of Germany and Vienna — being carried through a crowd of admirers on the backs of those same admirers. Perhaps this is his blackest, most self-evaluative moment — or should be.

After traveling to Paris and Biarritz in May, Sydney strayed to Lisbon on a trip meant to prepare the way there for Charlie's *City Lights* and found himself in the middle of a political situation that made his own look very unimportant. He related the events to cousin Aubrey Chaplin, and then more candidly to Jim Minney, of course, such that his account was soon published in Minney's *Everybody's Weekly*:

> I have only just returned from Lisbon where I had quite an exciting experience: the night I arrived I took a walk through the town, saw a large crowd outside a big theatre and a regiment of soldiers; I wondered what was going on within when suddenly two bombs exploded within a short distance of me — there was a stampede — and I was knocked down and trampled on in the rush. I found out afterwards that there was a huge political meeting within.[70]

His next notable experience was two days after when he was returning to his hotel about midnight. Suddenly another bomb exploded within 50 feet of him; there was another panic and the crowd and the police came rushing in his direction. "I thought it safer to retreat with them," he wrote. "Just then a woman with a baby in her arms, holding another child of about 3 years by the hand came rushing by me screaming."[71] Sydney picked up the little boy and carried him in order to help her. They tried to get access to a café, as there was no other place for shelter, all stores being closed, but the café refused to open the doors, in spite of the fact that he pointed out the two children. Just then, another bomb exploded in the center of the road. The woman became panic-stricken,

Minnie and Sydney Chaplin walking along the Promenade des Anglais in Nice, France, near their Palais Rosa Bonheur flat, circa 1931 (CHACHAA).

grabbed her little boy and rushed on. Sydney remembers that he "just lit a cigar and sat on the steps of the café, and waited to see what would happen. Just then a man rushed up to the café. The waiters evidently knew him, because they opened the doors immediately. I forced my way in behind him in spite of the protest of the waiters."[72] Sydney and his charges had no sooner entered the café, when it was immediately surrounded by police; they entered with drawn guns and compelled everyone to hold their hands up while they searched for firearms. They found a gun on the man whom Sydney had accompanied into the café, and he was immediately arrested and taken out. "They started asking me questions in Portuguese," Sydney recalled, "to which I simply answered: 'British,' showed them my passport, pointed to the name of 'Chaplin,' and profession 'Cinema,' then said in French: 'Frére de Charlot,' started giving an imitation of my brother and his walk twirling his cane."[73] Sydney believed the rest of the crowd thought he was mad. The police officials never broke a smile. However, they were all kept in the café for 15 minutes under armed guard until a high police official made his appearance, cross-examined everyone, and then told them all to get out. The following day there was a strong earthquake at three o'clock in the morning. The public was panic-stricken and the streets were crowded with people in pajamas and night-dresses. However, Sydney decided to stay in the hotel and take his chances:

> I prefer earthquakes to bombs. They have been throwing them almost every day. One bomb blew out the front of the store, right opposite my bedroom window. Another day there was a huge procession of fellows shouting and waving a newspaper called *Republic*. They were charged by the police with drawn sabers. I had an excellent view of the whole proceeding from my bedroom balcony.[74]

Then in February of 1931, Minnie Chaplin purchased a brand new flat on the sixth floor of a well-located building in Nice, the Palais Rosa-Bonheur, just a few blocks from the beach, with a "nice balcony outside & sun all day."[75] Her furniture arrived from the States in late March[76] and the two took residence shortly thereafter, with Sydney commenting, "I am looking forward to settling down. Hotels get a little tiresome."[77] While much has been made of the fact that Sydney never owned a house, because it made him feel tied down, in fact he did own this large apartment with his wife (all the money was in her name at this time, which was to cause him problems later) and lived there at least until the mid–1950s. But before he was able to settle down and realize what life on the French Riviera might entail, Sydney was to be scooped up by his touring brother Charlie and entourage.

Chapter 8

Travels with Charlie

> Well, Jimmie, old pal. It's too bad you are not my brother & yet perhaps it is just as well. I always remember the lines of Potash & Perlmutter after a quarrel. Potash says, "You treat me more like a relative than a friend." — Sydney to R. J. Minney, August 1930. WGC.

CHARLIE HAD EMBARKED ON A WORLD PUBLICITY tour in January 1931 for his new film, *City Lights*, a silent film made well after the advent of sound. As has been mentioned, the concurrence of this event with BIP's bankruptcy suit against him was not lost on Sydney. He was well aware of John Maxwell's calculation that Sydney would want to avoid bad publicity for Charlie's sake. As has been shown, Sydney's relationship with his brother Charlie was complicated, albeit loving. He supposedly never informed Charlie of his troubles,[1] and was adamant about shielding him from them throughout 1930, despite having received word from Arthur Kelly by June that "your troubles in England are well known here."[2] One letter Sydney wrote to Charlie from a refuge in Constantine, where he had fled for a time, illustrates the tenor of their relationship at that point:

> My dear Charlie, I am enclosing a cutting out of a cinema program here, that may interest you. I hope your picture is finished and that you are quite pleased with it. I heard that you intended taking a holiday & visiting the orient. If so I would advise you to get the book entitled "Finding the Worthwhile in the Orient."
> This town Constantine is very interesting, built on the side of a precipice with a deep gorge & caves, etc. Am just running away to see a talking picture. They have them even down here. So, must close. Hope you are keeping quite well. I had a long interesting letter from Chuck Reisner, telling me about your new tennis court, etc. All the best.
> Love, Sydney[3]

However, by February of 1931, he asked Jim Minney to bring up his affairs casually to Charlie when the hoopla of his initial arrival in London had died down a bit.[4] The obvious embarrassment of his situation was probably reason enough for this, but a letter dated December 10, 1930, suggests there was another reason — Sydney owed him "a very large sum of money."[5] Then, by February 1931, Sydney was hatching a plan for his own future and needed Charlie to help him out with it, so he began testing the waters. In a letter dated March 16, he responded to the knowledge that Jim Minney had failed to talk to Charlie about the matter, writing him that telling Carlyle Robinson (Charlie's publicity agent) was probably just as good a person to inform. Sydney's plan involved getting United Artists to agree to release either *The Submarine Pirate* or *Mumming Birds* (the unfinished Elstree film) as talking films, and Sydney needed Charlie's approval for this to occur.[6] A cable from Robinson to Jim Minney suggests that there might be even more to the tentative relationship between the two brothers at this time: "Seeing Sydney Sunday. Will advise Charlie practically assures release as suggested. Depends attitude Sydney."[7] In his own recounting of his experiences working as Charlie's publicity agent, Robinson offered this assessment of the brothers' relationship: "It was in Nice that Charlie was reconciled with his half brother. They had been at odds for many years."[8] May Reeves, in her memoir of the tour (as Charlie's lady friend) entitled *The Intimate Charlie Chaplin*, describes their relationship in more emotional terms:

> He was as changeable and thoughtless with his servant Kono as with his brother Sydney. For years, he and Sydney had not understood one another. Sydney, who lived at Nice, came to spend a day discussing some business matters at Juan-les-Pins. Charlie received him very coldly. Sydney swore that he had not participated in the intrigues hatched against me at Marseilles, that Robinson had been the sole instigator. I reconciled with him immediately and interceded for him with Charlie. I pitied Sydney, who had always had trouble with his brother. "No one will change him," Sydney assured me. "During long years of collaboration in Hollywood, not a day has passed without my heart being broken. Many times I have hidden and cried in the wings of the studio, me, a man of my age!"[9]

The press at the time, however, got wind of none of this, or at least chose to ignore it, the Edinburgh *Scotsman* on April 3, 1931, in an article entitled "April 1 Joke on Chaplin" reporting: "Chaplin found out to-day that it was April 1. He lunched with his brother Sydney and a large number of friends at a hotel, and one item on the menu was Charlie's favourite dish, 'crepes suzette,' the fascinating little rolled pancakes which are served with blazing rum." When the dish arrived Charlie took three, and began to tell everyone of the excellent pancakes he had eaten in all the four corners of the world. "'Ah!' said his brother Sydney, 'just eat these, Charlie; I'll bet you've never tasted any like them.' Charlie struggled with them for some time before he discovered that they were made of cheesecloth covered with batter." It then gradually dawned on him that he had forgotten the date. " 'These are too hard on a man,' he said, and then joined heartily in the laughter until he was otherwise occupied with some real 'crepes suzette.'"[10]

In the same March 16 letter referenced above, Sydney states he would not go to Berlin while Charlie was there, because: "I do not want to appear to be chasing him or trying to bask in his limelight." He hopes instead that Charlie will come to the Riviera, not because he wants to see him, but because he has a proposition: "It appears that on the 27th, 28th, and 29th of this month, [the City of Cannes is] having a big fête with army, navy & aeroplanes." They wanted to put on a big reception for Charlie with a military welcome and build a sort of Arche de Triomphe of flowers. Sydney wrote that it would be "a big gala where every lady will be requested to dress in blue & white, colors dedicated to Charlie. Also place at his disposal a suite in the best hotel. It will be a bigger affair than they have ever given any visiting king. The place is packed with titles and millionaires at the present moment & would be quite a fashionable affair."[11]

Sydney's participation in Charlie's tour was, although spotty, significant. Charlie did finally visit the area and spent a lot of time being entertained by Frank J. Gould and others, but, ironically, he didn't arrive until March 31—just after the dates outlined in Sydney's letter above as the dates of the Cannes fête. Sydney seems to have regained his old influence over Charlie there, however, and is soon (1) the cause of Charlie's attachment to the aforementioned May Reeves, a Czech dancer, whose acquaintance Sydney had made in Gould's casino shortly before Charlie's arrival, (2) the temporary firing of Arthur Kelly from United Artists, and (3) the permanent firing of Carlyle Robinson, who had worked loyally for Charlie since 1917.[12] Writing to Jim Minney about Robinson with seeming affection in early 1931,[13] it seems unreasonable that Sydney would lobby to have him fired by July, but as in many such affairs, a woman (Reeves) was central to the situation. This move also made Sydney Charlie's publicity manager for the remainder of the tour and the United Artists representative for Charlie's films in Europe throughout the 1930s. A brutal and more demanding representative Charlie had never had. Still, Sydney could not protect his own status with Charlie for long and was cast aside by the end of the summer over a disagreement involving the same woman—Reeves. According to Robinson, one of their battles resulted in Charlie's fleeing Nice for Marseilles, with intentions of traveling to Algeria on April 14, a short two weeks after his arrival.[14] Sydney became "enraged" (as Robinson describes it) both with his brother for having clamped onto a woman he had sought out for himself, and then later for Charlie's embarrassing himself by being seen in public with her so often and so exclusively. As Robinson recounts it, "It hardly matter[ed] whether Minnie [Sydney's wife] knew the truth; in any case she was furious, for one reason or another. Yet the more they scolded Charlie the higher his spirits rose. All these reproaches only served to fan the flames of his passion. He has always liked to double his attentions to those who are despised the most."[15] So, even though Robinson, Sydney and Minnie all expressed their disapproval, Charlie only slightly acquiesced to their wishes in terms of bringing May along on his tour of Algeria by asking them to accompany her on a second boat, following his by a few hours.[16]

Immediately upon his arrival in Algeria, Sydney began working his way back into Charlie's good graces through that one subject most important to them both: money. Sydney was able to convince Charlie that *City Lights* was not being marketed properly and also that he was not getting as much profit from the film in certain territories as he could be. The result was a tentative reconciliation between the two brothers and an order for both Sydney and Robinson to travel to France and investigate this situation. Once in Paris, however, Sydney soon lost interest in these business-oriented duties and, due to insistent cables from Minnie that strongly promoted the idea once again that Charlie was risking his fame and fortune on an unworthy female, his brother's relationship again assumed a position of top priority. Not wishing to risk his new status with his brother, though, Sydney decided to give Robinson the onerous task of breaking up the two lovers. Robinson admits in his memoir,

> It was a gigantic undertaking. I knew that Sydney wouldn't have attempted it for anything in the world. As for me, judging from my past experience, I genuinely doubted my ability to

tear Charlie from the arms of his mistress. And because I admitted as much, Sydney decided to tell me a secret which I am sure he would have preferred, in any other circumstance, to keep to himself. But for him it was worth the risk. By telling me this secret, he hoped to arm me with an unanswerable argument which would force Charlie to break off with May.[17]

This secret, that Sydney and May had been lovers, was to cause irreparable damage, but only to Robinson. Not intending to have to resort to revealing Sydney's secret, Robinson unsuccessfully tried every other recourse to break up Charlie and Reeves. In the end, he used this trump card, one that was to cost him a lucrative position as Charlie's publicity agent that he had held faithfully for 14 years. Charlie's rage only just matched that of Sydney when he found out that his secret had been revealed. Although initially jubilant that Charlie had finally been separated from Reeves, he became "pale with rage" at the news of how this separation had been accomplished. A week later, Charlie was also separated from Robinson, who, traveling to New York, ostensibly to replace Arthur Kelly, would shortly be off the Chaplin payroll himself.[18] In a letter to Jim Minney written on July 17 after Robinson had been sent packing, Sydney mentions his new occupation as Charlie's agent of sorts and its consequences, but nothing about Robinson or May Reeves:

> I am as busy as a one-armed paper-hanger with the hives, okaying Charlie's contracts and learning how to swear in French, whilst Charlie remains in a semi-comatose condition at Juan-les-Pins. He certainly has become enamoured of the place and from his conversation I gather that he is becoming reluctant to leave Europe, although I cannot see how he can possibly transfer his activities from America to here, as he has so many investments over there, including a studio, etc., and after all, there is no place in the world like America for making pictures.[19]

Charlie and Reeves, however, had not been separated at all, arriving back on the Riviera within the week. Sydney's plan had been foiled and once again he was in the doghouse, writing Robinson that "it was impossible to live on good terms with his half-brother, and he had therefore given up worrying about him and was on the point of taking a holiday, during which he would walk on the banks of the Rhine."[20] In a letter to Jim Minney, dated August 3, Sydney refers only to the physical manifestations of his last few months' involvement with Charlie: "I just wanted to drop you a line and wish you good-bye, as I expect to leave in a day or two for a walking tour through the Rhine country. I am sorry to say that my health is way below par, so I am adopting this as the best way of pulling myself together. As it is a matter of nerves, I have an idea that solitude will be the best remedy."[21]

Soon, however, he would be hiding out from the press in his solitary perch atop the high Cornish near Monte Carlo, but by the new year, Charlie had once again invited Sydney to join him, this time in St. Moritz, Switzerland. Sydney prettied up the story of time in St. Moritz in a letter to Jim Minney written much after the fact, on March 9, 1932, first starting with, "Let me tell you I have had a wonderful time with Charlie at St Moritz. It was so unexpected. I was just getting ready to hibernate for the winter and figuring out how I could reduce my debts by going off the Gold Standard or the end of the pier when I received a telegram from he of the quarter to three feet asking if I would care to join him in the solidified water sports." Because Charlie was covering costs, Sydney decided to travel first class. "The first thing that happened on crossing the border of

Traveling with Charlie, St. Moritz, Switzerland, 1932. Sydney was never confident on skis (CHACHAA).

Italy," he wrote, "was to have my two beautiful cigarette lighters confiscated by the customs as they are not allowed in the country. This lowered my opinion of Michaelangelo to zero. It left me with as much appreciation of him as the British had for Wagner during the War." Sydney found his brother looking well and madly enthusiastic about skiing. It was his first season and everyone told his brother of the great progress he was making. "I was invited to go with him and Mr Citroën and party on a skiing expedition the next day," he continues. "We started off in two of Mr Citroën's special built tractor cars, taking our lunch with us, which we thoroughly enjoyed in an out-of-the-way farmhouse miles from anywhere and well off the beaten track of skiers. Of course, we would be exclusive."

This was only Sydney's second time on skis and the guide assured him he had nothing to fear. But, in fact, twelve of the group started down and only eleven arrived. "After I came to," Sydney remembered, "I found myself buried in snow at the bottom of a ravine. The rest of the party had disappeared. I had visions of being left there for the night and frozen to death. I managed to pick myself up and continue on. I arrived an hour later at the station just as the rest of the party were about to take a train back to St. Moritz" looking like a snowman. Icicles were hanging from his nose and eyelashes. Everyone roared with laughter and Sydney was the joke of the evening. "I decided I had had enough of skiing and would confine my future activities to the bobsleigh, which I did. It's funny the different fears that people have," Sydney wrote. "Charlie would not go down the bob run for a £1000 and no one could persuade him to and yet he would go on night skiing expeditions that I would not have for any sum." St. Moritz proved incredibly rejuvenating for Sydney, which he partially attributed to the altitude: "Everyone would remark about my vitality; I would dance in the bar until two or three in the morning, rumbas and Tyrolean waltzes until my partners dropped from exhaustion. There was one little German girl there and how she could *dance*. When we got together, the floor would clear and our rumba would always finish up with a big round of applause." Of course, his energy was a great joke to Charlie, because on his arrival, Sydney had told him he did not think his heart would stand the altitude: "From then on in the middle of one my dervish whirls, Charlie would shout out 'mind your poor heart, Syd.'" Some of the best amusements in St. Moritz, to Sydney at least, involved members of the nobility who would gleefully enter into any kind of stunt the brothers arranged: "One night The Prince de Bourbon and I danced a waltz in a stooping position like two dwarfs. I also danced an eccentric rumba with the Princess de Hesse. They all seemed to enter into the spirit of fun, but you could always tell the *nouveau riche*. They would sit perpendicular and parallel with their starched shirt fronts and talk Einstein."[22]

Minnie, Sydney's wife, however, was worried from the outset about this trip, perhaps because she knew May Reeves would be there as well. She enlisted the one remaining United Artists representative in Europe at the time, Boris Evelinoff, stationed in Paris, to aid her in keeping an eye on her husband's state of mind. Evelinoff was to experience his own misfortune for having become involved within the year, but in early 1932, he reported on Sydney's attitude and demeanor to Minnie in at least two missives, one written February 7, 1932, in which he reports, "I have received lately several letters from your husband whom I see is quite in a good temper and feels quite all right, and up there are many people who have come back from St. Moritz, and who have there seen him. They are all in love with him who is charming everybody with his gaiety and his comic skillness."[23] However, Sydney returned to Nice well before Charlie was thinking of ending his own stay in Switzerland, haranguing Charlie's Japanese man Friday, Toraichi Kono, into arranging his invitation for the upcoming Southeast Asia tour before he left, or at least this is Kono's side of the story: "Syd had urged Kono to arrange for him to accompany them to the Orient. Kono did suggest it to Charlie, who, after a few days' hesitation, finally consented to take him along. Syd was informed by telegraph at Nice that he was to join them at Naples."[24] Sydney remembers this in a letter to Jim Minney only as "Kono, his Japanese secretary, was told to make all arrangements. The result is we are now comfortably installed in a suite on board the *Suwa Maru*."[25] Sydney did receive the aforementioned telegram, however, on February 23, which stated simply, "When can you come? Leave here Thursday. Sailing from Naples six March. Charlie."[26] Sydney complied, but Minnie was still worried about this situation with some justification, for Evelinoff reports to her on March 18, "I must tell you that before the departure, Sydney was very nervous during two days, because he did not know if Charlie would decide or not to go to Japan." Keeping close to Charlie was a man named Baron Plage, as well as a Mr. Luporini, who were doing their best to ensure that Charlie would stay longer in Italy, and this much annoyed and unnerved Sydney. Evelinoff wrote to Minnie that "at last he and I have won so that as you know Charlie sailed on the 6th with Sydney. [Later] I was with Sydney on board at the moment of leaving and his character and temper were then quite all right." Evelinoff claimed that he spoke a lot about her and asked him to always keep in touch and communicate with her, "But you know that I don't require his demand to be always very glad to personally communicate with you as you know quite well that I love you very much and that we are always good friends and comrades."[27]

On March 20, Sydney and Charlie were having their pictures taken by the media while they tried on fezzes and climbed atop camels, later enjoying the dusty sites provided by the Sphinx and the Great Pyramids at Giza. Charlie finally succumbed to Syd's nagging on the subject of May Reeves and she was left on the wharf in Naples in the company of Evelinoff, who was to lose his position with United Artists later due to his continual applications to Charlie on May Reeves' behalf. Syd's notes on the trip sum up their visit briefly, but fail to mention the woman:

> Motored through Cairo. Lunched at Shepheard's Hotel. Rushed around town shopping, white suits, tropical helmets, etc. Visited pyramids. Watched a man ascend and descend more than six minutes, very dangerous, stumble would be fatal. Photographed camels. Difficulty in purchasing movie camera. Everybody hunting Cairo. Dozen people and dozen camels arrive at Cook's office. Motored back to ship at night.[28]

After visiting Ceylon (Sri Lanka), where they enjoyed driving around Kandy and witnessing the devil dancers at work, a beautiful shot of the brothers sitting alfresco at table in Singapore appeared in the papers on Charlie's birthday. The result of this meal, however, was a case of dengue fever for Charlie. Sydney, essentially his new publicity agent by this point, was approached as to the patient's progress: "'His temperature was 103 yesterday,' Sydney Chaplin said, 'but he is much improved today. We hope to sail for Japan on the 24th.'"[29] On March 30, they arrived in Batavia, Java, meeting there a Dutch cameraman by the name of Henk Aalsem,[30] with whom they were to join up later. Here in Java, the brothers were to experience a Dutch delicacy, rijs tafel. In an unpublished manuscript, Sydney writes a sort of narrative of their experience with this dish: "Upon taking your seat at table, you will be given an extra large deep soup plate which you proceed to fill with rice. Then about thirty waiters immediately line up behind your chair in Indian file, each carrying a different dish containing everything but the kitchen sink & with smells ranging from a hen house to a burlesque chorus dressing room." The consumer than helps himself with a large spoonful of each until his plate resembles a snowy mountain range. Then another bunch of waiters arrives with a dozen dishes containing every kind of sauce, condiment and chutney possible. "You now take off your coat, roll up your sleeves, & unbutton your trousers (not too far down)," Sydney recalled. "Grab your spoon and dive in. Give your best imitation of a mole & every fifteen minutes come up for air. Shake the rice out of your ears & the sweat from the back of your neck, then dive in again. When you are nearing the bottom of the plate, you again emerge for respiration, also to see if the rest of the guests have departed & if the waiters are preparing to lock up the restaurant for the night." Having then played the waiting game with your table companion to the point of getting him to spring for the check, "You then belch your thanks like a well bred Japanese, hoist yourself out of your chair & walk bulgingly towards the door. Don't brush the rice off your waistcoat. Leave it. The orchestra will think you have just come from a wedding & will immediately burst forth into Mendelssohn's march as you exit."[31]

By April 1, the brothers reached Bali via a K.L.M. steamer, a place in the world both of them were looking forward to as uncluttered by Western morals and restrictive religion. Sydney had first entertained the idea of traveling to Bali after seeing a news report in June 1930, in the *New York Times*, entitled "Bali, the Last Garden of Eden" which was a review of a new book by Hickman Powell (and, more importantly, with illustrations by Alexander King) entitled *The Last Paradise*.[32] What the article encouraged, the book itself demanded, for it used soft pornographic imagery to display the more attractive aspects of Balinese culture.

Four perspectives on the brothers' time in Bali exist: two written by Sydney — one for his brother's use in writing his travel memoir for *Woman's Home Companion* and one for Jim Minney, part of which appeared in Minney's *Everybody's Weekly*- one written by Florence Hirschfield, spouse (at the time) of caricaturist Al Hirschfeld, who lived on Bali and, with her husband, entertained the brothers there more than once, and one written by Charlie well after the fact in the aforementioned *WHC* memoir. Sydney's notes list names and dates and places, but the preponderance of his information is on the local dances they witnessed: the kris dance, the "topeng" or mask dance, the Barong, the Legong, and the Baris. Because Charlie had purchased a hand-held movie camera before their departure in Cairo, Sydney was anxious to get these performances and the performers (many topless) on film and enlisted the help of cameraman Henk Aalsem to assist in this endeavor. The result is a brief and jumpy home movie of their stay with nearly all evidence of Charlie cut out — by Aalsem, who is believed to have taken the footage for his own uses. Sydney's letter to Jim Minney, though, provides the evidence of the real reason for their visit, describing, as he does, the Isle of Bali as "the enchanted garden of Eden that has been unspoiled by European intrusion, and where the young ladies walk around bare from the waist up — personally I'd sooner see it from the waist down; however, we must be grateful for small mercies in these days of alimony and gold-diggers."[33] Although Jim Minney did not include this portion of Sydney's letter in the *Everybody's Weekly* article, published in April 1932, Charlie does make mention of this particular Balinese attraction in his travel memoir.

Florence Hirschfeld, whose account was published in the *New York Times* in June 1932, fails to mention Sydney at all in her long article, even though he must have experienced all the moments and events she retells:

> Chaplin entered into the spirit of the place and ate rice with his fingers from dishes made of banana leaves, squatted on the ground to watch cockfights, and would go any distance to see a native dance or hear an orchestra. His understanding of the dancing and music was amazing. The music is entirely different from the white man's, and persons who have long been in Bali find it difficult to interpret, yet Chaplin went away from the performances humming entire passages with unerring instinct. And his imitations of the dancers would pack a Broadway house.[34]

Finally, in Charlie's *Woman's Home Companion* account, entitled "A Comedian Sees the World," he writes that "he first time I heard of Bali was during conversation with my brother. We were discussing the general unrest of the world. 'If it comes to the worst,' he said, 'I'll go to Bali. That is an island untouched by civilization, where you can sit under the sweltering palms and pick the fruit off the trees and live as nature intended. There one doesn't worry about depression,' Sydney offered. 'The problem of living is easy.

And the women are beautiful.'"[35] But, in fact, it was several hours after the brothers' arrival before they spotted their quarry. Finally taking a motor tour of the island, Charlie reports, "We had been riding about fifteen minutes when my brother Syd nudged me. 'Look there, quick!' I turned and saw a line of stately creatures walking along the road, dressed only in batiks wrapped around their waists and their chests bare."[36] Both Sydney and Charlie were to return to the island later, Sydney in 1938 and Charlie in 1936, possibly to convince themselves that such a place really existed.

The brothers' first initiation into Japanese culture occurred well before they landed on the Japanese shore. The crew of the *Suwa Maru* did their best to expose Sydney and Charlie to their culture on board the ship. Consistently, Sydney's clearest memories seem to involve food and in this case, his first Japanese meal: "Charlie and I sat for two solid hours in Japanese manner, and believe me the feeling after a first day's horseback riding is nothing in comparison with the aches and cramps on rising from the Japanese squat. Believe me, Japanese sitting, like skiing should be learned while young." He wrote that he "thought that Japanese meal was never going to end. They cook it right on the table in front of you and put everything in but the mountain of Fujiyama. When it's all finished, if you can guess what it is — you can have it. They gave us chopsticks to eat with." While Charlie had practiced with chopsticks before, Sydney claimed to be "about as graceful as an elephant trying to thread a needle with boxing-gloves on. Can you imagine trying to take a pea with two sticks in one hand? When it comes to eating peas you can have your chopsticks. Give me a knife — even though the peas do roll off."[37]

Sydney and Charlie landed in Kobe, Japan, on May 14 to adoring crowds that only got larger as they moved onto Tokyo by train. Their main purpose in traveling to Japan was to secure bookings for *City Lights* that would garner Charlie a decent profit on the film. At this, at least, they failed miserably. In fact, the trip as a whole seemed to be plagued with bad luck. Although Charlie never mentions it in "A Comedian Sees the World," Japan was beginning to cause problems already in 1931, through its constant aggressiveness towards China. On September 18, just a few months before his arrival with Sydney in Kobe and following the assassination of Captain Nakamura, the Japanese troops in Manchuria were mobilized and took Mukden.[38] During the brothers' visit, Japan's liberal Prime Minister Inukai was assassinated (he had hoped to forge a policy of friendly relations with China) and Charlie was soon to find out that his life was also in danger there during his stay.[39]

In giving his perspective on Japan in *Woman's Home Companion*, Charlie chose to focus mostly on the Kabuki-za Theater (and the fact that *kabuki* season was in full swing during their visit), Sumo wrestling, geisha girls and the tea ceremony: "More than anything I saw in Japan, the tea ceremony revealed to me the character and soul of the nation — perhaps not of modern Japan, but the Japan of yesterday. It exemplifies the philosophy of life, beautifying the simple action of preparing tea to please the senses, utilizing an everyday fact to express the art of living."[40] Sydney only gives his review of the place well after the fact, in a letter to Jim Minney written October 16, 1932, "I enjoyed the trip immensely. I always wanted to visit the Orient, so I am glad I got it out of my system. Of course, I haven't seen the half of it, dearie. I shall still look forward to seeing India, the interior of China, Indochina, etc., but the Orient should be taken in small doses and one should hold the nose while taking it."[41] He claimed, though, that he was glad to get home, having developed gout on the trip from too much rich food.

Kono remembers that the brothers' relationship was strained by the end of the tour, because Sydney "had been annoying Charlie with an unwarranted solicitation as to money spent on their travels. The money was Charlie's, but Syd disapproved of Kono's disposition of it."[42] Parting ways then in Japan on June 2, with Sydney returning to the Riviera and Charlie to Hollywood, the brothers were not to see each other for another five years. Sydney was in a hurry to return to his hedonistic lifestyle in Nice, although his life was now encumbered with Charlie's business deals, at least the European ones. Minnie, in Hollywood at the time of Sydney's Asian tour with Charlie, may or may not have known that she was visiting old friends there for the final time. Perhaps she had some intuition as to what lay ahead for her.

CHAPTER 9

Double Exposure: 1932–1938

> After a wonderful day at the beach, sunbathing, swimming and exercise, I come home, have my dinner, then spend the evening with my friends. These are usually well "lit up" by the time I get there, having spent the day mixing cocktails. I join them in a drink & listen to their conversation, which usually consists of smutty stories & shop, but you don't have to join in their "sez you." No, but you see they are old friends of mine, broad-minded and talk my language. I like a smutty story if it is clever and well-told. I also like a drink occasionally & besides their conversation is a relaxation from the high-brow discourses of the nudists. My evening friends would also like to be nudists, but unfortunately they like their Sunday afternoon cocktails, poker & bridge and are not very keen on exercise. What do I say? Nothing. It's none of my business. *Their bodies are their own.* Letter to R. J. Minney, October 7, 1932

WHEN SYDNEY ARRIVED BACK IN NICE at the Palais Rosa-Bonheur in June 1932, he did so as a resident alien and an exile. It looked like he and Minnie would be in Nice for a while, although he was not quite ready to admit to himself that there was not a film company in the entire world that would now hire him — that his film career was over. For Christmas 1931, Sydney had put on an outward show of both stability and affluence, even though he suggested that the celebration belied his actual financial status: "We had a great time & a large party of which I was the host with a 30% discount on the bill in return for my name. Such is fame. The management evidently hadn't read the newspapers or he would have paid me 30% to keep away."[1] By Christmas 1932, however, he was either unwilling or unable to "put on," claiming to Jim Minney that "my income has been reduced to a point where I am on the verge of sending out my unpaid tradesman's bills for Xmas cards. I was hoping this winter to have visited Paris and afterwards, taking in the winter sports, St. Moritz, but it looks very much as if I shall have to forego this pleasure unless by any chance the Wall Street Market takes a sudden turn and I can make a quick profit."[2] Of course, because Sydney had transferred his money and holdings to his wife, Minnie, by this time, in order to escape the bankruptcy mediators, financial information contained in such letters must remain suspect; in them he constantly bemoans his deficient finances and continues the refrain that he had, in fact, lost quite a bit in the Crash. Even so, he settled into the expatriate lifestyle as best as he could and seemed to enjoy what life in

9. Double Exposure: 1932–1938

the south of France had to offer. Minnie's Palais Rosa-Bonheur flat comprised three bedrooms, a living room, breakfast room, kitchen and two full baths. It was elaborately adorned with terrazzo mosaic flooring, crown molding and balconies that allowed them access to the out of doors on all sides. The lobby of the building, besides containing what might be high-quality marble, was dressed up with two *art nouveaux* murals of classical dancing ladies, with long flowing hair and filmy garments. And, a brand new elevator graced the center of the building, allowing them easy access to their penthouse accommodations. These were not the accommodations of a couple in any financial trouble, but of a couple enjoying the best that life and money had to offer.

In letters to Jim Minney, Arthur Kelly and others, Sydney sometimes wrote at length about how he spent his time — outside of writing lengthy letters, of course. One late 1933 letter contained an account of a typical night's entertainment: "The other night I was at the Hollywood Cabaret; they had a crazy night there in which nearly everyone dressed in eccentric costumes. I put on a burlesque make-up and did a number of funny stunts which got a great deal of laughter and applause. One stunt was a spring dance with a woman partner who must have weighed 250 pounds." Always ready to burst into song whenever the moment presented itself, Sydney writes, "I also sang them one of my own songs, which went over big. I received a bottle of Pommery champagne as a prize. Of course, that meant nothing. I was just in the mood and enjoyed myself immensely."[3] As this passage suggests, dinner, dancing, music, parties and other entertainments were of interest to both Sydney and Minnie and, by participating in them, the couple easily worked their way into the heady social life of the wealthy expatriates and local Niçoises. Add to these "the gentle art of lazing," and a fairly accurate picture of Sydney's life at the time can be constructed: "You cannot drag a sunworshipper away from his devotions and besides, I have been extremely busy practicing the gentle art of lazing. I can now accomplish the Yogi trick of relaxing every muscle of the body & making the mind a perfect blank." Falling into his usual bawdy rhetoric, he notes "That's not difficult for me—"sez you'— but unfortunately, *one muscle* remains relaxed, sometimes when I don't want it to.... I have been spending the mornings swimming and sunbathing, the afternoon in bed, evenings at the Thé dansant & my nights at the casinos." In relating to Jim Minney, at this point in the letter, that he had become an excellent swimmer and expert diver, he also reveals that in the Riviera he was continuing his relentless pursuit of women, this time through his "invention" of a "new aquatic sport":

> The game is played between two people of the opposite sex. The girl takes a water polo ball & places it between her thighs. The fellow then dives under the water & endeavors to wrest the ball away while the girl uses all her force to retain it. It is a case of his lung capacity against the strength of her legs. The first person I tried this on was a French college girl from Paris who was accompanied by a chaperone who did not swim, so we had no umpire. The first time I played it, I scored a touchdown right away. After this, there was a great deal of "fumbling" near the *back side* lines but I soon found an *opening* and started to *dribble* to the center forward & nearly *got a goal* but was offside again. I nearly scored, but her whistle blew, so I came to the surface for air. We played this game every day until she went back to Paris and you have no idea how it has developed my lungs. I can stay under water now almost as long as a piece of suburban real estate in winter. Of course, the game is not to really get the ball, but to make the girl think she is strong in the legs. I have tried this with

several other girls since & they all love the game. Even the fish have become interested. I feel sure that if the swimming season had not finished here it would have outdone the YoYo for popularity. I think I shall call the game "wavelengths."[4]

In addition to swimming and tennis (and pursuit of women), Sydney was also an accomplished duffer — he had won awards for his golfing skill in the United States in th '20s, and so, took up the art of golf with some enthusiasm in Nice, writing to Minney in late 1930, "am playing 27 holes of golf every day & am crazy about the game."[5] He also continued his interest in racing and gambling, developed in Hollywood, finding a 10–1 winner at the races in Nice in January 1931.[6] Sydney developed an interest in bridge in his new home, admitting to Minney, "I have been spending my time most pleasantly, having become a most enthusiastic tennis & Bridge player. I must have bought nearly every book written on Bridge & am studying the finer points of the game, preparing for my old age & future income."[7] And, his interest in photography continued to advance. One of the tragedies of his final heart-wrenching visit to London (really, to a London courtroom) was Sydney's loss of his Heidoscope camera stereoscopic on the train in July 1930. He writes Minney about the incident and, as usual, asks for his intervention: "I hate to trouble you again, but I have lost my camera. It is a Heidoscope camera stereoscopic, in a brown leather case with a shoulder strap. I remember distinctly taking it into the train with me on my way to London.... If you should find the camera, keep it until I tell you where to forward it to. Apologies for putting you to this trouble."[8] A later letter, in which he expresses his sorrow at the loss, clearly indicates his attachment to this diversion: "I am sorry you were not able to recover the camera. I'll charge this up to the arbitrator & buy a new one when I reach Germany as my travels would not be complete without my stereoscopic views. I have taken hundreds in every country I have been in."[9] Again, this loss, as sad as it might have been to Sydney, failed to keep him away from this diversion. At least by his 'round-the-world cruise in 1937 he had indeed replaced it and added at least two Bell & Howell hand-held movie cameras into the mix.[10]

Having plenty of free time, Sydney found himself taking up a suggestion of Jim Minney's from August 1930[11] that he write some music, and he actually had some success with the endeavor, getting two of his pieces written out in notation and disseminated about the dance bands there in Nice, where they became very popular. Of course, with this encouragement, he enlisted Minney to help him find a publisher for the music,[12] but instead, ended up finding one himself— a well-known music publisher based in America: "I have sold two of my songs, 'Give it to me' & 'I Love You' to Irving Mills, one of the America's biggest publishers. It appears he was in Nice & heard them played. After learning that I was the author & composer, he tried to get in touch with me at my Nice address, but I was in Paris at the time, so he left word for me to write him in America, which I did." Mills convinced Sydney that he was very enthusiastic about the songs and wanted to publish them before Christmas, Sydney then writing Minney that, in that case, "I left it to my NY attorney to close the deal. If these songs turn out successful on the market, I shall get busy on some more. Writing songs is like 'Duck Soup' to me. They come easy. You cannot imagine how pleased I am to think that Mills should choose a couple of songs in Europe, when he has all those professional writers of 'Tin Pan Alley' at his beck & call."[13]

Shortly thereafter, in January 1934, Sydney reports that "my contracts arrived today from America for my two songs. I do hope they turn out a big success. They are playing them here at the Palace & are quite popular. Last night, I was with Camilla Horne, the German star & she waltzed beautifully to I Love You. She insisted on writing down the title and the name of the publisher. I understand from New York, that Rudy Vallee is likely to record both numbers on his return from California to New York."[14] Although this information appears entirely positive, Sydney fails to mention the enterprise again, suggesting that the deal must have fallen through, or that Sydney simply lost interest in the project.[15] Still, just the lyrics from one of these songs, "Give It to Me," provide more evidence of Sydney's "interests." With "it" being the operative word in the title, he "just can't live without it," is always craving it and desiring it always. The song even contains a bit of a threat — the singer claiming that without "it," there will be misbehavior.[16] Even if Sydney was successful in placing a couple of these songs with publishers, his loss of interest in the enterprise suggests that perhaps it wasn't lucrative enough.

If he wasn't engaged in physical activity of some kind, however, chances are that Sydney was reading. Of the two brothers, Sydney was by far the more well-read and deeply intellectual, often spending full days within the pages of a book. Jim Minney often suggested possible titles and Sydney read every one of them. Some of his emotional reactions to his readings provide yet another level of the complexity of his personality, as in an August 1930 letter in which Sydney writes, "In the afternoon, I read *All Quiet on the Western Front* & after reading of men with their faces shot away & holding their entrails in while they struggled back to the base hospitals, I wondered if I had any troubles at all."[17] In a later letter, he mentions that he was reading French plays all afternoon: "I have purchased about fifteen bound volumes of very successful French plays. I think there must be about a couple of hundred plays in all. I find it not only improves my French but is also very instructive in getting the Frenchman's point of view & a knowledge of his technique."[18] Perhaps his deep love for books, though, is best illustrated in a letter to Aubrey Chaplin in which he bemoans the fact that his very expensive and best books have been ruined in the trip over to Nice from England, upsetting him terribly.

One of his new amusements, however, may have been inspired by his recent trip to the island of Bali (a trip inspired by the book by Hickman Powell and Alexander King entitled *Bali: The Last Paradise*) with his brother: nudism. In a letter written to Minney and dated June 11, 1931, Sydney casually mentions, "I have practically been living on the balcony, taking sunbaths 'à poil,' with no one but God and the sparrows to view my beautiful contour."[19] In fact, photos exist of an early 30-something Sydney à poil except for a canteen belt in a group of men clothed in hunting costumes, suggesting that perhaps this was not a new habit or occupation at all, but one he had been engaging in for some time, maybe even in Hollywood. A statement by nudist Harry Hermann of Hollywood, clipped from some periodical, found its way into Sydney's scrapbook. Entitled "Why Wear Clothes?" its narrative certainly would appeal to someone obsessed with cleanliness like Sydney: "The wearing of clothes is one of the filthiest habits of civilization, because clothes retain the excretions, prevent the proper contact of air and light with the surface of the body."[20] But it was not until Minney published two opposing views on the topic in September 1932 in his *Everybody's News*, though, that Sydney revealed himself — at least to Minney. In a 30-page handwritten letter sent from Nice and dated October 7, Sydney responded to these articles[21] and then told the story of his own experience as a nudist: "I know I can talk freely to you, Jim, & you know that what I say will be the truth & nothing but the truth. You have always been a confidante of mine & one of my best friends. So I have no fear of speaking my mind knowing that what I have to say is in strict confidence."[22]

Sydney claimed that he first visited a nudist organization in Berlin, but did not join at the time. Although he fails to indicate when this might have occurred, it is likely that it happened in 1919, when he was in Europe to film *King, Queen, Joker*. He relates that some time later, "I happened to notice a magazine in a bookstore in Nice with a photograph of several nudists on the cover. The magazine was called 'Vivre.' I purchased the book and found it was published by a nudist society of Paris, who had a private grounds in Paris called the Sparta Club."[23] Sydney discovered that the organization's committee consisted of some of the best-known doctors and statesmen in France: "This was a big surprise to me, as I was under the impression that nudism was strictly forbidden in France. I also discovered that they had an affiliated society in Nice so I decided to join."[24]

Given his admitted body obsession, one developed in childhood,[25] combined with what Sydney terms his second reason for being interested — "the strong streak of sensuality in my nature"— becoming a nudist almost seems a natural tangent to his constant pursuit of health and sexual gratification. Although he argues in the letter that there was no place in these organizations for perversion or sexual predation and seems to suggest that his own motives for pursuing this lifestyle were or at least soon became largely philosophical ("One becomes so used to nudity around them that one almost forgets that it exists."), of course, these aspects of his "conversion," as he terms it, cannot be ascertained. However, his statement that the majority of nudists he encountered "are intellectuals of advanced thought, some of them communists and some like myself, rebels at heart against the smug hypocrisy of convention, and above all, reformers with atrophied glands who make it their business to tell other people what they shall do with their bodies" seems very much consistent with manifestations of this philosophy in other areas of his life.[26]

Sydney's retelling of his day-to-day interaction with the group, unfortunately for him, does little to convince anyone of his supposed high-brow motivations for becoming involved in the group: "After joining and paying my dues of 60 francs for the year, I was given directions where to meet, which was a deserted part of the beach, where we could depend upon complete privacy. Of course, this was strictly against the law, as the beach is public and had anyone complained, we were all liable for arrest, but we kept strict lookouts, so felt safe in our retreat." He claims that this will soon no longer be a problem, because the club was negotiating to acquire its own grounds. "Our club meets every Sunday on the beach," he writes, "and twice a week during the evenings at the private gymnasium belonging to a doctor. On my first visit to the beach, I found about 20 members all in the nude & indulging in various sports — medicine ball, badminton, swimming, etc." Sydney was introduced around, meeting "a local doctor, his wife and two children — two painters, very well known — a Russian dancer from the well-known Russian ballet, stenographers, shop girls, etc., all of them quite unconcerned about their nudity. Some of the figures were beautiful and some fat & flabby." He claimed that he was not in the least embarrassed about undressing before them, but was, in fact, rather eager to do so. The average girl, he wrote, revealed herself as eagerly and without much fanfare: "But one day a German girl came. It was her first visit. She was completely dressed—silk underwear, stockings, suspenders, brassiere—in fact everything possible a woman could wear. She undressed like a slow-moving picture. It was the only erotic thing I have seen in the club."[27] It seems apparent from this candid description that Syd's motivations were as much exhibitionistic as voyeuristic. Of course, Minnie's perspective on this avocation is unknown, but it seems clear that she did not join her husband in this particular social circle.

The end of 1932 was marked by the early demise of Aubrey Chaplin from stomach cancer, and with this death, Sydney and Minnie became more involved in the life of one of Aubrey's children, May (Betty Tetrick) Chaplin. Sydney had unashamedly used Aubrey's ambitions to his own purposes, enlisting him whenever necessary to solve particular problems for him in London, such as housing his car, arranging a benefit performance of *The Better 'Ole* for the *Exmouth* boys, and acting as a liaison between himself and Jim Minney, when necessary. In a January 6, 1931, letter to Jim, he had this to say about his "cousin" (really only Charlie's cousin):

> I hope my cousin is not bothering you. I did not ask him to call upon you, but just to send you the whiskey, as I wish to throw the business his way. I incidentally mentioned in my letter that you had been very kind to me and had helped me greatly in my case. I have never discussed my case with him as he does not speak "my language." So I suppose he was curious to get some inside "dope" from you. I was sorry when I heard he was trying to see you as I know how busy you are & he is a trifle boring, lacking in a sense of humour & broadmindedness which is rather strange for a publican. Outside of that he is a nice fellow & one of England's great suburban churchgoing population. If you do not have the leisure to see him personally, you will see him in every newspaper photograph of Charlie, should he visit England. You will easily recognize him, as he will be as close to the brother as a toadstool on a tree trunk.[28]

By Aubrey's death, however, he had transferred whatever feeling he had about the event to a sense of caring for May (Betty), one perhaps initially motivated by his more predatory impulses. Betty herself reported in an interview with Matthew Sweet that Minnie Chaplin was careful never to allow Sydney to be alone with her.[29] For her own part, Betty worked Sydney to her own purposes. A letter Sydney wrote to Minney dated December 6, 1932, reveals her motives: "I feel awfully sorry for the poor kid. It appears she is not very happy at home since the death of her father, and is most anxious to try and obtain employment on the Riviera. I would like to help her if I possibly could, but it will be most difficult for her to obtain work here as they are so strict about Worker's Cards and will not issue them to anyone who is likely to compete with their own national out–of–works."[30] Still, Betty stayed in close contact with Sydney and his wives, in many ways was as close or closer to them as his own nieces and nephews. Betty was to benefit greatly from this relationship over the years, first when Sydney arranged for her to come to Hollywood in the late 1930s, while he was deeply involved with the production of *The Great Dictator*.

In addition to his various pastimes, Sydney spent 1933 and 1934 fighting hard to get his film contract renewed with British International Pictures, and he enlisted Jim Minney to help out with the process. In December 1930, when his film industry prospects looked especially bleak, he continued to state his willingness to negotiate: "I wrote a long letter to Sidney [Garrett] from Biarritz in which I said I would always be willing to return & complete my contract. I am still willing." Sydney continued in the letter his refrain that he did not want BIP to lose the money they had already invested, and that he was "willing to eliminate the second picture, also the percentage of profits that was to have been paid beyond the hundred thousand dollars. This of course providing it was agreeable to Sidney as he was to have shared in this profit, but this is the only sacrifice I will make. I am deeply in debt & have to live."[31] Tangentially, he had really never left the business, having temporarily taken over many of Charlie's publicity agent Carlyle Robinson's duties in 1931 following his firing. Then by May 8, 1933, Sydney was assigned the duty of approving all of Charlie's United Artists contracts in Europe due to the firing of UA representative Boris Evelinoff. He often complained of being "up to my eyes in business correspondence"[32] or, "I am afraid I have a terribly worrying disposition and had quite a lot of work to do in connection with Charlie's affairs."[33] Sydney announced to Arthur Kelly, however, in a letter dated September 23, 1933, that although Charlie still wanted him to approve his contracts, Sydney was happy to delegate that duty to Kelly, who was now located in Paris anyway, thereby ending Sydney's United Artists involvement for a time.[34] Just a few months later, in March 1934, and also connected (supposedly) to Charlie's business interests, Sydney tried to convince his brother to finance a trip to Russia. He hoped to accompany Jim Minney on an upcoming trip there, signing a March 16 letter, "Farewell Comrade Minnyvitch, Yours without a stitch, Comrade Chaplinski" and mentioning that he had started "taking the moth balls out of my red woolen underwear in preparation for our trip through the whiskered wilderness."[35] But a letter to Alf Reeves shows that Charlie turned down Sydney's "proposal": "It was too bad CC did not want me to visit Russia. I had a great opportunity to look the land over, as I would have gone the same time as a friend of mine who is editor of an English paper very friendly to the Bolshevic movement." Sydney claimed that Jim Minney was traveling with all kinds of letters of introduction to the highest government officials, which would have helped him to "feel out" the situation for Charlie. "Of course, I would not have gone there with the intention of peddling Charlie's pictures," he writes. "I would have given the impression of being on a holiday & would have waited for propositions to come from them. However, I suppose Charlie knows best."[36] Despite this rejection, by August 1934, Reeves was writing to ask Sydney to continue okaying contracts on the continent, in preparation for the start of *Modern Times*.[37]

Although Sydney often referred to himself as lazy, at least his epistolary report of his activities suggests otherwise, for being adept at learning new languages (Sydney became fluent in French shortly after deciding to relocate there, even translating for Charlie during their time together on his brother's world tour), he was determined to use this talent to make himself a more marketable actor, if possible:

> I am studying German now. Yesterday I learned forty words. From what I understand, nearly all the big American Companies are going to establish studios in Paris to take care of the continental versions of their American pictures & providing this recent case of mine does not put me clean off the map, I can see a great opportunity, because if an American Company makes a great comedy in Hollywood, it would be a big asset to them to have a comedian in Paris

who could make the continental versions in French, German and Spanish, surrounded by a company of artists from these different countries. My accent would add to the comedy, because nearly all comedy is based on imperfection. Anyhow, I am going to study hard on the three languages. The reason I include Spanish is because there is a tremendous sale of pictures in the Argentine. I am full of ambition at the present moment & if the worse comes to the worse & I cannot play, then there is nothing to prevent me from directing & they need directors over here.[38]

As this endeavor seems to suggest, getting back in the business was never far from Sydney's mind. His next attempt made in earnest occurred over the span of 1933 and involved both of his closest friends, Arthur Kelly and Jim Minney. In fact, Kelly was probably the one responsible for fostering Sydney's hopes and essentially got the ball rolling by offering him a contract for a French United Artists picture in January of that year, by telephone, but Sydney wrote to Minney, "The terms were so ridiculously small that I was compelled to turn it down. Of course, he thinks me foolish not to accept as he pointed out to me it would be an opportunity to re-establish myself over here on the continent."[39] By February 5 he was writing a letter to Minney with his plans: one quick film with Maxwell and British International Pictures to settle the judgment and then a diplomatic move over to Gaumont to continue his career. In this letter he let Minney know that he had been contacted by a colleague of John Maxwell's just before leaving for Asia with Charlie (spring 1932), who, upon gaining a promise of his interest, would return to Maxwell with the information, with the intention of then starting the process from there.[40] The fact that he had not heard from Maxwell since that time, coupled with the proposition from Kelly, meant that the compulsion to investigate further must have been overwhelming for Sydney. Somehow he was able to cool his heels until April, however, when he officially asked Minney to negotiate a contract for him with BIP. Maxwell had agreed by this time to contemplating a contract, but only if United Artists would release the film in America.[41] An agreement to this effect is first given by Charlie in a cable from early May and by May 25 from Joseph Schenck himself, then president of United Artists.[42] So, by the end of May, Maxwell should have had the assurances he needed. Sydney's initial contract requirements aimed high (as always), asking for $20,000 of the $40,000 still owed him from his first contract, with $5,000 in advance and the rest to be paid as a weekly salary once shooting began. All previous claims against him had to be relinquished by the contract upon signing.[43] By May 8 and continuing to May 25 Sydney was wondering what the delay could be, because he had received nothing as yet from anyone affiliated with BIP.[44] Finally, by June 20, he had received word from Minney that progress was indeed being made and Sydney began making up his wish list for the contractual elements, including, in addition to the above, that 50% of his fee would be paid directly to him and that he wanted the capability of transferring rights and monies due to any individual or corporation he chose.[45]

July came and went and Sydney had still received no contract or contract draft, although he received a cable from Silverstone the first week of August saying that Maxwell had received the United Artists agreement regarding distribution the previous week.[46] By August 3 he wrote a letter to Minney discussing his preferred and most successful film roles, with a tone that suggested his optimism in the matter:

First let me say that I prefer character parts instead of clean make-up. All my biggest successes have been character parts, the style of parts that suit me are as follows: Charley's Aunt, Old Bill, Fred Emney Dames, Drunks, Broken English parts, underworld Apache, Dude parts, Dialect, Cockney, Lancashire, Scotch Irish, etc. All these different parts I can play equally well in comedy or drama & am just as willing to play a dramatic picture as I am a comedy. Therefore, if a play could be found that would give me scope to display versatility, I feel sure it would be a big moneymaker.... I am very much in favor of fast-moving stories of adventure & mystery. Therefore, I could play an Arsene Lupin part with various disguises, or secret service story, but the story would have to be convincing and not burlesque, or it would not succeed. My laughs would not be obtained by my foolish antics, but by my fooling the higher ups & offending their dignity, the audience sharing in my secrets & laughing with me & not at me.... You remember the play "The Unholy Three" in which Lon Chaney played the part of a crook disguised as an old woman? There is a part I could have played & embellished it with half a dozen different character disguises if necessary.[47]

His wife, Minnie, too, chimed in, writing Jim Minney that "he feels great & all pepped up about his story & thinking out tons of gags, handing me plenty of laughs."[48] This note may have followed a brief meeting between the two parties—Jim Minney and Sydney and his wife—that occurred in Paris the second week of August. And so the roller coaster ride continued. By August 23 the tide turned when the first draft contract arrived and Sydney claimed to be "astounded" with the original offer, calling the whole thing "nothing but a joke." The contract provided him 50 percent of net receipts in America only, which translated to his receiving no money until after the cost of the production, the previous judgments and his now $1,000 salary had been recouped by the film's business elsewhere in the world. Naturally, Sydney analyzed the thing from a position of suspicion immediately, writing that he believed he was offered such an impossible contract so that he would have to say "no" to it, thereby placing the blame upon himself and not BIP, at least in the eyes of the all-important United Artists. His conclusion after reading this draft was that all their efforts had been wasted and that their negotiations were at an end.[49] By August 30, he was already contemplating other ways to get back into the business, suggesting that if this contract fell through, he would continue working on the "Old Bill" story for the remainder of the year in hopes that Charlie would finance that effort in 1934.[50]

And, yet again, the tide turned. By September 5, Minney had indicated to Sydney that Walter Mycroft was keen about the contract going through and wanted to talk "story" with him. This seemed to be enough to bolster Sydney's hopes a bit and he continued the letter, again discussing possible roles.[51] Less than a week later, Sydney had agreed to some changes in the contract and was so enthusiastic now that "it could be signed in five minutes." His agent, Heywood, had done a good job with the contract and seems to have protected Sydney in every way possible. Maxwell seems to have agreed now to offer Sydney 50 percent of the world box office, with the exception of England only.[52] Sydney wrote with considerable glee to Kelly, that "they give me to understand that they have a very good story for me written by an American author, the fellow who wrote 'The Cradle Snatchers.'[53] ...They even talk of getting me the best American director they can find."[54] But this optimism was not to last for long. On September 14, Sydney received the contract, which he now referred to as "the bad news." It did not cancel the judgment upon signing, perhaps Sydney's most adamant requirement, and so could not be signed.[55] These negotiations were now at an end.[56] Sydney must have indeed felt very dejected about the whole thing.

But, in fact, this ordeal was not the bloody end of his film career, because Sydney truly felt he had other options. By August of 1934, he seems to have been on the verge of signing some sort of contract to do a film for Alexander Korda and was uneasy about the thought of someone stealing any sort of scenario ideas he might be pondering, citing the case of Mack Sennett and Roscoe Arbuckle allegedly stealing the idea from him that shortly became Arbuckle's innovative film *He Did and He Didn't* (1916). In a letter to Minney dated November 8, 1934, however, this possibility had fallen through, because Sydney had now turned his venom on Darryl Zanuck, Korda and Douglas Fairbanks — the parties who were to be involved in the film deal discussed in August, recounting a time when another of his film ideas presented to this group was at first highly praised and then completely ignored, this being "the kind of treatment that makes me detest the movies and people associated with them. They are all talk and promises which mean nothing."[57]

By late 1934, though, Sydney left any thought of a film career behind, for Minnie and her plummeting health had become the main occupation of both. Most of their efforts from that date until her death in September 1936 were with one motive in mind — her survival. While Sydney had been preoccupied with Charlie's affairs at the time of the 1931–32 World Tour, Minnie had taken what would be her final trip to America to visit friends in April 1932.[58] While her condition received some coverage from Sydney in letters to old friends, it is interesting to note that it receives next to no coverage in his correspondence to Jim Minney. As late as March 1936, about six months before her death, Sydney wrote a lengthy and comical letter to Minney that focuses on his own hypochondria (as usual), this time over "a continuous feeling of nausea and a burning sensation in the rectum." His only mention of Minnie's condition in the letter is covered in one line: "I'm glad to tell you that Minnie is keeping quite well."[59] In a typical move, however, Sydney complains in a July letter to his half-brother Wheeler about Minney's insensitivity in the matter, which, by this point, seems to have caused a temporary rift in their relationship.[60]

At this time, Nice was crowded with processions of rebels coursing up and down the streets outside the Palais Rosa-Bonheur and elsewhere "wearing red flags in their buttonholes & ... sporting the tri-color" and creating their own tepid brand of civil unrest."[61] This background to Minnie's demise is only worth mentioning because it works as a fitting metaphor for the biological unrest occurring in Minnie's body and Sydney's mind at that time. However, his response to brother Charlie's recent short telegram, ending, "However, buck up. Don't be discouraged. Love, Charlie,"[62] reads like another of Sydney's exercises in deception. He begins: "You have no idea how much I appreciated the long sympathetic cable you sent me regarding Minnie's illness. I was in a terrible state of mind when it arrived. I had not touched feed for four days." He then tells Charlie that Minnie's illness came on without warning: "One day she noticed casually a hard lump in the breast. I advised her to go to the doctor. He informed her she should be operated on immediately. I wanted to be sure he was giving me the right advice, so consulted the two best surgeons in town. They both said the same thing." Of course, Minnie was terribly nervous about the operation, but Sydney claimed to have done "everything in the world to allay her fears and cheer her up." The doctors had to remove the left breast and the glands under that arm, but "she has been very brave and has taken it philosophically. She made a splendid recovery, but of course cannot yet use her arm, or go anywhere. She is at present taking X-ray treatments & resting quietly at home." Reverting back, then, to commentary on his own condition, he writes that "it has been a terrible shock to me. I have learned to realize that only two people in life mean a thing to me, yourself and Minnie. She has been a wonderful pal & we have grown more together in the last few years. I have at last realized how self-sacrificing she has been. I have been her only thought—she has mothered me for years—& it was not until her illness did I appreciate her at her full value." In a candid and self-effacing moment, Sydney admits, "Charlie, there are greater things in life than money. The rarest thing on God's earth is sincere friendship & when we are in the hour of sorrow, it is then that we realize it. Your cable was the most comforting and encouraging thing we had. It cheered us up tremendously & we are both grateful to you from our hearts. All Minnie's friends have been very kind to her. Her room was a mass of flowers."[63]

Desiring to continue their lives with as much normalcy as possible, Sydney next set about planning a getaway. Although the recent United Artists reorganization had engendered more correspondence than his wife's cancer to acquaintances like Alf Reeves, her condition was at least worth a mention: "I am glad to tell you that Minnie is still making progress & I am taking her tomorrow to Budapest, from there we shall go up into the mountains." But in his thoughtfulness to Minnie lay Sydney's usual financial manipulations: "I have Budapest bonds that defaulted in 1932 & my bank gives me to understand that I can cash the coupons there so long as I spend the money in Hungary, which means that I shall only have to make a cash outlay for my fare there & as I get a 50% deduction going through Italy, the fare will amount to very little, all the rest of my expenditures will be in Hungarian Pongoos. I could not get a holiday as cheap as that in France."[64]

In between all these episodes of misery, Sydney made the acquaintance of James A. FitzPatrick, whose voice as the narrator of MGM's *TravelTalks* short film series had already become familiar to moviegoers. In a letter responding to Sydney's mention of FitzPatrick, Alf Reeves details that "he is a very charming boy and he is a very hard worker. He does a one-man job. You may be able to hook up with him and carry out your ideas. You love to travel and he has to make a world's cruise every year and sometimes twice a year in order to get his travelogue material."[65] Indeed, working with FitzPatrick may have been a perfect opportunity for Sydney, but as he relates in a later missile to Minney, his past came back to haunt him and foiled the plan, at least for the time being: "Some time ago, [FitzPatrick] approached me to see if I would be interested in making a world tour with him on the 'Franconia' & playing the principal part in his picture. I accepted the proposition, but at the last minute it fell through exactly the same as all my other offers." Sydney brought it up in his letter, because FitzPatrick had just recently revealed the reason for the plan's failure: "It appears he sent a cable to one of the head officials of the M.G.M. in London asking him what my drawing value was in England. That official confidentially advised him to leave me alone, as I had been connected with some girl scandal over there & if I appeared on the screen, there might be complications." This admission proved to be an epiphany for Sydney: "I am now convinced that this has been the reason for all my other offers falling through." And, of course, he tried to persuade FitzPatrick that he was, in fact, in the process of taking care of the problem. FitzPatrick played along, told Sydney he could throw a lot of work his way (business had been booming for him), and then even offered to write Dent (BIP) and suggest adding Sydney to an upcoming production BIP had recently offered him. Sydney writes, "I thought it was a good idea and coming at the same time as your effort, would clinch the matter. We sat talking until four in the morning & I stayed at his apartment all night. The following day he took me to the R.C.A. recording rooms & I stayed there all day with him while he recorded with full orchestra the music for his coloured pictures of the Paris Exposition." His hours spent with FitzPatrick allowed Sydney to feel much easier in his mind: "I really felt I was back at work again. It was so interesting from beginning to end."[66] Of course, nothing was to come of it.

This wasn't to be the only disappointment 1936 had to offer. Just a few months later, as Charlie was enjoying the South Pacific with Paulette Goddard after the release of their new film, *Modern Times*, on May 26, 1936, Sydney appealed again to Dr. Rosanoff, who had recently recommended one or two convalescent houses located in Montreux, Switzerland, as possible refuges to which both Minnie and he could turn. But Minnie was not well enough now even for her X-ray treatments and was certainly not well enough to travel. Although she was taking the morphine Rosanoff had prescribed, Sydney knew the relief would only last her a mere four hours—"The pain has destroyed her appetite & she is losing weight. She shows great courage and tries hard to fight down the pain with sheer willpower.... If there is any other treatment, Doctor, she would be very glad to follow it."[67]

Losing her less than four months after this letter's writing on September 3 at 4 o'clock in the afternoon, Sydney wrote his half-brother Wheeler that "the loss of Minnie has been a terrible blow to me and I very much doubt I will ever get over it."[68] Well-wishers like Alf Reeves's wife, Amy, wrote with heartfelt sentiments intended to console him as best they could, despite being so far away: "Although you have lost the priceless love and loyalty of our brave Minnie you still have the love of your wonderful brother Charlie to help you over the rough spots. You are nearer his heart than any other being on *this* earth. I'm sure of that. Please do not think me maudlin or gushing, Syd. I only want you to remember the anchor you have in your great loss. *Wherever* you are, his love is with you."[69] Read Kendall marked her passing with a brief tribute in his column in the *Los Angeles Times*: "Sad news. Sydney Chaplin's wife's death in Nice, France, proved a shock to her hundreds of friends in Hollywood.... She was formerly Minnie Gilbert of the London stage."[70]

But there was really nothing unusual about the way Sydney responded to this over other such events in his life. His admission to Wheeler, "I feel very depressed at the moment and each day I seem to get worse. My health is none too good, so the future looks very gloomy"[71] followed his usual procedure exactly. He kept the death notice out of the papers, for financial reasons. Minnie's death certificate stated that she was not a resident of Nice, but of London, and had no worldly goods for anyone to inherit.[72] Of course, all of this subterfuge was to backfire. In the meantime, Sydney decided to employ his other survival tactic: escape. He wrote to Wheeler again almost exactly two months later, on November 25: "I think the best thing for me is to leave Nice for a while. So, I have therefore booked my passage on the 'Empress of Britain,' leaving Monte Carlo January 22nd for a world tour."[73] There's an old saying—"Everywhere you go, there you are"—that could easily be applied to Sydney and his predilection for travel, especially during times of crisis. Perhaps he knew that constant movement into and out of strange places was not going to offer him any kind of real relief. Nevertheless, his situation at the end of 1936 propelled him into yet another tour, this one on the *Empress of Britain* around the world.

The RMS *Empress of Britain* was built for Canadian Pacific in 1930,[74] the largest ship ever built for this company.[75] Canadian Pacific was trying to lure passengers away from the luxury liners that took a more southerly route. To that end, they employed the latest in art deco architecture and design on the ship. The Mayfair lounge, for example, was adorned in dark walnut, complemented with silver. Taking their inspiration also from Greek architecture, the designers included tall scagliola columns and pilasters. The ceiling of this lounge possessed a large vault that featured amber glass and zodiac signs around the base. The ship had a first-class gymnasium, equipped with stationary bicycles, punch balls, electric horses, and other mechanical devices. A *Fortune Magazine* advertisement for the line claimed that "to size and speed, the *Empress of Britain* adds something new in transatlantic travel ... space to live, and space to play. She has a big Sun Deck ... an entire Sports Deck carrying a full-size tennis court ... a racing swimming pool ... a championship squash-racquets court, and two gymnasiums. She has an entire Lounge Deck. More private and public square feet of space per individual passenger than any other ship."[76]

Although the *Empress of Britain* was launched with great fanfare and had a successful maiden voyage in 1931, her popularity soon declined, due to the Great Depression as well as the fact that passengers preferred the more southerly route. So, she immediately instituted the wintertime world-cruise to prospective passengers, with the first one starting out on December 3, 1931. Gordon Turner claims in an article on the line that "her passengers were mostly American. Most made the complete voyage; segments were available but were not widely advertised. It goes almost without saying that world-cruise passengers were wealthy; they were accustomed to demanding and receiving only the best in amenities and service, and these were exactly what the *Empress of Britain* provided."[77]

Accommodations spanned the range of small inside cabins to spectacular suites, two with their own balconies. Two-room apartments started at $2,300[78] and a five-room was approximately $500 more. The cruise booklet for Sydney's tour claimed that the cruise lasted about 125 days and covered some 30,000 miles. Passengers could choose from among 29 ports in 22 different countries. While the luxuriousness of the ship and its offerings would seem to suggest that Sydney had to have been wealthy in order to participate, chances are he was in attendance due to some accommodating acquaintance, or some sort of deal he was able to acquire. In fact, he seems to have been on the ship with an unattached male friend, seen in photos and home movies of the trip. This particular bespectacled friend also appears in the amateur movies Sydney and Charlie made in Bali in 1932, so perhaps he was more than just an acquaintance; their relationship, at least, would have had to have weathered five years or more.

Sydney climbed aboard the ship in Monaco, just a few miles from his home in Nice.

Fun with amateur theatricals aboard the S.S. *Empress of Britain* and its around-the-world tour, 1937–8. Sydney is seated (CHACHAA).

A poem he wrote entitled "on my world cruise on the 'Empress of Britain,'" about his comings and goings and adventures on board, provides adequate detail of his experiences on the trip:

> I'm tired of all this four months cruising
> Seeing things that's not amusing
> Tired of all the time I'm losing

I'm tired of Pompeii's lava ruins
Walking miles for private viewings
Of paintings of their naughty doings

I'm tired of pyramids & sphinx
Of King Tut's tomb and native stinks
Tired of signing chits for drinks

I'm tired of passports, tired of docks
Tired of always changing clocks
Tired of cabin doors with locks

I'm tired of Ceylon & its sapphires
Bits of glass they sell to "Sap" buyers
Tired of touring cars & flat tires

I'm tired of waiting hours for tenders
Buying drinks for tightwad spenders
Changing dough at money lenders

I'm tired of all the shore excursions
Sharing cars with pet aversions
Watching Hindu corpse immersions

I'm tired of mischief making "Janes"
Who won't let girls wear shorts on trains
The damned old hags have varicose veins

I'm tired of taxis without meters
Chauffeurs who are lousy cheaters
Tired of fevers & mosquitoes

I'm tired of spending my vacation
Taking pills & vaccination
Tired of arms with inflammation

I'm tired of temples, priests & sandals
Boat deck love affairs & scandals
Tired of girls who travel vandals

I'm tired of swimming, squash & ping pong
Keno shuffleboard & sing song
Tired of girls who get me in wrong

I'm tired of girls who keep on crabbing
Tired of all their scandal gabbing
Yet they'll sleep in some guy's cabin

I'm tired of news pushed through the door
Concerning Germany & war
I've read this same news before

I'm tired of those with heraldry
Who boast about their family tree
They're just the God damned sap to me

> I'm tired of the man who had to pay
> To become a Baron, so they say,
> Too bad his mother wasn't that way
>
> He suffered much with head inflation
> Said he owned a big plantation
> But all he had was constipation
>
> I'm tired of girls who take vacations
> Shun the law of sex relations
> And get a thrill from syncopations
>
> I'm tired of girls who dance & seldom
> Take a bath, that's why we smell them
> And their best friends will not tell them
>
> I'm tired of men who always dance
> As if their brain were in a trance
> Their thoughts are way down in their pants
>
> I'm tired of tangos, tired of trucking
> Yes, I'm even tired of— —-Gee! But I'm tired.[79]

The tour offered ports-of-call in, among a few other places, Naples, Athens, Haifa, Port Said, Bombay, Colombo, Penang, Singapore, Batavia, Bali, Manila, Hong Kong, Shanghai, Kobe, Tokyo, Honolulu, San Francisco, Los Angeles, Panama, and New York, where the voyage ended on May 14. Sydney appears to have left the ship in Los Angeles for good,[80] visiting his brother and later traveling east to New York to visit his lawyers and address his concerns about having Minnie's assets transferred back to him. He would have arrived in Los Angeles on May 2, and seems to have stayed around until shortly before Thanksgiving.[81] While in town, he was spotted and interviewed by Louella Parsons, who reported her findings in an article entitled "Syd Chaplin, Back in Hollywood, Amazed at Ten Years' Changes": "Flabbergasted, to use his own expression, Syd Chaplin just couldn't get over the changes in Hollywood in ten years. He's back now to visit his brother Charlie, and, although, when he left here he was a well known screen comic, he walked into the Brown Derby today without being recognized by anyone save this writer who used to review his comedies in the silent days." Sydney told Louella that he had been loafing for ten years "playing tennis, summering in Budapest, wintering in St. Moritz — why I'm so out of touch with movies, when someone mentioned a few present-day stars, I had to admit I had never seen them." Even this short piece portrays Sydney's continuing hopes of returning to film: "Charlie insisted that Syd make a voice test[82] while here, which so intrigued him that he is buying a special camera and sound apparatus to take back with him to Europe — that is, if he returns. Syd has always been a top comedian, and it wouldn't surprise me to hear that he had been signed by one of our Hollywood producers."[83] Most likely, however, it was not a great time to pay Charlie a visit. Following the success of *Modern Times*, Charlie was dabbling in several projects for Paulette Goddard, such as *Stowaway*, *Regency*, and a Napoleon Bonaparte story, and finding himself pleased with none of them. By mid–1937, he was about to dump the last of the projects, *Regency*, having nothing really to replace it. It is doubtful, given these irritations, that

Charlie would have been terribly sympathetic about Sydney's inheritance disaster at this time, but he was to come through for him in a big way a year later.

By the time he reached New York, Sydney's trip to Los Angeles had instilled in him the drive to re-energize his desire to return to movies, and he used his problems with the courts to provide an opening for him to ask Jim Minney to help him do it. He wrote a long letter from the New Weston Hotel in New York City to Minney December 5 that relates "unfortunately things are blacker than ever. After waiting here inactive & nervous for two weeks, my lawyer eventually called me to his office & informed me that the outlook was very bad, in fact, hopeless." Sydney's lawyer had told him that there was no possible way to make the government accept the viewpoint that his wife's property was really his and had been all along, even though he could prove it had been transferred to her out of his own bank account by an emergency cable in order to protect himself from a threatened lawsuit. In addition to this, Sydney related, "He informs me I will probably have to pay double taxes because I will have to swear under oath where my wife's domicile was at the time of her death & this will either have to be England or France."[84] This, of course, would make him liable to pay inheritance taxes from the country of domicile and, because the judgment would appear in the papers, there would be every chance that BIP could take advantage of the opportunity to press their suit. In other words, all the subterfuge Sydney had devised after Minnie's death had suddenly come back to haunt him. Needless to say, he was on the verge of a nervous breakdown,[85] or appeared to be in the letter. His next move (in the letter), then, was to suggest that his only way out of this quagmire was to clear up the business with BIP and get back into film, saying to Minney, "I am willing to place myself entirely in your hands in this matter & to leave everything to your good judgment." He pleads further, "In order to eliminate his judgment against me, I would be willing to make a talking picture for *nothing*. If you could get me a small salary weekly to take care of my hotel & traveling expenses, so much the better, but I do not insist upon it." And further, "*Time* is the most important thing." He ends the letter, "looks like a Black Xmas for me unless I get some good news. I feel I am now at the crossroads. One may lead to success and the other to God knows where. If it is to the former, I hope it will give you some satisfaction to know you were my guide & help."[86]

By February 2, Sydney was back in Nice and sounding much more hopeful about his situation and his new plan to get back into films. He energetically puts forth the idea to Minney that *The Submarine Pirate*, his final and most successful Keystone film, would make a great talkie: "What a comedy that would make today with the present Spanish situation, using British cruisers & their latest methods against submarines with nets and depth bombs, submarine trap escapes, oxygen diving suits without air pipes or overhead connections."[87] A March 8 letter indicates that Minney was at least still making some effort to achieve Sydney's request and that Sydney himself was fairly inured to the fact that it was going to take some time if it happened at all.[88] By April 22, Sydney was still talking strategy with Minney:

> I would like to pin him [John Maxwell] down to a new contract before anything broke in the papers about probation of a will. Maxwell is a fellow who will work quickly enough if he sees other companies after an artist. However hard he may be to deal with, I cannot believe in my heart that he bears me any malice or that he would want to stop me working for the

rest of my natural life. Even if he decided not to use me himself, or even try to rent me out, I think he might be persuaded to give me a clean bill of health and let me go ahead without interference on his part. I am sure it is this trouble that exists between us that prevents my making contracts elsewhere.[89]

Sydney left Cannes on the S.S. *Conte di Savoia* for New York again September 14, 1938, and this time he achieved some legal success there. He was able to see Wheeler in a play called *Blossom Time*, and to visit with Wheeler's wife, Alyce, and his new baby, Spencer.[90] Sydney wrote Minney from Nice in late November that "at last my luck has changed & I have some good news for you. I have won my case in America & have nothing to pay except a modest fee to the tax attorney who put it through in spite of all the gloom three other attorneys handed me besides their bills." While he doesn't give Minney all the details, it is clear from this letter that Sydney traveled to Washington, D.C., and with his bank's attorneys, met with the head of the tax department. He writes, "His attitude was so cold he sent pessimistic icicles down my back. He gave us to understand that there could be no question of joint property, the stocks were either my wife's or mine & by his manner I concluded he had already arrived at the final decision." But, only two days after he arrived back in Nice, he received a cable that told him his case had been settled completely to his advantage. He even had some good news on the film industry front during his visit to America. His old friend Arthur Kelly informed him that Eddie Small wanted to talk contract: "He was negotiating with the English comedian George Formby, according to Kelly, and wanted to put us both into the same picture." Sydney believed the picture Small had in mind for him was based on *Gunga Din*, a Rudyard Kipling poem for which Small owned the rights.[91] But, Minney was pushing the idea of Sydney accepting a contract with a French film company instead. By December 18, Sydney realized nothing was going to happen with either Eddie Small or George Formby and so he was ready to accept a French contract, even practicing the interview scene from Sacha Guitry's *Debureau*[92] to facilitate this plan. But, no sooner had the new year dawned than Charlie both changed Sydney's direction *and*, inadvertently, put an end to Sydney's remaining film business aspirations: "Charlie has just telephoned me from L.A. & asked me if I would help him on his next story, which is now almost ready to shoot. Needless to say, I did not have to make up my mind."[93] He left just two days later on the S.S. *Isle de France*, arriving in New York on the 17th, perhaps unaware that another ship's manifest provided evidence of a relationship that Sydney had heretofore told no one about, but which had probably been going on for years — one to a Romanian woman named Henriette, who would shortly become his second wife.

CHAPTER 10

Charlie, Gypsy and a Caravan

"I am through with films and Hollywood," he told a representative of this paper, on his arrival in Bombay by the "Empress of Britain" today. "Film fame was my heart's desire at one time. I worked hard for it and came into the limelight. Now I have decided to remain an ordinary picture–goer. I have no more interest in films and business." — "Syd Chaplin as Passenger," *The Evening News of India* [Bombay], 12 February 1937

I must admit that when I saw the name Sydney Chaplin on the screen I had a feeling of nostalgia. Although I have had lots of pleasure out of life & have seen a great deal of the world, there are times when I ask myself whether it would not have been better to have continued making pictures. It is only when I see a great picture like "Limelight" that I get the feeling of regret that I gave up the business. — letter to Charlie Chaplin from Los Angeles, June 27, 1953

WHILE SYDNEY'S SHORT TRIP TO THE United States in 1938 to settle his tax debt allowed him to briefly imagine the possibility of a resurrected film career, when he returned a few months later to work for Charlie on the set of *The Great Dictator* throughout 1939 and 1940 this fantasy finally came to rest after some twelve years of on-again-off-again negotiations, worry, and disappointment. Sydney had not lived in Hollywood since 1927 and things had changed — in the film business and in the general demeanor of the place and its people. It was no longer the playground of young and idealistic folks trying on a new lifestyle and way of making a living in the heady early days of silent film. Filmmaking was now big business and along with this transformation came unions and standards and rules, many of which were also foreign to brother Charlie, a fact exemplified by the fact that his new film would be his first talking picture, a full 13 years after the onset of this technology.

Sydney arrived in Los Angeles on January 21, 1939, his arrival having been announced in the papers the day before in a short note that named him co–director of Charlie's new film.[1] By March, it was being announced in bold print that Sydney would take the part of Goebbels (renamed Garbitsch in the film), Hitler's propaganda minister.[2] In fact, as a later letter to friend Jim Minney would indicate, Sydney had not received a work permit as part of his visa and so was not legally able to assume either position. Therefore, he is not listed in the film's credits at all. Likely, Sydney's purpose for not acquiring a work permit was to prevent himself from being subject to further American taxation, but this scheme was to backfire on him later, as nearly all his tax-evasion schemes had before.

March 1939 was also important in Sydney's life as this was the month that Henriette Leoneanu, the woman who was to become Sydney's second wife, arrived in Los Angeles. Henriette, who jealously guarded details about her early life, was a Niçoise of Romanian decent. Chaplin family legend has it that she spent part of her childhood in Canada and/or Peru, but this cannot be proven. Legend also has it that Sydney and Gypsy, the nickname he gave her because of her dark coloring and hair and the long gold earrings she liked to wear, had known each other in Nice well before the passing of Sydney's first wife, Minnie, but this is also conjecture. What is known is that Sydney asked her to join him in Los Angeles after he'd been there only two months, and her arrival marked the last time they would be apart until his death.

By the time Gypsy arrived, however, Sydney was in one of his black moods with seemingly no way out. He had written to Jim Minney a month earlier, "The first few days I was here I became homesick and my ambition faded away to nothing. Even now I doubt very much whether I shall remain here after the picture is completed. I think if I am to make pictures, I would much prefer to make them in Paris in the French language."[3] By March, his depression is clearly evident: "It is very nice of you both [Jim Minney and Arthur Kelly] to be working on my behalf, but I have been debating with myself whether I want to continue on in this business. I have grown very homesick for Nice. I miss the freedom, the sunny days on my balcony with my birds, fish & flowers. Also the tennis & swimming. Here I have not a moment to myself."[4] Warner Brothers had recently approached him with an offer to film *The Better 'Ole* as a talkie, but Sydney was still not willing to work off his debt to British International Pictures, and the offer came to nothing.[5]

Sydney found Hollywood very changed and the changes disconcerted him. Life there, he felt, seemed artificial. "So many people that I knew have passed on, the orange groves have been replaced with oil stations & hot dog stands. Studios that were sun-diffused & where we made pictures in God's fresh air have now been turned into stifling factories where even the artists must punch clocks," he wrote to Jim Minney, "gone are the practical jokes the stars played on each other, the cafés where we all used to meet, where Charlie & Arbuckle would conduct the orchestra, & where we used to raise Hades like a bunch of school boys."[6] Charlie's cousin Betty Chaplin Smith (later Tetrick — she was to marry Charlie's wardrobe man, Ted Tetrick) presented an additional perspective on life in Hollywood in a series of articles she was to write on the subject for the *Daily Express,* entitled "Mr. and Mrs. Smith Go to Hollywood." In one installment, Betty reported that the studios "were like cities, all with their own police force, powerhouses, theatres, carparks, with miles of roads and blocks of office buildings"[7] — hardly the romantic atmosphere of the small-town, do-it-yourself days.

Sydney took up residence at a posh apartment complex, right on Hollywood Boulevard, the Garden Court apartments. Having opened its doors on New Year's Eve 1919, the Garden Court was comprised of 190 rooms and boasted a baby grand piano in each of its 72 suites. Just a half-block from Grauman's Chinese Theatre, the Garden Court was adorned with an ornate façade, sculpted angels, and a trio of cherubs intertwining arms on the fountain.[8] Smith reported in her series that "everybody here lives in furnished apartments." Hollywood's hundreds of apartment buildings all made it easy for the prospective tenant; all a person had to do was arrive: "You are self–contained; you can live as you please. They supply linen, cutlery, china, glass. Gas, electricity, refrigeration (in no habitation in America are you more than two strides from the ice box) are included in your monthly rent."[9] In addition, all such apartments were cleaned daily and pretty much provided all the services of a first-class hotel. This convenience and luxury, however, seemed to do little to assuage Sydney's growing dissatisfaction with his former home.

Dan James, Charlie's assistant director on the set of *The Great Dictator*, noted in an interview to David Robinson that by 1939, Charlie had outgrown Sydney. This assumption is supported by the fact that in Charlie's autobiography, mention of his older half-brother drops out a full 150 pages before the end. Charlie's last memories of his brother seem to surround the time they spent together on his 1931–32 world tour, suggesting that the 30-some years since then provided the brothers no experiences of great significance. Charlie's eldest son, Charles Jr., recounted in his memoir an instance that lends even greater credence to this assertion when he relates that during *The Great Dictator* years, Sydney approached Charlie with an offer of two million dollars he had been given for Charlie's studio, now an old cavernous space that required nearly $1,000 a day to maintain. Of course, ever conscious of Charlie's spending, Sydney was excited about the offer, because, Charlie only really needed a studio once in five years anyway. But, as Charles Jr. relates, "At the time Uncle Sydney panted out his proposal Dad was making a test of some kind of sound effect. Uncle Sydney waited eagerly for Dad's reaction, but Dad didn't even lift his head from what he was doing. 'Oh, tell them to leave us alone,' he said. 'Just where would I play if I didn't have the studio?'"[10] Yet, one reporter credited Sydney with discovering and then recommending Jack Oakie for the Napaloni role. Oakie and his wife had run into Sydney at a Hollywood party and after they spent some time reminiscing about old Hollywood, Sydney suddenly interjected: "Stick out your jaw that way again, will you? Um-huh. Jack, I want you to come around and see Charlie tomorrow. I've got an idea." After a quick screen test in his street clothes the next day, Oakie had the part.[11]

Despite his growing uneasiness, Sydney kept busy at the studio during the early days of *The Great Dictator* production, even though he had no title or authority there. One of his first orders of business was to acquire a position for half-brother Wheeler Dryden, which he succeeded in doing—in the casting department. Wheeler now had a wife, Alyce, and a new baby to consider. He soon decided to make the move permanent and served in some capacity at the studio until Charlie left in 1952.[12] James remembered that Sydney was a part of the early gag meetings, being what he called "immensely ingenious." "Very few of them, he remarked, had any relevance to what we were doing, but that didn't matter. It was stimulating. A bad gag is always a challenge to do better."[13] In a letter to MInney, Sydney himself suggested that he was at least being consulted on the writing of the script, but does not concretely label his particular role on the production: "Charlie is exceedingly enthusiastic about his next picture. He has been working very hard on the script from nine in the morning until six at night—sometimes later—so I have had very

Rehearsal for a street scene in the ghetto of Charlie's film, *The Great Dictator* (United Artists, 1940). Charlie is in the hat in the foreground and Sydney is standing to the far right (LKSC).

little time to look around and for social activities. ... There is a possibility I may be playing in the picture myself, although I would much prefer to be behind the camera."[14] The projection logbook of Chaplin Studios projectionist B. J. Moody illustrates some of Sydney's other activities there. The Chaplin Studios production reports document Sydney at the studio first on January 21, with the projection logbook then showing his attending Charlie's preparatory screenings as early as January 27,[15] when he is listed among the viewers of *City Lights* that day. The first two weeks of February, Sydney, Rollie Totheroh, Charlie and Dan James, among others, seem to have been occupied with Josef von Sternberg's *The Sea Gull*, which, had it not been destroyed, would have starred Charlie's former leading lady Edna Purviance. One wonders what kind of input Sydney had in Charlie's decision to destroy it. Sydney and the others mentioned were also viewing episodes of *The March of Time* and what is labeled "Nazy stock film."

Sydney is mentioned in the projection logbook the next time in early August when he seems to have been given some responsibilities in the casting area. On August 1, both MGM's *Broadway Melody* and Universal's *When Love is Young* were projected ostensibly for "casting," with Sydney listed as the responsible party. On August 4, he viewed the wardrobe tests of actors Cy Kendall, Billy House, Luis Alberni and Maurice Moskovitch. On August 11, he had MGM's *Everybody Sing*, Fox's *My Lucky Star* and Grand National's

Panama Patrol screened for casting, as well as the tests of Gloria Holden and Leonid Kinsky. Production itself is listed as starting on September 9 and at that point, Sydney's name drops out of the logbook, never to be mentioned again. In addition, he is not listed by name in the Chaplin Studio Daily production reports until December 29, 1941, when he attended a Chaplin Studios meeting.

This documentation of Sydney's activities in Los Angeles is significant for two reasons. First, Sydney's scathing account of his experiences at the studios during *The Great Dictator* production, written to friend Jim Minney from Cuba on March 14, 1941, indicates he had been essentially deported from the United States for working without a permit. Second, without the mention of Sydney's presence at the studio meeting in December, there would be no indication of where he spent the war years, since his letter to Minney would leave him "at sea," so to speak, in a sort of exile once again. Instead, the production report information places him back in Hollywood, where he likely remained until 1948, when he is known to have ventured back to Nice, France, for the first time since the war had started.

Sydney's own account of his experiences during the production exist only in the March 14, 1941 letter to Jim Minney. In this account, Sydney describes the studio's severely deteriorated condition and his role in reversing its decline:

> When I arrived, I found everything in a dilapidated, run–down condition. There was no excuse for it, because Charlie does not limit the expenditures & the studio staff has years between pictures, when there is nothing for them to do but maintenance of the studio. I found the property room like a pig sty, filthy with dust and cobwebs. The Sunset house the same way, paper peeling off the walls & the place overrun with rats. You should see the difference now. They are using it as dressing rooms for "Stars." The still room where Charlie keeps all the negative stills of his early pictures was in the same neglected condition. Nothing was inventoried & dozens of plates were broken. These can never be replaced. They contained many photos of visiting celebrities taken with Charlie & would have been most valuable for a biography. Those that had not been broken, we had to spend hours trying to identify the people in the photographs. There was never any index kept. I had all this remedied. The property room cleaned from top to bottom, everything segregated and inventoried, requisition and double checking systems put in on both purchases & rentals & running inventories kept. Also graphs on labour.[16]

This work, he suggests, made him "Enemy #1." In addition, he was given the task of "supervising & the letting of contracts for the erection of new buildings & the installation of sound equipment," tasks that met with the daily passive resistance of what he labels Charlie's "senile staff." Unfortunately, his toe-trodding behavior came back to haunt him, for one of these disgruntled employees discovered that he was in the country with a visitor's permit only. Sydney relates: "I was hauled before the immigrant investigators & accused of working without a permit. I had to take along my lawyer and swear I had received no compensation, that I was trying to relieve Charlie from a lot of irksome responsibilities & everything I had done was out of brotherly love." This statement saved him from further government trouble, but as he had already received two extensions on his visitor's permit, he was advised to leave the country and come back in as a resident alien.[17]

In this same letter, Sydney mentioned Gypsy for the first time. He described her to Minney as a "charming girl, whom I married before leaving America." As in the case of his first wife, Minnie, however, there seems to be no evidence or documentation of the marriage, beyond this written mention. He described her as a French girl he knew previously in Nice: "She is brunette and looks decidedly Spanish. I have nicknamed her 'Gypsy.' We are spending our honeymoon here and are very happy. We have not decided yet whether we will return to America, or push on to some of the Caribbean islands. We both love the sun & nature in its primitive form."[18] This last comment suggests that they perhaps met at Nice's nudist club, which may indeed date their acquaintance prior to Minnie's death in 1936.

Back in Hollywood, then, in late 1941, Sydney came to the studio probably only when needed. The December 29th meeting, which included Bob White of Price, Waterhouse & Co., Hershel Green of Loyd Wright's office (one of Charlie's lawyers), Alf Reeves, Sydney and Charlie, was organized to dissolve the Charles Chaplin Film Corporation, moving everything into Charlie's personal accounts. Sydney then accompanied Alf and Bob White to the Bank of America, Highland Branch, where the Corporation's safe deposit box was transferred over and Reeves endorsed all of the Corporation's stock certificates. Beyond that, Sydney and his new "wife" Gypsy's activities are undocumented until Sydney is mentioned in the "Between Pictures" Chaplin Studios production reports on Tuesday, July 4, 1944, when it is noted that he had left for New York to attend a meeting of the

Sydney (center with hands in pockets) and wife Gypsy (next to him) attending a United Artists meeting in Charlie's stead, New York City, 1944 (CHACHAA).

United Artists, with Gypsy in tow. Charlie had asked Sydney to attend in his stead, most likely due to the fact that Charlie was deeply involved in the Mann Act trial and the paternity suit of actress Joan Barry against him. Also, Charlie had recently married fourth wife Oona O'Neill, daughter of playwright Eugene O'Neill, and they were expecting their first child, daughter Geraldine. It was, by all accounts, a poor time for Charlie to travel across country, and Sydney was probably happy to feel useful as his temporary replacement on the UA Board of Directors. He and Gypsy returned to Hollywood on October 16. This date marked Sydney's last mention in the Chaplin Studios production reports.

Sydney really only had the pleasure of playing the part of doting uncle after Charlie and Oona began having children in 1944. Charlie had two boys by a previous marriage to Lita Grey, Charlie Jr. and Sydney Earle (his namesake), born in 1925 and 1926, respectively. But due to the fact that Sydney left America for twelve years starting in 1927, when both boys were infants, and the fact that Lita herself had a low opinion of him,[19] it's certain that he never had the sort of relationship with these boys that he may have wanted. So, when Oona gave birth to Geraldine on August 1, 1944, Sydney must have embraced this new chance at uncle-hood with great expectations.

In the mid–to late 1940s, Charlie was occupied with what came to be known as his "Landru" or "Bluebeard" script, later the script for his film *Monsieur Verdoux* (1947). Sydney was not involved in this production. However, in his book, Robinson reports that

Sydney and wife Henriette (Gypsy) and their camping caravan touring the United States continent, circa 1946 (CHACHAA).

Charlie very much wanted Sydney to play the part of Detective Morrow, the character who first uncovers Verdoux's crimes, then unwisely gets himself poisoned before he can arrest him: "Sydney's wife Gypsy opposed this, since she did not want to see Sydney worried sick by Charlie's extravagance as, she said, he had been during *The Great Dictator*."[20] Perhaps to remove themselves from the situation entirely, Sydney and Gypsy purchased a "caravan," an Airstream luxury camping trailer that they then toured around America, just as soon as the gasoline rationing ceased following World War II.[21]

Jerry Epstein, Charlie's assistant on *Limelight* (1952) and the founder of the Circle Theatre in Hollywood in the late 1940s, wrote in his memoir about his distinct honor in being invited to attend Christmas at the Chaplin household: "The guests were usually the same: Charlie's older brother Sydney, with his lovely wife Gypsy; his half-brother Wheeler Dryden and his son; his cousins, Betty and Ted Tetrick; Amy Reeves, the widow of his studio manager; Constance Collier and Phyllis Wilbourne, her young English companion; Sydney Jr. and myself, and the children."[22] Sydney and Gypsy did attend Circle Theatre performances on occasion and to one in particular, called *The Circle Revue*, Sydney contributed some old music hall material that turned out to be the most popular aspect of the show. Epstein notes that the routine started with a tap-dance performed by what were supposed to be two brothers. As one of them retreated backstage, the other brother (played by Sydney Jr.), addressed the audience: "Ladies and gentlemen, my brother and I have decided to give up tap-dancing. My brother has developed a strong-man act, which he's been rehearsing for years." The brother then entered in tights, and invited the audience to feel his biceps. Then Sydney announced, "For the first time tonight, my brother will perform the *impossible*. We would like five members of the audience to stand on this table, while he lifts the table up WITH HIS TEETH!" Sydney then helped the five volunteers onto the small table, where they stood squashed together, feeling embarrassed. The brother then surveyed his task and flexed his muscles. To the sound of a drum-roll, he knelt down and bit the edge of the table, struggling to lift it. As he grunted and groaned, he spit out slivers of wood. Of course, he couldn't do it.

The strong-man pondered, stared at the table, then consulted his brother, who was ready again. Another drum-roll went off. Again he crouched on his knees, bit the table — and again couldn't lift it. Finally, Sydney walked forward and announced, "Ladies and gentlemen, my brother and I have decided to go back to tap-dancing." Blackout. Epstein remembered that their "audiences loved this ridiculous sketch, especially when the lights came on again, and the five volunteers were standing sheepishly on the table. There was so much laughter we couldn't go on with the show."[23] One night, however, Sydney Senior's impetuousness got the better of him and he volunteered to stand on the table. Then to everyone's surprise, he threw in an extra flip-flop: "But as he twirled, he hit his head against the edge of the table and fell to the floor. Gypsy and the audience gasped; it was dreadful seeing this elderly man lying prostrate. Luckily he rose unharmed, smiled, and the act continued. But we lost our laughs for the rest of the night."[24]

By late June 1948, Sydney and Gypsy were back in Nice, having decided it was finally safe enough for them to consider such a journey. In a letter to Charlie, Sydney commented that "things are still very unsettled over here & what little gaiety there is over here is very strained." Upon returning to their apartment at the Palais Rosa Bonheur, they found many things stolen: "Everything was in a hell of a mess & it took Gypsy and I nearly a month to straighten things up."²⁵ Nice was full of tragic war stories at this time, and Sydney often relayed them to Charlie by way of the mail. One focused on a jewelry and diamond-buying businessman whom Sydney had seen just before the war taking bars of gold out of his safe deposit box in a Monte Carlo bank. Over a drink, Sydney asked what had become of them during the war: "It appears he had been called up as a French aviator & had entrusted his gold and jewels to a friend who was a banker in Paris. Well, the history and adventures in hiding that gold from the Germans would make a good picture. The banker lived to tell the story & return the gold to my friend, but the banker's wife & family were killed & his house blown to pieces by the Gestapo." Worse, though, was the eyewitness account Sydney heard of the day the Germans evacuated Nice. "Just before the Americans arrived," he wrote Charlie, "over a thousand Frenchmen were killed as collaborators by other Frenchmen of the underground & their bodies littered the streets."²⁶

Initially disappointed and dejected by the situation that awaited them in Nice, Sydney and Gypsy decided to look at a few new apartments in Monte Carlo, where the tax situation for them was, of course, ideal. The one they fell in love with, right on the yachting harbor, had a price tag of $32,000.²⁷ But instead of committing themselves to such an immediate outlay of money, they decided to travel to Montreux, Switzerland. Perhaps Sydney's description of the place found its way into Charlie's memory and influenced his decision to purchase the Manoir de Ban, just five miles away from the spot, in Corsier-sur-Vevey, five years later. It was clear that Sydney and Gypsy, however, would continue to engage in exotic travel, for their plans for the winter of 1948 included a drive through Spain and Portugal, then a trip over to Madeira, then into South Africa if they could acquire tickets. Their initial dejection soon turned to contentment, however, as Sydney indicated that "the sun is shining brilliantly, the sea is calm and as blue as a sapphire, the table on the balcony is all set for lunch, so I must away and feed the inner man, as I have a hard game of tennis to play before dusk. Ye gods! What a life."²⁸

Oona Chaplin's desk diary shows that Sydney and Gypsy were back in Hollywood at least for part of the year in 1949 and 1950. They were frequent guests during September and October 1949, playing tennis with Charlie, attending the Ice Follies with the family, even coming over to the Summit house for breakfast on one occasion. This particular Christmas, they shared the company of Charlie's family with Betty and Ted Tetrick, Amy Reeves and Wyn Ritchie, Sydney Jr., Jerry Epstein, Wheeler and Spencer Dryden. Still in Hollywood and environs, Sydney and Gypsy visited on February 17 and then were treated to a caviar dinner on March 14, probably in celebration of Sydney's 65th birthday two days later.

Although Charlie's letter to his brother no longer exists, Charlie must have informed Sydney of his political troubles and his worry about leaving America for a European trip well before that fatal day in September 1952 in which his fears were realized. In January 1951, Sydney offers his counsel to Charlie on this issue from a holiday in St. Moritz, Switzerland, writing that he (Charlie) will surely not be able to return to America if he leaves without a re–entry permit. Instead of advising Charlie to consider this thoughtfully and carefully, however, he immediately begins to offer him residential alternatives throughout Europe, concentrating, of course, on locations favorable to the brothers' philosophy on personal taxation. While Sydney first recommends Monte Carlo, he most forcefully argues once again for Montreux, Switzerland, writing that "this is one of the most beautiful resorts. It is on the Lake of Geneva & is only about a 25-minute drive from Lausanne, a much larger town in which you will no doubt want to do your banking & also place the children in school." The rest of this letter contains detailed and specific information about Swiss bank accounts and how to keep the studio in Hollywood from being attached, just to name a few.

Christmas of 1950 had been one of sadness and bleak realization for Sydney and Gypsy. Back in St. Moritz after a long absence, Sydney claimed not to recognize any of the old crowd (from 1932!). The present bunch, he found to be *nouveau riche* Italians, who seemed to be "loaded down with DeBeer's crystallized merchandise. At the New Year's Gala the party got very rough. The champagne eliminated that dangerous veneer of refinement & Zola's slumbering hog came lumbering to the surface." One male guest at an adjoining table dropped a champagne bottle on the head of a fellow nearby. Sydney related that "he started to swear like hell, so I leaned over & whispered 'MUMMS' the word. He evidently did not appreciate the joke. What he said to me would have made a Billingsgate Bloater blush with shame."[29] Sydney and Gypsy were so crowded there on the dance floor that they turned in at one A.M.

Albert de Courville and his wife, Edie, provide a unique perspective on Sydney and Gypsy's relationship at this time, as well as on Sydney's continuing (and sometimes increasing) mental/emotional problems. De Courville, a variety show producer from the English music hall days who produced José Greco's premiere in America in October 1951, at the Shubert Theatre in New York City, probably knew Sydney and his first wife, Minnie, from those early days. Writing Albert and Edie from Montreux in July 1951, Sydney indicated his plan to motor through Spain and Portugal in the fall and then return to America in the summer of 1952.[30] Although he didn't mention this directly, it seems clear from this account that Charlie wanted Sydney in America when he left, in case the worst should transpire for him and his family. Also, as he was to do in practically every letter now, Sydney related the most recent of his many visits to the doctor: "Well, my cardiograph showed 'coronary insufficiency' & the doctor advised me to give up tennis & smoking, two of my three greatest pleasures (you can guess what the third is). I thought it advisable to consult another doctor, who, after examining my electrocardiograph, said, 'If that was my cardiograph reading, I would continue with my tennis.' His advice pleased me greatly, even if he is wrong."[31]

In October of that year, Sydney related to Edie de Courville that again their Palais Rosa Bonheur flat in Nice had been burgled, with 38,000 francs having been stolen from the mother-in-law's room. It is likely that Gypsy's mother, Mme. Fanny Olivieri, lived with them from around this time off and on until her death, which would certainly indicate the first time for such co-habitation in Sydney's life. Nice, Sydney related, "Is crowded and the weather like mid-summer. We were astounded on arrival here to see the terrace of the Ruhl [the Hotel Ruhl on the Promenade des Anglais] crowded, something we have never seen before, even in the height of the season. The sea is still full, bathers contributing a little extra liquid to the sewer outflow."[32] It would prove difficult for them to leave for Spain, given these warm and sunny conditions. But by the end of the year, Sydney and Albert had a severe falling out, one that was to mark the end of their relationship and provide ample evidence of Sydney's continuing inability to nurture relationships outside his immediate family. Albert's existing letter on the topic seemed to indicate that it had occurred over a misunderstanding on Sydney's part, that, as was usual for him, he had falsely accused Albert and Edie of choosing the company of Arthur Kelly and his wife over Sydney and Gypsy (notably all correspondence between Arthur and Sydney had halted some time before). Albert pleaded to Sydney in a letter dated January 23, 1952, from the Hotel Negresco in Nice:

> I need not tell you how extremely sorry we are that you hold such rancor against us for what happened.
> It would take much too long to recount what happened in a letter, but this I can write to you. If you feel that we had made any appointments for Arthur in preference to spending the day with you both, you are wrong, wrong, WRONG.
> Perhaps the conclusions you have jumped to are wrong. We really do not know where we are to blame and we always looked upon you and Gypsy as such good friends that the least you could do is to thrash the matter together and give us an opportunity to explain.[33]

By the fall of 1952, however, such experiences had to take a back seat to Charlie's situation in America. When Charlie took Oona and their four children abroad to attend the London premiere of his latest film, *Limelight*, he did so with trepidation. Although he had submitted himself to four hours of interrogation before his departure in order to secure his re–entry permit, Charlie's paranoia about the situation was not unfounded. Two days after he left New York harbor on September 17, Charlie was informed that, indeed, his re–entry permit had been revoked by Attorney-General, Judge James McGranery and he would have to submit himself to hearings once again in order to return to America.[34] Of course, this proved to be the last the United States would see of one of its founding actors for another 20 years. Prepared as he was mentally and emotionally for such a situation, of course, Charlie had not left with his affairs entirely in order. Instead, he left his brother Sydney behind in Hollywood, knowing full well that he could handle any contingency that arose. Upon receiving the news a short time later, Sydney immediately sprang into action.

Sydney and Gypsy took up residence this time at the Bermuda Apartments on Wilshire Boulevard, just on the border of Beverly Hills and Westwood, and very near what once would have been the Syd Chaplin Airfield. Having settled into what would be their home for 1953 and then seasonally throughout the 1950s, Sydney writes to Charlie and Oona, "We bought an excellent electric broiler & one that turns a chicken around on a spit, so, what with alternating with steaks & chickens, we are beginning to lose our sylphlike figures, especially as we are not playing tennis. We have been too busy adding homelike touches to our new apartment, which you said in your letter is a little on the 'posh side.'"[35] One of these "homelike touches" was a pet canary—something else new for Sydney (in addition to a resident mother-in-law). Sydney and Gypsy had just been invited to a private showing of Charlie's latest film, *Limelight*, even though it had been released to the public almost a year before. Sydney's often critical responses to Charlie's other films, like *Modern Times*, he replaced this time with a touching and emotional reaction, writing that "we think it is a 'masterpiece' & the greatest Charlie has ever made.

There are no superlatives I could use to do justice to it. It was so well acted, so beautifully balanced between laughter and pathos. Gypsy & I cried like kids, so much so, that we waited for everyone to leave the room before we left our seats. You did an excellent piece of acting Charlie & so did Claire Bloom." He related to Charlie that he and Gypsy discussed the film for hours and then the next morning, when they put the record on the phonograph, broke into tears once again. "It's a good thing," he writes, "you have not my brooding nature. If I had had to endure the persecution you have received in this country, someone would have been murdered. I think it is a damnable crime that such a picture as 'Limelight' should be banned in America."[36]

In late August, Charlie wrote one of his very rare missives to his brother, announcing both the arrival of son Eugene and the beginning of his new film project, one that would become *A King in New York*: "I play an ex–King character who escapes to Switzerland to get away from the revolution. It will afford me lots of opportunities for satire and comedy, etc. It will also have a great deal of music in it and perhaps I might go in for a little colour — it all depends, but I don't expect to have anything materialize until the end of the year; nevertheless, I have definitely made up my mind to do the ex–King."[37] With America's treatment of him still freshly smarting, Charlie candidly admits to his brother, "I shall be glad when I can cut all my ties with the U.S. While I still have interests over there I am not completely relaxed. They are like the sinews of cancer that eat into my concentration and until I can say goodbye and God damn them, I shall not completely enjoy the tranquility of Switzerland." Charlie freely offered his brother credit for taking on the huge project of the studio dissolution, among other of his remaining affairs in America:

> It is difficult, being so far away, to manage my affairs there but it is nice that you are on the job. Thanks a lot, Syd. The next issue, and a troublesome one, will be the dissolving of the Celebrated Film Corporation. It seems to be quite involved and neither Schwartz nor Wright nor the Government have a definite opinion. The only firm of lawyers that had an opinion were the Davis people of New York. They seemed to think that my status was clear with the U.S. and that I was no longer a resident there. However, I hope to dissolve the Company at the beginning of next year — keep that under your hat.[38]

The real work at the studio didn't begin, however, until the fall of 1953, when Sydney, working every day on the studio grounds — found himself in the middle of many territorial battles similar to those he experienced on *The Great Dictator* production, a fact that probably indicates that his ability to cooperate and manage had failed to improve over the years. In September, Sydney notifies Charlie that offers are still being considered in the sale of the studio and that he hopes some party will buy it with contents. He has already run into some problems with Lois Runser, a legal secretary, who will become a greater source of irritation in this endeavor as time moves on.[39]

Within a month or so of this communication, Sydney visited the Beverly House, Charlie and Oona's residence on Summit Drive in Beverly Hills, and took a complete inventory of its contents. From his narrative on the experience, Sydney creates an atmosphere of intrigue and conspiracy within the house and among its few remaining employees. He found the Chaplin butler, Henry, in the possession of a list of items that had been loaned out or borrowed by certain individuals at specific times, which Sydney claimed he was reticent to give over to him. He writes to Charlie, "I think Henry is honest in every way & has your interest at heart. He also told me that someone had taken 45 figurines or porcelains from the two glass cupboards that stand at the top of the stairs at the entrance of your library, but that you had requested that they be sent over to Switzerland & the party who took them had to bring them back again. Henry did not mention the person's name. *I sincerely hope you have received them?*"⁴⁰ And, by this point, the studio contents had also been inventoried and its contents appraised, although no sale had yet occurred. With great emotion, Sydney lists some of the dearest items for Charlie, nearly pleading for some added consideration on his part in terms of their real financial value:

> I have just finished reading the inventory of the whole studio & the appraisal value placed upon it by the General Appraisal Co. I think their figures are way under value & in some cases are ridiculous. For example, you have a playback machine that cost $5,000. You also have a boom that cost $3,000. These articles are both rented out. The appraisal co. values them at $500 for the two. Rollie [Totheroh] tells me there is a great shortage on booms & one cannot get them for love nor money. Rollie figures we could get the full price of $3,000 for the boom alone.⁴¹

The appraisal company had set the value of the complete studio contents at only $30,000. Sydney, having just placed advertisements for the material in *Variety* and *The Daily Reporter,* lobbied for doubling that value, promising not, however, to allow this figure to harm any chance for the studio's sale. Happily, his partnership with Kathleen Pryor in these matters seemed to have made the work a bit easier for him (he notes that Miss Runser was away at this time).

In addition to pleading for a fair price for much of the studio contents, this latest letter from Sydney in Hollywood clearly indicates his foresight in guarding and securing Charlie's personal documents — all of which can be found in the Charlie Chaplin archive today. Miss Pryor alerted Sydney to the fact that she had possession of files of personal correspondence dating back to the founding of the studio in 1918: "I opened one & the first letter I looked at was one from Professor Albert Einstein. So, I am having Wheeler take out all the *personal* letter folders & put them together. I hope he will find nothing of an embarrassing nature in them, or anything bordering on the Kinsey report?"⁴² Later, this became a priority of the entire project, and the saving of personal files became the saving of files, photos, pressbooks and many other important documents. At each stage of this process, Sydney found himself among short-sighted individuals: "The girls in the office were surprised when I told them your press clipping books were to be retained. If I had not mentioned it, I think they would have been thrown out. Good God! What do they think so much time was spent on these books for?"⁴³ Sydney lobbied strongly that Wheeler be placed in control of this particular aspect of the studio's dissolution,⁴⁴ probably due to his meticulousness in everything, but also due to the fact that Sydney and Gypsy were itching to get back to Europe and planned to do so by April 1954.

With Miss Runser's return in late October, however, Sydney found himself powerless to organize and manage things the way he felt his brother would have wanted. In regards to some household articles that Oona wanted to be sold, he devised a reasonable plan whereby Charlie's employees would benefit from the proceeds, a plan to which Miss Runser objected "& with a very autocratic air, 'snapped back,' 'I already have had my instructions from Mr. and Mrs. Chaplin what to do with these articles.' So I replied, 'Very well, then. I leave everything entirely in your hands.'"[45] Of course, in such situations — at least when he was acting on Charlie's behalf, he knew when to back down and told Charlie so, but not without his usual sarcastic commentary: "I did not ask her how she intended disposing of the various articles left in the house & the studio, but *mon petit doigt qui me l'a dit*,[46] that if she tries to get any more furniture into her house, the walls will burst."[47]

By this point in the dissolution process, Sydney writes that he signed an agreement selling the studio equipment for $12,500, but assuring his brother that this figure did not include certain pieces, including the complete contents of Charlie's bungalow (Charlie had already agreed to the sale of all equipment at only $12,000, so probably did not need this added assurance). Until this time, Rollie Totheroh and his assistants had been laboriously cutting up unwanted film in order to dispose of it. Sydney soon implemented what seemed like a more logical plan for what must have been a physically and emotionally exhausting procedure for everyone involved: "I had Wright's office make a special contract with the laboratory insisting that the drums of film should be accompanied by one of our employee's presence, which they agreed to. It would have taken months for Rollie & Eddie to have chopped up that film as they were doing. In the event it would cost too much to ship the good film, we may be able to rent a vault from the studio renting co. & keep the film there."[48]

Sydney and Gypsy brought in the New Year in Palm Springs ostensibly for the holiday, but actually to transact some of their own business, since Charlie's had been recently

Henriette (Gypsy) and Sydney, circa 1956 (CHACHAA).

concluded: "We went to Palm Springs primarily to sell our trailer, but in spite of its beautiful interior & excellent condition, we had no luck, although I spent a lot of money advertising it in the local newspapers. I am afraid there is a glut in the market for second-hand trailers. Now there is nothing left for us to do but store the old home during our trip back to Europe."[49] Having served out his period of usefulness to Charlie by this time, Sydney would find his mailbox empty and his place in the family one in which he and Gypsy waited long periods for rare invitations. He complained about this to old friend Jim Minney in January, 1954, and not for the last time: "I hear little or no news from Charlie, now all his business is taken care of, I am rewarded with his silence which is golden."[50] With Charlie and his family now situated in their new home, Manoir de Ban, in Corsier-sur-Vevey, Switzerland, Sydney and Gypsy expected to see them mainly when they were in the area, usually in the summer. Their lives began to assume a certain pattern; they spent winters in America, sometimes in Los Angeles, but also in Florida, then early spring in Nice, France, eventually leaving their Palais Rosa Bonheur apartment in the late 1950s to live in the Hotel Ruhl there, and finally spending summers in Montreux, Switzerland, where they usually stayed at the Montreux Palace.

Sydney and Gypsy's first visit to Charlie's new residence in Vevey, Switzerland occurred May 22, 1954 and pretty much every day thereafter for a week. Subsequent visits occurred in August and then for the next few months, with the Charlie Chaplins often meeting them for dinner at *their* residence, the Montreux Palace Hotel. Thus began a sort of tradition of Sydney and Gypsy's visits, ones that their nieces and nephews remember with great fondness. Geraldine remembers that her aunt and uncle arrived usually in the early afternoon and stayed then for dinner, with lots of performing (usually skilled magic tricks[51]) and joke-telling in between, for the benefit of the children and often to Charlie's horror: "They always arrived in Sydney's incredible Cadillac, which was an enormous thing. The biggest latest model. He would drive it so slowly, you wouldn't believe it — about 30 kilometers an hour.[52] It had these two things coming out of the bumper with rubber on them that looked like breasts and Sydney would say, 'These are my Marilyn Monroe's.'" Sydney's jokes were similarly off-color, probably the reason they were so enjoyed and so remembered. Geraldine remembered one such joke, not because it was funny or even because she understood it, but because since she and her siblings didn't understand what a "waffle" was — a word important to the punchline. They thought it must have some sexual connotation and was therefore all the more valuable for it.[53] More than that, Sydney was just generally funny and always on the lookout for some way to entertain the kids. Michael Chaplin recalled that "once, in Switzerland, out in the garden where my parents used to dine, I was with Josephine and there was a black cat that jumped on the dining room window. Josephine threw a stone at the cat and it smashed through the window into the dining room. Sydney, in the dining room, fell off his chair as if he had been shot. I guess Gypsy bawled him out, because he gave her a terrible fright, but we all thought it was hilarious."[54]

The children thought of Sydney not only as a humorous and entertaining guy, but as a gangster of some sort. He pasted his hair down with dressing, smoked big cigars and drove the huge Cadillac. He had a wife, Gypsy, who spoke with a foreign accent, wore Chanel suits and was adorned with gaudy jewelry Sydney had picked out for her or had acquired cheaply at the Nice pawnshops that served largely casino clientele. Gypsy was not the only recipient of Sydney's generosity, however. Oona received her first 16mm movie camera from Sydney and the children were overloaded with gifts. Josephine, for instance, received "a beautiful gold heart with a square emerald & two tiny emeralds & diamonds. It's supposed to be for her charm bracelet but I think it's too nice & should hang on her neck on a chain.... The stones came from some ring Syd had picked up cheaply long ago. Then a Nice jeweler made it and it has quite a sparkle."[55]

In 1955, their visits are listed in March for Sydney's 70th birthday, in June through August and then in November for a visit in which they say goodbye before leaving for Hollywood once again. They arrived back in New York on March 29, 1956, on the *Andrea Doria*. Sydney explained to Jim Minney that he and Gypsy had tried to get a three-month's extension on their American return permit at the time: "Gypsy is a bad sailor & we wanted to return to America in summertime. The Consul refused the extension so we sailed on the Italian liner 'Andrea Doria.' If we had received the extension, we would have been on the liner when she sank.[56] So you see, the Consul, like George Robey's song 'Had to be cruel to be kind.'" In December 1956, Sydney recalled one of his visits to Charlie and family to friend Jim Minney: "I don't think I told you that I went with Charlie, Oona & the kiddies to see the Chinese Opera Co. in Lausanne.... Next day, Charlie's kiddies were giving imitations of the Chinese in high-pitched voices. They sure are a bunch of clever youngsters and are surefire for a stage career."[57]

January 1957 found them in Hollywood at the Bermuda Apartments once again (Sydney had admitted to a friend that the luxury accommodations there, complete with new television set, were hard to beat), with plans to return to Nice in the summer, but at this point, both he and Gypsy had been back visiting the doctors. "We both have lost our appetites, also weight & feel bilious the greater part of the day," he wrote one correspondent. "My trouble has been an enlarged spleen & Gypsy has an ulcer."[58] Sydney and Gypsy had not heard from Charlie or Oona in some time, probably due to the upcoming release of Charlie's first European production, *A King in New York*, but Sydney really could never understand Charlie's communication lapses when it came to family: "Gypsy & I have been very anxious to know how his new picture is coming along. We get no news of it in American papers." He was able to discover at a Hollywood party, however, that Charlie's son Michael had been chosen to play the precocious school boy's part and quickly took credit for that decision, as if he was Charlie's casting director once again: "Charlie had no intention of giving him this part. He thought he was too young & not experienced, but I kept plugging for him & am glad to hear Charlie changed his mind. I think the boy has great acting ability."[59]

In fact, due to Gypsy's continually failing health at this time, the two would spend the rest of 1957 in Hollywood. By May, Sydney described Gypsy as not being able to bear the pressure of a girdle "& she has a continual taste in her mouth, like rusty iron or copper." The many doctors they consulted were perplexed and Sydney decided to take her first to Scripps Hospital in La Jolla, California, and failing that, the Mayo Brothers Clinic. The couple had still received no communication from either Oona or Charlie, despite the release of *A King in New York*.[60]

Gypsy improved to the extent that they could return to Europe in October, although doing so turned out to be a mistake. Sydney noted that the weather was terrible on the Riviera that winter, while Southern California was enjoying unbroken sunshine and 70 degrees in temperature. They spent a very quiet Christmas and New Year's Eve that year, taking in a terrible Chinese ballet and an enjoyable Spanish one. Their sailing in October also caused them to miss the sudden death of a dear family member, younger half-brother Wheeler Dryden. Wheeler had been worried about heart pain for some time, despite the fact that his doctor told him not to worry about it. He had dined with Sydney and Gypsy the day before their departure from Los Angeles and told them that he had had a premonition that he would die soon: "This scared Gypsy, so she immediately phoned the doctor for an appointment. The next day we started our journey to New York, but before leaving on the speedway, I went to the doctor's office to give Wheeler a check for his medical expenses." Despite this additional assistance, the couple received a cable from Tom Harrington (Charlie's first Hollywood butler and longtime family friend) as soon as they reached Nice that simply read: "Wheeler dead & buried."[61] Subsequently, Wheeler's ex-wife, Alyce, cleared out his apartment, probably hoping to take what she could use to supplement what would have been a meager inheritance for her son. Sydney declared, "I would have helped the boy through college, but he has no other ambition than to become a drummer in a night club orchestra & I'm not interested in that."[62] This boy, Wheeler's son Spencer, was to become the drummer for Jefferson Airplane.

Sydney's last existing letter, not surprisingly, was to Jim Minney. Gypsy and Sydney were staying in Montreux at the time and finding that things were just not the same there or anywhere else for that matter. He implored Minney for information on Majorca as too many people were swarming the beaches of Nice these days. In Montreux, he and Gypsy found a new manager at their usual hotel, the Montreux Palace, and were not happy with the new regime: "It has now become a one night stand for auto bus tourists who are here today & gone tomorrow. One can no longer rub shoulders (& other things) with society. The old timers who made a practice of spending six months here, are conspicuous by their absence."[63] But, being in Montreux, they could count on frequent visits with Charlie and his family, who had just returned from an African safari. Sydney also reported that his nephew Sydney was appearing often at the Chaplin estate with dancer Noëlle Adam and that there were rumors of wedding bells (they were indeed to be married soon thereafter). Charlie himself was busy with his memoirs, drafts of which he was sharing with his half brother on a regular basis.

From 1959 on, Sydney's life is portrayed only second hand, in letters Gypsy wrote to either Betty Tetrick or Oona, or in letters Oona and Betty wrote to each other. In 1959, for instance, Gypsy wrote Betty about the enormous tidal wave that destroyed much of Nice around the area of the Promenade des Anglais: "The whole thing disastrous!! The Promenade all under water, the back streets like a river. Never saw anything like it." It occurred quickly and unexpectedly after four days of rain. In a couple of hours everything was under water "with waves high up to our windows on the 4th floor of the Ruhl Hotel and saw it all. We stayed without lights, heat, elevators and food as the kitchens in the basement were of course flooded." The shopkeepers along the Promenade lost everything and workers spent days afterwards cleaning up the mess. In other parts of the Riviera matters were even more dire: "Families drowned, so many of them. Some parents and 4 or 5 children, etc. ... horrible, horrible. The whole coast from Mendon on the Italian side, way to San Tropez, etc. ... on the other side are part of the disaster and today the rain is on again (Who said "Sunny Riviera, a Winter Paradise"!!)."[64] At this point, although they were staying at the Hotel Ruhl and enjoying the service there — despite power outages due to the storm — the couple still owned the Palais Rosa-Bonheur apartment and the one in Monte Carlo. They would become attached to this service soon, however, and relinquish both apartments in favor of hotel life. Most likely, their increasing worry and preoccupation with health concerns resulted in this decision. In fact, Sydney and Gypsy seemed so like-minded by this point, in their concerns about health, money and family relationships that Gypsy began to sign her letters "GypSyd." Perhaps the letter that provides the most honest portrayal of the two, however, is the one Oona wrote to Betty in February 1961, reporting on a recent visit of Sydney and Gypsy to the Manoir de Ban. Oona writes,

> They both look extremely well, but they are as funny as ever. I guess he has honestly been terrifically depressed this past winter. She goes on & on about it — said he had crying spells — even cried in front of the doctor. So now he has some "pep" pills, & those plus the change of scene have cheered him up a bit. He cracked a few jokes & seemed gay enough, but then suddenly said, "I wonder what the percentage is?" Charlie said, "Percentage of what?" And with a long sad face he answered, "The percentage of people who live beyond 80."[65]

Gypsy had reported to Oona during this visit that Sydney was losing his memory, and it was increasingly up to her to take care of their business dealings. Uncharacteristically, Sydney even divulged his current worth to Oona and Charlie during this visit, casually commenting to them, "Well, according to the market reports these days, I'm worth about a million." This news flabbergasted Oona and Charlie both — Oona commenting in the letter to Betty: "I thought about half that. Selling his land[66] must have brought a lot —."[67] Just a few months later, Gypsy reported on their activities to Betty herself, bemoaning Sydney's continuing depression about growing old: "He has been very depressed lately and as you know, a depressed Chaplin is something!! I had to take him to the doctor so as to give him something to pull him up, but it doesn't help very well if he himself doesn't try to overcome his feelings. Of course, adding another year, instead of making him realize how wonderful he looks for his age, it depresses him more."[68]

In early 1962, Gypsy recounted a recent visit to the Manoir to Betty, noting that she and Sydney were very well received: "Everyone looks wonderful. We even stayed over for the night the first time we visited the Manoir. Oona looks beautiful and is a marvel the way she goes around like she wasn't carrying all those pounds,[69] doing things, taking care of everyone — remarkable." Sydney, on the other hand, "was so undecided and low" that Gypsy feared they would never begin the drive to Charlie's. Once at the manoir, Sydney began having his recurring breathing trouble: "He can take a nice walk — nothing happens — and then right after, just crossing the road or getting out of bed, it comes. He can't catch his breath. We thought the cold air was one of the causes, but today was a real summer day, and just going to open the window of the car, he came back puffing and blowing, walking slow."[70] Gypsy herself reported increasing heart trouble and both continued to spend a lot of time visiting doctors and chasing remedies.

When the end came for Sydney — on his brother's birthday, April 16, 1965, only a

Sydney clowning atop the Tusey "Meuse" statue, Prince Albert Gardens, Nice, France, 1963 (LKSC).

month after his 80th birthday — Gypsy was beside herself.[71] *Nice-Matin* reporter Marie Brun, reported on April 17 that Sydney had died at 30 minutes after midnight on Friday, the 16th, in his apartment on the fourth floor of the Hotel Ruhl, where he typically resided ten months of the year. Brun chose to portray the last two months of Sydney's life by focusing on his favorite Niçoise restaurant, Raynaud, where his favorite dish was the very rich bouillabaisse: "Son coeur avait commencé à donner des signes de faiblesse en novembre 1963, et cela avait du reste motive à l'époque un voyage de Charlie et d'Oona. L'état de santé de Sydney Chaplin n'avait cessé dés lors de se degrader, et chez [Raynaud] il ne mangeait plus que du bout des dents, ne buvait plus que du bout des levres le sautemes qu'il adorait."[72] Charlie and Oona arrived in Nice on Saturday, the 17th, to view the body and ensure its safe transportation to Marseille, where it would be cremated. Geraldine remembers being worried about her father's response to Sydney's death and whether or not he would be able to recover from it. But instead, although he was dreading the viewing, Charlie thought Sydney looked wonderful, like he could wake up and begin talking to him any second. And so he was at peace with it.

There was no funeral. And, even though the paper mentioned no final resting place, Gypsy chose the Cimitière de Clarens-Montreux in Montreux, Switzerland, and a plot there that looks poignantly over the beautiful Lac Leman, with the Alps framing it from behind. Gypsy was to mourn him openly for the rest of her life, claiming the spot next to him in Clarens 26 years later.

Sydney's obituary appeared in the *New York Times* and in papers throughout the world. As with most of Sydney's "life-stories," his obituary was rife with mistakes and misinterpretations, even claiming for him and for Charlie a never-before–heard-of brother,

Guy Dryden, and that Sydney's Keystone character, Reginald Gussle, was a "foil for the precisely hilarious antics of his brother." Despite such reports and what can be described as a quixotic life at best, Sidney John Hill died a man beloved by his wife, his nieces and nephews and his younger half-brother, Charlie Chaplin — in other words, he was a very rich man indeed. After he had seen *Limelight* for the first time, Sydney wrote to Charlie, "I get a great satisfaction when I hear people praise your work. It makes me very proud of you & I console myself with the thought that I am Charlie Chaplin's brother, which is my usual form of introduction & which does not arouse in me the slightest thought of jealousy. I glory in your success and bask in your 'Limelight.[73] In the final analysis, the squabbles Sydney and Charlie had had over the course of their lives had all but disappeared in later years, with the next generation remembering only an adoring and loving relationship between them. Michael Chaplin called it a "big attachment" and "a deep, deep connection."[74] If any truth exists today about the Sydney Chaplin story, perhaps this is it.

Appendix A

Filmography

1914

1. Fatty's Wine Party*

PRODUCTION: Keystone Film Company, released by Mutual Films
DIRECTOR: Roscoe Arbuckle
CAST: Roscoe Arbuckle (Fatty); Mabel Normand (Girl); Syd Chaplin (Waiter); Mack Swain (Restaurant owner); Al St. John, Harry McCoy (Men at soda fountain); Joe Bordeaux (Soda fountain operator); Phyllis Allen (Woman in restaurant); Frank Hayes, Alice Davenport (Couple seated at Allen's table); Fritz Schade, Cecile Arnold, Edwin Frazee, Billy Gilbert (People in restaurant)
FILMED: 10 October–31 October 1914
RELEASED: 21 November 1914

2. Among the Mourners

PRODUCTION: Keystone Film Company, released by Mutual Films
DIRECTOR: Unknown
CAST: Chester Conklin (A friend); Frank Opperman (A husband); Alice Davenport (His wife); Syd Chaplin (Drunk mourner); Phyllis Allen (Chester's wife); Edwin Frazee, Slim Summerville, Ted Edwards (Pallbearers); Glen Cavender (Mourner)
FILMED: 31 October–10 November 1914
RELEASED: 28 November 1914

3. His Prehistoric Past

PRODUCTION: Keystone Film Company, released by Mutual Films
DIRECTOR/SCENARIO: Charles Chaplin
CAST: Charles Chaplin (Weakchin); Mack Swain (King Lowbrow); Gene Marsh (Lowbrow's favorite wife); Fritz Schade (Cleo/Medicine Man); Cecile Arnold (Cave woman); Vivian Edwards (Cave woman); Grover Ligon (Cave man); Ted Edwards (Cave man); Syd Chaplin (Cop)
FILMED: 14 October–27 October 1914
RELEASED: 7 December 1914

4. Wild West Love

PRODUCTION: Keystone Film Company, released by Mutual Films
DIRECTOR: Walter Wright
CAST: Chester Conklin (Droppington) Syd Chaplin, Norma Nichols
FILMED: 24 November–7 December 1914
RELEASED: 21 December 1914

5. Gussle the Golfer

PRODUCTION: Keystone Film Company, released by Mutual Films
DIRECTOR: Unknown, possibly F. Richard Jones
CAST: Syd Chaplin (Reginald Gussle); Mack

---

*Syd Chaplin Keystone shooting dates provided in an email communication from Brent Walker, received September 10, 2008, and also from his book Mack Sennett's Fun Factory (McFarland, 2009), where more detailed information about the films may be found. Data for these dates was originally gleaned from the Aitken Papers/Wisconsin Historical Society and Sennett Collection/Academy of Motion Picture Arts and Sciences and other sources.

Swain (Ambrose); Dixie Chene (Mrs. Ambrose); Josef Swickard (Chief of Police); Eddie Cline (Card player with cigar; prisoner); Dick Smith (Card player with hat); Slim Summerville (Drunk in jail); Bobby Dunn (Caddie); Frank Opperman (Judge); Ted Edwards (First cop); Grover Ligon (Second cop); Dan Albert (Card player offering his seat to Gussle)
FILMED: 27 November–9 December 1914
RELEASED: 28 December 1914

1915

6. Hushing the Scandal

PRODUCTION: Keystone Film Company, released by Mutual Films
DIRECTOR: Unknown, possibly Walter Wright
CAST: Chester Conklin (Droppington); Syd Chaplin (Gussle); Norma Nichols (Bride); Frank Opperman, Alice Davenport (Older couple in park); Fritz Schade (Friend); Phyllis Allen (Washerwoman); Charles Lakin, Vivian Edwards (Younger couple at party); Cecile Arnold, Edwin Frazee, Grover Ligon, Frankie Dolan (Party guests)
FILMED: 13 November–23 November 1914
RELEASED: 4 January 1915

7. Giddy, Gay and Ticklish

PRODUCTION: Keystone Film Company, released by Mutual Films
DIRECTOR: Unknown, possibly F. Richard Jones
CAST: Syd Chaplin (Mr. Dash); Phyllis Allen (Mrs. Dash); Edgar Kennedy (Barber); Dixie Chene (Manicurist); Grover Ligon (First cop); Edwin Frazee (Second barber); Dan Albert (Customer with towel)
FILMED: 10 December–22 December 1914
RELEASED: 7 January 1915

8. Caught in a Park

PRODUCTION: Keystone Film Company, released by Mutual Films
DIRECTOR: Unknown, possibly F. Richard Jones
CAST: Syd Chaplin (Husband); Phyllis Allen (Wife); Slim Summerville (Boyfriend); Cecile Arnold (Girlfriend); Mack Swain (Bartender); Wesley Ruggles (Cop)
FILMED: 18 January–23 January 1915
RELEASED: 6 February 1915

9. That Springtime Feeling

PRODUCTION: Keystone Film Company, released by Mutual Films
DIRECTOR: F. Richard Jones
CAST: Syd Chaplin (Flirt); Cecile Arnold (Nursemaid); Ted Edwards (Cop); Jack Kennedy (Drunk)
FILMED: 2 February–6 February 1915
RELEASED: 25 February 1915

10. Gussle's Day of Rest

PRODUCTION: Keystone Film Company, released by Mutual Films
DIRECTOR: F. Richard Jones
CAST: Syd Chaplin (Gussle); Cecile Arnold (Girl in park); Slim Summerville (Boyfriend); Phyllis Allen (Mrs. Gussle)
FILMED: 25 January–22 February 1915
RELEASED: 29 March 1915

11. Gussle's Wayward Path

PRODUCTION: Keystone Film Company, released by Mutual Films
DIRECTORS: Syd Chaplin and Charles Avery
CAST: Syd Chaplin (Gussle); Phyllis Allen (Mrs. Gussle); Joy Lewis (Blond girl on train); Billie Brockwell (Clergywoman) Wesley Ruggles (Clergyman; Flirt on train); Frank Hayes (Conductor); Ollie Carlyle (Maid)
FILMED: 23 March–31 March 1915
RELEASED: 10 April 1915

12. Gussle Rivals Jonah

PRODUCTION: Keystone Film Company, released by Mutual Films
DIRECTORS: Syd Chaplin and Charles Avery
CAST: Syd Chaplin (Gussle); Phyllis Allen (Mrs. Gussle); Joy Lewis (Blond girl on boat); Frank Alexander (Her boyfriend); Minnie Chaplin (Sleeping passenger); Wesley Ruggles (First steward; passenger with moustache); Ivy Crosthwaite (Diving girl)
Filmed on a boat running between San Pedro harbor and Avalon, Santa Catalina Island, then on the Avalon docks.
FILMED: 6 March–20 March 1915
RELEASED: 26 April 1915

13. Gussle's Backward Way
PRODUCTION: Keystone Film Company, released by Mutual Films
DIRECTOR: Syd Chaplin and Charles Avery
PHOTOGRAPHY: R. D. Armstrong
CAST: Syd Chaplin (Gussle); Phyllis Allen (Mrs. Gussle); Joy Lewis (Blond girl); Frank Alexander (Fat man); Wesley Ruggles (Tourist in monocle); Dave Anderson (Hotel owner); Minnie Chaplin (Waitress)
Filmed atop Mt. Baldy.
FILMED: 3 April–20 April 1915
RELEASED: 3 May 1915

14. Gussle Tied to Trouble
PRODUCTION: Keystone Film Company, released by Mutual Films
DIRECTOR: Syd Chaplin and Charles Avery
PHOTOGRAPHY: R. D. Armstrong
CAST: Syd Chaplin (Gussle); Phyllis Allen (Mrs. Gussle); Joy Lewis (Blond girl); Frank Alexander (Fat Man); Wesley Ruggles (Tourist with monocle); Dave Anderson (Ski Instructor); Minnie Chaplin (Waitress)
Filmed atop Mt. Baldy.
FILMED: 3 April–20 April 1915
RELEASED: 6 May 1915

15. Lover's Lost Control
PRODUCTION: Keystone Film Company, released by Mutual Films
DIRECTOR: Syd Chaplin and Charles Avery
CAST: Syd Chaplin (Gussle); Phyllis Allen (Mrs. Gussle); Frank Alexander (Shoe customer); Joy Lewis (His daughter); Wayland Trask (Janitor); Wesley Ruggles (Shoe clerk with moustache); Jay Belasco (Shoe clerk); Billie Bennett (Customer who is slapped); Josef Swickard (Customer with cigar); Charles Lakin (Dishwear clerk); Grover Ligon (Man who calls police); Minnie Chaplin (Customer at counter)
FILMED: 22 April–10 July 1915
RELEASED: 2 August 1915

16. No One to Guide Him
PRODUCTION: Keystone Film Company, released by Mutual Films
DIRECTOR: F. Richard Jones
CAST: Syd Chaplin (Gussle); Phyllis Allen (Mrs. Gussle); Edgar Kennedy (Dark stranger); Josef Swickard (Smith, the bar owner); Slim Summerville (Bartender); Edwin Frazee (Butler); Ted Edwards (Mug; Cop); Charles Lakin (Drinker; Dinner guest); Cecile Arnold, Billy Gilbert, Dixie Chene (Dinner guests); Grover Ligon, Joe Bordeaux, Eddie Cline (Cops)
Originally shot as a three-reeler, but cut down to a two-reeler for release.
FILMED: 24 December 1914–14 January 1915
RELEASED: 30 August 1915

17. A Submarine Pirate
PRODUCTION: Keystone Film Company, released by Triangle Films
DIRECTORS: Syd Chaplin and Charles Avery, supervised by Mack Sennett
ASSISTANT DIRECTOR: Grover Ligon
PHOTOGRAPHY: R. D. Armstrong
CAST: Syd Chaplin (Waiter); Glen Cavender (Inventor; Ship captain); Wesley Ruggles (Inventor's accomplice; Sub officer; Ship officer); Phyllis Allen (Hotel guest); Harold J. Binney (Hotel manager); Grover Ligon, Harold Lloyd (Cooks) Louise Fazenda (Allen's dinner guest); Fritz Schade (Chef); Charles Lakin (Desk clerk); Cecile Arnold (Hotel guest); Shorty Hamilton (Wireless operator); Josef Swickard (Surplus store owner); Frank Alexander (Fat man with cast); Ted Edward (Waiter); Billy Gilbert, Al Hill (Torpedo loaders); Minnie Chaplin (Girl in hotel lobby); Mort Peebles
FILMED: 5 May–15 October 1915
RELEASED: 26 December 1915

1918

18. A Dog's Life*
DIRECTOR: Charles Chaplin
PRODUCTION: Chaplin–First National
PRODUCER: Charles Chaplin
SCENARIO: Charles Chaplin
PHOTOGRAPHER: Roland Totheroh
Filmed at Chaplin Studio on Sunset and La Brea
CAST: Charles Chaplin (Tramp); Edna Purviance (Bar singer); Mutt (Scraps); Sydney Chaplin (Lunch wagon owner); Henry Bergman (Employment agency applicant; woman in dance

---
*Thanks to David Robinson's Chaplin: His Life and Art for much of the information on Charles Chaplin productions.

hall); Charles Reisner (Employment agency clerk; drummer in dance hall); Albert Austin (Crook); Tom Wilson (Policeman); M. J. McCarty (Unemployed man); Mel Brown (Unemployed man); Charles Force (Unemployed man); Bert Appling (Unemployed man); Thomas Riley (Unemployed man); Slim Cole (Unemployed man); Ted Edwards (Unemployed man); Louis Fitzroy (Unemployed man); Dave Anderson (Unemployed man); Granville Redmond (Dance hall proprietor); Minnie Chaplin (Lady in dance hall); Alf Reeves (Man at bar); N. Tahbel (Hot tamale man); Rob Wagner (Man in dance hall); L. S. McVey (Musician); J. F. Parker (Musician); James T. Kelly (Customer at hot dog stand); Al Blake, Loyal Underwood, Fred Starr, Janet Miller Sully, Grace Wilson, Jerry Ferragoma, Park Jones, Jack Duffy, Richard Dunbar, Edward Miller, Billy Dul, Bruce Randall, Brand O'Ree, Bill White, John Lord, Jim O'Niall, H. C. Simmons, J. L. Fraube, Jim Habif, Florence Parellee, Miss Cullington, Margaret Dracup, Ella Eckhardt, Sarah Rosenberg, Lottie Smithson, Lillian Morgan, Jean Johnson, Fay Holderness, Dorothy Cleveland, J. Miller, Minnie Eckhardt, Mrs. Rigoletti (Dance hall patrons)

FILMED: 15 January–9 April 1918
RELEASED: 14 April 1918

19. The Bond

DIRECTOR: Charles Chaplin
PRODUCTION: Chaplin–First National
PRODUCER: Charles Chaplin
SCENARIO: Charles Chaplin
PHOTOGRAPHER: Roland Totheroh

Filmed at Chaplin Studio on Sunset and La Brea

CAST: Charles Chaplin, Edna Purviance, Sydney Chaplin (The Kaiser); Henry Bergman (John Bull); Dorothy Rosher (Cupid)

FILMED: 15 August 15–22 August 1918
RELEASED: 16 December 1918

20. Shoulder Arms

DIRECTOR: Charles Chaplin
PRODUCTION: Chaplin–First National
PRODUCER: Charles Chaplin
SCENARIO: Charles Chaplin
PHOTOGRAPHER: Roland Totheroh
CAST: Charles Chaplin (Recruit); Edna Purviance (French girl); Sydney Chaplin (Sergeant and the Kaiser); Jack Wilson (German Crown Prince); Henry Bergman (Fat German sergeant; Field Marshall von Hindenburg); Albert Austin (American soldier; German soldier; Kaiser's chauffeur); Tom Wilson (Training camp sergeant); John Rand (American soldier); Park Jones (American soldier); Loyal Underwood (Small German officer); W. G. Wagner, J. T. Powell, W. Herron, W. Cross, G. E. Marigold (Motorcyclists); C. L. Dice, G. A. Godfrey, L. A. Blaisdell, W. E. Allen, J. H. Warne (Motorcyclists, alternative group); Roscoe Ward, Ed Hunt, M. J. Donovan, E. B. Johnson, Fred Graham, Louis Orr, Al Blake, Ray Hanford, Cliff Brouwer, Claude McAtee, F. S. Colby, Jack Shalford, Joe Van Meter, Guy Eakins, Jack Willis, Charles Cole, T. Madden (American and German soldiers); Harry Goldman, Jack Willis, Mark Faber, E. H. Devere, Fred Everman, A. North, Charles Knuske, O. E. Haskins, Tom Hawley, W. E. Graham, James Griffin, W. A. Hackett, E. Brucker, J. H. Shewry, Sam Lewis, R. B. McKenzie, K. Herlinger, A. J. Hartwell (Additional players in street set, outside German headquarters)

FILMED: 27 May–16 September 1918
RELEASED: 20 October 1918

1921

21. King, Queen, Joker

PRODUCTION: Sydney Chaplin Productions, released by Paramount-Artcraft
DIRECTOR: Sydney Chaplin
SCENARIO: Sydney Chaplin and Alexander De Bray
PHOTOGRAPHY: Murphy Darling
ART DIRECTOR: Henry Clive
CAST: Sydney Chaplin (King of Coronia; Barber); Lottie McPherson (Queen of Coronia); Sylvia Grey (King's manicurist); Fontaine La Rue (Apache "queen"); Ivor McFadden, Harry Griffith (Crooks); Al Garcia (Head barber)

Exteriors filmed in France.
WORKING TITLE: "One Hundred Million"
RELEASED: 15 May 1921

1922

22. Pay Day

DIRECTOR: Charles Chaplin
PRODUCTION: Chaplin–First National

PRODUCER: Charles Chaplin
SCENARIO: Charles Chaplin
PHOTOGRAPHER: Roland Totheroh
Filmed at Chaplin Studio on Sunset and La Brea
CAST: Charles Chaplin (Laborer); Phyllis Allen (His wife); Mack Swain (Foreman); Edna Purviance (Foreman's daughter); Sydney Chaplin (Workman; Lunch wagon owner); Albert Austin (Workman); John Rand (Workman); Loyal Underwood (Workman); Henry Bergman (Drinking companion); Allan Garcia (Drinking companion); Pete Griffin, Joe Griffin, Harry Tenbrook, Ethel Childers, Edith Blythe, Virginia Bodle, Helen Kapp, La Belle Raymond, Sylvia Menier, Joe Kedian (Extras)
FILMED: 6 August–23 February 1922
RELEASED: 2 April 1922

1923

23. The Pilgrim

DIRECTOR: Charles Chaplin
PRODUCTION: Chaplin–First National
PRODUCER: Charles Chaplin
SCENARIO: Charles Chaplin
PHOTOGRAPHER: Roland Totheroh
CAST: Charles Chaplin (Escaped convict); Edna Purviance (Girl); Kitty Bradbury (Girl's mother); Mack Swain (Deacon); Loyal Underwood (Elder); Charles Reisner (Thief); Dinky Dean Reisner (Horrid child); Sydney Chaplin (Child's father; Eloping groom; ticket taker on train); May Wells (Child's mother); Henry Bergman (Sheriff on train); Tom Murray (Local sheriff); Monta Bell (Policeman); Jack Wilson (Clergyman whose clothes are stolen); Raymond Lee (Boy in church); Frank Antunez (Bandit); Joe Van Meter (Bandit); Phyllis Allen, Florence Lattimer, Edith Bostwick, Laddie Earle, Louis Troester, Beth Nagel, Mrs. C. Johnson (Members of congregation); Miss Evans, Frank Liscomb, S. D. Wilcox, Robert Traughbur, Carlyle Robinson, Jack McCredie, Charles Hafler, Bill Carey, Paul Mason McNeill, Sarah Barrows, Donnabelle Ouster, Gallie Frey, Della Glowner, Theresa Gray, Cecile Harcourt, Anna Hicks, Martha Harris, Mary Hamlett, Ethel Kennedy, Emily Lamont, Agnes Lynch, Mildred Pitts, Katherine Parrish, Edna Rowe, Mabel Shoulters, Georgia Sherrart, Rose Wheeler, George Bradford, George Carruthers, J. Espan, F. F. Guenste, Lee Glowner, Harry Hicks, Carl Jensen, Tom Ray, James J. Smith, S. H. Williams, Paul Wilkins, H. Wolfinger (Extras in Church Scene)
FILMED: 1 April–15 July 1922
PREMIERE: 26 February 1923

24. The Rendezvous

PRODUCTION: Marshall Neilan, distributed by Goldwyn-Cosmopolitan
DIRECTOR: Marshall Neilan
ASSISTANT DIRECTOR: Thomas Held
PHOTOGRAPHY: David Kesson
ART DIRECTOR: Cedric Gibbons
AUTHOR: Madeleine Ruthven
ADAPTATION: Josephine Lovett
CAST: Conrad Nagel (Lieutenant Walter Stanford); Lucille Ricksen (Vera); Richard Travers (Prince Sergei Tamiroff); Kathleen Key (Varvara Korenieva); Emmett Corrigan (Vassily Leonidoff); Elmo Lincoln (Juan Godunoff); Sydney Chaplin (Winkie Harrington); Kate Lester (Mrs. Stanford); Cecil Holland (Nichi Wandor); Lucien Littlefield (Samuel Klein); Eugenie Besserer (Nini Muskuin); E. O. Pennell (Czar)
RELEASED: 11 November 1923

25. Her Temporary Husband

PRODUCTION: Associated First National Pictures, Inc.
DIRECTOR: John McDermott
AUTHOR: Edward Paulton
CAST: Owen Moore (Thomas Burton); Sylvia Breamer (Blanche Ingram); Sidney Chaplin (Judd); Tully Marshall (John Ingram); Chuck Reisner (Hector)
RELEASED: 23 December 1923

1924

26. The Galloping Fish

PRODUCTION: Thomas Ince, released by First National, Inc.
DIRECTOR: Del Andrews
STORY: Frank Adams
CAST: Sidney Chaplin (Freddy Wetherill); Louise Fazenda (Undine); Ford Sterling (George Fitzgerald); Chester Conklin (Jonah); Lucille Ricksen (Hyla Wetherill); John Steppling (Cato Dodd); Freddie the Seal (Freddie the Seal)
RELEASED: 10 March 1924

27. Hello, 'Frisco!
PRODUCTION: Universal Pictures, Inc.
DIRECTOR: Slim Summerville
CAST: Slim Summerville (Cameraman); Bobby Dunn (Cameraman); Antonio Moreno, Wanda Wiley, Bryant Washburn, William Duncan, Edith Johnson, Norman Kerry, Hoot Gibson, William Desmond, Hobart Bosworth, Jack Hoxie, William S. Hart, Bebe Daniels, Jackie Coogan, Anna Q. Nilsson, J. Warren Kerrigan, Syd Chaplin, Ham Hamilton, Bull Montana, Barbara La Marr, Lew Cody, Fred Niblo, Enid Bennett, Ralph Lewis, Elliott Dexter (Wampas pageant attendees)
RELEASED: 9 December 1924

28. The Perfect Flapper
PRODUCTION: Associated First National Pictures, Inc.
DIRECTOR: John Francis Dillon
AUTHOR: Jessie Henderson
CAST: Colleen Moore (Tommie Lou Pember); Sydney Chaplin (Dick Trayle); Phyllis Haver (Gertrude Trayle); Lydia Knott (Aunt Sarah); Frank Mayo (Reed Andrews); Charles Wellesley (Joshua Pember)
RELEASED: 25 May 1924

1925

29. Charley's Aunt
PRODUCTION: Christie-Ideal, released by Producers' Distributing Corp.
DIRECTOR: Scott Sidney
AUTHOR: Brandon Thomas
ADAPTATION: F. McGrew Willis
CAST: Syd Chaplin (Sir Fancourt "Babbs" Babberley); Ethel Shannon (Ela Delahay); James E. Page (Spettigue); Lucien Littlefield (Brassett, the Scout); Alec B. Francis (Mr. Delahay); Phillips Smalley (Sir Francis Chesney); Eulalie Jensen (Donna Lucia D'Alvadorez); David James (Jack Chesney); Jimmie Harrison (Charlie Wykeham); Mary Akin (Amy); Priscilla Bonner (Kitty)
RELEASED: 8 February 1925

30. The Man on the Box
PRODUCTION: Warner Bros.
DIRECTOR: Charles F. Reisner (originally Fred Newmeyer)
AUTHOR: Harold McGrath
ADAPTATION: Charles Logue
CAST: Syd Chaplin (Bob Warburton); David Butler (Bob's Brother-in-law); Alice Calhoun (Betty Annesley); Kathleen Calhoun (Mrs. Lampton); Theodore Lorch (Mr. Lampton); Helene Costello (Bob's sister); E. J. Ratcliffe (Colonel Annesley); Charles F. Reisner (Badkoff); Charles Gerrard (Karloff or Karaloff); Henry Barrows (Bob's father)
RELEASED: 27 September 1925

1926

31. Oh! What a Nurse!
PRODUCTION: Warner Bros.
DIRECTOR: Charles F. Reisner
AUTHOR: Robert E. Sherwood
ADAPTATION: Darryl F. Zanuck
CAST: Syd Chaplin (Jerry Clark); Patsy Ruth Miller (June Harrison); Matthew Betz (Capt. Ladye Kirby); David Torrence (Big Tim Harrison); Gayne Whitman (Clive Hunt); Edgar Kennedy (Eric Johnson); Henry Barrows (Newspaper editor)
RELEASED: 7 March 1926

32. The Better 'Ole
PRODUCTION: Warner Bros.
DIRECTOR: Charles F. Reisner
AUTHORS: Bruce Bairnsfather and Arthur Eliot
ADAPTATION: Charles F. Reisner and Darryl Francis Zanuck
MUSICAL SCORE: Herman Heller, assisted by Maurice Baron, Fred Hoff and Dr. Edward Kilyeni
CAST: Syd Chaplin (Old Bill); Doris Hill (Joan); Harold Goodwin (Bert); Theodore Lorch (Gaspard); Edgar Kennedy (Corp. Quint); Charles Gerrard (The Major); Tom McGuire (The English General); Jack Ackroyd (Alf); Tom Kennedy (The Blacksmith); Kewpie Morgan (Gen. von Hinden); Arthur Clayton (The Colonel); Dick Gordon (Adjutant); Gordon Lewis (Female impersonator); Bill Hauber (Syd Chaplin double); Larry George, George Liggew, James Davis, Frederick Beck, Chick Collins (Stage hands); Jim Fulton, Otto Berringer, Charlie Dennis, Bill Dugwell, Steve Barrett, Billy Gilbert, Paul Malvern, Max Hawley (Band)
RELEASED: 7 October 1926 (New York); 18 November 1926 (Los Angeles)

1927

33. The Missing Link

PRODUCTION: Warner Bros.
DIRECTOR: Charles F. Reisner
STORY: Daryl Francis Zanuck and Charles F. Reisner
ADAPTATION: Darryl Francis Zanuck
CAST: Syd Chaplin (Arthur Wells); Ruth Hiatt (Beatrice Braden); Crauford Kent (Lord Dryden); Tom McGuire (Colonel Braden); Sam Baker (Missing Link); Akka (Chimp)
RELEASED: 6 May 1927 (New York); 18 June 1927 (Los Angeles)

1928

34. The Fortune Hunter

PRODUCTION: Warner Bros.
DIRECTOR: Charles F. Reisner
ASSISTANT DIRECTOR: Sandy Roth
PHOTOGRAPHY: Ed. Du Par
AUTHOR: Winchell Smith
ADAPTATION: Bryan Foy and Robert Dillon
CAST: Sydney Chaplin (Nat Duncan); Helene Costello (Josie Lockwood); Clara Horton (Betty Graham); Duke Martin (Harry West); Thomas Jefferson (Sam Graham); Erville Alderson (Blinky Lockwood); Paul Kruger (Roland); Nora Cecil (Betty Carpenter); Louise Carver (Store owner); Bob Ferry (Sheriff); Babe London (Waitress)
RELEASED: 9 January 1928 (U.S.); 17 September 1928 (U.K.)

35. A Little Bit of Fluff

PRODUCTION: British International Films (U.K.); released by Metro-Goldwyn-Mayer in America
DIRECTORS: Jess Robbins and Wheeler Dryden
AUTHOR: Walter A. Ellis
ADAPTATION: Wheeler Dryden
PHOTOGRAPHY: René Guissort and George Porknall
CAST: Sydney Chaplin (Bertram Tully); Betty Balfour (Mamie Scott); Nancy Rigg (Violet Tully); Annie Esmond (Mrs. Martin); Edmond Breon (John Ayers); Diana Wilson (Pamela Ayers); Clifford McLaglen (Henry Hudson); Enid Stamp Taylor (Susie West)
AMERICAN TITLE: *Skirts*
RELEASED: 24 May 1928 (U.K.); 26 July 1928 (U.S.)

Appendix B

A Selection of Sydney Chaplin Letters (WGC)

Feb. 22, 1931, Hotel de Paris, Monte Carlo
Saturday

My dear Jimmy,

So delighted to get your long letter & also to hear that you have both recovered from your accident. Thank heavens it was not too serious. What would I do without you? Well, Jim, I will try and give you all the news in a nutshell. I had seen the article in the Express before your wrote me. I quite agree with you. It is another attempt at blackmail, timed for the brother's arrival. Other newspapers placed their bloodhounds on my track, so I had to leave the Hotel Westminster suddenly then one of them traced me to a very small hotel & because I would not see him, wrote a piece in the Chicago Tribune that I had disappeared from the "fashionable" Hotel Westminster & was living in an obscure hotel Monty & had fifteen trunks with me. Of course, the trunk story was all d — d his. Also the "fashionable Westminster." Had he said I had left a third rate hotel for a cheap fifth class, the story would have suited me down to the ground, but he twists what I said to hurt me. Anyhow, I have left that hotel before the other hounds arrived. I thought it best not to take Minnie or they would have said "the bird has flown again." She stayed behind to spread the rumour that I had gone to London to meet Charlie. This will leave them guessing & the time coincided and sounds very reasonable. Whereas, I am living alone in a <u>very obscure hotel</u> on the high Cornish, perched on a rock one thousand feet above Monte Carlo. I am the only guest there and have been for days. The hotel has no heating system and I am gradually freezing to death. It has redeeming features — the view is wonderful. I see all Monte Carlo & the coast of Italy and at night I look down on a blaze of lights. While I sit having my dinner, I can well imagine I am flying over some city in a zeppelin. I get a little French practice, as no one speaks English & we are all in bed at 9:30. Except for the view and food, which is excellent, it is the nearest thing to a prison I can imagine. I shall stick it for a few days longer & then beat it to another sylvan retreat. You asked me in your last letter if there is anything I wanted to ask your solicitor. Yes, I would like to know just exactly what I gain by hiding away. In what way do I defeat the other side? What difference does it make whether I am served with papers or not? I have consulted a French solicitor here & he says they cannot do a thing to me except go to the French courts & ask them to recognize the English judgment & if the courts agreed to do so, they cannot do anything, so long as I have no banking account or safe deposit in my name. Since I wrote you, Minnie has taken a very pretty flat in Nice overlooking the sea, on the sixth floor. Nice balcony outside & sun all day. New building & right in the center of everything. Her furniture arrives from America next month. I was also wondering if the London crowd could step in, but the French solicitor tells me they can do nothing. She could kick the sheriff out of the door if it is her flat & her furniture. Do you know, I really don't know whether I have been made bankrupt or whether the receiver is holding off until I am served. I really would like to know what point they gain by serving me. And now for the next subject. I see the papers are all full of Charlie's arrival. I was afraid there was going to be a lot of counteraction—Campbell arriving at the same time, but everything turned out wonderful. I am so glad he had so great a welcome. I have just written him a long letter, saying how sorry I was I could not be there & I have asked him that when the excitement is all over to make a luncheon or dinner date with yourself. I know you will both like each other. I have extolled you to the skies & told him what a good pal you have been to me during my trouble. I also told him that you were the only one that I had taken into my confidence & that you could give him all the details of the rotten way I have been treated & the kind of justice I received. I know he will be glad to hear all the facts, because anything he knows must be just newspaper gossip & garbled hearsay. I have never written him about my case. I did not want to worry him as he had enough worry with his picture, but now when he can relax, he will no doubt like to hear the truth. I would also like you to meet Charlie's publicity manager, Mr. Carlyle Robinson. You will find him a good sport & has been with Charlie years. He talks the newspaper language backwards & his mother, I believe, owns "The Police Gazette." Don't talk quite so confidentially to him as you do to Charlie. You know what publicity men are. They are working for you today & maybe the B. I. tomorrow. I will drop a line to Carl & tell him to get in touch with you. I have just checked into Monte Carlo to write this letter and get warm. I cannot take my gloves off on the glacier. It is 8 P.M. & I am not going home to the bird's nest. When I tell you I go to bed with my socks on & my underwear underneath my pajamas, it's a great life & I still keep laughing.

Love to you both, Sydney

PS. When I read of Charlie's wonderful reception, I cannot help but feel my position. However, my time will come. "It is always darkest before the dawn."

* * *

Dec. 16, 1930, Hotel Westminster, Nice France

My dear Jim,

I am in receipt of all your letters, also cables. I did not answer your last cable as I did not want them to think I was anxious & I was prepared to take a chance and ask whether they would put me into bankruptcy or not, as I had already received publicity about the appointment of a receiver, so I could not have made much difference & might have been an advantage. It seems to me that as they did not go through with it, Garrett must have already discussed the possibility of a settlement with Maxwell. Anyhow, you are playing your cards splendidly & you are up against a d—d shrewd poker player in Garrett. You can always figure him 90% with Maxwell & 10% with me. For some reason or another, he is telling a lot of lies. For instance, when he said he did not receive a letter from me asking him to try & get a settlement. I told him in that letter that I would be willing to return to make the picture even though I had to wait two years, but I advised him to show my letter to the solicitors before doing anything & I have a letter from the solicitors saying that Garrett had shown them my letter, but that they had advised him not to approach Maxwell with it that time. So why is he lying about it? Also, why does he say that I was asked to pay the bill $50 a week for a year & that I refused. That also is a d—d lie. I would have been a blasted idiot not to have done so, guilty or not guilty. Does it sound reasonable that I would have wanted to risk the publicity & lose a $200,000 contract for the sake of $2500? I cannot understand what his object is in saying these things. I am also suspicious of his visit to California & his talk with my brother. He also discussed the matter with my New York lawyer. Why? He never goes to Los Angeles. He has a partner in America that takes care of all the American end of his business. It wouldn't surprise me if Maxwell had paid his expenses out there to find out if I had any property that they could put in their hands or if they won. It was a long time before they started suit against me & only after Garrett had arrived in L.A. However, I know your mind is just as shrewd as his & cannot put anything over on you. Even though they were willing for me to return & complete the picture at the contract price, I would be afraid they were preparing some trap for me. I would be in a pretty tough spot if they got me over there & then pulled one of Maxwell's slick moves. The safest place for me to make the picture is either France or Germany. I do not trust Maxwell. He has broken his word too many times with me.

The question that he has to decide is if they are convinced that they can get anything from me, then they must look upon the sixty thousand as a dead loss & ask themselves the question is Chaplin worth $40,000 to make a picture & if by engaging him at this figure can they retrieve their sixty thousand in a profit? Naturally, they would prefer to take their loss if they thought my picture would be a fizzle. They would not want to throw good money after bad & they may prefer to wait until their judgment & come down on me at some future time when I was working or had money. Personally, I shall be in a quandary what to do, even though they are willing to complete the picture. I *don't* trust them. However, don't worry, Jim. Don't show any anxiety. Bankruptcy can't hurt me. I'm not in a credit business, so a thousand thanks for all the trouble you're putting yourself to. I can never repay you. You will be glad to know I am very good health. I am playing 27 holes of golf every day & am crazy about the game. It is giving me a new lease on life. I have also made a number of nice friends here & have been to some wonderful house parties. I don't know whether I should hide away or not or whether I should enjoy myself. I hope you and Edith are quite well. I send very best wishes to you both. How's the Xmas number coming along? I saw a man killed by an auto outside my window. What a mess of blood everywhere.

Sydney

PS. Some time ago, I had sent you a gag that had been given me as original, but I afterwards discovered it had been used in Cochran's revue. I have just heard another & the party swears it is original & they witnessed the incident. It might make a good section for your paper.

A couple in a small town church are about to be married. They both kneel down before the clergyman & on the soles of both of their shoes written in chalk is "room 23," no doubt put their by the "boots" of the hotel. The congregation were hysterical.

Sydney

* * *

October 7th, 1932

My dear Jim,

    I was very interested in reading an article you published on "nudism" & intended writing you a letter of congratulation upon your courage in printing it. Then Wheeler handed me another cutting also from your paper, but written from the opposite angle. This article I resent from the fact that the person who wrote it is "talking out of the back of his neck," as the Americans say. It is quite evident he has had no personal experience in a nudist camp & shows his ignorance of the subject. I know I can talk freely to you, Jim, & you know that what I say will be the truth & nothing but the truth. You have always been a confidante of mine & one of my best friends. So I have no fear of speaking my mind knowing that what I have to say is in strict confidence. First let me tell you I have been a nudist for some considerable period. I was first converted to nudism when I first visited a nudist camp in Berlin. I did not at that time join their organization because I was only there for a few days, but I made up my mind that at some future date I would go back & spend a vacation in one of their camps, but I never did. The opportunity did not present itself. But sometime later, I happened to notice a magazine in a bookstore in Nice with a photograph of several nudists on the cover. The magazine was called "Vivre." I purchased the book and found it was published by a nudist society of Paris, who had a private grounds in Paris called the Sparta Club. Their committee consisted of some of the best known doctors & statesmen in France. This was a big surprise to me, as I was under the impression that nudism was strictly forbidden in France. I also discovered that they had an affiliated society in Nice so I decided to join. Now let me explain my motives. In the first place I have always had a great pride of body. As a boy & even now I was always fascinated by acrobats & strong men. I used to buy all the physical culture magazines & take my Sandow exercise every morning with 5lb. dumbbells. Also my cold baths & 10- and 20-mile walks. I was a fanatic in keeping fit. I worshipped the sun, what little I saw of it in England & would expose my body to its rays whenever an opportunity presented itself, being a firm believer in its curative properties. This desire for physical fitness plus the sunbathing was the main object in my joining the nudists. My second reason was the strong streak of sensuality in my nature. I was sex curious. I thought how wonderful it would be to indulge my passion for physical fitness & sunbathing surrounded by a bevy of maidens in complete nudity. I knew the laws of the club were very strict. It was a case of "you must look, but mustn't touch" but this did not deter me from joining the group. I felt I could cater to my aesthetic senses. I had always been interested in art & sculpture & if it was considered perfectly proper to gaze upon the sculptured form of an undraped woman with admiration, how much more interesting it would be to see that same form animated with the vibrant pulsations of life, youth & beauty, to watch the ever-changing contours & the harmonic coordination of muscles. This was the sex curiosity I had. For after all there is sex in all art & beauty. In fact, in nearly everything we do. Therefore this sex curiosity was the second impulse that prompted me to join. I will now try to give you an idea of my impressions & reactions based upon close observation, which is a faculty I have cultivated as being so necessary to my business of making moving pictures. After joining and paying my dues of 60 francs for the year, I was given directions where to meet, which was a deserted part of the beach, where we could depend upon complete privacy. Of course, this was strictly against the law, as the beach is public and had anyone complained, we were all liable for arrest, but we kept strict lookouts, so felt safe in our retreat. This inconvenience will shortly be overcome as the club is now negotiating for a private ground, the same as the Paris club & the various clubs in Germany. Our club meets every Sunday on the beach and twice a week during the evenings at the private gymnasium belonging to a doctor. On my first visit to the beach, I found about 20 members all in the nude & indulging in various sports — medicine ball, badminton, swimming, etc. I was introduced. The crowd was mixed. There was a local doctor, his wife and two children — two painters, very well known — a Russian dancer from the well-known Russian ballet, stenographers, shop girls, etc., all of them quite unconcerned about their nudity. Some of the figures were beautiful and some fat & flabby. Some of them rouged with long exposures to the sun & some pale & anemic, as though they had just joined. I was not in the least embarrassed in undressing before them. In fact, was rather eager to do so. The average girl turns up on the beach with a one-piece dress & no underwear. The dress is quickly stripped off & the girl is completely nude standing in sandals. But one day a German girl came. It was her first visit. She was completely dressed — silk underwear, stockings, suspenders, brassiere — in fact everything possible a woman could wear. She undressed like a slow-moving picture. It was the only erotic thing I have seen in the club. The men all lost interest in the ball game & even the women all became interested. It proved one thing to me and that is that a partially clothed body is much more arousing than complete nudity. I am much more interested in a tight-fitting bathing suit that shows the indentations of the body, than I am in a tuft of pubic hair. My final summing up of nudity is that it tends to make one blasé instead of arousing the sexual passions. I have often been asked by curious people what happens if one of the male members suddenly becomes aroused? I have yet to see this happen & I have attended many meetings. I know it has never happened to me. One becomes so used to nudity around them that one almost forgets that it exists. One becomes entirely unconscious of their own nudity. I have sat & talked to fully dressed lady visitors & have become so interested in the conversation that I have forgotten completely I was in the nude. It is one of the easiest things in the world to get used to, in spite of all our early training and conventions. On my first visit to the beach, I decided to watch very carefully the actions of the various members, to try & fathom what their real motivation was in becoming nudists & I came to this conclusion. The majority of them are intellectuals of advanced thought, some of them communists and some like myself, rebels at heart against the smug hypocrisy of convention, and above all, reformers with atrophied glands who make it their business to tell other people what they shall do with their bodies. It is not that nudists believe that they will not receive sufficient sunshine if they wear a slip, but it is an outward display of freedom and resentment against the dictates of Country and Society. We have no syphilis or other venereal diseases among our members. The majority of them take a great pride in their body & health for the benefit of your writer who refers to their "orgies." If throwing the medicine ball, badminton, and swimming are "orgies," then we have orgies. I have never seen an immoral act or gesture in all the time I have been with them. The girls are treated with every respect. Their disadvantage if I may put it that way, puts a man upon his honour. There may be sex thoughts in the mind & undoubtedly is & so there is in any church congregation, but the thoughts can find no physical outlet in the nudist camp, unless it is to work it off with strenuous exercise. As I said before, I think nudity has the tendency to make one blasé. I have seen fellows sleep for hours in the sun surrounded by female youth & beauty in every possible posture. I have also seen the same fellows inwardly resent being disturbed in order to be introduced to a new girl member. I have seen a young boy of fourteen, who had received a complete sexual education, shake hands with a new young girl member without showing the slightest curiosity and then disappear immediately into the sea for a swim & I wondered whether I would have done the same thing at his age, in spite of my membership in the "Christian endeavour." No, in my days there was too much mystery surrounding it, too much distorted information, too many marked pages in the bible about Lot and his daughters, etc., also too many shops in

Wlych & Claren Streets where one could buy erotic books and see every appliance in the window used for sexual intercourse and birth control. I am not holding the nudists up as a flock of angels. Outside of the camp, I suppose they are just as natural as anyone else, but I do say their movement is a step in the right direction. There are several middle-aged men who join purely out of sex curiosity. You can easily tell them. Their bodies are white and pot-bellied. It is their first appearance in the sun. They are immediately asked to join in the games which results in their either becoming enthusiastic members, improving both physically and mentally or you don't see them any more. I would be prepared to bet that if Germany continues the nudist movement with its present growth & popularity, in ten years, she will be the greatest athletic country in the world. Stadiums are taking the place of beer gardens. Your contributor is quite wrong when he states that Germany has prohibited the movement. The government has only stopped public athletic displays & nudity in public places, which is as it should be. I do not believe in nudists forcing their nudity upon people who don't want it. Neither do I believe in non-nudists interfering with people who do want it & have their own private grounds. I was amused at some of the silly arguments of your correspondent. He said nature did not intend us to be nudists or we would have fur like an animal. If Darwin was right, then at some time or other we must have had fur. He makes excuses for the savage by saying a pigment in his skin has a natural protection. Put any white race continually nude under a tropical sun & he would find that the sun would soon develop a protective pigment for them also. He also states that even savages cover their nudity. So they do, with boxes to make their sexual parts look larger. There are also a number of races that do not wear anything & whose morals are all of the highest standard. I would advise him to read "Untrodden Fields of Anthropology," by a French army doctor and published by the Librarie de Médicine—13 Faubourg, Montmartre, Paris. He would learn a great deal about nudity & morals. I have never seen a bitch out of heat fall for a dog yet, and dogs have plenty to show. I wonder when all this d — d canting? Hypocrisy will finish. If it was only for the sake of nudity that I had joined this society, then I would not have to go further than a certain licensed house I know in Paris, where for the price of a glass of beer, I can see 50 nude women, dance with them, have them sit upon my knee (not the fifty at one time) or expose themselves to me in any conceivable position. Yet all the months I have lived in Paris, I have been there three times, once out of curiosity, and twice to take my friends who were equally curious. No, you can take it from me, Jim. Nudism as it is carried out in the responsible clubs of Germany and France is a great beneficial and healthy movement. After a wonderful day at the beach, sunbathing, swimming and exercise, I come home, have my dinner, then spend the evening with my friends. These are usually well "lit up" by the time I get there, having spent the day mixing cocktails. I join them in a drink & listen to their conversation, which usually consists of smutty stories & shop, but you don't have to join in their "sez you." No, but you see they are old friends of mine, broad-minded and talk my language. I like a smutty story if it is clever and well-told. I also like a drink occasionally & besides their conversation is a relaxation from the high-brow discourses of the nudists. My evening friends would also like to be nudists, but unfortunately they like their Sunday afternoon cocktails, poker & bridge and are not very keen on exercise. What do I say? Nothing. It's none of my business. *Their bodies are their own.*

Kindest regards, Sydney

* * *

[Cuba] 14 March

My dear Jim,

Here I am again from out of the long distant past. I have no excuse to offer for my months of self-imposed silence towards humanity and the world in general. It started in Hollywood and increased in intensity as my nerves became on edge & I suffered loss of sleep through trying to assume the responsibilities of running a studio rife with jealousies & old fashioned ideas. I am not referring to Charlie's individual work, but to the working conditions with which he is surrounded. When I arrived, I found everything in a dilapidated, rundown condition. There was no excuse for it, because Charlie does not limit the expenditures & the studio staff has years between pictures, when there is nothing for them to do but maintenance of the studio. I found the property room like a pig sty, filthy with dust and cobwebs. The Sunset house the same way, paper peeling of the walls & the place overrun with rats. You should see the difference now. They are using it as dressing rooms for "Stars." The still room where Charlie keeps all the negative stills of his early pictures was in the same neglected condition. Nothing was inventoried & dozens of plates were broken. These can never be replaced. They contained many photos of visiting celebrities taken with Charlie & would have been most valuable for a biography. Those that had not been broken, we had to spend hours trying to identify the people in the photographs. There was never any index kept. I had all this remedied. The property room cleaned from top to bottom, everything segregated and inventoried, requisition and double checking systems put in on both purchases & rentals & running inventories kept. Also graphs on labour. Nothing like this had ever been done before, so naturally, I became "Enemy #1." However, I did give a damn, so long as I had Charlie's support. In addition to all these innovations, I had the supervising & the letting of contracts for the erection of new buildings & the installation of sound equipment. Well, it was the hardest and most disagreeable work I have ever undertaken, the work plus the passive resistance of the senile staff (who had been shell-shocked out of a two-year hibernation) got on my nerves. I would arrive home at night a tired wreck. I made no social engagements, or answered letters from friends. I had only one idea, that was to get away from it all & shut myself off from the world. When I thought of my home in Nice & the quiet life I had lead there, I realized I had left a Paradise. Hollywood was not the same, people had changed. Before it was fun making pictures. We worked together like a happy family, everyone ready to do anything that was needed. Now the game is in the hands of unions who are gradually throttling it. Here are a few examples of what the producer has to contend with: The property man wanted to nail a few vines to a garden wall set. The vines were to be cut from the Sunset house grounds. The work would have taken 15 minutes, but the union insisted that we telephone & obtain a union green man to do the work & the vine should be purchased from a union horticulture establishment. Result, work held up while the studio running expenditure is several thousand dollars a day. The property man makes a strap that is to support Charlie while (PTO) he is seated in an aeroplane which is upside down, the property man straps himself in the plane to see if it works right & if it is sufficiently strong enough to hold Charlie, the result is a union fight, the special effect union maintaining it is their work to test it & the property man maintaining that as he had made it, he was responsible for Charlie's safety. Charlie had a wardrobe woman who had handled successfully this department through all his previous pictures. We were now told that she would not be allowed to handle men's clothing. We must engage a wardrobe man at three times her salary. In addition we would have to put on other men according to the number of extras engaged. Sometimes we would have as many as six wardrobe men who would hand out uniforms in the morning & sit on their behinds for the rest of the day doing nothing. I could give you enough dope on unions that would fill a book. I have no objections to unions, I think every man is worthy of this hire, but they are making ridiculous rules. Here is a rule regarding extras: All property men must take on location ladies' Kotex, as if women have not the brains to know when they will need them & provide their own. Can you imagine the humiliation of a woman coming to the property man & saying, "I want a Kotex, medium size"? Here are some more of their rulings: We employed some extras at $8.50 a day. When the anti-aircraft gun revolved, they were told to pretend to be knocked down by the gun & to sit down on their fannies. They did the scene all right & then asked for $35 each, claiming they came under the heading of "stunt men" and the union upheld their claim. Ye gods, $35 a day? Why we Karno boys worked for half that salary a week, four shows a night & did every kind of ground tumbling under the sun, including head spins — and liked it. Here is another ruling: If you use an actor and weeks after decide you would like to use him in an added scene, which would mean more work for him, you have to pay him a salary for all intervening time. However, if he puts on a moustache, he becomes another character & intervening payment is not necessary. We availed ourselves of this, but instead of using a moustache, we placed a scar on his face and got away with it. It is not the actors themselves who make the trouble, but the union spies who work as extras. I tell you the game is getting childish and I was glad to get away from it. The climax came when some dirty skunk, whose toes I had trodden on, discovered that I was in the country with a visitor's permit only. I was hauled before the immigrant investigators & accused of working without a permit. I had to take along my lawyer and swear I had received no compensation, that I was trying to relieve Charlie from a lot of irksome responsibilities & everything I had done was out of brotherly love. This statement saved me from government trouble, but as I had already received two extensions on my visitor's permit, I was advised to leave the country & come in on a resident quota. Well, I packed up and headed for Havana, but I took with me a charming girl, whom I married before leaving America. She is French and I knew her previously in Nice. She is brunette and looks decidedly Spanish. I have nicknamed her "Gypsy." We are spending our honeymoon here and are very happy. We have not decided yet whether we will return to America, or push on to some of the Caribbean islands. We both love the sun & nature in its primitive form. Unfortunately our stay here has been marred by my illness. I have only just recovered from seven weeks in bed with a bad attack of flu. Well, Jim, that is all my news. Please forgive me not writing sooner & let me know how you are getting along, because I know you are having hell over there. I am glad you got Edith and the children out of it. I am so sorry I was not in Hollywood when they arrived. Please keep this letter confidential. Also keep your chin up and come through safe and sound, because we must see each other again. We'll have plenty to talk about. Gypsy & I send you our very best wishes for your happiness.

Yours as ever, Sydney

Chapter Notes

Introduction

1. Quoted in William H. Gass, "Go Forth and Falsify: Katherine Anne Porter and the Lies of Art," *Harper's* (January 2009), p. 76.
2. Sydney Chaplin, Palais Rosa-Bonheur, Nice, France, R. J. Minney, 4 June 1935, WGC.
3. Sydney Chaplin, Palais Rosa Bonheur, Nice, France, Charles Chaplin, Hollywood, 22 June 1948, CHACHAA.

Chapter 1

1. Charles Chaplin, *My Autobiography*, London: Bodley Head, 1964, p. 14.
2. Ibid., p. 6.
3. Sydney notoriously adopted March 17, St. Patrick's Day, as his official birthday, after he became a film star.
4. Chaplin, *My Autobiography*, p. 17.
5. Sydney Chaplin, Montreux Palace Hotel, Montreux, Switzerland, R. J. Minney, 22 September 1958, SOC.
6. A careful examination of documents in the Walter Gasparini Collection (WGC) revealed two envelopes dated 1930, sealed with wax and embedded with a signet ring. Unfortunately, it was a completely different ring, with completely different icons. This suggests that the rings had nothing to do with any actual ancestor, but were simply part of Sydney's ever-changing disguise.
7. Still, its existence and the story surrounding it must have provided an illegitimate boy (and man) a sense of relief from the issue that must have been palpable, unless the ring was only a joke between himself, his friends and family. Also, it seems likely that Hannah named her son for the man who impregnated her and, in this case, the census records offer up a man by the name of Sidney John Hawke (a more accurate spelling of the name, according to Wheeler Dryden), who lived alone in Lambeth for every census but 1890, and was born in 1859, a reasonable age for a mate of Hannah's. His occupation, though, was hotel proprietor, or at least it was by the 1900 census. Could this have been the man? Someone who lived just down the street all the time that his boy was growing up in poverty?
8. David Robinson, *Chaplin: His Life and Art* (London: Penguin, 2001), p. 5.
9. Ibid., p. 7.
10. Ibid., p. 22.
11. Chaplin, *My Autobiography*, p. 14.
12. Sydney Chaplin, "Some Reminiscences of Sid Chaplin," *Reel Life* (November 14, 1914), p. 21.
13. Sydney Chaplin, "Some Reminiscences," p. 21.
14. "Charlie's Mother in the Chorus," CHACHAA.
15. David Robinson, p. 15.
16. Wheeler Dryden was to force his way back into the lives of Sydney and Charlie in 1918, via Edna Purviance.
17. In one ironic twist of fate, late in life, Dryden won a part in a 1930 film written by James A. FitzPatrick, of *TravelTalks* fame, entitled *The Lady of the Lake* (an adaptation of Sir Walter Scott's novel); Sydney was to be courted by FitzPatrick on at least two occasions just six years later.
18. R. J. Minney, *Chaplin the Immortal Tramp: The Life and Work of Charles Chaplin* (London: George Newnes, 1954), p. 5.
19. Ibid., p. 8.
20. Ibid., p. 8.
21. Chaplin, *My Autobiography*, pp. 24–25.
22. David Robinson, p. 17.
23. Ibid.
24. Ibid.
25. Peter C. Higginbotham, "Lambeth (Paris of St. Mary), Surrey, London"; *The Workhouse*, 2008, 25 May 2008, http://www.workhouses.org.uk/index.html?Lambeth/Lambeth.shtml
26. David Robinson, p. 19.
27. Quoted in Simon Fowler, *Workhouse: the People, the Places, the Life behind Doors*, (Richmond, UK: The National Archives, 2007), p. 10.
28. Fowler, pp. 37–38.
29. Chaplin, *My Autobiography*, p. 55.
30. Fowler, p. 44.
31. Quoted in Fowler, p. 108.
32. Higginbotham, "Lambeth."
33. Higginbotham, *The Workhouse Cookbook* (Port Stroud, Gloucestershire, UK: History Press, 2008), p. 42.
34. Higginbotham, *The Workhouse Cookbook*, p. 136.
35. Chaplin, *My Autobiography*, p. 27.
36. Quoted in Higginbotham, "Central London School District," *The Workhouse*, 2008, http://users.ox.ac.uk/~peter/workhouse/CentralLondonSD/CentralLondonSD.shtml.
37. David Robinson, p. 19.

38. Sydney Chaplin, R. J. Minney, 7 October 1932, WGC.
39. Higginbotham, "Central London School District."
40. The death certificate of his second wife, Henriette (Gypsy), states it more clearly: she is recorded as "Henriette Hill dit Chaplin" (Hill called Chaplin).
41. Wheeler, in later life, however, once chastised R. J. Minney for referring to Sydney as "Syd" in an article he had written, claiming that his half-brother preferred to be referred to by his full name (Sydney); this preference is supported by the fact that Sydney signed his correspondence with it almost exclusively.
42. Dr. Ch. H. Leibbrand, "The Training Ship 'Exmouth,'" *The Strand* (1899), p. 88.
43. Fowler notes that "between 1876 and 1929, over 16,000 workhouse boys were trained on board; of these over 4,500 joined the Royal Navy, 6,400 joined the merchant marines and 1,600 became army musicians," p. 145.
44. Leibbrand, p. 88.
45. David Robinson, p. 22.
46. Leibbrand, p. 88.
47. In fact, Bourchier and Schoolmaster Hollamby both signed Sydney's Record book, CHACHAA.
48. Leibbrand, p. 89.
49. Ibid., p. 89.
50. Ibid., p. 92.
51. Ibid.
52. CHACHAA.
53. Sung to the tune of Gilbert and Sullivan's *HMS Pinafore*, CHACHAA.
54. CHACHAA.
55. Minney, 12.
56. Harry Carr, "Charlie's Brother Sid," *Classic* (April 1924), p. 21.
57. Chaplin, *My Autobiography*, p. 32.
58. Elizabeth Van Heyningen, "The Social Evil in the Cape Colony 1868–1902: Prostitution and the Contagious Diseases Acts," *Journal of South African Studies* 10.2 (1984), p. 179.
59. *Encyclopedia of Alternative Medicine* (Detroit, MI: Thomson/Gale, 2005).
60. Admittedly, the disease is only passed in the primary stage, and so, it is likely that only Sydney would have been in danger of contracting it this way.
61. Van Heyningen, p. 171.
62. Jonathan Martens, Maciej Pieczkowski and Bernadette Van Vuuren-Smyth, *Seduction, Sale & Slavery: Trafficking in Women & Children for Sexual Exploitation in Southern Africa.*, third ed. (Pretoria, South Africa: IOM International Organization for Migration, 2003), p. 20.
63. Philippa Levine, *Prostitution, Race and Politics: Policing Venereal Disease in the British Empire* (New York: Routledge, 2003), p. 235.
64. Van Heyningen, p. 172.
65. Ibid., p. 180.
66. *The Era*, 26 September, 14 & 31 November, and 3 December 1885, n. p.
67. David Robinson, p. 26.
68. Chaplin, *My Autobiography*, p. 33.
69. David Robinson, p. 27.
70. Chaplin, *My Autobiography*, p. 62.
71. Carr, "Charlie's Brother Sid," p. 21.
72. David Robinson, p. 35.
73. Minney, pp. 12–13.
74. Sydney Chaplin, "Some Reminiscences," p. 21.
75. Chaplin, *My Autobiography*, p. 82.
76. "Greater Opportunity in America, Actor Asserts," *Los Angeles Times* (26 June 1927), p. C19.
77. David Robinson, p. 51.
78. Chaplin, *My Autobiography*, pp. 85–86.
79. CHACHAA.
80. Tony Barker, *Round the Town: Following Grandfather's Footsteps* (Hambergen, Germany: Bear Family Records, 2002), p. 23.
81. David Robinson, pp. 55–56.

Chapter 2

1. *The Era* (7 April 1906), n. p.
2. Minney, p. 14.
3. *Referee* (5 May 1906), n. p.
4. Minney, p. 14.
5. A. J. Marriot, *Chaplin: Stage by Stage* (Hitchin, UK: Marriot, 2005), p. 219.
6. *The Era* (14 April 1906), n. p.
7. Ibid. (21 April 1906), n. p.
8. Ibid. (12 May 1906), n. p.
9. Ibid. (21 April 1906), n. p.
10. David Robinson, p. 64.
11. Minney, 14; Chaplin, *My Autobiography*, p. 93.
12. In fact, the advertisement for the "NEW WING" appeared in the same edition of *The Era* (6 October 1906) as the first-ever mention of the Sydney Chaplin name in reference to a Karno production.
13. *The Era* (6 October 1906), n. p.
14. Edwin Adeler and Con West, *Remember Fred Karno? The Life of a Great Showman* (London: John Long, 1939), p. 110.
15. David Robinson, pp. 86–87.
16. The ship manifest notes that Sydney had $50 with him, a huge sum considering he had just started with Karno.
17. "Syd Chaplin," *The Triangle* (18 December 1915), p. 5.
18. Adeler and West, p. 118.
19. Ibid., p. 120.
20. *Variety* (27 October 1906), included a discussion of the origin of the stage-upon-a-stage device: "The endless discussion as to the originality of the 'stage upon a stage' scene as given in the Karno act, and also in the similar sketch produced by Jean Bedini, might be settled through the fact that in 1871 at the Karl Theatre, Vienna, Austria, a travesty on 'Tannehauser' was written by Johann Nestroy, with music by Franz von Suppe. As produced at that time, thirty-five years ago, it contained, with a few minor differences, the essential characters and business of the disputed pieces."
21. *Variety* (15 September 1906), p. 4.
22. An article in the *New York Evening World* (3 January 1907), entitled, "Vaudeville Fight in the U. S. Courts," reported that Karno won an injunction to prevent Bedini from performing Karno's copyrighted skit in any other venues.
23. Bedini's version of Karno's sketch was entitled *A Night in English Vaudeville*, *Variety* (29 December 1906), p. 5.
24. *Variety* (8 September 1906), n. p.
25. *Variety* (10 December 1906), p. 6.
26. David Robinson, p. 76.
27. *The Era* (29 December 1906), n. p.
28. Adeler and West describe Kitchen: "Fred Kitchen was a revelation. He had his chance and grabbed it with both hands. There are all types of comedians. There is the comedian born, and the comedian who is manufactured. The latter's technique may be sheer perfection; he may have rehearsed every gesture to nicety; he may try his voice inflections in a thousand different ways till he gets the right one, and by sheer study and hard work he may get right to the top of the tree. But comedy was and is inherent in Fred Kitchen; it is 'bone of his bone and flesh of his flesh,' if a rather grisly simile may be used," pp. 91–92.
29. "The Football Match," *The Era* (29 December 1906), n. p.
30. Ibid.
31. "The Football Match," *The Era* (29 December 1906), n. p.

32. *The Era* (22 June 1907), n. p.
33. Adeler and West, p. 127.
34. *The Era* (31 October 1908), n. p.
35. *The Era* (13 March 1909), n. p.
36. One factor that may have led to this opportunity for Sydney was that the manager he worked with from nearly the beginning of his Karno career—Arthur Forrest—passed away the first week of October, *The Era* (10 October 1908), n. p.; perhaps this gave Sydney the impetus he needed to try to advance himself in the company.
37. *The Era* (8 May 1909), n. p.
38. Ibid.
39. Ibid.
40. Ibid.
41. David Robinson, 83–84.
42. "Shoreditch Olympia," *The Era* (5 June 1909), p. 16.
43. Ibid.
44. "Willesden Hippodrome," *The Era* (10 July 1909), n. p.
45. "Islington Empire," *The Era* (31 July 1909), n. p.
46. *The Era* (17 July 1909), p. 20.
47. *The Era* (28 August 1909), p. 16.
48. Adeler and West, p. 133.
49. "Studio Shots," *MPW* (21 February 1920), p. 1250.
50. Irvine Gilbert (Minnie's great-nephew), phone communication, 10 January 2010; Minnie's parents were Samuel Gilbert and Rebecca Harrison Gilbert and she had many siblings, among them Charlie, Norman, Israel, and Laura.
51. David Robinson, pp. 88–89.
52. Sydney was still garnering much acclaim for his performance in *Skating* on this night at the East Ham Palace; a reviewer noted, "Large and appreciative audiences are attending here this week to witness one of the most interesting and entertaining programmes to be obtained.... The company is undoubtedly one of Karno's best," *The Era* (13 August 1910), p. 18.
53. *The Era* (20 August 1910), p. 21.
54. Quoted in David Robinson, p. 89.
55. Adeler and West, p. 142–43.
56. Adeler and West, p. 143.
57. Quoted in Adeler and West, p. 144.
58. Adeler and West, p. 145.
59. CHACHAA.
60. *The Illustrated Chronicle* (13 June 1912), n. p., CHACHAA.
61. Ibid.
62. Ibid.
63. *The Standard* (Oldham) (1913), CHACHAA.
64. *The Illustrated Chronicle* (13 June 1912), n. p., CHACHAA.
65. Fred Karno, Sydney Chaplin, 13 February 1913, CHACHAA.
66. *The Era* (17 September 1913), p. 9.
67. The sketch was reincarnated for a time in 1914, beginning on March 16, *The Era* (11 March 1914), p. 9.
68. *The Era* (24 September 1913), p. 11.
69. *Flats* M.S., CHACHAA.
70. Sydney Chaplin, Palais Rosa Bonheur, Nice, France, R. J. Minney, 6 February 1956, WGC.
71. Fred Karno, Sydney Chaplin, 29 December 1913, CHACHAA.
72. Fred Karno, Sydney Chaplin, 7 April 1914, CHACHAA.

Chapter 3

1. Charlie Chaplin, Los Angeles Athletic Club, Sydney Chaplin, 9 August 1914, CHACHAA.
2. Chaplin, *My Autobiography*, p. 158.
3. Al P. Nelson and Mel R. Jones, *A Silent Siren Song: The Aitken Brothers' Hollywood Odyssey, 1905–1926* (New York: Cooper Square Press, 2000), p. 140; this information, retrieved from a copy of the original ship's manifest, completely refutes the version of these events related by Roy Aitken in taped interviews made in preparation for an autobiography and transcribed in the third person by Kalton C. Lahue:

> After Charlie Chaplin began to work at the Keystone lot in 1913, he asked Roy to look up his brother Sydney on his next trip to England. Charlie also wrote Sydney to expect Roy.
> So eventually the two got together over lunch in London. Roy could easily see many of Charlie's physical characteristics in Sydney, and in answer to his question, advised Charlie's brother that there might be a place for him in American films.
> Within six months, Charlie phoned Roy in New York and said that Sydney was coming in (sic) America and would arrive on the *Mauritania* within the week. He asked Roy to go down to Ellis Island and meet him, since he was in California working on a picture.
> Roy went to the "gateway to America" and met Sydney, who was very happy to see him. After all, Charlie and Roy were the only people in the United States he knew.
> To get off Ellis Island quickly, he needed an American sponsor, and so Roy performed that duty.

4. Sydney Chaplin, "Some Reminiscences," p. 21.
5. Ibid.
6. Chaplin, *My Autobiography*, p. 158.
7. Sydney Chaplin, Palais Rosa-Bonheur, Nice, France, R. J. Minney, 8 November 1934, WGC.
8. "Keystone Signs Syd Chaplin," *MPN* (31 October 1914), n. p.; interestingly, the same clip appeared much later in the small-town papers, well after Sydney's films began to be released, for instance, in *The Lima* (OH) *Sunday News* (17 January 1915), page 3, and *The San Antonio Light* (7 February 1915), n. p.
9. *MPN* (7 November 1914), n. p.
10. "Fatty's Wine Party," *Reel Life* (21 November 1914), p. 10.
11. Ibid.
12. *MPN* (28 November 1914), n. p.
13. *MPN* (29 December 1914), n. p.
14. Brent Walker, "*Wild West Love,*" *Mack Sennett's Fun Factory* (Jefferson, NC: McFarland, 2009), p. 306; thanks to Steve Massa for alerting me to this reference.
15. Kalton C. Lahue, *Mack Sennett's Keystone: The Man, the Myth, and the Comedies* (South Brunswick, NJ: A. S. Barnes, 1971), p. 157.
16. Lahue, *Mack Sennett's Keystone*, p. 158.
17. Ibid., p. 159.
18. Brent Walker, "Gussle the Golfer," *Mack Sennett's Fun Factory*, p. 307.
19. On page 40 of his book, *How to Become a Comedian* (London: F. Muller, 1945), Lupino Lane terms the fall "the Spin on the Head," and illustrates his description of the fall, that it "is managed by the performer falling straight back up on the head and on reaching the floor, pushing with one shoulder to give the body a twist," with a step-by-step cartoon of the trick being performed; silent comedy expert Richard M. Roberts, in a 10 February 2009 forum post, claimed that "the head spin was an old music hall standard, and most of the Karno star comics, Billie Ritchie, Billie Reeves, even brother Charlie did it, as well as various Lupinos. I think Dan Leno was also famous for it, and it probably goes farther back than that, I'd wager it's also in the *Commedia del Arte* bag of tricks."
20. *MPN* (9 January 1914), n. p.
21. *MPN* (20 February 1915), n. p.

22. "That Springtime Feeling," *MPN* (13 March 1915), n. p.
23. "That Springtime Feeling," *MPW* (20 March 1915), p. 1764.
24. "Doings at Los Angeles," *MPW* (20 March 1915), p. 1750.
25. Walker, "*Gussle's Day of Rest,*" *Mack Sennett's Fun Factory,* p. 314.
26. "Gussle's Day of Rest," *MPN* (10 April 1915), n. p.
27. Lahue, *Mack Sennett's Keystone,* pp. 159–160.
28. "Notes of the Trade," *MPW* (5 June 1915), p. 1633.
29. George Blaisdell, "New York Motion Picture Company," *MPW* (10 July 1915), p. 236.
30. Mack Sennett and Cameron Shipp, *King of Comedy* (Garden City, NY: Doubleday, 1954), p. 154.
31. Brent Walker, E-mail communication, 10 January 2009.
32. "Gussle's Wayward Path," *MPN* (1 May 1915), n. p.
33. "Gussle's Wayward Path," *MPW* (1 May 1915), p. 728.
34. *Frederick (MD) Post* (1 May 1915), p. 6.
35. *MPW* (3 April 1915), p. 49.
36. Grace Kingsley, "At the Stage Door," *Los Angeles Times* (24 March 1915), p. III4.
37. Grace Kingsley, "At the Stage Door," *Los Angeles Times* (8 April 1915): n. p.
38. "Doings at Los Angeles," *MPW* (22 May 1915), p. 1265.
39. Brent Walker, personal communication, 10 January 2009.
40. "Gussle Rivals Jonah," *MPN* (24 April 1915), p. 68.
41. "Gussle Rivals Jonah," *MPW* (1 May 1915), p. 728.
42. "Gussle's Backward Way," *MPN* (22 May 1915), n. p.
43. "Gussle Tied to Trouble," *MPN* (22 May 1915), n. p.; *Lancaster (OH) Daily Eagle* (11 June 1915), n. p.
44. "Gussle Tied to Trouble," *MPW* (5 June 1915), p. 1605.
45. Kalton C. Lahue and Terry Brewer, *Kops and Custards: The Legend of Keystone Films* (Norman, OK: University of Oklahoma Press, 1968), p. 78.
46. *MPW* (24 April 1915), p. 542.
47. *MPW* (8 May 1915), p. 886.
48. *MPW* (8 May 1915), p. 885.
49. *MPW* (5 June 1915), p. 1608.
50. "Doings at Los Angeles," *MPW* (3 July 1915), p. 50.
51. *MPW* (19 June 1915), p. 1926.
52. *Cedar Rapids (IA) Republican* (11 July 1915), p. 19.
53. *MPW* (19 July 1915), p. 1959.
54. "Jinx Still Follows Chaplin," *The Ogden (UT) Standard* (August 28, 1915), 8; also, *MPW* (28 August 1915), p. 1465.
55. "Keystone's Once a Week," *MPW* (19 June 1915), p. 19.
56. "N. Y. M. P. and Keystone Stars," *MPW* (10 July 1915), p. 316.
57. Charles Baumann, New York, Mack Sennett, Los Angeles Athletic Club, 4 June 1915, AMPAS.
58. A *New York Times* article entitled, "Personality in Vaudeville" (19 June 1912), n. p., describes his stage persona as "one who reveals himself on the stage of the Union Square blocks out his own lineaments with grease-paint, wears a couple of painted wafers over his eyes, and paints a black circle around his mouth. The general result is an exceedingly-funny make-up — one that looks like a grotesque toy."
59. CHACHAA.
60. "Keystone Company to Build $100,000 Studio," *MPW* (18 September 1915), p. 1981.
61. Gene Fowler, *Father Goose: The Story of Mack Sennett* (New York: Covici Friede, 1934), p. 339.
62. *MPW* (21 August 1915), p. 1390, also printed in *The Kokomo (IN) Daily Tribune* (n. d.), p. 11; this description fails in all respects to match the plot of the film that now exists, especially concerning the behavior of Mr. and Mrs. Lewis. It claims that while "Lewis wanders to another part of the store, Mrs. Lewis discovers that she has no money with which to pay for her purchases. Gussle comes gallantly to the rescue." In fact, it is Mrs. Gussle who finds she has no money for her purchases. Gussle takes up with Mrs. Lewis just for the adventure of it.
63. *Portsmouth (NH) Daily Times* (19 November 1915), p. 10.
64. Kalton C. Lahue, *Dreams for Sale: The Rise and Fall of the Triangle Film Corporation* (South Brunswick, NJ: A. S. Barnes, 1971), p. 40.
65. Simon Louvish, *Keystone: The Life and Clowns of Mack Sennett* (New York: Faber and Faber, 2003), p. 117.
66. "New York Motion Picture Company," *MPW* (10 July 1915), pp. 233–34, 236.
67. "Keystone Company to Build $100,000 Studio," *MPW* (18 September 1915), p. 1981.
68. British slang for a German U-boat.
69. "Written on the Screen," *New York Times* (14 November 1915), p. 191.
70. "A Submarine Pirate," *MPW* (11 December 1915), pp. 2088, 2090.
71. Ibid.
72. *A Submarine Pirate* continuity, AMPAS.
73. *Waterloo* (IA) *Times-Tribune* (5 December 1915), n. p.
74. "Use a Submarine in New Movie Play" *New York Times* (15 November 1915), p. 11.
75. Ibid.; "Written on the Screen," *New York Times* (14 November 1915), n. p.
76. "Change in Triangle Releases," *MPW* (11 December 1915), p. 20.
77. "Triangle Film Shows Working of Submarine" *The Triangle* (13 November 1915), p. 7.
78. Rob King, *The Fun Factory: The Keystone Film Company and the Emergence of Mass Culture* (Berkeley, CA: University of California Press, 2009), pp. 191–92.
79. King, 192.
80. "New York Elite Gives Private Triangle Show," *The Triangle* (4 December 1915), p. 5.
81. All reviews contained in *The Triangle* (4 December 1915), p. 7.
82. Louis Reeves Harrison, "A Submarine Pirate," *MPW* (27 November 1915), p. 1681.
83. "Keystone Repeated by Request, *The Triangle* (18 December 1915), p. 2.
84. *The Triangle* (18 December 1915), p. 8.
85. "Bally-Hoo Display for Syd Chaplin Comedy, 'A Submarine Pirate,'" *The Triangle* (18 December 1915), p. 5.
86. Lahue and Brewer, *Kops and Custards,* p. 162.
87. "Syd Chaplin Quits Keystone," *Waterloo* (IA) *Times Tribune* (n. d.), n. p.
88. "'A Submarine Pirate' Captures U.S. Navy," *The Triangle* (5 February 1916), p. 3.
89. Chaplin, *My Autobiography,* p. 160.
90. "Syd Chaplin Quits Keystone," *Waterloo* (IA) *Times Tribune* (n. d.), n. p.
91. Sydney Chaplin, Palais Rosa-Bonheur, Nice, France, R. J. Minney, 9 August 1934, WGC; this contention was also mentioned in "He Did and He Didn't," *Variety* (4 February 1916), n. p., which stated, "Incidentally there has been some discussion regarding this picture in film circles. According to certain folk who have the acquaintance of Sid Chaplin, that comedian is said to have had the idea for this comedy originally and to have outlined it to a party of picture players at a dinner at which Roscoe Arbuckle was one of the guests. Later, at another party, Arbuckle offered to let Chaplin in on a joke, and then told the English comedian that he had appro-

priated the idea and used it for a picture. But Mr. Chaplin need not worry for 'He Did and He Didn't' will not add materially to the glory of Arbuckle as a film comic. He did get the idea, but he didn't get it over in this two-reeler. Perhaps with Chaplin it would have gotten a greater number of laughs, but this production is so full of old tricks of the game that it will never create any great furor."

Chapter 4

1. David Robinson, 150–52.
2. It should be noted that the original company, Charlie Chaplin Advertising Service Company, set as its goal the advertising of products, rather than the licensing of the image—a goal which proved to be too ambitious. David Robinson notes in his Chaplin biography (pg. 153) that James Pershing, the manager of the service the brothers hired, found the task impossible, because "there seems to be hundreds of people making different things under the name of Charlie Chaplin," p. 153.
3. In the real estate business initially, John Freuler came to be a partner in a nickelodeon, the Comique, in Milwaukee, Wisconsin, for a small investment of $450, and the business prospered. Soon he became interested in the distribution end, forming the Western Film Exchange, and still later, he became the president of Mutual Film Corporation, "Where John Freuler Got His Start in Pictures," *MPW* (15 July 1916), p. 378.
4. Mutual Pressbook #5.1, Louella Parsons interview of John Freuler, *Chicago Herald* (4 March 1916), n. p., CHACHAA.
5. Mutual Pressbook #5.1, unidentified news clipping, CHACHAA.
6. A photograph of the three men was published in the *Boston Sun Post* (May 7, 1916) n. p., showing Charlie standing with his arm through Sydney's, a brotherly image that seems to suggest Sydney's importance in the negotiations.
7. Mutual Pressbook #5.1, *Chicago Daily News* (12 March 1916), n. p., CHACHAA.
8. "Syd Chaplin Given $75,000 by Charlie," *New York Review* (18 March 1916), n. p.; "Syd and Charles Still Best of Pals," *Racine* (WI) *Journal-News* (24 July 1916), p. 6.
9. David Robinson, p. 164.
10. Cable Tom Harrington, Los Angeles, Sydney Chaplin, New York City, 2 August 1916, CHACHAA.
11. "No Chaplin Split," *New York Telegraph* (7 July 1916), n. p.
12. Cable Sydney Chaplin, New York, Charlie Chaplin, Los Angeles, 8 August 1916, CHACHAA.
13. David Robinson, p. 185.
14. David Robinson, p. 187; "Auditorium Notes," *Newark* (OH) *Daily Advocate* (5 February 1918), p. 6.
15. Mutual Pressbook #5.2, *Allentown* (PA) *Democrat* (9 June 1917), n. p., CHACHAA.
16. Mutual Pressbook #5.1, *Los Angeles Record* (22 December 1917), n. p. CHACHAA.
17. The pajama at this time was a lounging article of clothing, not simply an item for the boudoir; American travelers to the French Riviera, beginning in the 1920s caused the pajama to catch fire, offering, as it did, both style and comfort—and allowing women a new access to the freedom of slacks.
18. R. H. Goodell, "Builders of Business: June Rand," *System* (July 1920), pp. 46–48.
19. Victor H. Levy v. Commissioner of Internal Revenue, 16 U. S. Board of Tax Appeals Reports, p. 653, quoted in David S. Ort's unpublished biographical essay on Sydney Chaplin, 5 November 1990, CHACHAA.
20. "Comedian Not Good in Ready-to-Wear," *Waterloo* (IA) *Daily Courier* (24 May 1930), p. 8.
21. Mutual Pressbook #5.1, *Akron* (OH) *Journal* (15 May 1917), n. p., CHACHAA.
22. Mutual Pressbook #5.1, newspaper clipping, no title or source, 12 June 1917, CHACHAA.
23. "Sydney Chaplin Interview," *Exhibitors' Trade Review* (28 April 1917), n. p.
24. Sydney Chaplin, Los Angeles, John Freuler, New York City, n. d., CHACHAA.
25. John Freuler, Sydney Chaplin, Los Angeles, n. d., CHACHAA.
26. First National, coincidentally, was only formed (in April 1917) by Williams and Tally as a way of competing with Adolph Zukor's Paramount-Artcraft; it's interesting that Sydney decided to go with Zukor when the time came for his own film contract, just over a year later.
27. "Seen on the Screen," *The Syracuse Herald* (5 August 1917), p. 8.
28. Sydney Chaplin, Claridge Hotel, New York City, Charlie Chaplin, Los Angeles, 3 July 1917, CHACHAA.
29. David Robinson, p. 199.
30. Sydney received a letter from Alf dated September 14, stating that everything was arranged for his departure the first week of October, CHACHAA.
31. Sydney Chaplin, Claridge Hotel, New York City, Charlie Chaplin, Los Angeles, 3 July 1917, CHACHAA.
32. Jack Jasper, Los Angeles, Sydney Chaplin, New York City, 30 July 1917, CHACHAA.
33. Ibid.
34. Tom Harrington, Los Angeles, Sydney Chaplin, New York City, 20 July 1917, CHACHAA.
35. Wheeler Dryden, Bombay, India, Edna Purviance, Los Angeles, CA, 8 September 1917, CHACHAA.
36. "Two Directors for Wheeler Dryden," *MPN* (26 April 1919), p. 2682; Wheeler's directors are listed as Charles Ranson and Charles Morgan Seay; his leading lady was Grace Harte; no other information could be located on either the film or Wheeler's contract.
37. Mutual Pressbook #5.2, *Motography* (13 October 1917), n. p., CHACHAA.
38. Mutual Pressbook #5.2, no source, no title (29 October 1917), n. p., CHACHAA.
39. Mutual Pressbook #5.2, *MPW* (3 November 1917), n. p., CHACHAA.
40. Sydney Chaplin, Los Angeles, Aubrey Chaplin, London, 12 June 1918, CHACHAA.
41. Daisy Dean, "News Notes from Movieland," *Janesville* (WI) *Daily Gazette*, 15 December 1917, p. 6.
42. Sydney Chaplin, Los Angeles, Aubrey Chaplin, London, 12 June 1918, CHACHAA.
43. Sydney Chaplin, Los Angeles, Aubrey Chaplin, London, 20 July 1917, CHACHAA.
44. Sydney Chaplin, Los Angeles, Aubrey Chaplin, London, 12 June 1918, CHACHAA.
45. Aubrey Chaplin, London, Sydney Chaplin, Los Angeles, 18 August & 26 August 1919, CHACHAA.
46. David Robinson, p. 229.
47. Ibid., pp. 230–31.
48. A. P. Michael Narlian, Sydney Chaplin, 5 February 1918, CHACHAA.
49. Sydney Chaplin, A. P. Michael Narlian, 12 February 1918, CHACHAA.
50. Grace Kingsley, "Flashes: Chaplin Incorporates," *Los Angeles Times* (26 February 1918), p. II3.
51. Sydney Chaplin, Los Angeles, Aubrey Chaplin, London, 12 June 1918, CHACHAA.
52. Ibid.
53. David Robinson, p. 244.
54. "'Sunnyside' Ready," *MPW* (19 April 1919), p. 360.

Notes — Chapter 4

55. Sydney Chaplin, A. H. & H. G. Stocker, Peckham House, London, 30 November 1918, CHACHAA.
56. Telegram, Charlie Chaplin, Sydney Chaplin, 21 April 1919, CHACHAA.
57. A. H. Giebler, "Rubbernecking in Filmland," *MPW* (1 February 1919), pp. 607–08; also quoted in Tino Balio, *United Artists: The Company Built by the Stars* (Madison: University of Wisconsin Press, 1976), pp. 12–13.
58. "United Artists Association Formed," *MPW* (25 January 1919), p. 455.
59. Grace Kingsley, "Flashes: Syd Enters Denial," *Los Angeles Times* (23 January 1919), p. II3.
60. Carlyle R. Robinson, "A Speed Star" (1919), suggests that this interest of Sydney's dated from 1907, CHACHAA.
61. A scrapbook of these clippings still exists in the Chaplin archives.
62. Sydney Chaplin, Palais Rosa Bonheur, Nice, France, R. J. Minney, London, 6 December 1932, WGC.
63. The agreement was to last ten years.
64. "To Buy Airplanes," *Los Angeles Times* (16 April 1919), p. II1.
65. "School Contract," Al Wilson Aviation Co., 6 March 1919, CHACHAA.
66. William M. Henry, "Southern California Soon to See Commercial Aircraft," *Los Angeles Times* (20 April 1919), p. V13.
67. "Syd Chaplin Is Flying High," *MPW* (3 May 1919), p. 651, and "To Establish Airline," *The MPW* (3 May 1919), p. 661, respectively.
68. Rogers had most recently been the officer in charge of flying at Souther Field in Americus, Georgia, "The Syd Chaplin Airline," *The Ace* (October 1919), p. 63.
69. Emery H. Rogers, Jr. was born on March 21, 1921, just four months before his father lost his life (on November 27) at what was then Rogers Airport on Wilshire Boulevard in an air race; E-mail communication, 22 September 2007.
70. Syd Chaplin Aircraft Corp. Corporate Records, CHACHAA.
71. Some of these fliers included Lieut. A. C. Burns, former flight commander at Rockaway Beach, L. I., Lieut. H. F. Salisbury, head of the engineering department at Southfield, Georgia, W. S. Eaton, general manager of the St. Louis Aircraft Corporation during the war, and others, "The Syd Chaplin Airline," *The Ace* (October 1919), p. 63.
72. "Whole Flock of Airplanes His," *Los Angeles Times* (11 June 1919), p. II10.
73. "Fly to Catalina Thursday," *Los Angeles Times* (28 June 1919), p. II3.
74. "Passenger Service by Plane Deferred," *Los Angeles Times* (5 July 1919), p. II2.
75. "Sky-Bus to Fly Today," *Los Angeles Times* (12 July 1919), p. II8.
76. "Chaplin Secures 400 Planes," *Manitoba* (Winnipeg) *Free Press* (12 July 1919), p. 23.
77. "Patrons Hear of War Tax on Flying," *Los Angeles Times* (13 July 1919), p. II6.
78. "Insurance Tickets for Flying Arrive," *Los Angeles Times* (26 October 1919), p. VI8.
79. "Not Guilty Is Verdict in Aviator's Case," *Riverside Enterprise* (20 June 1920), n. p., Syd Chaplin Aircraft Corp. Pressbook, CHACHAA.
80. "Ten Thousand Visit Aircraft Showroom," *Los Angeles Examiner* (13 December 1919), n. p., Syd Chaplin Aircraft Corp. Pressbook, CHACHAA.
81. Syd Chaplin Aircraft Corporation ad, CHACHAA.
82. Ibid.
83. "Los Angeles Should Establish Municipal Aero Landing Field," *Los Angeles Express* (27 January 1920), n. p.
84. "Crozier and Parr Found Not Guilty," *Riverside (CA) Press* (20 June 1920), n. p. Syd Chaplin Aircraft Corp. Pressbook, CHACHAA.
85. Chaplin-Curtiss Flying School ad, *Los Angeles Times* (14 September 1919), p. II10.
86. "Flying Course at Auto School," *Bulletin of the Young Men's Christian Association* Vol. IX (19 June 1920), n. p., Syd Chaplin Aircraft Corp. Pressbook, CHACHAA.
87. "Mary Roberts Rinehart Takes First Air Trip," *Manitoba* (Winnipeg) *Free Press* (8 November 1919), p. 39.
88. Mary Roberts Rinehart T. S., CHACHAA.
89. Alma Sierks, "Admiral Rodman to Clouds in Sea-Plane," *The Catalina Islander* (28 October 1919), p. 1.
90. "Chaplin to Give Rick Club Prize," *Los Angeles Examiner* (17 January 1920), n. p., Syd Chaplin Aircraft Corp. Pressbook, CHACHAA.
91. "Fliers to Aid Hospital Fund," *Los Angeles Examiner* (6 June 1920), n. p.; "A Big Show Put over in a Big Way," *Artcraft and Aircraft* (July 1920), n. p., Syd Chaplin Aircraft Corp. Pressbook, CHACHAA.
92. Chaplin Aircraft Corporation ad, *Los Angeles Times* (9 August 1919), p. II6.
93. "Fly" brochure, Syd Chaplin Aircraft Corporation, LKSC.
94. *Catalina Airline Record* (no title, date or page), Syd Chaplin Airline Corp. Pressbook, CHACHAA.
95. "Movies up in the Air over Aviation," *Moberly* (MO) *Democrat* (10 November 1919), n. p.
96. Syd Chaplin Aircraft Corporation Records, 4 December 1919, CHACHAA.
97. Syd Chaplin Aircraft Corp. Records, 5 January 1919, CHACHAA.
98. Syd Chaplin Aircraft Corp. Records, 12 February 1919, CHACHAA.
99. Emery Rogers Resignation Letter, 26 March 1920, CHACHAA; Rogers's resignation notice in the press indicated no animosity between parties and did not mention any financial problems the company was currently experiencing; "Emery H. Rogers Resigns," *Los Angeles Saturday Night* (13 May 1920), n. p., Syd Chaplin Aircraft Corporation Pressbook, CHACHAA.
100. "The Field of Aeronautics," *Los Angeles Saturday Night* (20 May 1920), n. p., Syd Chaplin Aircraft Corporation Pressbook, CHACHAA.
101. "Chaplin Promises Some Surprises in Aviation," *Los Angeles Express* (27 May 1920), n. p., Syd Chaplin Aircraft Corporation Pressbook, CHACHAA.
102. "Representatives of the Aircraft Industry Invited and Attending the Third Pan-American Aeronautic Congress and Exposition," *Flying* (May 1920), p. 248.
103. "Sid Chaplin Has Relapse Caused by Mystery Visitor," *Los Angeles Examiner* (13 October 1920), n. p.
104. Waldo Waterman described the event: "Emory had been ill; rumor had it that he had a brain tumor which was causing blackouts. As was customary, a little excitement was built-up on Sunday afternoons at Rogers Field to attract onlookers who would then be solicited for rides. On the day of his death, one of Rogers' pilots took the plane up and put on a lukewarm show. As I understand it, Emory then jumped into the plane and proceeded to put on a good show finalized by a 'pylon' turn at the intersection of Fairfax and Wilshire. The turn ended in Emory's fatal crash. His plane was a complete washout, hitting the pavement of Fairfax Avenue, about 100-yards north of Wilshire, not far from where Ormer Locklear crashed. No one else was involved"; Waldo Dean Waterman and Jack Carpenter, *Waldo, Pioneer Aviator: A Personal History of American Aviation, 1910–44* (Carlisle, MA: Arsdalen, Bosch, 1988), p. 239.

105. Jesse L. Lasky, *I Blow My Own Horn* (Garden City, NY: Doubleday, 1957), pp. 152–27.
106. It was advertised or reported as his "million-dollar" deal, because the press reported the contract to require four films; "Chaplin to Find Rival in Brother," *St. Paul Pioneer Press* (29 June 1919), n. p.; the existing copy of the contract in the Chaplin archive, however, requires only two films.
107. "Famous Players–Lasky Chiefs Give Outlines of Next Season's Plans," *MPW* (28 June 1919), p. 1919.
108. Famous Players Lasky/Sydney Chaplin Contract, 14 May 1919, CHACHAA.
109. "Sydney Chaplin Signs with Famous Players," *MPN* (7 June 1919), p. 3810.
110. Paramount–Artcraft Pictures ad, "Syd Chaplin," *MPW* (31 May 1919), n. p.
111. Sydney and party left Los Angeles on July 10. "Syd Chaplin to Sail," *MPW* (26 July 1919), p. 505.
112. "Sydney Chaplin Going Abroad to Produce First of Four Pictures for Famous Players," *MPW* (26 July 1919), p. 517.
113. "Good Luck to Sydney Chaplin," *MPW* (2 August 1919), p. 658.
114. "Famous Players Dines S. Chaplin," *MPN* (6 August 1919), p. 1078.
115. Sydney's preoccupation with getting his mother to the States would play a part in this scenario in the coming year.
116. An excerpt from these "Greek" remarks appeared verbatim in *MPW* (9 August 1919), p. 750; it was "loosely" translated as "I'm going away to that fair land — /The land where the *toot sweet* grows;/where the comic spirit has not been canned/And the fair flower *finnee* blows./Ah, well-a-day, it's *au revoir*;/The ocean's very wet;/but I'm coming back *esprit de corps*/With film you'll want to get."
117. Famous Players Lasky Corporation ad, *MPN* (16 August 1919), p. 1336.
118. Famous Players–Lasky Corporation ad, *MPN* (23 August 1919), p. 1051.
119. "Sydney Chaplin Going Abroad to Produce First of Four Pictures for Famous Players," *MPW* (26 July 1919), p. 517.
120. "Éclair," http://ftvdb.bfi.org.uk/sift/organisation/7184; Éclair acquired an American studio in Fort Lee, New Jersey, having become a major film organization in France just the year before; no evidence exists that Éclair had undergone a renovation or updating prior to Sydney's residence there.
121. James Henry Bernard, Stoll Film Co., Ltd., London, Sydney Chaplin, 5 August 1919, CHACHAA.
122. Jack Green, E-mail communication, 2 August 2009.
123. Ricky Green, E-mail communication, 3 November 2009.
124. "Syd Says," *Photoplay* (July 1920), p. 63.
125. "Chaplin Finds Europe Is Unsettled," *MPN* (27 September 1919), p. 2615; "Syd Chaplin Returns from France," *MPW* (27 September 1919), p. 197.
126. Grace Kingsley, "Flashes: Syd Is Coming Back," *Los Angeles Times* (12 September 1919), p. III4.
127. "Sid Chaplin Finds Studio Home," *MPN* (1 November 1919), p. 3327.
128. "Sydney Chaplin in 'King, Queen, Joker' Rialto Next Saturday," *Hamilton* (OH) *Evening Journal* (10 August 1921), p. 5.
129. "Sydney Chaplin in 'King, Queen, Joker' Rialto Next Saturday," *Hamilton* (OH) *Evening Journal* (10 August 1921), p. 5.
130. "Has Game of Golf before Breakfast," *Anniston* (AL) *Star* (3 June 1921), n. p.
131. "Syd Chaplin Flies to Location," *MPW* (15 November 1919), p. 337.
132. #11 Pressbook clipping, CHACHAA.
133. "Sydney Chaplin in 'Queen, King, Joker' (*sic*) at Rialto Tomorrow," *Hamilton* (OH) *Evening Journal* (12 August 1921), p. 13.
134. "At the Rex," *Sheboygan Press & Sheboygan Telegram* (29 August 1921), p. 9.
135. "Handcuffed! Key Lost!" *The Mexia* (TX) *Evening News* (30 May 1921), p. 4.
136. "First Syd Chaplin Paramount Artcraft Comic Written by Star," *MPN* (6 December 1919), p. 4126; "Sydney Chaplin Names First Comedy," *MPW* (13 December 1919), p. 823.
137. "Studio Shots," *MPW* (17 January 1920), p. 398.
138. "Heustis Finds Brother Syd Chaplin Mixes 'Artistics' with His Business," *Los Angeles Evening Herald* (19 January 1920), n. p., CHACHAA.
139. "Studio Shots," *MPW* (21 February 1920), p. 1250.
140. Telegram, Tom Harrington, Los Angeles, Sydney Chaplin, New York City, 15 April 1920, CHACHAA.
141. "Charles Chaplin Takes Latest Film to Utah to Evade Wife's Process Servers," *MPW* (28 August 1920), p. 1143.
142. Grace Kingsley, "Flashes: Chaplin Rents Plant," *Los Angeles Times* (8 October 1920), p. III4.
143. "Syd Chaplin is Sued," *Los Angeles Times* (15 October 1920), p. II12.
144. "Film Flickers," *The Lima* (OH) *News & Times Democrat* (16 November 1920), n. p.; Daisy Dean, "News Notes from Movieland," *The Olean* (NY) *Evening Herald* (15 November 1920), p. 4.
145. "Syd Chaplin to Leave Hospital Today," *Los Angeles Times* (13 November 1920), p. II5.
146. Daisy Dean, "News Notes from Movieland," *Eau Claire* (WI) *Leader* (4 December 1919), p. 4.
147. Edward Weitzel, "'King, Queen, Joker'" *MPW* (25 June 1921), n. p.
148. "'King-Queen-Joker': Press Notice-Story" *MPN* (11 June 1921), p. 3609.
149. "'King, Queen, Joker' Synopsis," Paramount Scripts Collection, AMPAS.
150. "Syd Chaplin Diverts in Big Vaudeville-Majestic," *La Crosse Tribune and Leader-Press* (7 May 1922), p. 17.
151. "Synopses: Chaplin Outtakes, *King, Queen, Joker* (Production Material) Syd Chaplin Co. HARTMAN 264-3 104–106 MS, side view. British Film Institute Film & TV Database, found at <http://ftvdb.bfi.org.uk/sift/title/753326?view=synopsis>.
152. [Charlie the Barber scenario] T. S., CHACHAA.
153. This point is also one made by Frank Scheide in his work.
154. Lasky Returns Enthusiastic over New Paramount-Artcraft Specials," *MPW* (24 January 1920), p. 584.
155. "Paramount Lists Its Features," *MPN* (29 January 1921), p. 1050.
156. Paramount-Artcraft ad, "Sydney Chapin in 'King, Queen, Joker,'" *MPN* (5 March & 16 April 1921), n. p.
157. "Advance Information on All Film Releases," *MPN* (7 May 1921), p. 2958.
158. "Many Paramounts in May," *MPN* (14 May 1921), p. 3064.
159. "Deception Issued May 15," *MPN* (21 May 1921), p. 3194; Paramount-Artcraft ad, "Deception," *MPN* (28 May 1921), n. p.
160. Laurence Reid, "'King-Queen-Joker'" *MPN* (11 June 1921), p. 3609.
161. Ibid.
162. "What the Big Houses Say," *MPN* (11 June 1921), p. 3545.
163. Ibid., p. 53.

164. Edward Weitzel, "'King, Queen, Joker'" *MPW* (25 June 1921), n. p.

Chapter 5

1. David Robinson, pp. 270–71.
2. Joan Jordan, "Mother O' Mine," *Photoplay* (July 1921), p. 45.
3. Charles R. Hughes, "Mother of Charlie Chaplin Comes to America—'Behold My Sweetheart,' Says Chas.," *The* (Lorain, OH) *Chronicle Telegram* (10 May 1921), n. p.
4. "Mr. Charles Chaplin's Mother," *London Times* (24 May 1922), n. p.
5. "Plan to Deport Mother Chaplin," *Los Angeles Times* (11 March 1925), p. A6.
6. "Sid Chaplin May Appeal to Coolidge," *Los Angeles Times* (12 March 1925), p. A8.
7. Alf Reeves, Los Angeles, Sydney Chaplin, 13 September 1920, CHACHAA.
8. David Robinson, p. 295.
9. "Back Alley Quartette Revived in 'Pay Day,' *Pay Day Press Book,* First National Pictures, Inc., 1922, LCLPA.
10. More on the negotiations can be found in Robinson's *Chaplin: His Life and Art.*
11. "Chaplin Sends His Brother to S. L.," *The Ogden* (UT) *Standard Examiner* (26 April 1922), p. 3.
12. "Lawyer Witness in Chaplin Suit," *The Ogden* (UT) *Standard Examiner* (29 April 1922), p. 4.
13. "Charlie Chaplin Loses Law Suit," *Des Moines* (IA) *Capital* (4 May 1922), p. 1.
14. "Food for Stars," *Edwardsville* (IL) *Intelligencer* (18 October 1922), n. p.
15. Cable, Sydney Chaplin, Nathan Burkan, 23 January 1923, CHACHAA.
16. Cable, Nathan Burkan, Sydney Chaplin, 29 January 1923, CHACHAA.
17. Tino Balio, *United Artists: The Company Built by Stars* (Madison: University of Wisconsin Press, 1976), pp. 58–60.
18. Sidney Garrett, London, Sydney Chaplin, Los Angeles, 23 August 1921, CHACHAA.
19. Sidney Garrett, New York, Sydney Chaplin, Los Angeles, 3 February 1921, CHACHAA.
20. Quoted in Sidney Garrett, New York, Sydney Chaplin, Los Angeles, 3 October 1922, CHACHAA.
21. Sidney Garrett, New York, Sydney Chaplin, Los Angeles, 13 October 1922, CHACHAA.
22. "Picture Plays and People," *New York Times* (25 January 1920), p. 78.
23. Quoted in Sidney Garrett, New York, Sydney Chaplin, Los Angeles, 24 October 1922, CHACHAA.
24. Sidney Garrett, New York, Sydney Chaplin, Los Angeles, 24 October 1922, CHACHAA.
25. "Sydney Chaplin Signs for Part in Slav Picture," *Los Angeles Times* (27 April 1923), p. I11.
26. "Unusual Cast in 'The Rendezvous,'" *The Daily Northwestern* (Oshkosh, WI) (16 August 1924), p. 6.
27. "Ah! The Villain Gets His Due, at Last!" *The Kokomo* (IN) *Daily Tribune* (27 December 1923), p. 12.
28. "'The Rendezvous,' A Marshall Neilan Production at Palace Starting Tomorrow," *Hamilton* (OH) *Daily News* (16 September 1924), n. p.
29. Harry Oliver was known for designing the Willat Studio in Culver City.
30. "Built Complete Russian Village for Film Play," "The Rendezvous,' A Marshall Neilan Production," Pressbook, LKSC.
31. "Russian Circus in Film," "The Rendezvous," A Marshall Neilan Production, Press Book, LKSC.
32. "Marshall Neilan and Company," *Oakland Tribune* (3 June 1923), n. p.
33. *The Rendezvous* by Madeleine Ruthven, "Title Synopsis," MGM Collection, USCCAL.
34. Madeleine Ruthven, "The Rendezvous," vault copy, MGM Collection, USCCAL.
35. *The Rendezvous*, "Silent Cutting Continuity," December 5, 1923, MGM Collection, USCCAL.
36. George Landy, "The Greatest Tribute," "*Camera!*" *The Digest of the Motion Picture Industry* (12 January 1924), p. 17.
37. In fact, Laurence Reid makes this comparison in his review of the film: "A heavy melodrama painted in drab colors except for a flash of comedy relief furnished by Sydney Chaplin, who as a British Tommy, suggests 'Ol Bill of 'The Better 'Ole,'" "The Celluloid Critic," *Classic* (March 1924) pp. 94–5.
38. "'Rendezvous' Proves Baby Star Triumph," *Los Angeles Times* (24 December 1923), p. I17.
39. "Was Charlie Correct about Brother Syd?" *Hamilton Daily News* (23 February 1924), p. 11.
40. Daisy Dean, "News Notes from Movieland," *Ada* (OK) *Evening News* (3 March 1924), p. 6.
41. "'Rendezvous' Proves Baby Star Triumph," *Los Angeles Times* (24 December 1923), p. I17.
42. "Was Charlie Correct about Brother Syd?" *Hamilton Daily News* (23 February 1924), p. 11.
43. "It Has Syd Chaplin," *Syracuse* (NY) *Evening Telegraph* (15 May 1923), p. 10, and "The News Review of the Stage and Screen," *The Mansfield* (OH) *News* (13 May 1923), p. 8.
44. "Comedy and Crook Drama at Century," *Oakland* (CA) *Tribune* (3 May 1925), p. W-3.
45. "News of the First National Pictures: Unwelcome Husbands Never Die," *The Saturday Evening Post* (1 December 1923), p. 49.
46. George Landy, "The Greatest Tribute," "*Camera!*" *The Digest of the Motion Picture Industry* (12 January 1924), p. 17.
47. "Whole City Takes Part in Farce," *Los Angeles Times* (28 February 1924), p. A11.
48. "You're Wonderful, Sydney Chaplin," First National ad, *The Film Daily* (4 December 1923), n. p.
49. Sydney Chaplin, Arthur Kelly, [December 1923], CHACHAA.
50. Sidney Garrett, New York, Sydney Chaplin, Los Angeles, 5 October 1923, CHACHAA.
51. Quoted in Sidney Garrett, New York, Sydney Chaplin, Los Angeles, 1 October 1923, CHACHAA.
52. Patrick Robertson, *Film Facts* (New York: Billboard Books, 2001), p. 19.
53. "Galloping Fish" Synopsis, AMPAS.
54. Ibid.
55. Ibid.
56. During the film's publicity, Ince emphasized the fact that he had so many well-honed comedians in the film; "'Galloping Fish' Is Filled with Hilarious Fun," *The Billings* (MT) *Gazette* (18 May 1924), p. 4.
57. Sydney Chaplin, Arthur Kelly [December 1923], CHACHA.
58. "Poor Fish Fell Hard for Louise," *Los Angeles Times* (8 June 1924), p. B19.
59. "Understudying Venus," *Los Angeles Times* (15 June 1924), p. 19.
60. "At the Movies," *Hamilton Daily News* (29 December 1923), p. 11.
61. "'The Galloping Fish,'" *The Hamilton Daily News* (2 August 1924), p. 9.
62. Lew Cody (1884–1934) often played roles of suave lady-killers in the silents.
63. "Chatter of the Make-believers," *Oakland* (CA) *Tribune* (25 April 1924), n. p.

64. "Romance in the Dance," *The Sunday State Journal* (22 June 1924), p. B8.
65. Ibid.
66. "New Film Star and Chaperone," *Los Angeles Times* (1 February 1924), p. A3.
67. "Where Are Imitations?" *Los Angeles Times* (20 April 1924), p. B11.
68. Quoted in "Comedy Special Conquers Gotham," *The Silver Sheet* (February–June 1924), p. 14.
69. Thomas C. Kennedy, "'The Galloping Fish,'" *MPN* (3 May 1924), p. 2015.
70. Quoted in "Box-Office Reports," *The Reel Journal* (13 September 1924), p. 18.
71. Sydney Chaplin, Arthur Kelly, [December 1923], CHACHAA.
72. Arthur Kelly, New York, Sydney Chaplin, Los Angeles, 30 November 1923, CHACHAA.
73. Sydney Chaplin, Los Angeles, Arthur Kelly, New York, [December 1923], CHACHAA.
74. Arthur Kelly, New York, Sydney Chaplin, Los Angeles, 6 December 1923, CHACHAA.
75. George Landy, "The Greatest Tribute," "*Camera!*" *The Digest of the Motion Picture Industry* (12 January 1924), p. 18.
76. Grace Kingsley, "Flashes: Which Shall It Be?" *Los Angeles Times* (8 February 1924), p. A11.
77. Jack Jungmeyer, "Syd Chaplin Hangs to Desert Movies," *The Lowell* (MA) *Sun* (27 June 1924), p. 8.
78. "'Hello, 'Frisco!'" *Universal Weekly* (6 September 1924), p. 40.
79. Stetson hat advertisement, New York Hat Stores, *Los Angeles Times* (20 March 1924), p. 5.
80. Crown Army Shirts ad, *Oakland Tribune* (2 December 1924), p. 1.
81. "Film Folk Buy Encinitas Sites for Residences," *Los Angeles Times* (31 August 1924), p. D5.
82. "Gags Come to Him as He Works Ranch," *Los Angeles Times* (10 May 1924), p. 13.
83. Grace Kingsley, "Now It's Sid Chaplin," *Los Angeles Times* (21 March 1924), p. A11; "News Nuggets," *The Reel Journal* (12 April 1924), p. 9.
84. Alma Whitaker, "Aesthetic or Ascetic—Which?" *Los Angeles Times* (30 March 1924), p. B21.
85. "Chaplin Surgeon in Denial," *Los Angeles Times* (4 April 1924), p. A8.
86. "Beauty Quest Ruins Nose," *Los Angeles Times* (7 March 1924), p. A1.
87. "Sydney Chaplin Is Loser to Brokers," *Los Angeles Times* (6 April 1924), p. C13; Nathan Burkan, New York, Sydney Chaplin, Los Angeles [April 1924], CHACHAA.
88. "Syd Plays Hunch and Wins a Pot," *Los Angeles Times* (4 May 1924), p. B12.
89. "Colleen Depicts Flapper Again," *The Kokomo Daily Tribune* (29 May 1924), p. 12.
90. John Springer and Jack Hamilton, *They Had Faces Then: Superstars, Stars and Starlets of the 1930s* (Secaucus, NJ: Citadel Press, 1974), p. 317.
91. William M. Drew, *Speaking of Silents: The First Ladies of the Screen* (Vestal, NY: The Vestal Press, 1989), pp. 172–73.
92. "The Perfect Flapper," *Hamilton* (OH) *Daily News* (10 January 1925), p. 13.
93. "'Perfect Flapper' Pleases Many," *Charleroi* (PA) *Mail* (n. d.), p. 5.
94. "Separate Movies for Children is Urged by Chaplin," *The Olean Evening News* (23 August 1924), p. 4.
95. "2000 Persons in Crowd to Meet Movie Comedian," *Olean Evening News* (25 November 1924), p. 1.
96. Lita Grey Chaplin and Jeffrey Vance, *The Wife of the Life of the Party* (Lanham, MD: Scarecrow Press, 1998), p. 91; Lita also explains that this incident was the reason she changed her son Sydney's name to Tommie for a time following their divorce.
97. "Chaplin Brother to Compete," *Hamilton* (OH) *Daily News* (26 April 1924), p. 16.
98. "Amusement Notes: B. F. Keith's Theatre," *The Lowell* (MA) *Sun* (1 June 1925), p. 11; similar articles erroneously report that Sydney played the part of Babs on the London stage.
99. "Syd Chaplin Stars in Real Film Comedy," *The Charleston* (SC) *Daily Mail* (15 March 1925), p. 3.
100. Grace Kingsley, "Flashes: Star in Big Role," *Los Angeles Times* (5 June 1924), p. A9.

Chapter 6

1. "Al. E. Christie," *MPW* (20 February 1915), p. 1148.
2. "Christie Studios Announce Strong Line-up of Comedies for Fall Production," *MPN* (27 September 1924), p. 1627.
3. "'Charley's Aunt' is Capitol Film," *Manitoba Free Press* (14 March 1925), p. 1.
4. The Brandon Thomas Estate had already earned $3 million over the course of its 33-year stage run; Cal York, "Studio News & Gossip East and West," *Photoplay* (April 1925), n. p.
5. Grace Kingsley, "Flashes: Chaplin Grooms for *Aunt*," *Los Angeles Times* (3 October 1924), p. A9.
6. Grace Kingsley, "Flashes: Cast for 'Charley's Aunt,'" *Los Angeles Times* (23 October 1924), p. A9; "English Actor Here to Play in 'Charley's Aunt,'" *MPN* (25 October 1924), p. 2084.
7. "Christie Names Cast for 'Charley's Aunt,'" *MPN* (1 November 1924), p. 2201.
8. Grace Kingsley, "Flashes: To Distribute 'Charley's Aunt,'" *Los Angeles Times* (26 November 1924), p. A9.
9. "Old-Time Farce a Scream on Screen," *Helena* (MT) *Daily Independent* (21 August 1925), p. 2.
10. "Christie Completes Film of 'Charlie's Aunt,'" *MPN* (10 January 1925), p. 145.
11. Laurence Reid, "'Charley's Aunt,'" *MPN* (21 February 1925), n. p.
12. Ibid.
13. Ben Shlyen, "'Charley's Aunt,'" *The Reel Journal* (7 February 1925), p. 6.
14. W. W., "Real Comedy," *Los Angeles Times* (14 January 1925), p. C9.
15. "'Charley's Aunt' Off to Record in N. Y.," *The Reel Journal* (28 February 1925), p. 10.
16. "Exhibitors Box Office Reports: 'Charley's Aunt,'" *MPN* (21 March 1925), p. 1230-h.
17. "Rialto Patrons Are Insured," *Hamilton Evening Journal* (6 May 1925), p. 4.
18. "Feline Mascot Won Fame for Charley's Aunt," *Los Angeles Times* (19 April 1925), p. 21.
19. Photo caption: "Syd Chaplin recently re-enacted his role in 'Charley's Aunt' (Producers' Dist. Corp.) at an Orphan Benefit at Grauman's Million Dollar Theatre, Los Angeles," *MPN* (18 April 1925), p. 1716.
20. Alma Whitaker, "Syd Sees 'Charley's Aunt,'" *Los Angeles Times* (26 February 1925), p. A9.
21. "Coach to Carry Wampas Stars," *Los Angeles Times* (1 February 1925), p. B2.
22. "Stage Set for Wampas Frolic," *Los Angeles Times* (1 February 1925), p. 17.
23. "New Projects Are Announced," *Los Angeles Times* (25 January 1925), p. E1.
24. Devore was reported to be

hosting a party of guests — including Sydney — at the Montmartre on Hollywood Boulevard the evening of Saturday, 19 September 1925; Sydney was one of the guests; "Society of Cinemaland," *Los Angeles Times* (27 September 1925), p. 26; Devore was also signed by Warner Bros. at the same time as Sydney; "Freelancers Are Signing up," *Los Angeles Times* (22 March 1925), p. D12.
25. "Film Stars Will Receive Guests for Sixty Club," *Los Angeles Times* (13 March 1925), p. All.
26. "Paulais in Hollywood Is Opened," *Los Angeles Times* (10 October 1924), p. 7.
27. "Radio: Latest News and Inventions," *The Charleston* (SC) *Daily Mail* (1 March 1925), p. 3.
28. "Engage John Barrymore," *New York Times* (12 March 1925), p. 17.
29. "Hollywood Pauses for Baby Star," *Los Angeles Times* (16 March 1925), p. 16.
30. "Warner-Vitagraph through to Merger," *The Reel Journal* (2 May 1925), p. 8.
31. "Warners Plan Larger Output," *Los Angeles Times* (9 April 1925), p. A10.
32. "Warner Brothers Sign Syd Chaplin as Star," unknown newspaper (13 April 1925).
33. "Newmeyer to Direct Syd Chaplin," *Los Angeles Times* (27 March 1925), p. A9.
34. *The Man on the Box*, story digest, Warner Bros. Archive, USCCAL.
35. Of course, Reisner had a long history with the Chaplin brothers; he had just finished co-directing on Charlie's *The Gold Rush* when he took this assignment.
36. "Newmeyer Quits Post at Warners," *Los Angeles Times* (15 May 1925), p. A10.
37. Jack Jungmeyer, "Daily Movie Chat," *Olean* (NY) *Evening Times* (3 October 1925), p. 10.
38. Mordaunt Hall, "Out Slapsticking Slapstick," *New York Times* (28 September 1925), p. 24.
39. Quinn Martin, "California Musician Solicits Attention," *Oakland* (CA) *Tribune* (11 October 1925), p. 2-W.
40. Helen Klumph, "'Man on Box,'" *Los Angeles Times* (4 October 1925), p. 27.
41. "The Pick of the Pictures," *Sunday Chronicle* (Manchester UK) (4 October 1925), n. p.; "Syd Chaplin, Comedian," *Evening Standard* (22 September 1925): n. p.
42. "'Man on the Box' Held at Forum for Second Week," *Los Angeles Times* (14 October 1925), p. 15.
43. *The Man on the Box*, shooting script, Warner Bros. Archive, USCCAL.
44. "Cinema Celebrities Dine," *Los Angeles Times* (9 April 1925), p. A1.
45. "Film Stars to Fete Shriners," *Los Angeles Times* (29 May 1925), p. A1; "Film Stars Participate in Pageant," *Los Angeles Times* (5 June 1925), p. All.
46. "Egyptian Theatre Mecca," *Los Angeles Times* (26 June 1925), p. A9.
47. "'Good Night Nurse' for Syd," *Los Angeles Times* (23 July 1925), p. A7.
48. Alma Whitaker, "Syd's New Role Not All Comedy," *Los Angeles Times* (11 October 1925), p. 31.
49. "Exits and Entrances," *Oakland* (CA) *Tribune* (28 August 1925), p. 36.
50. Leonard Mosely, *Zanuck: The Rise and Fall of Hollywood's Last Tycoon* (Boston: Little Brown, 1984), p. 49.
51. Yet Sydney worked tirelessly to make his mother as comfortable and happy as she could be, sparing no expense to do so.
52. Quoted in Mosely, p. 50.
53. "Syd Chaplin Visits at Yosemite Park," *Los Angeles Times* (18 August 1925), p. 6.
54. Grace Kingsley, "Patsy Ruth Miller Comedienne," *Los Angeles Times* (17 September 1925), p. All.
55. Miller was never a star, but is best remembered for her role as Esmeralda in Lon Chaney's *The Hunchback of Notre Dame*, filmed in 1923; John Springer and Jack Hamilton, *They Had Faces Then: Superstars, Stars and Starlets of the 1930s* (Secaucus, NJ: Citadel Press, 1974), p. 316.
56. William M. Drew, *Speaking of Silents: The First Ladies of the Screen* (Vestal, NY: Vestal Press, 1989), p. 49.
57. "Film Star Recovers from Flu," *Los Angeles Times* (2 October 1925), p. A5.
58. "With the Producers and Players," *New York Times* (25 October 1925), p. X5; "Syd Chaplin Hurt," (26 September 1925), n. p., Syd Chaplin Clippings, CHACHAA.
59. "Syd Chaplin — the Ideal Female Impersonator," *Girls' Cinema* (20 March 1926), p. 15.
60. Don Ryan, "How Laughs Are Built," *Photoplay* (February 1926), p. 64.
61. "Syd Chaplin — the Ideal Female Impersonator," *Girls' Cinema* (20 March 1926), p. 15.
62. Alma Whitaker, "Syd's New Role Not All Comedy," *Los Angeles Times* (11 October 1925), p. 31.
63. "Syd Chaplin Passes Test in Patience," *Mansfield News* (15 November 1925), n. p.
64. Mordaunt Hall, "The Screen: 'Oh! What a Nurse!," *New York Times* (22 February 1926), n. p.
65. Laurence Reid, "Syd in Disguise," *Movie Monthly* (May 1926), p. 52.
66. Mordaunt Hall, "The Screen: 'Oh! What a Nurse!," *New York Times* (22 February 1926), n. p.
67. Edwin Schallert, "Syd's Film Hilarious," *Los Angeles Times* (14 June 1926), p. All.
68. "Syd's Comedy Enters on Third Week," *Los Angeles Times* (27 June 1926), p. C22; the film premiered on Friday, June 11 in Los Angeles.
69. "How Comedies Evolve" Photograph in *Los Angeles Times* (7 March 1926), p. 12; "Warners to Produce Six New Films," *Los Angeles Times* (7 March 1926), p. 27.
70. "Syd Swaps Skirts for Army Togs," *Los Angeles Times* (14 March 1926), p. 29.
71. Mosley, p. 95.
72. "Old Acquaintances Meet on Warner Lot," *Los Angeles Times* (13 May 1927), p. A9.
73. *The Better 'Ole*, story digest, Warner Bros. Archive, USCCAL.
74. Bruce Bairnsfather and Arthur Eliot, *The Better 'Ole, or the Romance of Old Bill*, Synopsis T. S. Warner Bros. Archive, USCCAL.
75. "Bruce Bairnsfather's Idea of Chaplin," *Newark* (OH) *Advocate and American Tribune* (19 May 1927), p. 17.
76. Barbara Miller, "Chaplin Understands 'Better 'Ole' Role," *Los Angeles Times* (14 November 1926), p. C21.
77. "The Better 'Ole." *Oakland Tribune* (17 August 1926), p. 2.
78. Bruce Bairnsfather, "How 'Old Bill' Came to Life on Stage and Screen," The Better 'Ole *Souvenir Book* (Los Angeles, CA: Warner Bros., 1926), n. p., LCLPA.
79. "Bairnsfather Play down in Greenwich," *New York Times* (21 October 1918), n. p.
80. Ibid.
81. Mark Warby, "*The Better 'Ole, or the Romance of Old Bill*," www.brucebairnsfather.org.uk, 21 September 2009; <http://www.brucebairnsfather.org.uk/index_files/page0010.htm>.
82. "'The Better 'Ole,' T. and D. Feature," *Oakland* (CA) *Tribune* (15 May 1919), p. 9.
83. "'Old Bill,' World's Most Popular Fighter in 'The Better 'Ole,'" *Lethbridge* (Alberta, Canada) *Daily Herald* (5 March 1919), n. p.

84. "'Better 'Ole' Week at the Strand," *MPW* (15 March 1919), p. 1466.
85. Ibid.
86. *The Better 'Ole, shooting script,* Warner Bros. Archive, USC-CAL.
87. Bruce Bairnsfather and Arthur Eliot, *The Better 'Ole, or the Romance of Old Bill,* Synopsis T. S. Warner Bros. Archive, USC-CAL.
88. Edwin Schallert, "Syd Chaplin Scores Hit," *Los Angeles Times* (19 November 1926), p. A9.
89. Sydney Chaplin, Palais Rosa Bonheur, Nice, France, R. J. Minney, 16 March 1934, WGC.
90. "Big Pictures Coming," *New York Times* (28 November 1926), p. X7.
91. Scott Eyman, *The Speed of Sound: Hollywood and the Talkie Revolution 1926–1930* (New York: Simon & Schuster, 1997), p. 98.
92. Mordaunt Hall, "The Vitaphone and 'The Better 'Ole,'" *New York Times* (8 October 1926), p. 23.
93. "*The Better 'Ole* Starring Sydney Chaplin," *Picture Play* (January 1927), n. p.
94. "Critics Enthusiastic in Praise of 'Better 'Ole,' Chaplin Film," *Lethbridge* (Alberta, Canada) *Herald* (19 February 1927), p. 12.
95. "Big Crowds See 'The Better 'Ole,'" *Fitchburg* (MA) *Sentinel* (4 April 1927), p. 2.
96. Cable Arthur Kelly, New York, Sydney Chaplin, Los Angeles, 8 July 1926, CHACHAA.
97. Sydney Chaplin, Arthur Kelly, New York, 21 July 1926.
98. Arthur Kelly, New York, Sydney Chaplin, Los Angeles, July 31, 1926, CHACHAA.
99. "Sydney Chaplin's Next," *Los Angeles Times* (12 August 1926), p. A10.
100. Sydney Chaplin, Arthur Kelly, New York, 24 August 1926, CHACHAA.
101. Arthur Kelly, New York, Sydney Chaplin, Los Angeles, 30 August 1926, CHACHAA.
102. "Society of Cinemaland," *Los Angeles Times* (4 & 18 July, 22 August 1926), pp. C11; C6; C12.
103. "Syd Chaplin in Africa" T. S., CHACHAA.
104. Ibid.
105. "The Missing Link" Warner Bros. Press book, LCLPA.
106. "The Missing Link" Warner Bros. Press book, LCLPA.
107. "Slapstick Held Factor," *Los Angeles Times* (21 November 1926), p. C23.
108. "Well, Well!" Photograph printed in *Los Angeles Times* (17 October 1926), p. 13.
109. Irene Thirer, "Syd Chaplin Ill, Link Missing in 'Missing Link,'" *Daily News* (23 December 1926), p. 30.
110. "Chaplin Comedy Closes Tonight," *Los Angeles Times* (4 July 1927), p. A7.
111. Mordaunt Hall, "Sydney Chaplin and Wild Animals," *New York Times* (7 May 1927), p. 15.
112. Quinn Martin, "At the Colony Syd Chaplin in 'The Missing Link,'" unknown source (9 May 1927), n. p., CHACHAA.
113. Presumably, this accounting was made *after* the release of *The Better 'Ole.*
114. H. Mark Glancy, "Warner Brothers Film Grosses, 1921–51: The William Schaefer Ledger," *Historical Journal of Film, Radio and Television* (March 1995), n. p.
115. Sidney Garrett, London, Sydney Chaplin, Los Angeles, 17 November 1926, CHACHAA.
116. Sidney Garrett, London, Sydney Chaplin, Los Angeles, 30 December 1926, CHACHAA.
117. David Robinson, p. 372.
118. Sydney Chaplin, Charlie Chaplin, New York, [January 1927], CHACHAA.
119. "Syd Chaplin's Next," *Los Angeles Times* (11 December 1926), p. A6.
120. "Movieland," *Manitoba Free Press* (Winnipeg) (26 March 1927), p. 27.
121. "Six Added to Roster of Writers," *Los Angeles Times* (13 February 1927), p. C19.
122. Grace Kingsley, "No Hidden Sorrows for Syd," *Picture-Play* (May 1927), p. 97.
123. Sydney Chaplin, the Desert Inn, Palm Springs Arthur Kelly, New York, [February 1927], CHACHAA.
124. Behavior such as this probably didn't do much to endear Sydney to his nephews, Charlie, Jr. and Sydney Earle.
125. *The Fortune Hunter* (1927) Warner Bros. Press Book, CHACHAA.
126. Grace Kingsley, "No Hidden Sorrows for Syd," *Picture-Play* (May 1927), p. 97.
127. "For & Against — Movie Stars on Marriage," *The Capitol News* (Melbourne, Australia) [July 1927], p. 50.
128. Stella, "Your Birthday," *Evening Graphic* (17 March 1927), p. 19.
129. Mordaunt Hall, "Sydney Chaplin," *New York Times* (10 January 1928), p. 28.
130. Mordaunt Hall, "A Clown as an Artist," *New York Times* (15 January 1928), p. 111.
131. Irene Thirer, "'The Fortune Hunter' Conceals Syd Chaplin's Comic Talents," *Daily News* (11 January 1928), p. 40.
132. "Chaplin Film Is Held Over Second Week," *Los Angeles Times* (29 January 1928), p. C10.
133. Cable, Douglas Fairbanks, Sydney Chaplin, 10 May 1927, CHACHAA.
134. "Chaplin May Go Abroad," *New York Times* (8 June 1927), p. 23.
135. Sydney Chaplin, Aubrey Chaplin, London, 22 July 1926, CHACHAA.
136. Aubrey Chaplin, London, Sydney Chaplin, Los Angeles, 12 October 1926, CHACHAA.
137. Aubrey Chaplin, London, Sydney Chaplin, Los Angeles, 27 November 1926, CHACHAA.
138. Captain Currey, T. S. *Exmouth,* Grays, Essex, Sydney Chaplin, Los Angeles, 3 December 1926, CHACHAA.
139. Richard Care, T. S. *Exmouth,* Grays, Essex, Sydney Chaplin, Los Angeles, [December 1926], CHACHAA.
140. Aubrey Chaplin, London, Sydney Chaplin, Los Angeles, 12 November 1926, CHACHAA.
141. "Mr. S. Chaplin's Offer to the Exmouth," *London Times* (26 July 1927), n. p.
142. "British International Pictures Prospectus," *London Times* (22 November 1927), n. p.
143. Earle E. Crowe, "British Picture Loan Made," *Los Angeles Times* (20 August 1927), p. 12.
144. Sydney Chaplin, Montreux Palace Hotel, Montreux, Switzerland, Sidney Garrett, London, 28 July 1927, CHACHAA.
145. Sydney Chaplin, Arthur Kelly, New York, 8 February 1929, CHACHAA.
146. "Comedian Not Good in Ready-to-Wear," *Waterloo* (IA) *Daily Courier* (24 May 1930), p. 8.
147. Sydney Chaplin, Arthur Kelly, New York, 8 February 1929, CHACHAA.
148. Sydney Chaplin, Montreux Palace Hotel, Montreux, Switzerland, Sidney Garrett, London, 28 July 1928, CHACHAA. Little did Sydney know then that this would be his view throughout eternity.
149. Sydney Chaplin, Montreux Palace Hotel, Montreux, Switzerland, Sidney Garrett, London, 28 July 1928, CHACHAA.
150. Sidney Garrett, Sydney Chaplin, Montreux Palace Hotel,

Montreux, Switzerland, 21 July 1927, CHACHAA.

151. Sydney Chaplin, Bill George, Los Angeles, 1 September 1927, CHACHAA.

152. Sydney Chaplin, Charlie Chaplin, Los Angeles, 1 September 1927, CHACHAA.

153. "Mrs. Chaplin Is Buried at Hollywood," *Amarillo Globe* (31 August 1928), p. 10.

154. Sidney Garrett, London, Sydney Chaplin, London, 23 September 1927, CHACHAA.

155. Wheeler Dryden, Sydney Chaplin, London, 8 June 1928, CHACHAA.

156. "Chasing Charley's Aunt: An Intimate View of Mr. Syd Chaplin ... and a Pipe," *The Photoplayer* (n. d.), T. S., CHACHAA.

157. "Sydney Chaplin in 'Skirts,'" Press Material, Metro-Goldwyn-Mayer, LCLPA.

158. "'A Little Bit of Fluff' Reviews," *The Kinomatograph Weekly* (31 May 1928), n. p.

159. "A British Film," *Daily Mirror* (12 September 1928), n. p.

160. Wheeler Dryden, Sydney Chaplin, London, 8 June 1928, CHACHAA.

161. Sidney Garrett, London, Sydney Chaplin, Rome, Italy, 4 April 1928, CHACHAA.

162. Arthur Kelly, New York, Sydney Chaplin, Paris, France, 18 May 1928, CHACHAA.

163. On this trip, Minnie and Sydney were the victims of a band of American thieves canvassing the Riviera at the time; "The French Police," *The Marion* (OH) *Star* (9 March 1929), p. 6.

164. Arthur Kelly, New York, Sydney Chaplin, Paris, France, 18 May 1928, CHACHAA.

165. Ibid.

166. Ibid.

167. J. P. Gallagher, *Fred Karno: Master of Mirth and Tears* (London: Robert Hale, 1971), p. 135.

Chapter 7

1. Sydney Chaplin, Hotel Napoleon, Avenue Friedland, Paris, R. J. Minney, November 15, 1930, WGC.

2. Actually, Syd probably took off during the first week of June 1929; "Sydney Chaplin Missing," *New York Times* (3 August 1929), p. 13; "A Missing Comedian," *The Englishman* (27 August 1929), n. p.; "Syd Chaplin's Vanishing Causes Stir in Hollywood," *The Film Daily* (6 August 1929), p. 2.

3. *Columbus* (OH) *Dispatch*, 24 August 1929, n. p., CHACHAA.

4. Matthew Sweet, "A Life in Full: The Other Chaplin," *The Independent Sunday* (19 October 2003), p. 16.

5. In an undated and uncited newspaper clipping entitled, "Mumming Birds: Film Comedies to Be Based on Famous Show" (CHACHAA), a reporter details how the "Mumming Birds" project came about, writing that Syd, while in England filming at BIP, "heard that the famous show was on the road again. He went to see it, and immediately said: 'That's the stuff I want.' He has arranged to produce a series of 'Mumming Birds' comedies. It is likely that Fred Karno, who revived the stage show, will be called in to assist in direction."

6. Sydney Chaplin, Ambassador Hotel, Paris R. J. Minney, October 1930, WGC.

7. A *Washington Post* article entitled "Actress Sues Brother of Chaplin, in London" and dated 28 July 1930, reports that Wright had officially sued Sydney the day before, a suit that BIP settled out of court.

8. In a letter to R. J. Minney, written in about August 1930 and sent from the Grand Hotel Osborne, Digue Mer, Ostende, Syd wrote that Wright claimed in her suit for libel defamation that he had accused her of blackmail to two members of the press, WGC.

9. Sydney Chaplin, Palais Rosa-Bonheur, Nice, France, R. J. Minney, 10 December 1930, WGC.

10. Ibid.

11. Wright was born in 1907 and appeared in at least three BIP silents, *Squib's Honeymoon* (1923), *Reveille* (1924), and *The Arcadians* (1927)—two of which starred Betty Balfour; Matthew Sweet to Kate Guyonvarch, E-mail communication, 5 October 2003.

12. In a letter to R. J. Minney, written in October 1930 and sent from the Ambassador Hotel, Paris, Syd offers this rationale for his actions: "If you make a law that is contrary to the laws of nature, you are immediately setting the stage for a tragedy. Supposing I had wanted this girl. It would have been a compliment to herself and to her mother. How should the mother feel if her daughter attracted no one? Like an artist who had painted a picture that no one wanted. However, our laws will not justify an immoral overture & whatever I might think on that particular point means nothing. People could accuse me of immorality & I would laugh at them. I am a novice compared to David whose psalm they sing & whom they hold up as a saint, but what I do resent is the accusation of cruelty. I would as much think of acting cruel to a girl as I would of maltreating my own mother. I have too much of the idealist in my nature & the aesthetic. It is these rotten lies that hurt," WGC.

13. Sydney Chaplin, Hotel Europäischer Hof, Baden Baden, Germany, R. J. Minney, 1 September 1930, WGC.

14. Sydney Chaplin, Ambassador Hotel, Paris, R. J. Minney, July 17, 1930, WGC.

15. Sydney Chaplin, Ambassador Hotel, Paris, R. J. Minney, 15 June 1930, WGC.

16. Sydney Chaplin, Grand Hotel Osborne, Digue de Mer, Ostende, R. J. Minney, [August 1930], WGC.

17. Minnie Chaplin, Ambassador Hotel, Paris, R. J. Minney, July 15, 1930, WGC.

18. Sydney Chaplin, Ambassador Hotel, Paris, R. J. Minney, July 16, 1930, WGC.

19. "Monty Banks?" *To-day's Cinema* (24 July 1929), p. 14.

20. Sydney Chaplin, Ambassador Hotel, Paris, France, R. J. Minney, 19 June 1930, WGC.

21. Sydney Chaplin, Grand Hotel Osborne, Digue Mer, R. J. Minney, [August 1930], WGC.

22. Aubrey Chaplin is first cousin to Charlie (not Sydney).

23. Matthew Sweet, "A Life in Full: The Other Chaplin," *The* (London) *Independent* (19 October 2003), p. 16.

24. Syd identifies this gentleman later in the letter as Mr. S. G. Donble (Double?), 71 Parkside Drive, Cassiobury Park, Watford, Herts.

25. Sydney Chaplin, Ambassador Hotel, Paris, France, R. J. Minney, 19 July 1930, WGC.

26. David Cunninghame, a soundman at Elstree, reported in his journal that one of two sound recorders was not working from June 1 to at least June 11; other problems with the sound department, he believed, were due to "1) Lack of a good head, 2) Misuse of equipment and 3) Lack of a specialized mechanical electrician," BFI.

27. "'White Cargo' Finished," *To-day's Cinema* (5 July 1929), p. 11.

28. "More 'Sound' Stages for Elstree," *To-day's Cinema* (24 July 1929), p. 15.

29. In a letter to Sydney from close friend Arthur Kelly written 12 June 1930, Kelly advises that "you

must have confidence in people and not get suspicious."

30. The Swiss Corporation Sydney referred to here is Regent Finance Corporation, a dummy company Sydney had first set up in Delaware in 1924 in order to keep himself from paying income taxes in the U. S. He's obviously still using this gimmick five years later.

31. Sydney Chaplin, Hotel Grande Osborne, Digue Mer, Ostende, R. J. Minney, [August 1930], WGC.

32. *London Times* obituary for John Maxwell, dated 4 October 1940; interestingly, although Walter C. Mycroft fails to mention Sydney in his biography, Sydney is one of only a handful of actors mentioned in Maxwell's obituary as being a star of one of Elstree's earliest films.

33. Walter Mycroft, *The Time of My Life*, Filmmakers Series (Lanham, MD: Scarecrow Press, 2006), p. 130.

34. Walter Mycroft only mentions Syd once in his autobiography (despite Syd's *many* references to Mycroft in his letters) and in such a way that the reference fails to appear in the index: "*Charley's Aunt* has been filmed several times; the first version I saw being a silent made in Hollywood, with Charlie Chaplin's brother Syd. The *Tivoli*, where it was shown, fitted loudspeakers outside the cinema to relay to passers-by in the Strand the shouts of laughter within," p. 165.

35. Victor Porter, in his introduction to Walter Mycroft's biography, *The Time of My Life*, Filmmakers Series (Lanham, MD: Scarecrow Press, 2006), outlines the situation around the firings of Brunel and Hitchcock, who told Truffaut and others that Mycroft had it in for him and was working out his demise. Mycroft himself states in the autobiography that "The enmity occurred over a very simple issue. We were both at Elstree and from the moment of my arrival there I had only one interest in life. That was Elstree—and John Maxwell its creator. Hitchcock saw it differently. He insisted that the thing that mattered was not Elstree nor Maxwell but the given picture. He was not at all caught by the ideal of an English Hollywood: he scorned my hero worship of John Maxwell. His only concern was the picture he was making—and he didn't much care where he made it," p. 33. In Brunel's case, *Elstree Calling* (1930) required the filming of a burlesque sketch from Shakespeare's *Taming of the Shrew*: "Brunel, reluctant to turn the sketch into a broad farce, and apparently with Mycroft's approval, had filmed the sequence straight, planning instead to get his laughs by splicing intermittent surprises into the performances.... But when Maxwell saw the rushes out of their correct sequence, he was not amused, and insisted that 'this won't do—it isn't funny.' Although Mycroft cautiously interceded with Maxwell on Brunel's behalf, he was unsuccessful, and Maxwell instructed Alfred Hitchcock, who was also on the BIP payroll, to reshoot the burlesque according to his instructions. That was the end of Brunel's employment at Elstree, although Mycroft managed to survive," p. xvii.

36. Mycroft, p. 150.

37. Victor Porter, p. xx.

38. Rachel Low, *The History of the British Film 1929–1939: Filmmaking in 1930s Britain* (London: Routledge, 1985), p. 117.

39. Victor Porter, p. xix–xx.

40. The evidence that exists about salary amounts paid to Hitchcock and Sydney respectively would seem to countermand the argument that Hitchcock was the more important of the two and therefore, received preferential treatment, at least in 1929; Tom Ryall in *Alfred Hitchcock and the British Cinema* (London: Athlone, 1996) reports that "the contract that Hitchcock had signed made him the highest paid film director in the country with an annual income of £13,000," p. 92; Syd, on the other hand, lists his contract agreement to have been for two pictures with his salary amounting to £200,000, of which £60,000 was paid in advance; these figures are repeated in many letters, to R. J. Minney, Arthur Kelly and others, otherwise the fact that Maxwell oftentimes signed stars for as little as £1500 a film would make these amounts highly suspect.

41. The *Mumming Birds* project was officially scrapped by early August ("Retrospect" *To-day's Cinema* (7 August 1929), p. 11, a fact underscored in the press by an article entitled, "Fred Karno for 'Talkies,'" that indicated Karno's defection to America and a Paramount contract; *To-day's Cinema* (10 August 1929), p. 2.

42. Tom Ryall, *Alfred Hitchcock and the British Cinema* (London: Athlone, 1996), p. 47.

43. F. L Minnistrode's report in "British Film Optimism," *New York Times* (24 March 1929), p. 135, and in "London Screen Notes," *New York Times* (31 March 1929), 107, offer additional evidence that Syd's *Mumming Birds* was scheduled to be a talkie from the onset.

44. Patrick McGilligan *Alfred Hitchcock: A Life in Darkness and in Light* (New York: Harper Collins Publishers, 2003), p. 120.

45. McGilligan, p. 120.

46. This report occurred a week after *Blackmail*, in its talking version, had been released commercially on June 21.

47. Quoted in Tom Ryall, *Blackmail*, BFI Film Classics (London: BFI, 1993), pp. 19–20.

48. Howard Maxford, *The A–Z of Hitchcock* (London: B.T. Batsford, 2002), p. 49.

49. Low, p. 117.

50. "British International Surprise," *To-day's Cinema* (21 August 1929), p. 1.

51. Ibid.; also McGilligan, p. 126; the journal of soundman David Cunninghame records that on August 19, a "tremendous number of people have been given notice to quit at the end of the week," BFI.

52. Low, p. 122.

53. "British Film News," *To-day's Cinema* (4 September 1929), p. 9.

54. Sydney Chaplin, Hotel Ambassador, Paris, France, R. J. Minney, October 1930, WGC; also, a letter from Sydney to Jim Minney (dated November 1930) contained a clipping from *Variety* entitled, "'Express' Film Critic out on Economy Wave," that describes G. A. Atkinson's dismissal.

55. In a letter to Minney, sent by Sydney's wife Minnie, from the Ambassador Hotel in Paris on July 15, 1930, she writes of Minney's exceptional behavior in the matter: "Every letter I receive, Syd just raves about you and yours, how marvelous & hospitable you both have been," WGC.

56. R. J. Minney to Sydney Chaplin, 18 September 1933, WGC.

57. Ibid.

58. Ibid.

59. Sydney Chaplin, Grand Hotel Osborne, Digue Mer, Ostende, R. J. Minney, August 1930, WGC.

60. "A Film Actor's Failure," *London Times* (19 March 1931), n. p.

61. Sydney Chaplin, Hotel des Deux Villes, La Haye, R. J. Minney, August 22, 1930, WGC.

62. Sydney Chaplin, Hotel de Paris, Monte Carlo, R. J. Minney, 22 November 1931, WGC.

63. Sydney Chaplin, Ambassador Hotel, Paris, R. J. Minney, 16 July 1930, WGC.

64. Sydney Chaplin, Grand Hotel Osborne, Ostende, R. J. Minney, [August 1930], WGC.

65. Sydney Chaplin, Hotel des Deux Villes, La Haye, the Netherlands, R. J. Minney, 22 August 1930, WGC.
66. Sydney Chaplin, Hotel Europäischer Hof, Baden Baden, Germany, R. J. Minney, 1 September 1930, WGC.
67. "Syd Chaplin, Film Actor, Ill in Paris," *Los Angeles Times* (29 September 1930), p. A6.
68. Sydney Chaplin, Hotel de Paris, Monte Carlo, R. J. Minney, February 22, 1931, WGC.
69. Ibid.
70. Sydney Chaplin, Palais Rosa-Bonheur, Nice, France, R. J. Minney, 11 June 1931, WGC.
71. Ibid.
72. Ibid.
73. Ibid.
74. Ibid.
75. Sydney Chaplin, Hotel de Paris, Monte Carlo, R. J. Minney, 22 February 1931, WGC.
76. March 24, according to Sydney Chaplin, Monty Hotel, Promenade des Anglais, Nice, France, R. J. Minney, 16 March 1931, WGC.
77. Sydney Chaplin, Monty Hotel, Promenade des Anglais, Nice, France, R. J. Minney, 16 March 1931, WGC.

Chapter 8

1. Sydney Chaplin, Grand Hotel Osborne, Ostende, R. J. Minney, [August 1930], WGC.
2. Arthur Kelly, Sydney Chaplin, 12 June 1930, CHACHAA.
3. Sydney Chaplin, Grand Hotel Cirta, Constantine, Charlie Chaplin, 26 April 1930, CHACHAA.
4. Sydney Chaplin, Hotel de Paris, Monte Carlo, R. J. Minney, 22 February 1931, WGC.
5. Sydney Chaplin, R. J. Minney, 10 December [1930], WGC.
6. In a letter to R. J. Minney from the Monty Hotel, Promenade des Anglais, Nice, France, dated 16 March 1931, Sydney exclaims, "I cannot understand why they say that 'Mumming Birds' would be no use now. It is not topical & would be just as funny 10 years from now. There is no doubt about 'The Submarine Pirate' being a big possibility. I have always considered this so & have been keeping that up my sleeve for myself in case I wanted to do my own financing," WGC.
7. Cable Carlyle Robinson, Vienna, Austria, R. J. Minney, March 17, 1931, WGC.
8. Carlyle Robinson, *La Vérité sur Charlie Chaplin: Sa vie, ses amours, se déboirs* (*The Truth about Charlie Chaplin: His Life, His Loves, His Disappointments*) Constance Brown Kuriyama, trans., in May Reeves and Claire Goll (Paris: Société Parisienne D'Édition, 1933); Constance Brown Kuriyama, ed. and trans., *The Intimate Charlie Chaplin* (Jefferson, NC: McFarland, 2001), p. 135.
9. May Reeves and Claire Goll, *The Intimate Charlie* Chaplin, ed. Constance Brown Kuriyama (Jefferson, NC: McFarland, 2001), p. 62.
10. 1931–32 Chaplin Studios Pressbook, CHACHAA.
11. Sydney Chaplin, Monty Hotel, Nice, France, R. J. Minney, 16 March 1931, WGC.
12. Cable Charlie Chaplin, Sydney Chaplin, incorrectly attributed to 1930, but most likely late May 1931— the date David Robinson gives in *Chaplin: His Life and Art* as that of Carlyle Robinson's departure for New York (p. 436) provides evidence of the latter two acts: "Send Carl to New York.... Notify Reeves to OK American contracts. Dismiss Kelly. Get copy of foreign contract. Why not see Paris lawyer be sure of evidence of booking in the meantime. Further contracts must be okayed by you or me. Try and hold up bad contracts. Do what you think is best on my behalf. That's all that can be done. Will phone you Sunday evening seven. Charlie," CHACHAA.
13. In a letter to R. J. Minney, 22 February 1931, Hotel de Paris, Monte Carlo, Sydney writes of Carlyle Robinson, "You will find him a good sport & has been with Charlie [for] years.... Don't talk quite so confidentially to him as you do to Charlie. You know what publicity men are. They are working for you today & maybe the B. I. tomorrow," WGC.
14. 1931–32 Chaplin Studios Pressbook clipping, CHACHAA, attributed only to an article in *The Star* entitled "Charlie Chaplin Travels," 14 April 1931.
15. Carlyle Robinson, p. 138.
16. Ibid., p. 139.
17. Ibid., p. 141.
18. This occurred shortly after Charlie's arrival in St. Moritz, in December 1931; Carlyle Robinson, p. 144.
19. Sydney Chaplin, Palais Rosa-Bonheur, Nice, France, R. J. Minney, 17 July 1931, WGC.
20. Carlyle Robinson, p. 143.
21. Sydney Chaplin, Palais Rosa-Bonheur, Nice, France, R. J. Minney, 3 August 1931, WGC.
22. Sydney Chaplin, on board *Suma Maru*, R. J. Minney, 9 March 1932, WGC.
23. Boris Evelinoff, Paris, Minnie Chaplin, 7 February 1932, CHACHAA.
24. Gerith von Ulm, *Charlie Chaplin: King of Tragedy* (Caldwell: ID, Caxton Printers, 1940), p. 345.
25. Sydney Chaplin, on board *Suma Maru*, R. J. Minney, 9 March 1932, WGC.
26. Cable, Charlie Chaplin, Sydney Chaplin, 23 February 1932, CHACHAA.
27. Boris Evelinoff, Paris, Minnie Chaplin, 18 March 1932, CHACHAA.
28. Unpublished T. S., CHACHAA.
29. "Charlie Chaplin Ill in Singapore," *Los Angeles Evening Herald* (20 April 1932.), n. p., CHACHAA.
30. Proper name spelling provided by Stephen J. Fleay, E-mail, 6 August 2009.
31. Unpublished M. S., CHACHAA.
32. Syd mentions reading this article to R. J. Minney, in a letter written on board the *Suwa Maru* 9 March 1932: "The Island of Bali: this is the island that Roosevelt has been raving about in the papers as being the last unspoiled paradise on earth, so Charlie is going to see what impression he gets from it."
33. Sydney Chaplin, on board *Suma Maru*, R. J. Minney, 9 March 1932, WGC.
34. "Charlie Chaplin, Balinese," *New York Herald* (12 June 1932), n. p., CHACHAA.
35. Charlie Chaplin, "A Comedian Sees the World, Part V," *Woman's Home Companion* (January 1934), p. 21
36. Ibid.
37. Sydney Chaplin, on board *Suma Maru*, R. J. Minney, 9 March 1932, WGC.
38. Martin Gilbert, *A History of the Twentieth Century. Volume One, 1900–1933* (New York: William Morrow, 1997), p. 806.
39. Donald Richie, *The Honorable Visitors* (Rutland, VT: Charles E. Tuttle, 1994), pp. 110–111.

Donald Richie writes:
> Prime Minister Inukai was one of Japan's foremost liberals. He had long fought for parliamentary democracy and had initiated a policy of friendly relations with China that would, it was hoped, somewhat counter Japan's military adventures in that country. It was only many years later that Chaplin learned of the connection between his own experiences and the assassination. At the trial of those who

had killed the prime minister, Lieutenant Seishi Koga, the leader, testified that there had been plans for another assassination—that of Charlie Chaplin.

The famous comedian was to have met Inukai on May 15 and both he and the prime minister were to have been killed. During the proceedings, the judge asked Koga what the significance of killing Chaplin was to have been. The young man answered (in the words of Hugh Byas, from whom this account is taken) that "Chaplin is a popular figure in the United States and the darling of the capitalist class. We believed that killing him would cause a war with America." Japanese sources, however, say the assassination of the comedian was merely to cause such confusion that the coup d'état could be more easily consolidated.

40. Charlie Chaplin, "A Comedian Sees the World, Part V," *Woman's Home Companion* (January 1934), p. 86.

41. Sydney Chaplin, Palais Rosa-Bonheur, Nice, France, R. J. Minney, 16 October 1932, WGC.

42. von Ulm, p. 361.

Chapter 9

1. Sydney Chaplin, Hotel Westminster, Nice, France, R. J. Minney, 6 January 1931, WGC.
2. Sydney Chaplin, Palais Rosa-Bonheur, Nice, France, R. J. Minney, 6 December 1932, WGC.
3. Sydney Chaplin, Palais Rosa-Bonheur, Nice, France, R. J. Minney, 5 September 1933, WGC.
4. Sydney Chaplin, Palais Rosa-Bonheur, Nice, France, R. J. Minney, 16 October 1932, WGC.
5. Sydney Chaplin, Hotel Westminster, Nice, France, R. J. Minney, 16 December 1930, WGC.
6. Sydney Chaplin, Hotel Westminster, Nice, France, R. J. Minney, 6 January 1931, WGC.
7. Sydney Chaplin, Palais Rosa-Bonheur, Nice, France, R. J. Minney, 19 November 1933, WGC.
8. Letter to R. J. Minney, Ambassador Hotel, Paris, July, 1930, WGC.
9. Letter to R. J. Minney, Grand Hotel Osborne, Digue de Mer, Ostende, [August, 1930], WGC.
10. It is likely that the movie cameras were presented to Sydney in partial remuneration for his appearing in a magazine advertisement for the brand that year.
11. Letter to R. J. Minney, Grand Hotel Osborne, Digue de Mer, Ostende, August 1930, WGC.
12. Sydney Chaplin, Palais Rosa-Bonheur, Nice, France, R. J. Minney, 26 January 1933, WGC.
13. Sydney Chaplin, Palais Rosa-Bonheur, Nice, France R. J. Minney, 19 November 1933, WGC.
14. Letter to R. J. Minney, Palace Hotel, St. Moritz, 28 January 1934, WGC.
15. A request to the present owner of Irving Mills Music in April 2008 resulted in the discovery of no entries for Sydney.
16. "Give It to Me," music manuscript, CHACHAA.
17. Letter to R. J. Minney, Grand Hotel Osborne, Digue de Mer, August 1930, WGC.
18. Sydney Chaplin, Palais Rosa-Bonheur, Nice, France R. J. Minney, 16 March 1934, WGC.
19. Sydney Chaplin, Palais Rosa-Bonheur, Nice, France, R. J. Minney, 11 June 1931, WGC.
20. Harry Hermann, "Why Wear Clothes?" (n. d.), CHACHAA.
21. Sydney's half brother Wheeler Dryden showed him one of the articles, with the conclusion that Sydney's predilection was known at least to this particular family member.
22. Sydney Chaplin, Palais Rosa-Bonheur, Nice, France, R. J. Minney, 7 October 1932, WGC.
23. Nudism, or naturism, as it is more commonly termed in Europe, most likely began with Marcel Kienné de Mongeot, nobleman and World War I aviator, in 1920. He started the magazine Syd refers to as *Vivre*, which was originally titled *Vivre intégralement*, in 1926 and the first Sparta Club at Garambouville, France the same year. The one in Paris (among others) opened shortly thereafter. He was able to establish in court that nudism was legal on privately owned, fenced and screened property; excerpted and translated from Marc-Alain Descamps, *Vivre Nu: Psychosociologie du Naturisme*, Édition Trismégiste, 1987.
24. Sydney Chaplin, Palais Rosa-Bonheur, Nice, France, R. J. Minney, 7 October 1932, WGC.
25. See Chapter 1
26. Sydney also presents the following argument in an effort to support his supposed intellectual motivations: "If it was only for the sake of nudity that I had joined this society, then I would not have to go further than a certain licensed house I know in Paris, where for the price of a glass of beer, I can see 50 nude women, dance with them, have them sit upon my knee (not the fifty at one time) or expose themselves to me in any conceivable position. Yet all the months I have lived in Paris, I have been there three times, once out of curiosity, and twice to take my friends who were equally curious," Sydney Chaplin, Palais Rosa-Bonheur, Nice, France, R. J. Minney, 7 October 1932, WGC).
27. Sydney Chaplin, Palais Rosa-Bonheur, Nice, France, R. J. Minney, 7 October 1932, WGC.
28. Letter to R. J. Minney, Hotel Westminster, Nice, France, 6 January 1931, WGC.
29. Matthew Sweet, "A Life in Full: The Other Chaplin," *The Independent Sunday* (19 October 2003), p. 16.
30. Sydney Chaplin, Palais Rosa-Bonheur, Nice, France, R. J. Minney, 6 December 1932, WGC.
31. Sydney Chaplin, Palais Rosa-Bonheur, Nice, France, R. J. Minney, 10 December 1930, WGC.
32. Sydney Chaplin, Palais Rosa-Bonheur, Nice, France, R. J. Minney, 8 May 1933, WGC.
33. Sydney Chaplin, Palais Rosa-Bonheur, Nice, France, R. J. Minney, 11 June 1931, CHACHAA.
34. Sydney Chaplin, Palais Rosa-Bonheur, Nice, France, Arthur Kelly, 23 September 1933, CHACHAA.
35. Sydney Chaplin, Palais Rosa-Bonheur, Nice, France, R. J. Minney, 16 March 1934, WGC.
36. Sydney Chaplin, Palais Rosa-Bonheur, Nice, France, Alf Reeves, 17 May 1934, CHACHAA.
37. Alf Reeves, Charlie Chaplin Studios, Hollywood, CA, Sydney Chaplin, 6 August 1934, CHACHAA.
38. Sydney Chaplin, Hotel des Deux Villes, La Haye, R. J. Minney, 22 August 1930, WGC.
39. Sydney Chaplin, Palais Rosa-Bonheur, Nice, France, R. J. Minney, 26 January 1933, WGC.
40. Sydney Chaplin, Palais Rosa-Bonheur, Nice, France, R. J. Minney, 5 February 1933, WGC.
41. Sydney Chaplin, Palais Rosa-Bonheur, Nice, France, R. J. Minney, 3 April 1933, WGC.
42. Sydney Chaplin, Palais Rosa-Bonheur, Nice, France, R. J. Minney, 25 May 1933, WGC.
43. Sydney Chaplin, Palais Rosa-Bonheur, Nice, France, R. J. Minney, 3 April 1933, WGC.
44. Sydney Chaplin, Palais Rosa-Bonheur, Nice, France, R. J. Minney, 8 May 1933 & 25 May 1933, WGC.
45. Sydney Chaplin, Palais Rosa-Bonheur, Nice, France, R. J. Minney, 20 June 1933, WGC.

46. Cable Sydney Chaplin, Paris, France, R. J. Minney, 2 August 1933, WGC.
47. Sydney Chaplin, Hotel Ambassador, Paris, France, R. J. Minney, 3 August 1933, WGC.
48. Minnie Chaplin, En route to Nice, France, R. J. Minney, [July] 1933, WGC.
49. Sydney Chaplin, Palais Rosa-Bonheur, Nice, France, R. J. Minney, 23 August 1933, WGC.
50. Sydney Chaplin, Palais Rosa-Bonheur, Nice, France, R. J. Minney, 30 August 1933, WGC.
51. Sydney Chaplin, Palais Rosa-Bonheur, Nice, France, R. J. Minney, 5 September 1933, WGC.
52. Sydney Chaplin, Palais Rosa-Bonheur, Nice, France, R. J. Minney, 10 September 1933, WGC.
53. Russell G. Medcraft; the story in question could have been *The Camels Are Coming* (1934), *So You Won't Talk?* (1935), in which Monty Banks plays the lead, or *It's in the Bag* (1936)—all UK productions.
54. Sydney Chaplin, Palais Rosa-Bonheur, Nice, France, Arthur Kelly, 10 September 1933, CHACHAA.
55. In a letter to Arthur Kelly, dated 16 September 1933, Sydney writes, "[Maxwell] refused to cancel the bankruptcy judgment, which is outstanding against me before the completion of the picture. You can readily see what this means to me, that in the event that anything happened in England, such as adverse newspaper propaganda that would make it impossible for me to go through with the picture, my being in England at the time would make it possible for Maxwell to do what he liked with me by legal proceedings for the recovery of his judgment.... Upon my agent asking Maxwell why he would not cancel the judgment, he said he looked upon it as an asset, & he had no guarantee that I would go through with the contract. Good God, does he think I want to make my name stink with the United Artists, my brother, & the whole movie business in general?" CHACHAA.
56. Sydney Chaplin, Palais Rosa-Bonheur, Nice, France, R. J. Minney, 14 September 1933, WGC.
57. Sydney Chaplin, Palais Rosa-Bonheur, Nice, France, R. J. Minney, 8 November 1934, WGC.
58. "Mrs. Sydney Chaplin Arrives at L.A.," *Oakland* (CA) *Tribune* (5 April 1932), B11.
59. Sydney Chaplin, Palais Rosa-Bonheur, Nice, France, R. J. Minney, 14 March 1936, WGC. The body of this letter is worth including here, if only for the beauty of its construction and word-play:

You have no idea the number of fingers that have violated my posterior virginity. During the exploration of my artistic background, I was reminded of Grey's beautiful lines, "Full many a gem of beauty ray serene, the dark unfathomed caves of ocean bare." One doctor went as far as to stick a telescope up there with an electric light attached, evidently looking for discrepancies in my income tax. He said my muscle was contracted and that I should have my anus dilated with ether. I said why ether when I knew so many nice boys on the Riviera that knit their own socks and ride horseback with both legs on one side, who would be only too glad to dilate me without costing me a nickel. Besides if it was going to be painful, I prefer to start off with a Singer's midget. I told him I would have no difficulty in finding a dilator; Nice was so full of them. I suppose I shall have to sit around the house on pegs all day, first a one-inch, tomorrow one-and-three-eighths. So long as they don't give me a six-and-seven-eighths, thinking I wish to block my hat, everything will be OK. One doctor suggested I should take medicated enemas. One of the ingredients suggested was fleurs de mauve. I have had flowers in my button hole but never a bouquet up the other hole. Again, I was reminded of Grey's "Elegy," "many a flower is born to blush unseen & waste its perfume on the desert air." One doctor here in Nice has x-rayed me from every angle. He gave me bismuth to swallow, then watched it through the fluoroscope. It took the curves of my tonsils on high, swerved around the thorax, pulled up at the lungs for a little air in the tyres, made a speedy getaway & went all out until it reached the lower bowels where it filled up with gas, went off again at a full throttle, skidded badly around the big intestine, then coming full speed through the Blackwall tunnel, gave a loud blast on the Klaxon, which caused the doctor to jump clear & warned me in time to enable me to reach the parking station without backfiring in my exhaust box. The doctor said that, by the way, it had skidded around the big intestine. He was sure I had inflammation of that particular part of my anatomy, so he has placed me upon a very strict diet. I am making gradual progress, but I still have to visit his insulting room & take the Arab prayer posture while he examines my rear axle. I am beginning to wonder what the bogey is for this hole.

60. In a letter to Wheeler Dryden, dated 5 July 1936, Sydney writes, "I don't know what has come over Minney. He seems changed completely.... I told him in my previous letter that I had been very ill, also that Minnie was in a very bad way, but this meant nothing to him. I don't think he even commented on it," CHACHAA.
61. Sydney Chaplin, Palais Rosa-Bonheur, Nice, France, Wheeler Dryden, 5 July 1936, CHACHAA.
62. Cablegram, Charlie Chaplin, Sydney Chaplin, 17 April 1935, CHACHAA.
63. Sydney Chaplin, Palais Rosa-Bonheur, Nice, France, Charlie Chaplin, 7 May 1935, CHACHAA.
64. Sydney Chaplin, Palais Rosa-Bonheur, Nice, France, Alf Reeves, 11 June 1935, CHACHAA.
65. Alf Reeves, Charlie Chaplin Studio, Hollywood, CA, Sydney Chaplin, 24 January 1936, CHACHAA.
66. Sydney Chaplin, Palais Rosa-Bonheur, Nice, France, R. J. Minney, [Spring 1936], WGC.
67. Sydney Chaplin, Palais Rosa-Bonheur, Nice, France, Dr. Rosanoff, 26 May 1936, CHACHAA.
68. Sydney Chaplin, Palais Rosa-Bonheur, Nice, France, Wheeler Dryden, 23 September 1936, CHACHAA.
69. Amy Reeves, Playa del Rey, CA, Sydney Chaplin, 12 September 1936, CHACHAA.
70. Read Kendall, "Odd and Interesting," *Los Angeles Times* (13 September 1936), p. C3.
71. Sydney Chaplin Palais Rosa-Bonheur, Nice, France, Wheeler Dryden, 23 September 1936, CHACHAA.
72. Also, her body was listed "transport," which would remove any remaining evidence of her existence; it is not known where she is buried.
73. Sydney Chaplin, Palais Rosa-Bonheur, Nice, France, Wheeler Dryden, 25 November 1936, CHACHAA.
74. She was launched on 11 June 1930, being christened that day by Edward, Prince of Wales.
75. Her specifications included 760.6 feet in length, a 97.8-foot beam, and a weight of 42,348 gross tons. She could reach 24 knots in speed with her four engines and could serve 1,195 people; "Empress of Britain" @ http://www.greatoceanliners.net/empressofbritain2.htm.
76. "*Empress of Britain*" ad, *Fortune Magazine* (n. d.), p. 23.

77. Gordon Turner, "Vacations at Sea, 1930s-style: The *Empress of Britain* Set the Standard for Cruise Travel during the Great Depression," (Gale Group, 2005).
78. "Your Apartment for a World Cruise," from the *Empress of Britain* World Cruise from New York, 9 January 1937 cruise booklet (Canada, 1936), p. 5, provides a detailed description of these accommodations:

Entire floor space carpeted. Ceiling flush ... all beams, girders and piping encased. Walls in natural woods ... sapelli, zebrano, mahogany, walnut, bird's-eye maple, sycamore, satinwood, oak, birch, pearwood, ash and black bean. Full-size beds ... 6 feet long, 3 feet wide, inside measurements. Ceiling light ... wall lights ... bed lights ... telephone ... electric noiseless signal for steward and stewardess. Steam radiator ... electric radiator ... electric fan. Modern ventilation system under passenger's control. Up-to-the-minute wardrobes with automatic lighting, sliding trays, full-length door mirror, commodious shelf and drawer space, tie rails, and shoe rack. Smart dressing table with triple mirrors, sliding leaves, ample drawer space, and dressing stool. Full-length wall mirror. Hot and cold running water. Silver thermos jug for drinking water. Modern bathroom fittings ... tub and shower ... fresh water and salt water.

79. Sydney Chaplin, "Comments on my world cruise on the 'Empress of Britain,'" typescript, CHACHAA.
80. *Empress of Britain* ship manifest.
81. Sydney was on a visa, with his time expiring 9 January 1938; Sydney Chaplin, New Weston Hotel, New York, R. J. Minney, 5 December 1937, WGC.
82. In fact, this voice recording still exists and is the only known recording of Sydney's (and second wife Henriette's) voice, CHACHAA.
83. Louella O. Parsons, "Syd Chaplin, Back in Hollywood, Amazed at Ten Years' Changes," *Los Angeles Examiner* (8 May 1937), n. p.
84. Sydney Chaplin, New Weston Hotel, New York, R. J. Minney, 5 December 1937, WGC.
85. It is interesting to note that although his lawyer suggested that he might get a break if he became an American citizen, and that he could arrange it for Sydney without his having to wait for the quota, Sydney's immediate response was: "I hate like the devil to do this. Most Englishmen would feel the same way," Sydney Chaplin, New Weston Hotel, New York, R. J. Minney, 5 December 1937, WGC.
86. Sydney Chaplin, New Weston Hotel, New York, R. J. Minney, 5 December 1937, WGC.
87. Sydney Chaplin, Palais Rosa-Bonheur, R. J. Minney, 2 February 1938, WGC.
88. Sydney Chaplin, Palais Rosa-Bonheur, R. J. Minney, 8 March 1938, WGC.
89. Sydney Chaplin, Palais Rosa-Bonheur, R. J. Minney, 22 April 1938, WGC.
90. Spencer Dryden later made a name for himself as the drummer for Jefferson Airplane.
91. Unfortunately, Sydney was correct in saying that the film was planned for production the following year (1939), but Small had nothing to do with it.
92. Postcard Sydney Chaplin, Palais Rosa-Bonheur, R. J. Minney, 18 December 1938, WGC.
93. Sydney Chaplin, Palais Rosa-Bonheur, R. J. Minney, 9 January 1939, WGC.

Chapter 10

1. "Sydney Aids Charlie," *Nevada State Journal* (Reno), (20 January 1939), 3, and also a month later in "Screen Notes" *McKean County Democrat* (Smethport, PA) (9 February 1939), p. 3.
2. "Syd Chaplin as Goebbels," *Syracuse Herald* (20 March 20, 1939), p. 9.
3. Sydney Chaplin, Garden Court Apartments, Hollywood, CA, R. J. Minney, 18 February 1939, WGC.
4. Sydney Chaplin, Garden Court Apartments, Hollywood, CA, R. J. Minney, 27 March 1939, WGC.
5. Ibid.
6. Ibid.
7. Betty Smith, "We Dress for the Brown Derby and Find the Stars in Slacks," *Daily Express* (20 February 1939), p. 4; Betty Chaplin Smith, later Tetrick, was, at this time married to Albert Smith.
8. Russell Leavitt, "In California: A Fading Hollywood," HPTime.com (14 June 1982). <http://www.time.com/time/magazine/article/0,9171,950674,00.html>.
9. Betty Smith, "We Dress for the Brown Derby and Find the Stars in Slacks," *Daily Express* (20 February 1939), p. 4.
10. Charles Chaplin, Jr., *My Father, Charlie Chaplin* (New York: Random House, 1960), p. 219.
11. Don Ryan, "Dog Food to Filet Mignon," *Los Angeles Times* (29 September 1940), p. H3.
12. David Robinson, p. 493.
13. Quoted in David Robinson, p. 493.
14. Sydney Chaplin, Los Angeles, R. J. Minney, 18 February 1939, WGC.
15. Daily Production Reports, 1939–40, January 21, 1939, CHACHAA.
16. Sydney Chaplin, Cuba, R. J. Minney, 14 March 1941, WGC.
17. Sydney Chaplin, Cuba, 14 March 1941, WGC.
18. Ibid.
19. Lita's hatred of Sydney was so great that she refused to call her second son by that name, referring to him as "Tommy" instead.
20. David Robinson, p. 534.
21. Sydney and Gypsy were to tour America from coast to coast three times.
22. Jerry Epstein, *Remembering Charlie* (New York: Doubleday, 1989), p. 47.
23. Ibid., pp. 63–64.
24. Ibid., p. 64.
25. Sydney Chaplin, Palais Rosa Bonheur, Nice, France, R. J. Minney, 22 June 1948.
26. Ibid.
27. Sydney bought this apartment and was later to turn it over for a hefty profit.
28. Sydney Chaplin, Palais Rosa Bonheur, Nice, France, R. J. Minney, 22 June 1948.
29. Sydney Chaplin, Palace Hotel, St. Moritz, Switzerland, Charlie Chaplin, 29 January 1951, CHACHAA.
30. The manifest for the *Vulcania* documents that Sydney and Gypsy arrived in New York from Cannes on 12 July 1952.
31. Sydney Chaplin, Palace Hotel, Montreux, Switzerland, Albert and Edie de Courville, 16 July 1951, CHACHAA.
32. Sydney Chaplin, Palais Rosa Bonheur, Nice, France, Edie de Courville, 2 October 1951, CHACHAA.
33. Albert de Courville, Hotel Negresco, Nice, France, Sydney Chaplin, 23 January 1952, CHACHAA.
34. David Robinson, p. 622.
35. Sydney Chaplin, Bermuda Apartments, 10354 Wilshire Blvd., Los Angeles, CA, Charlie and Oona Chaplin, 27 June 1953, CHACHAA.
36. Ibid.
37. Charlie Chaplin, Manoir de Ban, Vevey, Switzerland, Sydney Chaplin, 26 August 1953, CHACHAA.

38. Ibid.

39. Sydney Chaplin, Bermuda Apartments, Los Angeles, CA, Charlie Chaplin, [September 1953], CHACHAA.

40. Sydney Chaplin, Bermuda Apartments, Los Angeles, CA, Charlie Chaplin, [October 1953], CHACHAA.

41. Ibid.

42. Ibid.

43. Sydney Chaplin, Bermuda Apartments, Los Angeles, CA, Charlie Chaplin, 3 November 1953, CHACHAA.

44. Sydney writes to Charlie, "He will see that nothing of an autobiography nature is destroyed. I have no confidence in anyone else handling it." (Sydney Chaplin, Bermuda Apartments, Los Angeles, CA, Charlie Chaplin, 3 November 1953, CHACHAA).

45. Ibid.

46. Sydney has constructed the French saying incorrectly, but it means "My little finger told me...."

47. Sydney Chaplin, Bermuda Apartments, Los Angeles, CA, Charlie Chaplin, 3 November 1953, CHACHAA.

48. Ibid.

49. Sydney Chaplin, Bermuda Apartments, Los Angeles, CA, R. J. Minney, 27 January 1954, LKSC. Sydney and Gypsy ended up leaving the caravan to one of Charlie's children.

50. Ibid.

51. Christopher remembers hearing that Sydney carried a mysterious magician's bag of tricks each time he visited; personal interview, 4 July 2007.

52. Michael remembers that you could see a long line of cars snaking through the Swiss countryside following Sydney's huge car; personal interview, 7 July 2007.

53. Personal interview, Geraldine Chaplin, Miami Beach, FL, 23 May 2009.

54. Personal interview, Michael Chaplin, Hotel Baglioni, Bologna, Italy, 7 July 2007.

55. Oona Chaplin, Manoir de Ban, Corsier-sur-Vevey, Switzerland, Betty Tetrick, 22 February 1961, CHACHAA.

56. The *Andrea Doria* sank just off the coast of Nantucket, MA on 25 July 1956; 46 passengers lost their lives.

57. Sydney Chaplin, Bermuda Apartments, Los Angeles, CA, R. J. Minney, 13 December 1956, WGC.

58. Sydney Chaplin, Bermuda Apartments, Los Angeles, CA, R. J. Minney, 21 January 1957, SOC.

59. Ibid.

60. Sydney Chaplin, Bermuda Apartments, Los Angeles, CA., R. J. Minney, 7 May 1957, LKSC.

61. Wheeler died on 30 September 1957.

62. Sydney Chaplin, Bermuda Apartments, Los Angeles, CA, R. J. Minney, 7 May 1957, LKSC.

63. Sydney Chaplin, Montreux Palace Hotel, Montreux, Switzerland, R. J. Minney, 22 September 1958, SOC.

64. Gypsy Chaplin, Hotel Ruhl, Nice, France, Ted and Betty Tetrick, 7 December 1959, CHACHAA.

65. Oona Chaplin, Manoir de Ban, Corsier-sur-Vevey, Switzerland, Betty Tetrick, 22 February 1961, CHACHAA.

66. The land Oona refers to in this letter is Sydney's property in Encinitas, California. Sydney must only have sold part of this property by this time, however, because Gypsy reports putting more of it on the market at $80,000 per lot (4 lots) to Betty Tetrick in a letter dated 25 August 1967, CHACHAA.

67. Oona Chaplin, Manoir de Ban, Corsier-sur-Vevey, Switzerland, Betty Tetrick, 22 February 1961, CHACHAA.

68. Gypsy Chaplin, Hotel Ruhl, Nice, France, Ted and Betty Tetrick, 12 April 1961, CHACHAA.

69. Oona would have been carrying her last child, Christopher, at this time.

70. Gypsy Chaplin, Montreux-Palace Hotel, Montreux, Switzerland, Betty Tetrick, 20 June 1962, CHACHAA.

71. Just as for Minnie, Sydney's death certificate contained the following narrative:

> *Le défunt n'avait pas de residence en France et ne possédait aucun mobilier. Il n'a fait aucune donation de biens français de son vivant.* (Translation: The deceased did not reside in France and possessed no furniture. He did not leave any French goods to his living heir).

72. His heart had started to show signs of weakness in November 1963, which at the time had been the reason for a visit from Charlie and Oona. Sydney Chaplin's health never improved after that. At the Chez Reynaud restaurant, he did no more than pick at his food and take small sips of the sauternes he loved so much. (Marie Brun, "Sydney Chaplin est mort ... le jour du 76e anniversaire de son frère cadet 'Charlot,'" *Nice-Matin* (17 April 1965), p. 2; translation courtesy of Kate Guyonvarch.

73. Sydney Chaplin, Bermuda Apartments, Los Angeles, CA, Charlie and Oona Chaplin, 27 June 1953, CHACHAA.

74. Personal interview, Michael Chaplin, Hotel Baglioni, Bologna, Italy, 7 July 2007.

Bibliography

Books

Adeler, Edwin, and Con West. *Remember Fred Karno? The Life of a Great Showman.* London: John Long, 1939.

Balio, Tino. *United Artists: The Company Built by the Stars.* Madison: University of Wisconsin Press, 1976.

Barker, Tony. *Round the Town: Following Grandfather's Footsteps.* Hambergen, Germany: Bear Family Records, 2002.

Chaplin, Charles. *My Autobiography.* London: Bodley Head, 1964.

Chaplin, Charles, Jr., with N. and M. Rau. *My Father, Charlie Chaplin.* New York: Random House, 1960.

Chaplin, Lita Grey, and Jeffrey Vance. *The Wife of the Life of the Party.* Lanham, MD: Scarecrow Press, 1998.

Descamps, Marc-Alain. *Vivre Nu: Psychosociologie du Naturisme.* Paris: Édition Trismégiste, 1987.

Drew, William M. *Speaking of Silents: The First Ladies of the Screen.* Vestal, NY: Vestal Press, 1989.

Encyclopedia of Alternative Medicine. Detroit: Thomson/Gale, 2005.

Epstein, Jerry. *Remembering Charlie.* New York: Doubleday, 1989.

Eyman, Scott. *The Speed of Sound: Hollywood and the Talkie Revolution, 1926–30.* New York: Simon & Schuster, 1997.

Fowler, Gene. *Father Goose: The Story of Mack Sennett.* New York: Covici Friede, 1934.

Fowler, Simon. *Workhouse: The People, the Places, the Life behind Doors.* Richmond, UK: The National Archives, 2007.

Gallagher, J. P. *Fred Karno: Master of Mirth and Tears.* London: Robert Hale, 1971.

Gilbert, Martin. *A History of the Twentieth Century. Volume One, 1900–1933.* New York: William Morrow, 1997.

Higginbotham, Peter C. *The Workhouse Cookbook.* Port Stroud, Gloucestershire, UK: The History Press, 2008.

King, Rob. *The Fun Factory: The Keystone Film Company and the Emergence of Mass Culture.* Berkeley: University of California Press, 2009.

Lahue, Kalton C. *Dreams for Sale: The Rise and Fall of the Triangle Film Corporation.* South Brunswick, NJ: A. S. Barnes, 1971.

_____. *Mack Sennett's Keystone: The Man, the Myth, and the Comedies.* South Brunswick, NJ: A. S. Barnes, 1971.

_____, and Terry Brewer. *Kops and Custards: The Legend of Keystone Films.* Norman: University of Oklahoma Press, 1968.

Lane, Lupino. *How to Become a Comedian.* London: F. Muller, 1945.

Lasky, Jesse L. *I Blow My Own Horn.* New York: Doubleday, 1957.

Levine, Philippa. *Prostitution, Race and Politics: Policing Venereal Disease in the British Empire.* New York: Routledge, 2003.

Louvish, Simon. *Keystone: The Life and Clowns of Mack Sennett.* New York: Faber and Faber, 2003.

Low, Rachel. *The History of the British Film 1929–1939: Film Making in 1930s Britain.* London: Routledge, 1985.

Marriot, A. J. *Chaplin: Stage by Stage.* Hitchin, UK: Marriot, 2005.

Martens, Jonathan, Maciej Pieczkowski, and Bernadette Van Vuuren-Smyth. *Seduction, Sale and Slavery: Trafficking in Women and Children for Sexual Exploitation in Southern Africa* (third edition). Pretoria, South Africa: IOM International Organization for Migration, 2003.

Maxford, Howard. *The A–Z of Hitchcock.* London: B. T. Batsford, 2002.

Minney, R. J. *Chaplin the Immortal Tramp: The Life and Work of Charles Chaplin.* London: George Newnes, 1954.

Mosely, Leonard. *Zanuck: The Rise and Fall of Hollywood's Last Tycoon.* Boston: Little, Brown, 1984.

Mycroft, Walter C. *The Time of My Life.* Edited by

Vincent Porter. Filmmakers Series. Lanham, MD: Scarecrow Press, 2006.
Nelson, Al P., and Mel R. Jones. *A Silent Siren Song: The Aitken Brothers' Hollywood Odyssey, 1905–1926*. New York: Cooper Square Press, 2000.
Porter, Vincent, ed. Introduction, *The Time of My Life*, by Walter C. Mycroft. Filmmakers Series. Lanham, MD: Scarecrow Press, 2006.
Reeves, May, and Claire Goll. *The Intimate Charlie Chaplin*. Edited and translated by Constance Brown Kuriyama. Jefferson, NC: McFarland, 2001.
Richie, Donald. *The Honorable Visitors*. Rutland, VT: Charles E. Tuttle, 1994.
Robertson, Patrick. *Film Facts*. New York: Billboard Books, 2001.
Robinson, Carlyle. *La Vérité sur Charlie Chaplin: Sa vie, ses amours, se déboirs* (*The Truth about Charlie Chaplin: His Life, His Loves, His Disappointments*). Translated by Constance Brown Kuriyama. Paris: Société Parisienne d'Édition, 1933.
Robinson, David. *Chaplin: His Life and Art*. London: Penguin, 2001.
Ryall, Tom. *Alfred Hitchcock and the British Cinema*. London: Athlone, 1996.
_____. *Blackmail*. BFI Film Classics. London: BFI, 1993.
Sennett, Mack, and Cameron Shipp. *King of Comedy*. Garden City, NY: Doubleday, 1954.
Springer, John, and Jack Hamilton. *They Had Faces Then: Superstars, Stars and Starlets of the 1930*. Secaucus, NJ: Citadel Press, 1974.
Turner, Gordon. *Vacations at Sea, 1930s-style: The Empress of Britain Set the Standard for Cruise Travel during the Great Depression*. Gale Group, 2005.
Van Heyningen, Elizabeth B. "The Social Evil in the Cape Colony 1868–1902: Prostitution and the Contagious Diseases Acts," *Journal of South African Studies* 10.2 (1984).
Von Ulm, Gerith. *Charlie Chaplin: King of Tragedy*. Caldwell, ID: Caxton, 1940.
Walker, Brent. *Mack Sennett's Fun Factory: A History and Filmography of His Studio and His Keystone and Mack Sennett Comedies, with Biographies of Players and Personnel*. Jefferson, NC: McFarland, 2009.
Waterman, Waldo Dean, and Jack Carpenter. *Waldo, Pioneer Aviator: A Personal History of American Aviation, 1910–44*. Carlisle, MA: Arsdalen, Bosch, 1988.
Walkowitz, Judith R. *Prostitution and Victorian Society: Women, Class and the State*. Cambridge: Cambridge University Press, 1980.

Newspapers

Ada (OK) *Evening News*
Allentown (PA) *Democrat*
Amarillo (TX) *Globe*
Anniston (AL) *Star*
Billings (MT) *Gazette*
Boston Sun Post
Capitol News (Melbourne, Australia)
Catalina Islander (Avalon, CA)
Cedar Rapids (IA) *Republican*
Charleroi (PA) *Mail*
Charleston (SC) *Daily Mail*
Columbus (OH) *Dispatch*
Daily Express (UK)
Daily Mirror
Daily News
The Daily Northwestern (Oshkosh, WI)
The Des Moines (IA) *Capital*
Eau Claire (WI) *Leader*
Edwardsville (IL) *Intelligencer*
Evening Graphic (UK)
Evening Standard (UK)
Fitchburg (MA) *Sentinel*
Hamilton (OH) *Daily News*
Hamilton (OH) *Evening Journal*
Helena (MT) *Daily Independent*
Janesville (WI) *Daily Gazette*
Kokomo (IN) *Daily Tribune*
La Crosse (WI) *Tribune and Leader-Press*
Lethbridge (Alberta, Canada) *Daily Herald*
The Lima (OH) *News & Times Democrat*
The Lima (OH) *Sunday News*
The (Lorain, OH) *Chronicle Telegram*
London Times
Los Angeles Evening Herald
Los Angeles Examiner
Los Angeles Express
Los Angeles Saturday Night
Los Angeles Times
The Lowell (MA) *Sun*
Manitoba Free Press (Winnipeg)
The Mansfield (OH) *News*
Marion (OH) *Star*
McKean County Democrat (Smethport, PA)
The Mexia (TX) *Evening News*
Moberly (MO) *Democrat*
Nevada State Journal (Reno)
New York Evening World
New York Herald
New York Telegraph
New York Times
Newark (OH) *Advocate and American Tribune*
Newark (OH) *Daily Advocate*
Oakland (CA) *Tribune*
The Olean (NY) *Evening Herald*
The Olean (NY) *Evening News*
Ogden (UT) *Standard-Examiner*
Portsmouth (NH) *Daily Times*
Racine (WI) *Journal-News*
Riverside (CA) *Enterprise*
Riverside (CA) *Press*
The San Antonio (TX) *Light*
St. Paul (MN) *Pioneer Press*
Sheboygan (WI) *Press & Sheboygan Telegram*
Sunday Chronicle (Manchester UK)
The Sunday State Journal
Syracuse (NY) *Herald*
Washington Post
Waterloo (IA) *Daily Courier*
Waterloo (IA) *Times Tribune*

Bibliography

Trade Publications

"Camera!" The Digest of the Motion Picture Industry
The Era (1885–1914)
Exhibitor's Trade Review
The Film Daily
Kinomatograph Weekly
Motion Picture News (1914–1928)
Moving Picture World (1914–1928)
The Reel Journal
The Silver Sheet
To-day's Cinema
The Triangle
Universal Weekly
Variety (1906)

Other Periodicals

Ace
Classic
Girls' Cinema
The Englishman
Flying
Harper's
Historical Journal of Film, Radio and Television
Nice-Matin
Movie Monthly
Photoplay
Picture-Play
Reel Life
Saturday Evening Post
The Strand
System
Time
Woman's Home Companion

Archival Collections

Archives des Alpes-Maritîmes Collection, Nice France.
British Film Institute Collection, London, UK.
Charlie Chaplin Archive, Cineteca di Bologna, Bologna, Italy.
Billy Rose Theatre Collection, Lincoln Center Library of the Performing Arts.
Library of Congress Film Collection.
Mack Sennett, Thomas Ince and Core Collections, Margaret Herrick Library, Academy of Motion Picture Arts and Sciences, Beverly Hills, CA.
Warner Bros. Archive and MGM Collections, USC Cinema Arts Library, Los Angeles, CA.

Personal Interviews and Communications

Chaplin, Christopher. Personal interview. 4 July 2007.
Chaplin, Geraldine. Personal interview. 23 May 2009.
Chaplin, Michael. Personal interview. 7 July 2007.
Fleay, Steven J. E-mail communication. 6 August 2009.
Gilbert, Irvine. Telephone communication. 10 January 2010.
Green, Jack. E-mail communication. 2 August 2009.
Green, Ricky. E-mail communication. 3 November 2009.
Rogers, Emery H. E-mail communication. 22 September 2007.
Walker, Brent. Personal communication. 10 January 2009.

Index

Numbers in ***bold italics*** indicate pages with photographs.

Aalsem, Henk 184–185
Ackland, Rodney 171
Ackroyd, Jack 232
S.S. *Acquitania* 156
Adams, Frank 114, 231
S.S. *Adriatic* 94
The Adventurer 47
Aitken, Harry 61–62
Akin, Mary 232
Akka 149–150, 233
Al Christie Studios 114, 122–123, 125–126, 129
Al Wilson Aviation 83
Alberni, Luis 209
Albert, King of Belgium 82, 86
Albert, Dan 228
Alderson, Erville 233
Alexander, Frank (Fatty) 56–57, 58, 61, 228–229
Allen, Phyllis 50, 52, 58, 62, 65, 227–229, 231
Allen, W.E. 230
Among the Mourners 47, 227
Anderson, Dave 229–230
Andrea Doria 221
Andrews, Del 116, 231
Andrews, Phillips 67
Andrews, William 26
Antunez, Frank 231
Appling, Bert 230
Arbuckle, Roscoe (Fatty) 46, 50, 59, 67, 89–90, 197, 207, 227
Arcache, Claude 5
Archives de Montreux (Montreux, Switzerland) 2, 5–6
Archives des Alpes Maritîmes (Nice, France) 2
Armstrong, R.D. ("Army") 59, 229

Arnold, Cecile 50, 52, ***53***, 54, 227–229
Arts Novelty Company 69
Associated Exhibitors 107
Association Chaplin 5
Atkinson, G.A. 172
Atlantic 169
S.S. *Aurania* 165
Austin, Albert 70, 230–231
Avery, Charles 54–56, 58, 60–61, 228–229

Bacon, Lloyd 70
The Bad Boy 121
Bairnsfather, Bruce 78, 111, 139–144, 232
Baker, Sam 233
Baldwin, Charley 38
Balfour, Betty 161–163, 170, 233
Bali 184–185, 191, 200
Balio, Tino 107
Banks, Monty 168–169
Barden, Wyn 96
Baron, Maurice 232
Barrett, Steve 232
Barrows, Henry 232
Barrows, Sarah 231
Barry, Joan 212
Barrymore, John 130, 152
Baumann, Charles 60
Beau Rivage Hotel (Switzerland) 4
Beck, Frederick 232
Bedini, Jean 30–31
Behoteguy, Henri 84
Belasco, Jay 229
Bell, Monta 105, 231
Bennett, Billie 229
Bennett, Enid 232
Bergman, Henry 229–31

Berringer, Otto 232
Besserer, Eugenie 231
The Better 'Ole 78, 111, 137–139, ***140***, 141–144, ***145***, 147, 156, 159, 193, 207, 232
Betz, Matthew 232
Binney, Harold J. 229
Blackmail 169–171
Blaisdell, L.A. 230
Blake, Al 230
Bloom, Claire 217
Blythe, Edith 231
Bodle, Virginia 231
Bomberg, Serge 6
The Bond 230
Bonner, Priscilla 127, 232
Bordeaux, Joe 227, 229
Bostwick, Edith 231
Bosworth, Hobart 232
Bourchier, Arthur 141
Bourchier, W.S. 17
Bow, Clara 129
Bradbury, Kitty 231
Bradford, George 231
Breamer, Sylvia 112–113, 231
Breon, Edmond 162, 233
British-Canadian Recruiting Committee 77
British Film Institute 2, 6, 70, 95, 99, 100
British International Pictures 69–70, 108, 151, 156, 158, 161, 163, 166–167, 169–173, 178, 193–195, 199, 204, 207, 235
Broadway Melody 209
Brouwer, Cliff 230
Brown, Mel 230
Brucker, E. 230
Brun, Marie 224
Brunet, Paul 108

265

Index

Burkan, Nathan 74, 107, 151, 159
Burlesque on Carmen 68
Burns, A.C. 84
Butler, David 232

Calhoun, Alice *131*, 132, *134*, 232
Calhoun, Kathleen 232
California Draft Board 71
Calvert, Frank 39
Campbell, Eric 70
Cane Hill Asylum 19–20, 22, 24, 26
Cape Town (South Africa) 9–10, 19–20
Care, Richard 156–157
Carey, Bill 231
Carlyle, Ollie 228
Carney, George 170
S.S. *Caronia* 29
Carr, Harry 21
Carruthers, George 231
Carver, Louise 233
Caught in a Park 52, *53*, 228
Caulfield, Henry P. 69–71, 74
Cavender, Glen 60, 62, 64, 227
Cecil, Nora 233
S.S. *Celtic* 103
Cenciarelli, Cecilia 6
Champagne 161
Chaney, Lon 196
Chaplain's Instructions 13–14
Chaplin, Aubrey 69, 76, 78–79, 103, 105, 156–158, 168, 175, 191, 193
Chaplin, Charles (Charlie) 1–17, 19, 21, 24–26, 28–38, 41, 43–47, 49, 52, 54–55, 61, 67–82, 86, 92, 95, 97–98, 100–105, *106*, 107, 112, 118, 122–123, 125, 130, 133–134, 136, 146, 148, 150–154, 156, 167–168, 171, 173–187, 194, 197–200, 203–204, 206–208, *209*, 210, 212–225, 227, 229–231, 235–236, 241–242
Chaplin, Charles, Jr. 133, 208, 212
Chaplin, Charles, Sr. 9–11, 14, 40
Chaplin, Geraldine 10, 212, 220, 224
Chaplin, Hannah Harriet Pedlingham Hill 9–13, 15–16, 19–21, 23–27, 69, 75–76, 79, 103–104, 161
Chaplin, Henriette (Gypsy) 1, 4–5, 205, 207, *211*, *212*, 213–215, 217, *219*, 220–224, 242
Chaplin, Josephine 220–221
Chaplin, Michael 220–221, 225

Chaplin, Minnie Gilbert 1, 4–6, *33*, 36, *39*, *40*, 41, 44, *45*, 56, 71–73, 75–77, 79, 89–90, 92, 94, 96–97, 104, 108, *120*, 121, 129, 148, 153, 159–161, 163, 168, 173–174, *176*, 177, 180, 183–184, 187–189, 193, 196–199, 203–204, 207, 211, 215, 228–230, 235
Chaplin, Oona 212, 214, 215, 217–218, 221, 223–224
Chaplin, Sydney Earle 133, 212–214
Chaplin Airdrome *82*, 84, 87, *88*, 90, 216
Chaplin-Curtiss Flying School 85, 87
Chaplin: His Life and Art 5, 13
Chaplin: The Immortal Tramp 22, 28
Charles Chaplin Studios 75–77, 79–80, 95, 107, 209–210, 212
Charles Ray Studios 108
Charley's Aunt 41, 109, 111, 114, 119, 123, 125–129, 133, 137, 144, 161, 232
Charlie Chaplin Advertising Service Company 69
Charlie Chaplin Music Corporation 69
Charlie Chaplin's Own Story 71
Charlot, Andre 141
Chene, Dixie 50, 228–229
Childers, Ethel 231
Christie, Al 125–126, 128
Christie, Charles 127
Cimitière de Clarens-Montreux (Montreux, Switzerland) 224
Cinema Museum (London) 2, 6
Cineteca di Bologna 2, 5–6
Circle Theatre 213
The Circus 54, 97, 150, 154, 156
City Lights 174, 180, 186, 209
Clark, Bert 7
Clark, Robert 173
Clayton, Arthur 232
Cleveland, Dorothy 230
Cline, Eddie 229
Clive, Henry 92, 95, 230
Coburn, Charles 141
Coburn, Ivah 141
Cody, Lew 232
Colby, F.S. 230
Cole, Charles 230
Coleman, Frank J. 70
Collier, Constance 213
Collins, Chick 232
Conklin, Chester 47, 50, *51*, 54, 113–114, 227, 231
Consolidated Shipbuilding Corporation 84
Contagious Diseases Act 20
S.S. *Conte di Savoia* 205

Coogan, Jackie, 232
Coolidge, Calvin 104
Corrigan, Emmett *110*, 231
Costello, Helene 153–154, 232–233
The Count 70
Creelman, J.A. 92
Cross, W. 230
Crosthwaite, Ivy 228
Crown Army Shirts 119
Crozier, R.L. 85
Cullington, Miss 230
Curtiss Aeroplane and Motor Corporation 81–85, 89–90, 98

Daniels, Bebe 119, 232
Darling, Murphy 97, 230
Davenport , Alice 50, 227–228
Davies, Marion 134
Davis, James 232
Day, Shannon 116
A Day's Pleasure 122
Dean, Daisy 111
Dean, Priscilla 129
De Bray, Alexander 92, 230
Deception 101
De Courville, Albert 215–216
De Courville, Edie 215–216
De Haven, Carter 97
DeMille, Cecil B. 89
Dennis, Charlie 232
Dent, Arthur 169, 199
Deshon, Florence 97
Desmond, William 119, 232
Devere, E.H. 230
Dexter, Elliot 119, 232
Dice, C.L. 230
Dillon, John 119, 232
Dillon, Robert 152, 233
Dodd, Neal 130
A Dog's Life *77*, 229–230
Doheny, E.L. 65
Dolan, Frankie 228
Donovan, M.J. 230
Dover Castle 25
Dracup, Margaret 230
Drew, William 136
Dryden, Leo 11–12, 148
Dryden, Spencer 222
Dryden, Wheeler 11–12, 20, 148, 159, 161, 163, 199, 205, 208, 213–214, 218, 222, 233, 238
Duncan, William 232
Duffy, Jack 230
Dugwell, Bill 232
Dul, Billy 230
Dunbar, Richard 230
Dunn, Bobby 119, 232
Du Par, Ed. 233
Dupont, E.A. 169

Eakins, Guy 230
Earle, Laddie 231
Early Birds 29
Eastman, Max 97
Eckhardt, Ella 230
Eckhardt, Minnie 230
Éclair Studios 93–94
Educational Films 118
Edwards, Ted 52, 227–228, 230
Edwards, Vivian 227–228
Eifelt, Cliff 97
1834 Poor Law Amendment Act 14
Ellis, Walter 159, 170, 233
Elstree Studios 158, 163, 166, 169–171, 179
R.M.S. *Empress of Britain* 200, **201**, 202–203, 206
Encinitas (CA) 119
Epstein, Jerry 213–214
Esmond, Annie 233
Espan, J. 231
Essanay Studios 68
Estee Studios 75
Evelinoff, Boris 183–184, 194
Everybody Sing 209
Everman, Fred 230
E.W. Wagner & Co. 121
T.S. *Exmouth* 17–19, 70, 156, **157**, 158–159, 193
The "*Exmouth*" Song 18–19

Faber, Mark 230
Fairbanks, Douglas 62, 78, 80–81, 107, 134, 197
Famous Players–Lasky 80, 83, 89–93, 96–97, 108–109
Fatty's Wine Party **46**, 227
Fazenda, Louise 113–114, **115**, 116, 229, 231
Ferragoma, Jerry 230
Ferry, Bob 233
Fiedler, H.J. 20
Fields, Gracie 168
First National Film Company 74, 79–80, 105–106, 108–109, 117–119, 146
FitzPatrick, James A. 198–199
Fitzroy, Louis 230
Flaming Youth 121, 123
Flats 41–42
The Floorwalker 61
The Football Match 32, 35
Force, Charles 230
Formby, George 205
Forrest, Arthur 29
The Fortune Hunter 6, 151–152, **153**, 154, **155**
Fowler, Simon 15
Foy, Bryan 152, 233
Foy, Eddie 60
S.S. *France* 169
Francis, Alec B. 232

Fraube, J.L. 230
Frazee, Edwin 227–229
Freddie the Seal 231
Freuler, John 69, 71, 73, 75
Frey, Gallie 231
Fulton, Jim 232

The Galloping Fish 113–114, **115**, 116–117, 119, 231
Gans, J.A. 84
Garcia, Al **91**, 97, **98**, 230–231
Garrett, Sidney 107–108, 113, 151, 158–159, 163–166, 194, 236–237
Gasparini, Walter 2, 5
Gass, William 3
Gay, Charlie 150
Gay's Lion Farm 150
George, Larry 232
Gerrard, Charles 232
Giannini, A.H. 158
Gibbons, Cedric 231
Gibson, Hoot 119, 232
Giddy, Gay and Ticklish 50, 228
Giebler, A.H. 81
Gilbert, Billy 139, 227, 229, 232
Glowner, Della 231
Glowner, Lee 231
Goddard, J.D. 167
Goddard, Paulette 199, 203
Godfrey, G.A. 230
The Gold Rush 112, 123, 133–134
Goldman, Harry 230
Goldwyn, Sam 107–108
Goodwin, Harold 232
Gordon, Dick 232
Gould, Frank J. 180
Graham, Fred 230
Graham, W.E. 230
Grauman, Sid 129, 134, 145
Gray, Theresa 231
The Great Dictator 100, 193, 206, 208, **209**, 213, 217
Green, Hershel 211
Green, Jack 94
Green, Ricky 94
Grey, Lita 123, 133–134, 148, 151, 153, 212
Grey, Sylvia 97, 230
Griffin, James 230
Griffin, Joe 231
Griffin, Pete 231
Griffith, D.W. 62, 81
Griffith, Harry 97, 230
Griffith, Raymond 129
Griffith, Robert 121
Grosse Isle, Quebec 45
Guenste, F.F. 231
Guissort, René 233
Gunga Din 205
Gussle Rivals Jonah 56, 228
Gussle the Golfer 49

Gussle Tied to Trouble 57–58, 229
Gussle's Backward Way 57–58, 229
Gussle's Day of Rest 54, 228
Gussle's Wayward Path 55, 228
Guyonvarch, Kate 5
Gwyn, Nell 9

Habif, Jim 230
Hackett, W.A. 230
Hafler, Charles 231
Hale, Georgia 123, 134
Hall, Danny 95
Hall, Mordaunt 133, 137, 145, 150, 154
Hamilton, Ham 232
Hamlett, Mary 231
Hanford, Ray 230
Hanwell Schools 14, 16
Harcourt, Cecile 231
Harrington, Tom 70–71, 75, 77, 97, 103, 106, 121, 222
Harris, Martha 231
Harris, Mildred 79, 86, 97, 107, 121
Harrison, James 127, 232
Harrison, Louis Reeves 65
Harron, Robert 121
Hart, William S. 75, 81, 119, 232
Hartwell, A.J. 230
S.S. *Harvard* 63, 109
Haskins, O.E. 230
Hauber, Bill 139, 232
Haver, Phyllis 121, 232
Haverford 22
Hawke (Hawkes), Sidney 9
Hawley, Max 232
Hawley, Tom 230
Hayes, Frank 227–228
Hays, Will 90
He Did and He Didn't 67, 197
Hearst, William Randolph 65, 117–118, 145
Heifetz, Jascha 86
Held, Thomas 231
Heller, Herman 232
Hello, 'Frisco 119, 232
Henderson, Jessie 232
Henry, William n. 68
Her Temporary Husband 6, 103, 109, 111, 113, 231
Herlinger, K. 230
Hermann, Harry 191
Herron, W. 230
Heustis, Reid 96
Heyningen, Elizabeth Van 20
Hiatt, Ruth **149**, 233
Hicks, Anna 231
Hicks, Harry 231
Hiers, Walter 126
Hill, Al 229

Hill, Charles 9
Hill, Doris 144, 232
Hill, Mary Ann (Smith) 9, 13
Hirschfeld, Al 185
Hirschfeld, Florence 185
His Prehistoric Past **47**, 227
Hitchcock, Alfred 161, 169–171
Hitchcock, Raymond 60, 62
Hodges, John George 13
Hodges, Joseph 10
Hoff, Fred 232
Holden, Gloria 210
Holderness, Fay 230
Hollamby, W. 18
Holland, Cecil 231
Hollywood Athletic Club 117
Hollywood Sixty Club 129
Horton, Clara **153, 155**, 233
Hotel Ruhl 5, 215, 222–224
Hotel Westminster 174, 235
Houdini, Harry 96
House, Billy 209
Hoxie, Jack 232
Hudson, Earl 118, 146
Hughes, Howard 163
Hunt, Ed 230
Hushing the Scandal 50, **51**, 52, 228
The Hydro 26, 39, **40**, 41

Ideal Films 114, 118, 120, 123, 125–127
The Idle Class 54, 97, 104, 123
Ince, Thomas 62, 89, 113–114, 116–117, 231
Ingram, Rex 159–160
Inter-Globe Export Corporation 107–108, 151, 164
Internal Revenue Service 4, 152, 158–159, 205
Inukai, Tsuyoshi 186
The Iron Strain 62
S.S. *Isle de France* 205
Ives, Burl 139

Jackson, Joe 60
James, Daird 127
James, Dan 208–209
James, David 232
Janis, Elsie 94, **106**
Jasper, John 74–75, 78
Jasper Studios 95–96
The Jazz Singer 166
Jefferson, Thomas 233
Jeffrey, R.E. 171
Jensen, Carl 231
Jensen, Eulalie 126, 232
Johnson, C. 231
Johnson, Dick 95
Johnson, E.B. 230
Johnson, Edith 232
Johnson, Jean 230
Johnson-Reed Act 142

Jolson, Al 145, 166
Jones, "Buck" 87
Jones, F. Richard 61, 227–228
Jones, Park 230
Jordan, Joan 103
Jourjon, Charles 93
Joy, Leatrice 129
Jungmeyer, Jack 118, 133

Kabuki-za 186
Kane, Arthur 108
Kapp, Helen 231
Karno, Frederick Westcott 27, 29–41, 43, 61, 67, **164**, 165, 167, 242
Karno London Comedians 2, 4, 29
Keaton, Buster 49
Kedian, Joe 231
Keenan, Frank 65
Kelley, James T. 70, 230
Kelly, Arthur 113, 116, 118, 134, 146, 148, 152–153, 159, 163–164, 178, 180–181, 189, 194–195, 205, 207, 216
Kendall, Cy 209
Kendall, Read 199
Kennedy, Edgar 50, 139, 144, 228–229, 232
Kennedy, Ethel 231
Kennedy, Jack 52, 228
Kennedy, Thomas C. 117
Kennedy, Tom 139, 232
Kent, Crauford 233
Kerrigan, J. Warren 232
Kerry, Norman 232
Kessel, Adam 52, 54
Kesson, David 231
Key, Kathleen 109, 231
Keystone Studios 44–47, 49–50, 52, 55–57, 59–60, 66–68
The Kid 97, 106–107, 123
Kilyeni, Edward 232
Kinfairns Castle 22
King, Alexander 185, 191
A King in New York 217, 221
King, Queen, Joker (*One Hundred Million*) 6, 10, 50, **88**, **91**, 92–93, 95–96, **98**, **99**, 100–101, 104, 107–108, 111, 192, 230
Kingsley, Grace 56, 118, 125, 154
Kinsky, Leonid 210
Kipling, Rudyard 139–140, 205
Kirkham, M.G. 117
Kit Kat Club 162
Kitchen, Fred 32, 35, 40
Kitchen, Karl K. 166
Kitts, Charles 41
Klumph, Helen 103, 117, 133
Knott, Lydia 232
Knuske, Charles 230

Koenekamp, Hans **74**
Kono, Torachai 71, 179, 183, 187
Korda, Alexander 197
Kruger, Paul 233

Lahue, Kalton C. 49, 58, 66
Lakin, Charles 228–229
La Marr, Barbara 232
The Lamb 62
Lambeth Workhouse 13, 16
Lamont, Emily 231
Lane, Rose Wilder 71
La Rue, Fontaine 97, 230
Lasky, Jesse 90, 100
Lattimer, Florence 231
Lauder, Harry 77, **86**
Law, Arthur 152
Lee, Raymond 231
Leibbrand, Charles H. 17–18
Lester, Kate 231
Levine, Phillippa 20
Levy, Benn 170–171
Levy, Bert 60
Levy, Victor H. 72–73, 84, 159
Levy's Café 50
Lewis, Gordon 232
Lewis, Joy 56–57, 228–229
Lewis, Ralph 232
Lewis, Sam 230
Library of Congress 2, 6
Liggew, George 232
Ligon, Grover 139, 227–229
Limelight 206, 213, 216, 225
Lincoln, Elmo 111, 231
Lincoln Center Library of the Performing Arts 2
Liscomb, Frank 231
A Little Bit of Fluff (*Skirts*) 41, 75, 159, 161, **162**, 163, 166, 170, 233
Littlefield, Lucien 127, 231–232
Lloyd, Harold 166, 229
Lobster Films 6
Loew, Marcus 145
Logue, Charlie 130, 232
London, Babe **122**, 233
London Suburbia 32
Lone Star Studio 69–70, **74**
Lorch, Theodore 232
Lord, John 130
Lovers Lost Control 57, 60, 229
Lovett, Josephine 110, 231
Low, Rachel 170
Lubitsch, Ernst 101
R.M.S. *Lusitania* 65
Lynch, Agnes 231

Mace, Fred 60
MacPherson, Lottie 95, 97, 230
Madden, T. 230
Malvern, Paul 232
The Man on the Box 41, 130, **132**, 133, **134**, 137–138, 232

Mann, Hank 139, *140*
Manoir de Ban (Corsier-sur-Vevey, Switzerland) 220, 223
Margaret Herrick Library (AMPAS) 2, 6
Marigold, G.E. 230
Marinelli, H.B. 31
Marsh, Gene 227
Marshall, Tully *112*, 231
Marshall Neilan Productions 108
Martin, Duke 233
Martin, Quinn 133, 150
Matchett, Billy 41
Maxwell, John 158, 161, 164, 167–173, 178, 195–196, 204, 236–237
Mayfair Hotel 161
Mayo, Frank 121, 232
McAdoo, William Gibbs 145
McAttee, Claude 230
McCarty, M.J. 230
McCoy, Harry 227
McCredie, Jack 231
McDermott, John W. 111, 113, 231
McFadden, Ivor 97, 230
McGranery, James 216
McGrath, Harold 130, 232
McGuire, Tom 148, 232–233
McKellan, R.S. 75
McKenzie, R.B. 230
McKern, John 65
McLaglen, Clifford 161–162, *164*, 233
McNeill, Paul Mason 231
McVey, L.S. 230
S.S. *Megantic* 44–45
Meighan, John 95, 97
Menier, Sylvia 231
Menjou, Adolphe *80*
Mercury Aviation 89
Metro-Goldwyn-Mayer (MGM) 158, 160, 163, 198
Miami University (Oxford, OH) 2
Miller, Edward 230
Miller, J. 230
Miller, Patsy Ruth 136–137, 232
Mills, Irving 190–191
Mineau, Charlotte 70
Minney, Rubeigh James (R.J.) 3–4, 10, 12, 16, 21–3, 28, 42, 81, 144, 166–170, 172–175, 178–181, 183, 185–186, 188–192, 195–197, 204–208, 210, 220–222, 235–242
The Missing Link 146, 148, *149*, 150–151, 233
Modern Times 97, 194, 199, 203, 216
Monsieur Verdoux 212–213
Montana, Bull 232

Monte Carlo 175, 214–215, 223, 235
Montreux (Switzerland) 159–160, 199, 214–215, 220, 222
Montreux Palace Hotel 160, 220
Moody, B.J. 209
Moore, Colleen 119, 121–123, 232
Moore, Owen 112–113, 231
Moreno, Antonio 119, 232
Morgan, Kewpie 232
Morgan, Lillian 230
Morton, Maggie 22
Mosely, Leonard 135
Moskovitch, Maurice 209
Mowbray, Kate 11, 68–69, 76
Mozart, George 25
Mumming Birds (A Night in an English Music Hall) 29, *30*, 36, 39, 165–167, 170, 173, 179
Murray, Tom 231
Mutual Film Corporation 69–71, 73, 75, 79, 100
My Lucky Star 209
My Trip Abroad 105
My Valet 62
Mycroft, Walter 169–170, 196

Nagel, Beth 231
Nagel, Conrad 109, *110*, 231
Neilan, Marshall 109, *110*, 113, 118, 231
The New Boy 152
New York Aeronautical Show 89
New York Motion Picture Company 60–62
Newmeyer, Fred C. 130
Niblo, Fred 232
Nice (France) 5–6, 159–160, *161*, 177, 179, 183, 187–199, 205, 207, 213–216, 221–222, *224*, 235, 238, 241–242
Nichols, Norma 228
Nilsson, Anna Q. 232
No One to Guide Him 44, 61, 229
S.S. *Norman* 21–23
Normand, Mabel *46*, 52, 227
North, A. 230
Numa 150

Oakie, Jack 208
Oh! What a Nurse! 6, 41, 133–135, *136*, 137–138, 232
Oliver, Harry 109
Olivieri, Fanny 215
One A.M. 70
O'Neill, Eugene 212
O'Niall, Jim 230
Opperman, Frank 47, 227–228
O'Ree, Brand 230

Orr, Louis 230
Ort, David 73
Ouster, Donnabelle 231

Page, James E. 126, 128, 232
Palais Rosa Bonheur 5, 177, 188–189, 197, 213, 215, 220
Palm Springs (CA) *138*, 152, 219–220
Palmer, Sam 92
Panama Patrol 210
Parallee, Florence 230
Paramount-Artcraft 80, 92, 101
Parker, J.F. 230
Parr, S.C. 85
Parrish, Katherine 231
Parrott, Charles (Charley Chase) 60
Parsons, Louella 69, 117, 203
Pathé Pictures 108, 118
The Pawnshop 54
Paulais 129
Paulton, Edward 231
Pay Day 50, 105, 230
Pearson, George 141, 161
Peckham House 68, 79, 103
Peebles, Mort 229
Pennell, E.O. 231
Percy Williams Circuit 31
The Perfect Flapper 119–121, *122*, 123, 232
Pickford, Charlotte 81
Pickford, Mary 78, 80–81, 107, 109, 114, 134
Pierce, Carl 92
The Pilgrim 47, 105, *106*, 107, 231
Pink, Wal 27
Pitts, Mildred 231
Plunkett, Joseph L. 142
Polanski, Roman 4
Police 47
Poor Law Commission 15
Porknall, George 233
Porter, Katherine Anne 3
Porter, Vincent 170
Powell, Hickman 185, 191
Powell, J.T. 230
Producers Distributing Corporation 127–128
The Professor 106
Pryor, Kathleen 218
Purviance, Edna 70, 75, 84, 86, 134, 209, 229–31

Quarry, Marcus 26

Rand, John 70–71, 230–231
Rand, June B. 71–73
Randall, Bruce 230
Rappe, Virginia 90
Ratcliffe, E.J. 232
Ray, Charles 65

Index

Ray, Tom 231
Raymond, La Belle 231
Raynaud (Nice, France) 224
Redmond, Granville 230
Reeves, Alfred (Alf) 29, 74, 78, 104, 194, 198, 211, 230
Reeves, Amy (Minister) 104, 199, 213–214
Reeves, Billy 30
Reeves, May 179–181, 183–184
Regent Finance Company 117, 119, 158
S.S. *Regina* 165
Regina, Fred 27
Reid, Laurence 101, 111, 128
Reisner, Charles 60, 105, 112, 130, 133, 135–136, 139, *140*, 142–143, 146, 148, 152, 230–233
Reisner, Dean (Dinky) 105, 231
The Rendezvous 6, 103, 108–109, *110*, 111, 113, 116, 118, 231
Repairs 27, *28*, 29
Ricksen, Lucille 109, *110*, 111, 114, *115*, 116–117, 129–130, 231
Rigg, Nancy 162, 233
Riggoletto Brothers 174
Riley, Thomas 230
Rinehart, Mary Roberts 86
The Ring 170–171
Ritchie, Billy 30
Ritchie, Wyn 104, 214
Robbins, Jess 159, 163, 233
Robinson, Carlyle 74, 92, 95, 97, 179–181, 194, 231, 235
Robinson, David 5, 13, 25, 29, 32, 37, 71, 77, 105, 208, 212, 229
Rock, Charles 141
Roger, Emery H. 83–84, 86–90, 97–98
Rolph, James 145
Rosenberg, Sarah 230
Rosher, Dorothy 230
Roth, Sandy 233
Rowe, Edna 231
Rowson, Harry 127
Roy Export S.A.S. 5
Royston, Harry 29
Ruggles, Wesley 58, 60, 62, 64, 228–229
Runser, Lois 217–218
Russell, Jimmy 29, 32, 36
Ruthven, Madeleine 108, 110, 231

St. John, Al 227
St. Louis 22
St. Moritz (Switzerland) 181, *182*, 183, 188, 214–215
Santa Catalina Island (CA) 56, *57*, 81–84, 87, 123, 146, 228

Santa Catalina Island Historical Society 2
Sassy Jane Manufacturing Company 71, *72*, 73, 96, 119, 158
Scanlan, D.F. 171
Schade, Fritz 227–228
Schallert, Edwin 138
Scheide, Frank 100
Schenck, Joseph 107, 134, 163, 195
Schwalbe, Harry 105–106
Seaver Center (Los Angeles Natural History Museum) 2
Selig Zoo (Los Angeles, CA) 54
Sennett, Mack 44, 50, 52, 55, 60, 62, 66–67, 116, 135, 163, 197, 220
Shalford, Jack 230
Shaner, Emel 92
Shannon, Ethel 126–127, 232
Shepheard's Hotel (Cairo) 184
Sherlock Holmes (Charles Frohman Co.) 24, *25*, 40, 67
Sherrart, Georgia 231
Sherwood, Robert E. 134–135, 232
Shewry, J.H. 230
Shlyen, Ben 128
Shoulder Arms 78, 79, 111, 141–142, 230
Shoulters, Mabel 231
Shute, Nerina 166
Sidney, H.C. 20
Sidney, Scott 126, 128–129, 232
Sierks, Alma 87
Simmons, H.C. 230
Sims, George R. 14–15
Skating 27, *33*, 34–35, 39, 48
Slaton, John Marshall 65
Small, Eddie 205
Smalley, Phillips 126, 232
Smith, Edward 16
Smith, James J. 231
Smith, Winchell 152, 233
Smithson, Lottie 230
The Smoking Concert 29
Sparta Club (Paris) 192
Spoor, George K. 68
Starr, Fred 230
Steppling, John 114, 231
Sterling, Ford 50, 113–114, 231
Stetson Hats 119
Stout, George 55
A Submarine Pirate 57, 61–62, *63*, 64–67, 179, 204, 229
Summerville, Slim 52, *53*, 54, 119, 227–229, 232
Sunnyside 79
Suwa Maru 183, 186
Swain, Mack *46*, 50, 227, 231
Sween, A. 84
Sweet, Matthew 167, 193
Swickard, Josef 229

Syd Chaplin Aircraft Corporation 80, 83–85, *86*, 87–89, 96–97
Syphilis 19–20

Tahbel, N. 230
Tally, Thomas L. 74, 80
Talmadge, Constance 129
Tambourine 170
Taylor, Enid Stamp 233
Taylor, Rex 152
Taylor, William Desmond 90
Tenbrook, Harry 231
Tetrick, Betty Chaplin 168, 193, 207–208, 213–214, 222–223
Tetrick, Ted 213–214
That Springtime Feeling 52, 54, 228
Third Pan-American Aeronautic Congress and Exposition 89
Thirer, Irene 154
30 Years of Fun 67
Thomas, Brandon 125–126, 133, 232
Thorpe, John 169
Tiller Girls *162*, 163
Tolstoy, Leo 3
Torrence, David 232
Totheroh, Rollie 77, 209, 218–219, 229–31
The Tramp 52
Trask, Wayland 61, 229
Traughbur, Robert 231
TravelTalks 198
Travers, Richard *110*, 231
Triangle Films 61–67
Troester, Louis 231
Truffaut, François 171
Turner, Gordon 200
The Two Little Drummer Boys (Walter Howard) 22

Under the Greenwood Tree 170
Underwood, Loyal 230–231
The Unholy Three 196
Union Castle Mail Steamship Company 21
United Artists 2, 80, 107–108, 118, 146, 184, 194–196, 198, 212

Vandal, Marcel 93
Van Meter, Joe 230–231
Vernon, Bobby 126
Vitagraph Films 130, 152
Vitaphone 145
Vivre 192, 238

Wagner, Rob 75, 78, 230
Wagner, W.G. 230
Wakefield Prison 42
Walker, Brent 6, 47, 227
Wampas Frolic 129

Ward, Roscoe 230
Wardour Films 170
Warne, J.H. 230
Warner, Jack 130, 146
Warner Bros. Archive (USC Cinema Arts Library) 2, 139, 143
Warner Bros. Film Company 112, 130, 135–137, 139, 142–144, 146–148, 150–152, 154, 156, 158–159, 207
Washburn, Bryant 119, 129, 232
Waverley Films 169
Weber (Joe) and Fields (Lew) 60
Weitzel, Edward 101
Weldon, Harry 32, 35
Wellesley, Charles 232
Wells, May 231
Welsh, Thomas A. 141
Welsh, Pearson & Co., Ltd. 141–142
West, Walter 168
West Norwood Schools 13
Wheeler, Rose 231
When Love Is Young 209
Whistler, Margaret 137
Whitaker, Alma 129, 137
White, Bill 230
White, Bob 211
White Cargo 169
Whitman, Gayne 232
Wilbourne, Phyllis 213
Wilcox, S.D. 231
Wild West Love 47, 227
Wiley, Wanda 232
Wilkins, Paul 231
Williams, Earle 152
Williams, J.B. 169
Williams, J.D. 74
Williams, S.H. 231
Willis, F. McGrew 232
Willis, Jack 230
Wilson, Diana 233
Wilson, Grace 230
Wilson, Jack 230–231
Wilson, Tom 230
Wolfinger, H. 231
Woman's Home Companion (WHC) 185–186
The Wontdetainia 38
Woodall, Jean-Paul 5
The Wow-Wows (A Night in a London Secret Society) 36, *37*
Wright, Arthur 90, 97
Wright, Loyd 107, 219
Wright, Molly 166–169, 171–174
Wright, Walter 47, 227–228
Wrigley, William 81, 83

YMCA Auto School 85
Yosemite National Park 135
Youngson, Robert 67

Zanuck, Darryl Francis 135, 139, *140*, 142–143, 146, 148, 152, 197, 232–233
Zetland, Louise 41
Zukor, Adolph 80, 90

www.ingramcontent.com/pod-product-compliance
Lightning Source LLC
Chambersburg PA
CBHW060258240426
43661CB00060B/2826